Battling for Saipan

Battling for Saipan

Francis A. O'Brien

Ballantine Books • New York

A Presidio Press Book
Published by The Ballantine Publishing Group

Copyright © 2003 by Francis A. O'Brien

Library of Congress Cataloging-in-Publication Data

O'Brien, Francis (Francis A.)
    Battling for Saipan / Francis O'Brien.
        p. cm.
    Includes bibliographical references and index.
    ISBN 0-89141-804-0
        1. Saipan, Battle of, 1944. 2. United States. Army. Infantry
Division, 27th—History—20th century. 3. World War, 1939–1945—
Regimental histories—United States. 4. O'Brien, William J.,
d. 1944. 5. United States. Army—Officers—Biography. 6. Medal
of Honor—Biography. I. Title.

D767.99.S3 06 2002
940.54'26—dc21
[B]

                                          2002025337

Maps © StyloGraphix, Mary Craddock Hoffman

Manufactured in the United States of America
First Edition: February 2003
1 3 5 7 9 10 8 6 4 2

Contents

Acknowledgments

In preparation for writing this book, I read every book, article, or pamphlet that I could find on the Saipan battle; they are listed in the bibliography. I relied on Capt. Edmund G. Love's excellent, detailed history entitled *The 27th Infantry Division in World War II*, first published in 1949, for much of the narrative of the Makin and Saipan battles. I also read and relied on Professor Harry A. Gailey's book, *Howlin' Mad vs. the Army*, published in 1986. His cogent analysis in defense of the army in the dispute which arose out of the relief of army major general Ralph C. Smith by "Howlin' Mad" Smith in the midst of the Saipan battle convinced me that I did not have to discuss this subject in my book.

In my research, I consulted operations reports, unit journals, and official histories of the 27th Division and the 105th and 165th Infantry Regiments at the National Archives new facility near College Park, Maryland, the National Guard Museum in Washington, D.C., and the New York State Military Museum, Division of Military and Naval Affairs, in Saratoga, New York, for information regarding the Saipan battle. I owe a special debt of gratitude to Michael Aikey, Deputy Director of the New York State Military Museum and his staff, for their assistance in locating relevant materials for my manuscript. The Rensselaer County Historical Society, Troy, New York, the Hoosick Falls Historical Society, Hoosick Falls, New York, and the Troy Public Library also contributed to my research. Ms. Ruth Zink of the Troy Public Library was most helpful in providing me with access to newspaper microfilm records.

In addition to these sources, I interviewed, in person or by telephone, dozens of former members of the 105th Infantry who served at Saipan and Makin. Many of them sent me letters, memoranda or diaries they had prepared during and after their period of service, providing first-hand accounts of their battle experiences. These individuals are identified in the bibliography.

Several of them deserve special recognition. Doctor June Hoyt, of Cushing, Maine, provided me with transcriptions of audiotapes recorded by Sgt. Ronald Johnson about his experiences on Saipan. He was communications sergeant for Lieutenant Colonel O'Brien and spent much of his time on Saipan in close contact with the dead hero. His recollections of first hand conversations with Colonel O'Brien are especially memorable. Luther "Luke" Hammond of Gainesville, Florida, O'Brien's S-2 officer on Saipan, provided me with copies of his precious notes, recounting his observations while he was on Saipan. His frequent references to O'Brien were helpful in preparing my manuscript. Francois V. Albanese, S-4, 1st Battalion, 105th Infantry, of Syosset, Long Island, New York, shared with me his personal conversations with O'Brien before and during the Saipan battle.

John A. "Jack" Armstrong of St. Petersburg, Florida, a close friend of O'Brien, and who served with him on Saipan, was helpful in providing me with information regarding the history of the 105th Infantry, as well as the role of Headquarters Company in repulsing the Japanese suicide attack on the morning of July 7. Vince Busone of Northport, Florida, served as clerk of A Company, 1st Battalion, 105th Infantry, when it was commanded by then Captain William J. O'Brien. He provided me with anecdotal information about Company A in general and Captain O'Brien in particular. Charles J. Stephani of East Patchogue, New York, who served as first sergeant of B Company on Saipan, shared with me the daily diary he kept during the fighting on Saipan. John Domanowski, now deceased, who served with Company B, 105th Infantry, on Saipan, wrote me a long letter in October 1996 outlining, in marvelous detail, his combat experiences on Saipan.

Others who provided me with valuable information include Richard Bishop of Bradley, Arkansas, son of Colonel Leonard Bishop, who commanded the 105th at Saipan, and W. Taylor Hudson, Lexington, Kentucky, who served with Antitank Company,

105th Infantry at Saipan. Seymour "Sy" Krawetz of Skokie, Illinois, who served with Company F, 2d Battalion, on Saipan, sent me twenty-three letters detailing his experiences during the battle. Arthur G. Hansen, Council Bluffs, Iowa, George O'Donnell, Riverside, California, and Donald P. Spiering, Beaverton, Oregon, who served as lieutenants with G Company, 2d Battalion, on Saipan, shared with me letters and memoranda describing their combat experiences in that battle. Lieutenant Joseph J. Meighan, Cohoes, New York, who served with M Company, 3d Battalion, on Saipan, provided me with photographs and memoranda describing his experiences during the battle. The late Carl E. Rohner of Hilo, Hawaii, who served as executive officer of the 3d Battalion, also provided me with his written recollections of combat on Makin and Saipan.

My editors at Presidio Press, Bob Kane, publisher emeritus and E. J. McCarthy, executive editor, were most helpful to me in writing this book. They provided me with invaluable advice for my first full-length book. I learned a great deal from them about writing techniques, which will be helpful in any future books I write. I owe thanks also to Iskandar (Alex) Baday, an old friend from Vienna, Virginia, who helped with the initial preparation of the maps that appear in the book. Mary Craddock Hoffman, of course, is responsible for the final version of the maps.

Finally, I want to thank several members of my family for their help and assistance in preparing this book. My cousins, William J. O'Brien Jr. of Jamestown, New York, and Gary Prout of Schenectady, New York, provided me with a wealth of information about our uncle, the 105th Infantry and the Saipan battle in the form of newspaper clippings and photographs from their family scrapbooks. My son, Dennis A. O'Brien, an attorney in New York City, read and commented on my manuscript in its early stages. My twin daughters, Kathleen O'Brien Krug and Eileen O'Brien Prophett, helped me from a technical standpoint. Their knowledge of the computer rescued me in several instances from losing the story altogether. My wife, Maryanne D. O'Brien, was a tower of strength as I struggled with the intricacies of preparing the manuscript on my word processor.

Preface

I decided to write a book about the Battle of Saipan for two reasons. First, my uncle, Lt. Colonel William J. O'Brien, Troy, New York, fought and died there in World War II. While commanding the 1st Battalion, 105th Infantry, 27th Infantry Division at Saipan, he was killed in action on July 7, 1944, and awarded the Medal of Honor. One of his men, Sergeant Thomas A. Baker, of Troy, New York, was also killed there and awarded the Medal of Honor for his heroism in that battle. Just recently a third member of the 105th, Capt. Ben L. Salomon, surgeon for the 2d Battalion, was awarded the Medal of Honor posthumously for heroism on Saipan. It is rare for three men from the same regiment to receive the Medal of Honor for heroic actions in the same battle.

Researching and writing this book has been a labor of love for me. During my research, I learned a lot about my uncle, not only as a war hero, but as a person and family man. I was too young to know him; the 105th Infantry was mobilized in October 1940 when I was four years old. My father was his younger brother and he told me about Uncle Bill and what he had accomplished during the war. My research has confirmed that he was a true hero, and I am grateful to Presidio Press for giving me the opportunity to share his story with my family, my sister's family, the families of the men of the 27th Division who served with him at Saipan, and with those people who enjoy reading about soldiers who fought and died honorably in the service of their country during World War II.

My research also discovered a second reason why a book about the army's role at Saipan should be written. Apart from Captain Edmund G. Love's 1949 book, *The 27th Infantry Division in World War II*, most of the books and articles written about Saipan during and after the war describe the Marine Corps role in the battle; the 27th Division is hardly mentioned. When the 27th is mentioned, its role is minimized and its performance disparaged.

The 27th had the unfortunate experience at Saipan of being under the command of a Marine Corps officer of superior rank—Lt. General Holland M. Smith, known as "Howlin' Mad" Smith to the veterans of the Saipan battle. General Smith was a cantankerous old man (age sixty-two at the time of the battle) who had an extreme dislike for the United States Army and the 27th Division in particular. Not surprisingly, Saipan was the first and only Pacific battle in which Marine officers commanded army troops in the field.

In August 1944, *Life* magazine published an article about Saipan that barely mentioned the 27th Division. It was written by Robert Sherrod, a Time-Life correspondent, who spent much of his time on Saipan at "Howlin' Mad" Smith's headquarters. In September 1944, *Time* published an article, which Mr. Sherrod subsequently acknowledged he wrote, disparaging the men of the 27th Division by claiming that at Saipan they "froze in their foxholes," and "were held up by handfuls of Japs in caves." As Sherrod admitted forty-six years later, these intemperate remarks had "a devastating effect on the morale of the 27th Division then retraining for combat at Espiritu Santo," and he apologized for publishing them in the *Time* article.

These insults were followed in November 1948 by publication of three articles by H. M. Smith in the *Saturday Evening Post* highly critical of the 27th Division, and by publication in 1949 (over the objection of the navy) of his memoirs, *Coral and Brass*, that further demeaned and maligned the division and its leadership. These publications perpetuated the twin myths that the 27th Division had failed in combat in the Pacific, and that the army in general is inferior to the Marine Corps in terms of personnel and combat training. Many of the World War II veterans I interviewed for this book still rankle when "Howlin' Mad" Smith's name is mentioned. A recent manifestation of Marine contempt for the army appears in *Flags of Our Fathers* by James Bradley. On page 71 newsman Jim Lehrer is quoted as saying that in Marine boot camp: "I learned that Marines never leave their dead and wounded behind, officers always eat last, the U.S. Army is chickenshit in combat, the Navy is worse, and the Air Force is barely even on our side."

In 1986, Professor Harry A. Gailey, in *Howlin' Mad vs. the Army*, convincingly demonstrated that "the slurs cast upon the officers and men of the 27th Division by H. M. Smith in his articles and books were totally unwarranted and unconscionable." Content with this refutation of H. M. Smith's tactics of ridicule and disparagement, I have shown in this book, through objective evidence, that the 27th Division, at Saipan, as well as at other battles in the Pacific, conducted itself in accordance with the highest standards of the army and that its reputation should be restored in the fullest measure. Its men fought and died for their country in heroic fashion—more than one thousand of them were killed in combat at Saipan.

Thus, I have stressed that the 27th Division was one of the best-trained combat divisions in the army when it left the United States for Pearl Harbor in February 1942. When it was selected to participate in the invasions of the Gilberts and Marshalls Islands in 1943, it was praised by Gen. George C. Marshall, chairman of the joint chiefs of staff, as a division that "has been in Hawaii for over a year and is a well-trained division with excellent leaders." Its commander, Maj. Gen. Ralph C. Smith, was described as "very much liked by Admiral Nimitz and Admiral Spruance." As Admiral Spruance is to command the task force, "I am sure that there will be a most harmonious relationship between Gen. Smith, his staff, and the navy."

At the time the invasion of the Marianas (code name Forager) was being planned, General Marshall visited the 27th Division in Hawaii and said: "We have the Japs beaten but we have to keep pushing. The Japs had jungle training long before the war and we didn't, but they're restricted and lack variation. Our great advantage is our enterprise and resourcefulness. Your training here is the best that can be given, and it is up to you to push the enemy through the jungle."

The combat scenes described in the book show beyond doubt that the men of the 27th had courage, discipline and fortitude, and were as ferocious in battle as any marine. Witness Pfc. Nicholas Johannes Timmens, five feet two inches tall and a native of Holland, who served with Company M, 105th Infantry, at Makin. On the first day there, he killed six Japanese soldiers with his rifle and later saved two of his buddies by throwing a live enemy grenade out of a foxhole. Examples of heroism at Saipan by men of the 27th are legion. Lieutenant Colonel O'Brien, Captain Salomon, and Sergeant Baker won the Medal of Honor; while dozens of other men from the division were awarded Silver and Bronze stars for heroic acts and deeds in combat.

I hope this book helps bring closure to the 27th Division soldiers who survived the Saipan battle and are still with us today. For the families of those men who did not survive the battle, or who have since passed on, I trust I have shown them that their fathers, sons, uncles and brothers served their country honorably and well during World War II, at Saipan and other places, and that they are entitled to our undying gratitude. If I have accomplished this, my efforts in writing this book have been worthwhile.

1 Prelude to World War II

Following Germany's attack on Poland on September 1, 1939, the U.S. War Department accelerated the training of the National Guard. Annual weekly drills increased from forty-eight to sixty per year, and summer field training was increased from fifteen to twenty-two days. President Franklin D. Roosevelt signed an executive order authorizing an increase in the size of the army. The cycle of field maneuvers was changed so that in the summer of 1940, all of the available army divisions in the First Army area (both regular and National Guard) were able to participate in the maneuvers held at De Kalb Junction, New York (near the Canadian border). One of the first obvious facts observed by the commanders of the participating units was that the National Guard units, in particular, were seriously understrength. The 27th Infantry Division, for example, had only 10,414 personnel, about one-half of the 22,000 authorized personnel. It was clear that these divisions had to be bulked up to full strength before they could become effective forces in the new war that had exploded in Europe.

Under these circumstances, the National Gusrd's summer camp of 1940 was given high priority. The war in Europe was almost a year old, and it was inevitable that the United States would soon become involved. Large-scale maneuvers and war games between regular army and National Guard units from New York and other states took place August 13–14, 1940. More than 100,000 troops participated, including a mechanized brigade of tanks from Fort Knox, Kentucky, and more than 600 planes of all kinds. It was clear to everyone that something big was up.

• • •

On August 23, 1940, the day before summer training at De Kalb Junction ended, the men were reviewed by President Roosevelt. The 105th Infantry (known as the "Apple-knocker" Regiment) was lined up along the roadway as the president and his entourage sped by in open vehicles. It was brutally hot, and the men were passing out by the score. It was clear to everyone, and certainly the Apple-knockers, that they would shortly be inducted into federal service and would soon be at war.

On September 16, 1940, President Roosevelt signed the Selective Service and Training Act, the first peacetime conscription law in U.S. history, a tacit confirmation that the country would soon be involved in the brutal war in Europe. The act required that all men aged twenty-one to thirty-five years register and, if selected, serve for a training and service period of twelve consecutive months and then serve in one of the reserve forces for ten years or until age forty-five. Moreover, under the act, if Congress declared a national emergency, the president could extend the period of service indefinitely. One month after the signing of the bill, 16 million men were registered for military service. The "selectees," as they became known, would augment the understrength National Guard divisions about to be mobilized.

On September 25, 1940, the mobilization order was signed inducting the 27th Division into federal service beginning October 15, 1940, for one year of active duty. Under the terms of the mobilization order, all men with dependents were authorized to request honorable discharges. On October 1, 1940, those men in the 105th Infantry Regiment who were not eligible for dependency discharges received notices from their company commanders. They were directed to report to their respective armories in their local communities on October 15 at 0800 for induction. The "Apple-knockers" were going back into active service.

Since World War I, there had been several changes in the structure of the 27th Infantry Division, many of which were significant. The 107th Infantry Regiment (formerly the 7th New York of Civil War fame) was transferred out of the division and redesignated the

207th Coast Artillery. To replace the 107th, the 165th Infantry Regiment (formerly "the Fighting 69th" New York) famous from Civil War and World War I, was assigned to the division. The 165th and the 108th Infantry Regiment from the Syracuse area of New York formed the 54th Infantry Brigade.

In September 1940, the 106th Infantry Regiment from Brooklyn, New York, was redesignated the 186th Field Artillery Regiment and was transferred out. Its place in the 53d Infantry Brigade was taken by the 10th New York Infantry from Albany, Utica, and other New York communities. In November 1940, the 10th New York was designated the 106th Infantry and became known as the "Knickerbocker" Regiment. The Apple-knockers, which had served with the 27th during World War I, joined the Knickerbockers to form the 53d Brigade.

For the 105th Infantry, this was the fourth time in less than one hundred years that the regiment, or one of its predecessor units, had been called into active duty to serve the United States. One of the oldest military organizations in the country, the 105th's predecessor militia units served in the French and Indian War during the 1750s, the Revolutionary War in the 1770s, and the War of 1812. The New York State Militiamen particularly distinguished themselves at the Battle of Saratoga, where the British were forced to surrender in September 1777. One of the 105th's core units, Company A, was formed as the Troy Citizen's Corps by the New York state legislature on September 23, 1835. During the American Civil War, this unit served as Company A of the 2d New York Volunteers for two years, from April 1861 to April 1863, and participated in numerous battles throughout the state of Virginia. Company A existed as a separate unit until the late 1870s when it was incorporated into the New York National Guard.

The National Guard in the northeastern part of New York had its origins in the late 1870s and 1880s when twelve separate companies of militia were formed in a number of upstate New York communities and organized as the 2d New York Infantry Regiment. This unit was called into active service during the Spanish-American War in 1898 and the Mexican border war in 1916. On July 12, 1917, shortly after the United States declared war on Germany, Pres. Woodrow Wilson called the entire National Guard into federal service. The 2d New York then became a part of the newly designated 27th Infantry Division, also known as the New York Division. On October 1, 1917, the 2d New York was redesignated the 105th Infantry Regiment and was augmented by approximately 1,500 officers and enlisted men from the 12th and 71st Infantry Regiments of the New York National Guard. It served with distinction in France and Belgium and participated in the successful assault on the Hindenberg line. It was mustered out of federal service on April 1, 1919, after precisely two years and seven days of service, and after demobilization, reverted to National Guard status and once again became the 2d Regiment, New York National Guard.

During the period between the notice of induction and the actual induction, an extensive reorganization took place. The division needed to be brought up to war strength as soon as possible, with some 7,000 men needed immediately. Details were sent to Fort Dix, New Jersey; Camp Upton, New York; and Fort Niagara, New York to begin the process of moving recruits from reception centers to Fort McClellan, an abandoned military reservation near Anniston, Alabama. The new recruits were expected to begin arriving in January 1941. On October 9, 1940, approximately six weeks after completion of the De Kalb maneuvers, Lt. Gen. Hugh Drum, in command of the II Army Corps, ordered the 27th Division to concentrate at Fort McClellan for field training. Major General William N. Haskell, commander of the 27th Division since 1926, established a regiment to facilitate initial combat training of the recruits. After completing their training, these men would be added to the four infantry regiments—105th, 106th, 108th, and 165th—already at Fort McClellan.

Meanwhile, on October 9, 1940, plans for rail and motor movements of the 105th Infantry were discussed at a meeting of the commanders and staff at the Troy Armory. The plans called for the main body of troops to leave by train for Fort McClellan on October 23, 1940, a trip of more than 1,100 miles. One train of twenty cars would carry units of the 1st Battalion, 105th Infantry, from Troy, Cohoes, and Hoosick Falls. A second would originate at Malone, New York, and pick up the 3d Battalion along the Delaware and Hudson Railroad Line. A third train would move from Schenectady, New York, with Companies E, F, and H of the 2d Battalion; G Company of the 2d Battalion would be picked up at Amsterdam. All trains were scheduled to arrive at Anniston no later than October 25.

On a rainy Tuesday morning, October 15, formal ceremonies took place at the Troy Armory inducting nearly 700 men of the 105th Infantry Regiment into federal service. When the ceremonies concluded, the 105th Regimental Band played "You're in the Army Now," and the armory was closed to the public. A guard detail from Company A was stationed at the entrance to the armory, under the command of 2d Lt. John G. Cocoa.

Private George P. Kelly, Headquarters Company, 105th Infantry, remembered that day: "On October 15, 1940, I was standing on the corner of Dauw Street and River Street in Troy, New York, waiting for a bus to take me to the Troy Armory—purpose to be inducted into the Army. I had just celebrated my eighteenth birthday the previous September 16. An officer came along and seeing my buck private's uniform offered me a ride. It was Col. O'Brien [at the time a captain]. Naturally, I was in awe and very appreciative. I was often assigned to Col. O'Brien as his radio operator during maneuvers in Tennessee, Arkansas, and Louisiana. The Col. was always concerned for the welfare of his men including myself and everyone else who served under him. The Col. was well liked and respected by everyone."

Immediately upon reporting to their armories, the men were given physical examinations. All personnel were required to remain until the main body of the regiment left for Fort McClellan on October 23. Before the Apple-knockers could move south, however, there was a great deal of clerical and technical paperwork to do. Five field kitchens were set up to provide food, and cots were provided for those who stayed overnight. The men who lived nearby spent the night with their families.

On October 18, 1940, a motor convoy of thirty-seven vehicles carrying five officers and ninety-five enlisted men left Troy for the 1,125-

mile trip to Alabama. They expected to take five days to complete the trip. Three days later, on October 21, 1940, a second party of five officers and 145 enlisted men left by rail and arrived at the same time as the truck convoy. Corporal Edwin Luck from Amsterdam, New York, a member of Company G, was with the truck convoy. He recalled that the "trucks broke down a lot," but they finally completed the trip.

Saturday, October 19, was a beautiful day in Troy. That afternoon the citizens turned out by the thousands for "105th Infantry Day" to bid farewell to the hundreds of sons leaving for Fort McClellan. The military parade was led down Fifth Avenue by Capt. William J. O'Brien, commander of Company A. Marching with them were former members of the unit, dressed in the uniform of the Troy Citizen's Corps—scarlet jackets, blue trousers, and plumed helmets.

Captain O'Brien, born in Troy on September 25, 1899, had joined the 2d New York Infantry on August 6, 1917, during World War I. He remained in the state Guard until February 3, 1920, when he enlisted in Company A. He had advanced through the ranks and, on May 29, 1939, was promoted to captain in Company A of the 105th Infantry.

At the departure of the 1st Battalion (Companies A, C, and D) on October 23, the citizenry of Troy turned out in one of the largest demonstrations ever witnessed to see the boys off. At Union Station, they were joined by the 1st Battalion Headquarters Detachment from Hoosick Falls, New York, as well as men of Company B from Cohoes, New York.

Private Anthony J. Wirmusky, 1st Battalion Headquarters Detachment, remembered seeing Captain O'Brien at the train station that morning. He described him as "a short officer with a trench coat" who carried a pistol at his side. Captain O'Brien was trying to keep the crowd of people on the platform away from the train cars and the troops of the 105th, who were hanging out the windows, yelling, waving, and screaming at their friends and family members. Earlier that day a report was received that a citizen in Glens Falls, New York, had fallen under the train while trying to touch members of Company K who had just boarded the train. According to Wirmusky, Captain O'Brien was simply trying to prevent a similar incident from happening in Troy.

When the regiment left Troy on October 23, 1940, it was commanded by Col. Christopher B. DeGenaar, who had previously served with the New York State Adjutant General's office. When it left, the regiment was composed mostly of men from small towns and cities scattered across the state's northeastern corner. Men of Regimental Headquarters, Headquarters Company, Medical Detachment, and Service Company came from Troy, New York; and the Antitank Company came from Whitehall. First Battalion Headquarters personnel were from Troy and the 1st Battalion Headquarters Detachment was from Hoosick Falls. Companies A, C, and D were from Troy; and Company B came from Cohoes. The 2d Battalion Headquarters and Headquarters Detachment were based in Schenectady, New York, while its rifle companies—E and F—and H Company, heavy weapons, also came from Schenectady. G Company originated in Amsterdam. The 3d Battalion Headquarters was from Schenectady, with the Headquarters Detachment from Saranac Lake. The 3d Battalion's rifle companies were located as follows: I, Malone; K, Glens Falls; L, Saratoga Springs; and M (heavy weapons), in Gloversville.

Five years later, when the 105th was demobilized, it would be represented by men from the entire United States and its territories.

The train trip from Troy to Anniston took almost three days, and for most, it was a nightmare. They rode in railway coaches with hard benches, while officers rode in Pullman cars with sleeping berths. Nobody was able to sleep much except for short naps. Sergeant John J. Daurio from Valley Falls and Company A recalled that the coaches were not comfortable and there was a lot of "hollering and drinking" aboard the train. Corporal Ernest L. Pettit from Wynantskill and Company D recalled that the guys were "raising the devil," and there were a lot of "card games" and "crap games." Private Samuel Di Nova of Troy and Company D also recalled that the hard wooden seats were quite uncomfortable.

When the 105th left Troy, it was snowing, so the men were dressed for cold weather. Three days later, however, the temperature was in the low 80s, and they sweltered in their heavy wool uniforms and "wrapped leggins." Morale plummeted further when they arrived and learned they had to carry their equipment almost a mile to Fort McClellan.

2 Training at Fort McClellan

Fort McClellan, named for Union Gen. George B. McClellan of Civil War fame, was an abandoned military reservation comprising 19,600 acres and located three miles from Anniston. It began its existence as an infantry training center in July 1917. In July 1929, it was home to a regular army regiment prior to the arrival of the 27th Infantry Division in late October 1940.

The facilities at the post were clearly inadequate for a full infantry division; so the division's engineers, aided by civilian labor, constructed billets and rifle ranges on the main post. While these were being constructed, the regiments camped on the fringes of the main post in squad tents pitched on wooden platforms. Temporary wooden mess halls were erected at the end of each company street, with latrines at the opposite ends. When men from Company D's advance detail began to prepare the camp for the arrival of the main body, they found a major snafu. Instead of floors and wall frames for the tents, they found a bunch of civilian carpenters lying around, claiming they were waiting for surveyors to lay out the camp area. Not a single nail had been driven. To expedite matters, 1st Lt. Kenneth J. Dolan, Company D, from Watervliet, used a little Yankee ingenuity. With the help of several enlisted men, he laid out the perimeter of the regimental camp site and lined up the company streets. The carpenters were able to set up the camp site, which was occupied for about one month, in short order, before the men moved into more permanent structures on the main post.

On first sight, Fort McClellan was a mess. Private Frank Standarski of Company A, from Wynantskill, described the fort as a "hell hole" and a "dirty, stinking, muddy hole." Living conditions were primitive. Six to eight men lived in each tent, a space about sixteen-by-sixteen feet square. The men slept on straw mattresses laid upon cots, with the scratchy straw breaking through the mattresses, itching and sticking in men's backs. The tents were heated with Sibley stoves placed on wooden platforms four inches deep and filled with sand. After several months, the stoves burned through the platforms and sparks from the stoves frequently burned holes in the tent material, creating fires that constantly had to be extinguished.

The woods had been cleared so recently, when the 105th first arrived at Fort McClellan, the company streets were still full of tree stumps. The men had to dig out the stumps themselves to permit formations and drilling. When it rained, the streets became seas of mud. Latrine facilities were extremely primitive; fifty-gallon drum "piss" cans were set up in the middle of the streets instead of at their ends as planned originally. The last two men to leave the tents each morning had to carry the cans 100 yards to the end of the company street and to empty them, a formidable problem if they expected to be on time to answer roll call.

Mess facilities were worse than primitive; the mess hall was simply a cook shack. Because there were no mess tents, the men had to eat out in the open, rain or shine, within 200 yards of the latrines. The food itself was adequate, but neither nutritional nor well cooked. Most of the trained cooks were discharged prior to leaving New York because of age or dependency status. Despite the lack of training, the cooks improved by the time the men moved into the permanent facilities on the main post. Heading into the nearby town of Anniston for a meal was not a viable solution, as the locals charged the Apple-knockers outrageous prices for simple food.

Equipment and weapons were inadequate. World War I wrap leggins were still required, and the men hated them just as much as the leftover wool uniforms from World War I that were the only issue. The riflemen carried Springfield '03 rifles, also World War I relics. They wore World War I "Smoky Bear" hats or World War I pot-type helmets. Because real mortars and machine guns were in short supply, makeshift mortars were created using pieces of stove pipe or wood. Trucks bore signs identifying them as "tanks" while artillery pieces served as logs, and old vehicles were crafted to resemble antitank pieces. The machine guns in the heavy-weapons companies were loaded onto two-wheel carts that were pulled by two men in front and pushed by two men behind.

By the Christmas holidays 1940, the troops had moved into their new camp in the interior of the fort. The living arrangements were much improved. Although the men were still billeted in tents, they now had hot showers, decent mess halls, and acceptable latrines.

With improved living facilities came improvements in the training and available equipment. In their first several weeks at Fort McClellan, the men completed basic training. During this period, the 102d Engineers constructed two rifle ranges, capable of accommodating two regiments at a time. The vacancies in cooks, bakers, clerks, technicians, and mechanics were also filled during this three-month period. Private John "Jackie" Breen from Cropseyville, who had joined Company A just before the move to Fort McClellan, trained as a cook after his arrival.

In January and February 1941, some 7,000 new recruits began pouring into Fort McClellan to augment the understrength 27th Division. All National Guard divisions had been given the choice by the War Department of training recruits themselves or accepting recruits after they had been trained at a replacement training center. Major General Haskell, the 27th Division commander, opted to do the training within his division. The War Department further agreed that the first draft of new men to the 27th Division would come from New York State. Many came from the New York City area and volunteered for army service under the terms of the 1940 Selective Service and Training Act. It obligated them to serve only one year of active duty, unless a national emergency were declared.

To indoctrinate the new recruits, Haskell ordered that each regiment set up an ad hoc unit to train its new men. Recruits assigned, for example, to Company A were placed in a corresponding training unit manned by a cadre of officers and experienced noncommissioned officers (NCOs) from the parent company. Upon completion of a thirteen-week basic-training period, the recruits were assimilated into their permanent unit. Following the initial training period, there was another thirteen-week period of advanced training, lasting into May 1941.

Training consisted of close-order drills, extended-order formations, calisthenics, tent pitching, pack assembling, and bayonet drills. As the men progressed, their training incorporated route marching, formation and conduct of the advance guard, approach marching, infantry-scout performance, small-unit tactics, and classes of fire, fire distribution, and fire control. They underwent preparatory rifle marksmanship (although there were only enough M1 rifles for one regiment) and training with .30-caliber light machine guns and 60mm mortars. Each day ended with the trainees marching into the encampment while the regimental band played.

Captain O'Brien was a stickler for tough training. Private John Domanowski, a new recruit from New Hyde Park, recalled the first time he saw O'Brien during bayonet training. He didn't know exactly who O'Brien was, but he knew he was Irish by the twinkle in his eye. O'Brien, a short man, "walked over to this big recruit and just took his rifle away from him with the greatest of ease. I'll never forget that. He had the respect of all that knew him." On another occasion, O'Brien and Sgt. Charles Whalen of Watervliet were on their way to pick up the company payroll at the paymaster's office. Pursuant to regulations, they were wearing Class A uniforms and carrying side arms. As they passed a group of soldiers running and dropping into position to fire their weapons, O'Brien remarked, "Look at those SOBs; they are not doing it right." He ran over to the men and proceeded to demonstrate the proper technique, muddying his uniform in the process, knowing he'd have to change into a new one before he could meet with the paymaster. Sergeant Whalen described Captain O'Brien as a "soldier's soldier."

The regimental coat of arms of the Apple-knockers was designed in February 1928, to reflect the history and service of the regiment. Its shield is blue and white; blue for the present infantry colors and white for the color of the old Revolutionary War infantry facings. The badge is a red apple with a stem and two leaves with a white number 2 superimposed thereon. At the top of the shield in gold is a Roman sword-in-sheath representing service in the Spanish-American War in 1898; a gold cactus (or prickly pear) represents service during the Mexican border incident in 1916; and a gold fleur-de-lis represents service in France during World War I. The motto of the 105th Infantry Regiment, *semper invicti terra* ("always victorious on land"), in red on a gold background, appears in a semicircle along the bottom and sides of the shield.

The first thing a soldier learned upon joining the regiment was the meaning of the insignia and the 27th Division patch. The Apple-knocker insignia flew on the flags carried at parades and appeared over barracks, mess halls, and recreation centers utilized by the soldiers of the 105th.

The regiment was short of junior officers when it reported to Fort McClellan in October 1940. Prior to mobilization, it had not promoted enough enlisted men to officer rank. In addition, many of its officers were overage and physically unfit for active service. One enlisted man from the 105th even described many line officers as "elderly"; too old to serve in combat. They had to be weeded out if the regiment was to be brought to full combat strength. Fortunately, during the fall of 1940, many newly commissioned, younger officers from the 107th Infantry Regiment were available for transfer to the 105th.

The 107th Infantry of New York City had operated its own Officer Candidate School (OCS) in the late 1930s, based on U.S. Army criteria. It was a self-study course and took about one year to complete. Each Friday evening, several candidates from each company in the regiment attended training sessions at the armory on 23d Street. They took turns commanding the men in formations and drill and were graded on various command functions by senior officers. Their summer training was held at Fort Benning, Georgia. The Friday unpaid meetings at the armory were in addition to regular unit drills on Wednesday and Thursday nights. Candidates who successfully completed this OCS program received a second lieutenant's commission in the Army Reserve. They were permitted to wear gold bars on their fatigues and diamonds on the epaulets of their uniforms, but they were not assigned command responsibilities.

When the 107th Regiment was redesignated as the 207th Coast Artillery in September 1940, many of those who had received reserve commissions were informed that there weren't enough officer vacancies for them in the newly established antiaircraft regiment. They would have to transfer to other units if they wished to become line officers. Lieutenant Francois Albanese from Queens recalled that his commanding officer, Colonel Tobin, recommended they consider joining the 27th Division, which was short of officers. Knowing that war was imminent, Lieutenant Albanese and two of his closest friends, Roger Peyre and William Baxter, decided to take the colonel's advice. Albanese and Peyre joined the 105th Infantry while Baxter became a military police officer with the 27th Division.

In total, sixteen of these lieutenants transferred to the 105th in the fall of 1940. Five of the sixteen transferred out of the 105th before it entered combat. Of the remaining eleven officers, five who commanded rifle companies in the 105th were killed in combat.

After more than six months of hard work, specialist schools, and marksmanship training, the 105th Infantry was directed to participate in combat maneuvers in Tennessee during May and June 1941, under the command of Lt. Gen. Ben Lear, the commander of Second Army. The division, along with the 5th and 30th Infantry Divisions and the 2d Armored Division commanded by Brig. Gen. George S. Patton, constituted the VII Corps.

To prepare for the maneuvers, Captain O'Brien had his men sleep on the ground outside their barracks. At first, it was for one night, then for three consecutive nights, then for one week, and later for three weeks. By the time the maneuvers began, the Apple-knockers were already accustomed to living off the land. On May 24, 1941, the division began moving to the maneuver area, travel that took three days. From then until June 27, the men lived in the field and marched almost 500 miles. Sergeant Charles Plante recalled that the unit marched through central Tennessee, bivouacking at Murfreesboro, Junction City, Chattanooga, and Nashville. Sleeping on the hard ground was "uncomfortable," according to Sergeant Plante. A member of Company C described the maneuvers as "endless marching up and down the hills of Tennessee. They marched us 500 miles in twenty days! But we wound up in fabulous condition."

The maneuvers lasted for six weeks and involved almost half a million men. They took place in an area almost 400 miles wide and was one of the army's first attempts to manage large numbers of troops in the field, both logistically and tactically. Troop movements, hospital support, communications among units, and overall coordination were the objectives of the exercise. Though some critics such as Col. J. Lawton "Lightning Joe" Collins, VII Corps chief of staff, claimed, "We were cramming too much, too soon, in these early exercises." It was undeniable that these early corps maneuvers in 1941 helped the army prepare for the army-versus-army maneuvers planned for the fall of 1941.

When the 27th Division reassembled at Fort McClellan on July 10, it immediately started to prepare for two months of extended maneuvers in Arkansas and Louisiana during the months of August and September. These maneuvers would be the largest in peacetime ever staged by the U.S. Army, involving more than 400,000 men of Second and Third Armies and culminating in a great mock battle between them in the area between Louisiana's Red and Sabine Rivers.

Ominously, on July 21, 1941, the U.S. Congress, at the behest of President Roosevelt, extended the Selective Service and Training Act of 1940 to require those men who had been inducted for one year in October, 1940, to extend their period of service for an additional six months. This meant that the men who expected to go home on October 15 would be kept in the army until at least April 15, 1942. This prospect, plus the extensive preparations being made for the new maneuvers, convinced the men that they would be kept in military service indefinitely if the United States entered the war in Europe. For some, this eventuality created dissension. Most, however, considered the prospect of defending their country in war to be their obligation as citizens.

On July 29, 1941, the division, as part of the VII Corps of the Second (Red) Army, trucked from Fort McClellan. The march went west through Birmingham, Alabama, then southwest through Bessemer and Tuscaloosa to the Mississippi state line. The column then moved west from Columbus to Greenville on the east bank of the Mississippi, 162 miles from the Alabama line. After crossing the river, it proceeded west to El Dorado, Arkansas, where it bivouacked on August

10. There the division prepared for the maneuvers against the Blue Army commanded by Lt. Gen. Walter Krueger.

The climate and conditions faced by the 105th Infantry in Arkansas and Louisiana were "abysmal." The climate was hot and humid, and the men, wearing heavy, dark uniforms, frequently passed out from heat exhaustion. There were swamps and diamondback snakes and all manner of bugs, chiggers, wood ticks, and black widow spiders. The roads upon which they marched, for what seemed forever, were nothing but wheel tracks. According to one soldier, this area was the "asshole of the world."

By this time, the quality of the equipment available had vastly improved. Now there were real tanks and mortars and machine guns that fired real ammunition. The regimental heavy-weapons companies, D, H, and M, now had .50-caliber water-cooled machine guns and 81mm mortars. Sergeant Vince Lombardi, Company E, admitted that the division was "adequately equipped" and that it was "more aggressive, better equiped [sic], better conditioned" for the maneuvers than it had been before. Sergeant Helmut Haag of Company C stated, "We had the Garand (M1) rifle by then and we had better vehicles—for example we were equipped with the two-and-one-half-ton trucks and other more modern military vehicles."

The first combat phase of the maneuvers took place August 17 through August 29 and was held in Arkansas, south of the Ouachita National Forest. The second phase, from August 30 to September 12, was held in an area to the southeast of the forest, extending to the Louisiana state line. The third phase—the important General Headquarters phase—took place from September 15 to September 30, in the north central and western parts of Louisiana. It included the battles of the Red River on September 15–16 and Shreveport on September 24.

The division performed "creditably" during the maneuvers. On several occasions during the last, critical phase, the Blue Army's 36th Division from Texas and the 27th went head to head. There was much simulated combat, in which men under fire were required to lay down, pretending that they were dead or wounded. Several 105th soldiers were captured by the Texas Division and put in a prison in Lake Charles, Louisiana.

Though grueling, the maneuvers were extremely valuable. Sergeant Haag thought they created a "well-functioning and well-trained organization, which unit-for-unit was comparable to the best the army had to offer." One unknown member of the 105th Infantry, in the midst of the battle of Saipan in June and July 1944, was heard to say, "If it wasn't for the shootin', I'd say the Louisiana-Arkansas maneuvers were as tough as this."

The 400,000 troops who slept on the ground and maneuvered through the mud in these war games came out of their ordeal, several officers said, "toughened and with high spirits and improved morale." The men were "hard as nails." As one officer said: "Their morale is better now than it was two months ago and it is getting better all the time." General George C. Marshall, chief of staff of the U.S. Army, called the maneuvers "a great success," praising the troops for their "zeal and energy, endurance and spirit," which he termed a model of excellence. General Dwight D. Eisenhower, who served as General Krueger's chief of staff for the Blue Army, later said that "the maneuvers were necessary and filled a great need. Not one of our officers on the active list had commanded a unit as large as a division in World War I." Lieutenant General Lesley J. McNair, maneuver director and chief of the General Headquarters staff, said the stamina the troops displayed was one of the outstanding developments of the maneuvers and added, "We can never be entirely satisfied with the performance of our troops, but the soldier of 1941 will give a better account of himself than the soldier in any other period in our history."

When the 27th Division reassembled at Fort McClellan on October 8, the word was rampant that many changes were in store. On August 19, 1941, the War Department had issued a statement providing for the release of approximately 200,000 soldiers from active duty: approximately 150,000 National Guardsmen, 10,000 Reserve officers, 20,000 selectees who had enlisted in the Army of the United States (AUS) and whose one year of service had expired, and 20,000 National Guard officers. The priorities for discharge were: (1) hardship cases (i.e., those men or women whose continued service was causing undue hardship to their families at home); (2) all enlisted men over twenty-eight years of age who had not achieved noncommissioned rank and NCOs over twenty-eight years of age who wished to be discharged; and (3) draftees whose one year of service had expired. These soldiers, upon their release from active duty, were to be transferred to the Enlisted Reserve Corps or to the inactive National Guard with the stipulation that they could be recalled into active service in the event of national emergency.

The War Department's order affected approximately 3,000 men in the division. By December 7, its strength dropped to 920 officers and 13,334 enlisted men; authorized strength was 1,012 officers, 12 warrant officers, and 21,314 enlisted men. The release of enlisted men twenty-eight years of age and older had a severe impact on the NCO's strength. Many experienced NCOs had already been transferred out of the division to OCS and higher headquarters' staffs shortly after the division assembled at Fort McClellan. Those twenty-eight and older who opted to be released had to be replaced by men from the division whose only experience was the recent maneuvers. Sergeant Ronald Johnson recalled that the War Department's order "left us with a very small cadre of people. And after October 15 we went into a kind of garrison situation. Training was at a minimum. There weren't all that many people remaining. Of course, all activities were short of staff, so our ranks were decimated at this time."

There were also changes at the top echelons. Shortly after the completion of the maneuvers, Major General Haskell, at age sixty-three, already one year past retirement age, announced that he would voluntarily retire effective November 1. Haskell, who had commanded the 27th Division since 1926, was reassigned to become the national director of civil defense at First Army Headquarters. The new commander was Brig. Gen. Ralph McT. Pennell, age fifty-nine, commander of the 52d Field Artillery Brigade since 1940. A regular army officer, Pennell had graduated from the U.S. Military Academy in 1906, the Army's Command and General Staff School in 1923, and the Army War College in 1928. He was succeeded at the 52d Brigade by Col. Redmond F. Kernan Jr., a 1917 graduate of West Point.

Many officers of the 105th Infantry Regiment who had served during World War I were released from active service under the War Department's August 19 ruling. Major Joseph A. Forgett, plans and training officer, was discharged at the age of fifty-two; Lt. Col. Charles B. Plumley, executive officer, was discharged at the age of fifty-eight; Capt. Thomas R. Horton, commander of the Regimental Headquarters Company, was discharged at the age of fifty; and Capt. Edwin F. Livingstone, commanding service company, was discharged at the age of fifty-one.

3 The Japanese Attack on Pearl Harbor

When word of the Japanese attack on Pearl Harbor was received around 1330 on December 7, the 27th Division was immediately mobilized, all leaves cancelled, and all men on pass rounded up. Military policemen went through movie houses, stores, and restaurants in Anniston and the neighboring communities telling the soldiers to report immediately. Sergeant John J. Daurio, of Company A, was on a weekend pass in Atlanta when he received word that all army personnel had to be back by 2000 that night. Everyone wondered: What and where is Pearl Harbor?

By 1800, the 53d Brigade under the command of Brig. Gen. Ogden J. Ross, including the Apple-knocker Regiment, whose commander was Col. Christopher B. DeGenaar, was immediately assigned to guard railroads, highways, plants, bridges, and other important installations in Alabama and Florida. By early morning on December 8, two of the brigade's regiments were on duty all the way from Mobile to Huntsville, Alabama. Elements of the 3d Battalion of the 105th Infantry were deployed as far as the naval base at Pensacola, Florida.

Private John Domanowski of Company B recalled that his unit was assigned to guard dams in Tennessee and Alabama. Several members of Company D were assigned to guard the Guntersville Dam on the Tennessee River north of Gadsen, Alabama. Corporal Ernest L. Pettit, of Company D, recalled that he and his men (accompanied by several riflemen) set up a machine gun on top of the dam. The next morning several local citizens in a rowboat were spotted in the river below the dam. Pettit yelled for them to go back, and when they kept coming, his men opened up with the machine gun, making sure to fire well in front of the boat, but it was enough to scare them off. Other men were assigned to Gadsen to guard an armory that produced 105mm artillery shells.

After a few days of chaos and sporadic guard duty, these units were recalled, with all assignments of the 27th Division taken over by the 33d Division of the Illinois National Guard. The brigade was ordered to return to Fort McClellan by December 11 for movement within forty-eight hours to an undisclosed destination. All leaves and furloughs were canceled. By December 11, the division was again assembled at Fort McClellan, and on December 13 it was formally alerted for movement.

Beginning December 14, the division began boarding trains to move to a destination still undisclosed. Seventy-two trains were required to move all the troops and equipment, and the accommodations were less than desirable, as the troops traveled in old coaches removed from storage for the mobilization. Each train was composed of six to ten Pullman cars, twenty flat cars, two boxcars, and two kitchen cars. On December 19, after a 2,500-mile trip, the 27th Division arrived in Los Angeles, California. Amazingly, nearly 30,000 troops had moved more than 2,000 miles on schedule—a logistical miracle!—and there had been only one accident.

The division headquarters was established in Ontario, California, with other division units spread all over Southern California to protect the coast from possible Japanese nuisance raids. The 53d Brigade Headquarters, along with the 105th Infantry, was set up at Camp Hahn, the great military installation at the edge of the desert, just ten miles outside Riverside. The 106th Infantry was at Corona about twenty miles away, and the 54th Brigade Headquarters was located in Pomona, as was the headquarters of the 108th Infantry. The 165th Infantry Regiment was temporarily attached (until January 1, 1942) to the 40th Division in the Los Angeles area.

The 105th's principal mission was to guard March Air Field, just across the road from Camp Hahn. Sergeant Daurio recalled that there were numerous B-25 bombers at March Field that needed protection. Guard duty was tedious and dull, but important work. One evening, Sgt. Vincent Busone of Company A was in command of the guard detail at the air field. It was a wet, cold night and the men were miserable, so he gave them hot coffee and let them out of the rain for a few minutes. When Captain O'Brien found out about the lax behavior, it was said he "complained like hell," yet disciplined no one.

On December 26 the division was ordered to requisition enough men to bring it up to war strength. The next day Lt. Col. Gerard W. Kelley, the division G-1, requisitioned 5,693 infantry, 1,067 field artillery, 346 engineers, 353 medics, 289 quartermaster troops, and 114 replacements from miscellaneous branches. This grand total of 7,862 enlisted men and 196 officers brought the division up to war strength. At the same time, many of the enlisted Reserve and inactive National Guardsmen at Fort McClellan were ordered by telegram to report to the nearest induction center and make their way to California to rejoin the division by December 28.

On January 2, 1942, the War Department ordered 3,200 men from Camp Wolters, the new infantry replacement training center at Mineral Springs, Texas, to report to the division at Fort Ord, California. Most men from Camp Wolters were Midwesterners from Indiana, Illinois, Kentucky, and Wisconsin. Among them was Sgt. W. Taylor Hudson from Louisville, Kentucky, who would serve with the 105th Antitank Company throughout the war. The Camp Wolters contingent was the first large group from outside New York to join the division. Fresh out of basic training, these men had to be trained by the remaining veterans of the Arkansas-Louisiana maneuvers in order for the division to reach the same high level of readiness it once possessed for overseas combat.

On January 17, after assembling at Pomona, Camp Hahn, and Arlington, California, the 53d and 54th Infantry Brigades and the 52d Field Artillery Brigade began movement north to Fort Ord, arriving January 24. An advance party went by truck with the bulk of the men following by train. Fort Ord, overlooking Monterey Bay, was about eight hours distant from the San Francisco port of embarkation. No formal alert orders had been received yet, but all signs were there. The regiment was quartered in Tent City, where "you roasted in daytime sun and froze as soon as that departed."

By February 23, the division received approximately 8,000 officers and men to bring total division strength up to 21,719. New jeeps and enough new M1 rifles and carbines for each man were ready at Fort Ord, and the artillery received new howitzers. The artillerymen engaged in extensive gunnery practice in preparation for what everyone believed was to be an overseas assignment, and new clothing was issued. The Apple-knockers were a long way from home, and things were not going to get any better in the near future—APO 27, c/o Postmaster, San Francisco, California, would be their address for the next four years.

While stationed at Fort Ord, there were several major changes in the divisional command structure, as well as in the Apple-knocker Regiment. On January 10, Col. Russell G. Ayers, age fifty, an Organized Reserve Corps officer, replaced Col. Thomas C. Dedell, age fifty-nine, as commander of the 106th Infantry Regiment; Colonel Martin H. Meany, executive officer of the 165th Infantry, transferred to the 108th Infantry as its commander; Col. Gardiner Conroy, age fifty-two, continued to command the 165th Infantry; and Col. Redmond F. Kernan Jr. was promoted to brigadier general and took command of the 52d FA Brigade.

On February 15, Lt. Col. Leonard E. Bishop, age forty-six, was promoted to full colonel and assumed command of the 105th Infantry, replacing Colonel DeGenaar, who was sick in the hospital at Fort McClellan. Bishop had been the executive officer of the regiment since November 1941. Prior to that, he was in command of the 2d Battalion and was replaced as 2d Battalion commander by Lt. Col. Leslie M. Jensen, age forty-four, of Schenectady.

Bishop was a veteran fighter, enlisting in the 2d New York Infantry on June 19, 1916, and had served in the Mexican Border incident. When the unit was called up for World War I, he was a sergeant in Company F. On July 18, 1918, he was promoted to 2d lieutenant in Company F while the unit was stationed in Belgium. After returning home in July 1919, he immediately rejoined the Guard. On January 13, 1920, he was appointed first lieutenant, and on January 12, 1926, when he was promoted to captain, he took command of Company E. Bishop subsequently was promoted to major and appointed adjutant of the 105th. On July 20, 1937, he became commander of the 2d Battalion with the grade of lieutenant colonel.

While at Fort Ord, the 1st Battalion, 105th Infantry, was commanded by Lt. Col. George H. "Hopalong" Hopkins, age forty-seven, of Whitehall, New York. He had served in the Reserve Corps from February to November 1918 and became a 1st lieutenant in the 105th's Headquarters Company on December 23, 1921. He was promoted to captain in April 1924, major in August 1940, and lieutenant colonel in charge of the 1st Battalion, 105th Infantry Regiment, on October 11, 1940.

Within the 1st Battalion, there were a number of organizational changes before the regiment moved to Hawaii. On February 25, Capt. William J. O'Brien, age forty-two, commander of Company A, was promoted to major and appointed regimental supply officer (S-4). Company A's new commander was 1st Lt. Albert A. Butkas of Hoosick Falls who had been executive officer of Company A. Butkas had previously served with Company D and as a sergeant in Headquarters Detachment.

On February 15, Capt. John P. Hennessey, age forty-two, who had commanded Company B, was transferred to the 98th Division. Command of Company B was given to Capt. Richard F. Ryan, an ROTC graduate from the University of California. Joining the unit at Fort Ord, Ryan was a lawyer but wanted to join a combat unit instead of the FBI. First Sergeant Charles J. Stephani, who served on Saipan, felt that Captain Ryan, tall and slim, was the kind of man he would "follow anywhere." Sergeant Domanowski recalled that on Saipan, Colonel O'Brien "took a great liking to our new Captain Ryan. They really made a good pair." At battalion staff meetings, Ryan was always the first officer O'Brien would call upon for his opinion.

Company C was commanded by Capt. Philip E. Smith of Troy. When he was assigned to the regimental staff as operations officer, his place as commander of Company C was taken by Capt. Edward J. McGlynn, also of Troy. Company D, the heavy weapons company, was commanded by Capt. William S. O'Toole until February 1942 when he was placed on detached service at the Infantry School, Fort Benning, Georgia. His place was taken by 1st Lt. Emmett T. Catlin who was promoted to captain on June 29, 1942, shortly after the battalion arrived in Hawaii.

Formal orders alerting the division for overseas duty were received on February 1. Physical screening of troops and inoculations began immediately, and on February 20, General Pennell ordered all advance details of the division to move to San Francisco. The first elements boarded the steamship *Republic* on February 27 and sailed the next day. The advance party consisted of representatives of practically every element of the division, including three infantry platoons from Company K, 106th Infantry; Company E, 108th Infantry; and Company C, 165th Infantry. When the men of the advance party landed in Hilo Harbor, Hawaii, on March 10, the division was to begin the longest wartime overseas tour of any army National Guard division. It was also the best-trained and first square army combat division to leave the United States for the Pacific after Pearl Harbor.

In early March, the rest of the division began to move by rail, in darkness and under blackout conditions, from Fort Ord to the embarkation point. Private Anthony J. Wirmusky of Headquarters Detachment recalled that the train was made up of wooden railway cars. When it arrived in San Francisco, the men were assembled in the San Francisco Cow Palace, which served as a staging area.

On March 8, two luxury liners requisitioned by the government—the *Lurline* of the Matson Line and the *Aquitania* of the Cunard Line—began loading the units of the division. On March 8, the 1st Battalion, 105th Infantry, and the Antitank Company (as well as other units), boarded the *Aquitania*. The 2d and 3d Battalions of the 105th Infantry did not leave San Francisco until April 1. The *Aquitania* was the sister ship of the British *Luisitania*, which was sunk by the Germans in 1916, while hundreds of Americans were aboard. With about 10,000 men aboard, the *Aquitania* sailed from San Francisco on March 10 bound for points unknown. Initially, because the ship had an APO number for Corregidor, the men thought they were headed to the Philippines to relieve the men still fighting the Japanese on Bataan and Corregidor. Apparently, the APO number was a ruse, because approximately ten days later, the *Aquitania* docked in Honolulu.

The *Aquitania* was a four stacker, eight stories high. It was a beautiful ship, and one of the largest transports in the world. It was manned by a British crew who, unfriendly toward their American allies, were difficult and condescending. The ship was extremely crowded, with Company A quartered on D and G decks and Headquarters Detachment seven decks below the main deck in bunks stacked six high!

The trip over on the *Aquitania* was a nightmare with many soldiers sick as dogs during the entire trip. Sergeant W. Taylor Hudson of Antitank Company remembers being "deathly ill" the whole time he was on board. Waiting for meals, the men formed long lines up and down the ship ladders, although the quality of the food was unspeakable. In contrast, the officers dined in the officers' mess with tablecloths and silverware. For the enlisted men, there was no room for physical exercise, so many spent their days playing interminable crap games.

The *Aquitania*, because of its thirty-five-knot speed and ability to maneuver, did not require an escort against submarine attack. However, the ship, as a converted luxury liner, did not have any armaments to protect against enemy air or surface attacks. Company D set up its .50-caliber machine guns on the ship's turrets, railings, and sundeck. Sergeant W. Taylor Hudson recalled that one of Antitank Company's 37mm guns was removed from its carriage and placed on a mount by the ship's rail as protection from submarines. The field artillery had a similar mission: placing field pieces for surface defense on the decks. It was primitive, but it was all the *Aquitania* had to protect itself against an enemy attack.

After five days at sea, the men began to hear radio reports from the infamous propagandist Tokyo Rose that the *Aquitania* had been sunk by a Japanese submarine. Over the next several days, these false reports continued. Although the reports were bogus, they indicated that the Japanese knew the ship was at sea and bound for Hawaii.

One night, Sgt. Felix Giuffre, Company A, went on deck to see how his squad was doing. He was startled to see lots of "beacons sticking out of the ocean, with red lights on the top." He asked a sailor about them, and was told, "We have eleven submarines charging up their batteries and they are right with our ship heading towards the

combat field in the Pacific." Giuffre recalled feeling a sense of relief, "because I thought we were traveling without an escort of any
kind." In truth, however, the submarines were not part of any escort;
they had simply come up for air.

The men manning the machine guns had lonely vigils. Private
First Class Dennis W. Roche of Point Pleasant, New Jersey, recalled
what it was like one evening:

> I was on the *Aquitania* going overseas to Hawaii in early
> March of 1942. My cousin Edward Doran and I were on guard
> duty aboard ship, and we were to man a .50-caliber machine-
> gun. We were on guard 12:00 midnight to 2:00 in the morning.
> At that time, I thought, and I still think today, "What in God's
> world could we see or hit in the dark?" As you can imagine, it
> was cold crossing the Pacific doing 22 knots in March.
>
> An officer came to our guard mount and told us that he was
> Captain O'Brien of the 105th Infantry and he was the O.D. We
> identified ourselves and talked a few minutes about how cold
> it was. The captain left and came back in about 15 minutes later
> with coffee and buttered rolls, apologizing that that was all he
> could get.
>
> I have never forgotten his kindness. . . . If the army had had
> more officers like him, it would have been a much better army.

The *Aquitania* arrived at Honolulu on March 14. Sergeant Giuffre recalled that "Pearl Harbor was a mess. It was bottled up very bad.
Our ships . . . sunk and still steaming . . . there were ships turned
over. . . . It was unbelievable to see." The troops were transshipped
to the army transport USS *Republic* because the *Aquitania* was too
large to enter the harbor at Hilo. The 1st Battalion was one of the
first combat units of the division to arrive, landing on the "big island"
of Hawaii on March 17.

At Hilo, the division's units were spread throughout the outer islands to defend against a possible Japanese attack on the coastlines.
General Pennell set up his headquarters on the island of Hawaii, defended by the 53d Brigade commanded by Brigadier General Ross.
The 105th Infantry's principal area of responsibility was the south-

eastern coast of the island near Pahala and Black Sands Beach. The island of Kauai was garrisoned by the 165th Regiment, with the 108th Regiment and later the 52d FA Brigade stationed on Maui. A battalion of the 108th garrisoned the smaller islands of Molokai and Lanai. On the island of Oahu, the Hawaiian Division, the forerunner of the 24th and the 25th Infantry Divisions, provided the defense of Honolulu and Pearl Harbor.

Although the threat of a Japanese invasion was ever present, during the first two months of manning the beach defenses, nothing much happened on the island of Hawaii. On April 26, 1942, however, the volcano Mauna Loa erupted, causing quite a commotion among the troops. Then in late May the division went on alert upon hearing that a Japanese task force was headed toward the Hawaiian Islands. Fears were allayed, however, when it was learned that the navy and its air forces had soundly defeated the Japanese at Midway on June 7. After the Midway victory, the danger to the Hawaiian Islands lessened, but the divisional units remained dispersed throughout the outer Hawaiian Islands until October.

With the war in Europe and North Africa heating up, the need for officers increased significantly. The division had already been deprived of some of its top officers and NCOs at Fort McClellan in 1941 and in California in early 1942. To fill new divisions with qualified officers and NCOs, existing units were called upon to provide cadre (i.e., trained soldiers with proven ability to train other soldiers). The 27th Division, one of the best-trained combat divisions in the army at the time, was a prime source of officer and NCO candidates. In July, some top enlisted men were offered the opportunity to attend OCS at Fort Benning. Many elected to go and were commissioned second lieutenants.

In July 1942, General Pennell received orders that the division was to be triangularized by August 31. Its size was to be reduced from four to three infantry regiments and its brigade structure abandoned. Brigadier General Ross, the previous commander of the 53d Brigade, became assistant division commander. Triangularization reduced the division's size from 21,000 men to approximately 14,000 men. Pennell's choice of which infantry regiment to drop was made for him, when the 108th Regiment, largely from the Syracuse area, was suddenly transferred to the 40th Division by the Hawaiian Department of the U.S. Army. It later fought in New Britain, New Guinea, and the Philippines. After triangularization, the 27th Division consisted of three infantry regiments: the 105th, 106th, and the 165th, plus supporting units. The 104th Field Artillery Regiment was split into two battalions, the 104th and the 249th. The 249th Battalion supported the 105th Infantry Regiment, while the 104th Battalion supported the 106th Infantry Regiment. The 105th Field Artillery Regiment was also split into two battalions, with the 105th Battalion supporting the 165th Infantry Regiment, and the 225th Artillery Battalion assigned to the Hawaiian Department.

On August 7 the 1st Marine Division landed on Guadalcanal, the first offensive move of the war against the Japanese. By the end of September, two months of hard fighting, the heat, and tropical disease had taken their toll on the marines. On October 16, 1942, General Pennell was ordered to relieve the 1st Marine Division. Preparations began almost immediately, and the 105th and the 106th Regiments began moving from their defensive positions on the outer islands to Oahu to prepare for Guadalcanal. On October 20, however, a change of orders came from the War Department. Instead of going to Guadalcanal, the division was to relieve the army's 25th Division on Oahu, and the 25th was being sent to Guadalcanal to relieve the 1st Marine Division. In addition, the 27th Division was ordered to furnish 3,500 replacement soldiers to bring the 25th Division up to strength before it shipped out. Several members of the 105th Regiment volunteered to go to Guadalcanal with the 25th Division, and bulletin boards at the barracks provided an opportunity to sign up. Sergeants Ernest L. Pettit, Ralph Perrett, and Charles E. Bell of Company D, were among those who volunteered, but at the last minute, Sergeant Perrett took his name off the list. Several weeks later, as Sergeant Pettit and Sergeant Bell approached Guadalcanal in separate landing barges, they waved to each other. Just then a Japanese shell hit Sergeant Bell's barge and blew it to smithereens. Sergeant Pettit recalled that Charlie Bell just disappeared.

• • •

In late October, the entire 27th Division moved to Oahu. For the first time since it left Fort McClellan almost a year ago, it was assembled in a reasonably compact area. Division Headquarters was established at Aiea on the north shores of Pearl Harbor across from Ford Island. Each regiment was assigned to a sector in the southern defense area of Oahu. The 105th was responsible for the defense of the Ewa Plain, the broad expanse of fertile land between the mountain ranges, adjacent to Pearl Harbor on the north. The Antitank Company, 105th Infantry, was positioned to stop any Japanese attacking force who might try to bring armor up the plain. The 106th Regiment defended the part of the island between Diamond Head and Pearl Harbor, including Honolulu. The 165th guarded the east side of the island with its principal mission the defense of Kaneohe Naval Base. This disposition of the division was to remain in effect for nine months.

On November 20, Maj. Gen. Ralph C. Smith, age forty-eight, took command of the 27th Division replacing General Pennell, who felt that he was too old at age fifty-nine for extended field service and had requested relief. He subsequently commanded the Field Artillery Replacement Training Center at Fort Sill, Oklahoma. Ralph Smith was a regular army officer who had joined the army in 1917. He had graduated from the Army's Command and General Staff School and was known as an expert French linguist and an authority on tactics. Pennell's chief of staff, Col. John Haskell, son of the former commanding general, was reassigned to the War Department General Staff. The new chief of staff was Col. Albert K. Stebbins, age forty-two, a 1925 graduate of West Point and a Command and General Staff School graduate.

Sergeant Ronald L. Johnson, Headquarters Detachment, 1st Battalion, and O'Brien's communications sergeant on Saipan, recalled the first time he met Major General Smith in Hawaii:

I was C.Q. this particular day, and we were in Schofield in the quadrangles there. It was a training day and all the troops were in the field. I was in the 1st sergeant's office where the desk was located. The 1st sergeant was out, and few people were working in the mess hall—I could hear pots and pans rattling around and what not—I heard the screen door in the hallway open and close coming into the quadrangle. I immediately jumped to my feet and went to the door to see who it was and be ready to call attention in the event it was an officer approaching. When I got to the door I was confronted by a man slightly shorter than I with two stars on his shoulder. Before I could get the word *attention* out of my mouth, he thrust out his hand to me, and said, "Hello. I'm Ralph Smith, your new division commander," and he shook my hand.

This was a most pleasant experience. I found the general to be a very warm, down to earth type of person, unimpressed with himself or rank, a very warm and feeling person. I don't recall ever seeing him after we had our short chat, but I was very comfortable with him, and felt great confidence in knowing this man was our division commander.

For the duration of their stay on Oahu, many of the units were quartered at Schofield Barracks north and west of Pearl Harbor. Sergeant Felix Giuffre described Schofield Barracks as "a beautiful set up. It was gloomy and dark, but there was plenty of air. We had double bunks there." Private Sam Di Nova of Company D agreed that the place looked like the barracks in *From Here to Eternity*.

The Antitank Company was stationed at Ewa Plantation. Sergeant W. Taylor Hudson described the facilities:

We were billeted in a big gymnasium complex, built by one of the sugar companies for its employees. This was a huge gym with a full-size basketball court, around the perimeter of which we had double-decked bunks. There was a sizeable shower room, several rooms which were used as company HQ, company PX, offices for regimental dentists and one Hawaiian dentist, as well as sleeping quarters for officers. This building sat on a large plot of land, which included in its bounds an Olympic-size swimming pool and several tennis courts. Just outside the perimeter fence sat an excellent restaurant (also built by the sugar company) to which we could go when the mess hall menu was not appealing. Everyone in the regiment envied our good fortune.

In the first several months at Schofield Barracks, the unit conducted a strenuous training program to prepare for short notice deployment to the far Pacific area. The soldiers were trained to use all the weapons organic to their units; each soldier had to qualify with his individual weapons, as well as with grenade throwing. Combat veterans from Guadalcanal were brought in to demonstrate battle-tested methods for fighting the Japanese in jungle conditions. At training centers at Makaha and Waianae on the western coast of Oahu, the men conducted maneuvers and live fire exercises, assaulted pillboxes with demolitions, operated tanks, and adjusted live artillery fire. During the period March 25–29, 1943, the entire division maneuvered over the Waianaes Mountains at night. Infiltration courses were set up in which the men had to crawl under barbed wire while live ammunition was fired over their heads. They were also taught how to climb fully equipped over fences and jump off towers.

The training was grueling. When jumping from a tower into water, the soldiers were instructed to hold their helmets upside down. After they hit the water, they would strap on the helmets. When going through the infiltration course, it was important to keep the rifle barrel out of the dirt. During jungle training, the men were instructed to shoot at the first thing they saw. This proved valuable when they were in combat on Makin and Saipan, where it was likely that anyone with his head above ground after dark was likely to be shot. Because the Japanese frequently operated at night, chances were that anybody moving above ground at night was the enemy. Any soldier who left his foxhole at night for any reason, including calls of nature, was liable to be shot.

Most new recruits who joined the 105th at Schofield Barracks in late 1942 felt that the training was good, but one recruit who joined Company G stated, "We were training for battle so I expected it to be harder. It was okay." A draftee who joined Company E said, "The regular NCOs of the division did most of our training. In retrospect I think they did a good job." Private First Class Arthur Herzog, of Antitank Company, 105th Infantry, described the training on Hawaii as "a period of just work and more work." It was "useful." His commanding officer, Capt. Frank Martin, sent his transport personnel to radio school. Captain Martin's theory was "You won't be able to repair much during combat. You will be better used as radio men." Private First Class Herzog thought his commanding officer was "a wise man."

Effective April 5, 1943, Major O'Brien, who had been serving as Regimental Supply Officer (S-4) since February 15, 1942, was promoted to lieutenant colonel and placed in command of the 1st Battalion. He replaced Lt. Col. George Hopkins who became regimental executive officer. O'Brien had been away from the 1st Battalion, 105th Infantry, for more than a year and, except for the Troy men still with Company A, not many of those men in the other companies knew him well. That would soon change.

After O'Brien took over, the number of battalion parades increased significantly. He liked to review his troops in formation, and he always appeared out in front with an immaculate uniform.

On July 4, after returning from a three-week assignment with a regular army division, Lieutenant Colonel O'Brien wrote his brother in the States: "I was over to the Old Company today [Company A] and looked over the roster very carefully and found just a football team left of the gang I brought south. It used to be a New York outfit. Now I'd say it was strictly 'continental.' They are from all over—North, South, East and West." It was true. The regiment was no longer exclusively from the Apple-knocker country of northeastern New York. Through transfers and the addition of draftees, it now had men from the Carolinas, California, North and South Dakota, Tennessee, Iowa, Indiana, Michigan, and Wisconsin. Rigorous physical examinations had weeded out many men—those with flat feet, bad legs, hernias, and a number of other handicaps. Personnel-wise, the 27th Division was only a shadow of the unit mobilized in October 1940.

On July 24, O'Brien wrote to his brother, "Our old friend Jack Purcell now has the 1st Battalion S-4 job," and that although Lieutenant Colonel O'Brien aspired to come home with a brigadier general's star on his shoulder, he doubted he would, because, ". . . a Nat'l

Guardsman has little chance of getting even an 'Eagle' (a full colonel's rank insignia). If the war goes on 'til 1949, as the navy says it will, I might still do the job. Frankly, I could do it now but there really is quite a lot of competition as there are still quite a lot of West Pointers above ground, and I don't mean in the Air Corps."

In that same letter, O'Brien described a typical day's training for the 1st Battalion on Oahu in the summer of 1943:

> If you think walking over the golf courses was a job, you should follow Brer Bill around some day. Thirty miles in 14 hours, up hills that rival the Adirondacks ain't no fun, no fooling! Of course we have to come down too, but one day even the mules quit and the gang had to carry the 81mm mortars and the ammo by hand. We have a good outfit, Frank, and I don't have to snap the whip too often. I try to sell 'em before I drive 'em and again I find that faculty a happy one.

4 The 105th at Makin

On July 27, 1943, the 27th Division, the first trained combat division to leave the continental United States, received its first combat assignment. The joint chiefs of staff decided to launch an attack across the Central Pacific, first against the Gilbert Islands followed by the Marshall Islands, located north and west of the Gilberts. In the Gilberts, the primary targets were the Tarawa and Apamama Atolls (to be assaulted by the 2d Marine Division under the command of Maj. Gen. Julian Smith) and Nauru (a small island about 390 miles west of Tarawa), a mission for the 27th Division. The assaults were initially scheduled for November 15. When navy planners concluded that it would take a large force to overcome the considerable Japanese garrison on Nauru, it was decided instead to attack Makin Atoll, about 100 miles northwest of Tarawa. Makin was important because it would be a base from which the Marshall Islands could be attacked, the next scheduled stop on the road to Tokyo. The task of capturing Makin was assigned to the 165th Infantry Regiment, reinforced by the 3d Battalion of the 105th Infantry Regiment, the 193d Tank Battalion, and the 105th Field Artillery Battalion. The assault date for Tarawa and Makin was changed to November 20, 1943.

Preparations for Makin began immediately. On August 1, the division was relieved of its beach defensive assignments. Division headquarters was relocated from the village of Aiea to Schofield Barracks, and on August 13, its three regiments began extensive training, which included long strenuous marches over mountainous areas, familiarization firing of weapons, rotations to the jungle training center on Oahu's north shore, and assaults on pillboxes.

Veterans of earlier campaigns against the Japanese on Guadalcanal, Papua, and Buna on New Guinea were brought in to teach the men how the Japanese fought. "From small unit problems in jungle fighting to battalion and regimental combat team exercises, the troops reviewed what was involved in daylight attack in close terrain, hasty and prepared defenses of position, perimeter defense, day and night withdrawal, the attack of fortified positions in jungle terrain, and the elimination of snipers."

Amphibious training intensified. An army amphibious school was opened and from April 7 to May 12, regimental and battalion commanders and their executive officers attended. Between May and August, each battalion landing team was given specialized instruction in landing operations at Schofield Barracks and at the Waianae Amphibious Training Center on Oahu. The men were instructed in the use of cargo nets, ropes, boat team drill, debarking, deployment from mock-up boats, and passage through wire entanglements and other obstacles. Some men recalled that they were required to scale an eight-foot wall carrying full packs and climb down a rope into LCVPs or "Higgins boats." Airplanes overhead dropped bags of flour to simulate exploding bombs. After the men hit the beach, they set up their weapons and began simulated firing. Other men recalled getting out of the Higgins boats and into smaller boats.

The decision to employ the 27th Division in the invasions of the Gilberts and Marshalls was reached at the highest levels. General George C. Marshall, chairman of the joint chiefs of staff, wrote to Admiral King on July 29, 1943, stating that the division "has been in Hawaii for over a year and is a well-trained division with excellent leaders. All of the advanced training facilities of Oahu, including jungle, shore-to-shore, and some mock-up ship-to-shore facilities, are now available for special intensive training of the 27th in preparation for an amphibious operation." He ended the memorandum by asking, "If the use of the 27th Division for the Gilberts operations is agreeable to you, we will take the necessary steps to initiate its training without delay." Deputy Chief of Naval Operations Richard S. Edwards replied, "The designation of the 27th Division for the Gilbert Operations, as proposed in your memorandum of July 29, is agreeable, and Admiral Nimitz is being advised to that effect." A week later on August 5 Marshall advised Lt. Gen. Robert C. Richardson, commander of the Hawaiian Department, that under the circumstances he wanted Maj. Gen. Ralph C. Smith "to be made aware of the critical importance of his training preparations for the operation and of the cooperative spirit of himself and of his staff." Lieutenant General Richardson replied on August 13 that Major General Smith was "very much liked by Admiral Nimitz and Admiral Spruance. As the latter is to command the task force, I am sure that there will be a most harmonious relationship between Gen. Smith, his staff, and the Navy."

Command of the Tarawa and Makin invasions did not reside with marine Lt. Gen. Holland M. Smith, even though he had operational control of the V Amphibious Corps on Hawaii. For planning and preparation purposes, the 27th Army and 2d Marine Divisions were subordinate to the corps, but it was itself subordinate to Adm. Raymond Spruance, who commanded the central area of the Pacific Theater. During the invasions, moreover, operational control of the two combat divisions was in the hands of Adm. Richmond "Kelly" Turner. When the troops landed on the beaches, command of the 2d marine division passed directly to Maj. Gen. Julian Smith, whereas command of the 27th went to Maj. Gen. Ralph C. Smith. Lieutenant General "Howlin' Mad" Smith was a supernumerary during the Gilberts operation and was excluded from command of both the Tarawa and Makin operations. Instead, he went along as an observer at Makin on Admiral Turner's flagship, the battleship *Pennsylvania.*

The Northern Landing Force (NLF), assigned to capture Makin, was composed of 6,470 officers and enlisted men from the 165th Infantry Regiment and the 3d Battalion, 105th Infantry Regiment. There were about 3,000 combat troops facing the 800 or so Japanese troops, who were dug in on the island of Butaritari, the main portion of Makin Atoll.

The 165th Regimental Combat Team was commanded by Col. Gardiner Conroy, age fifty-four, who had served with the New York National Guard as an infantryman and as a lawyer with the Judge Advocate General's Corps. The 3d Battalion, 105th Infantry Regiment, was led by Maj. Edward T. "Ted" Bradt, age forty-five, from Schenectady, New York. Major Bradt had served in combat as an enlisted man with the 105th during World War I. His leadership was considered outstanding because he instilled confidence in his men. Several officers from the 1st and 2d Battalions volunteered to join the 3d Battalion for the Makin assault: 1st Lt. Seymour P. Drovis, Company A, 1st Battalion; 2d Lt. Arthur G. Hansen, Company G, 2d Battalion; and 2d Lt. Robert D. Young, Antitank Company, 105th Infantry.

While the main assault force was to go ashore in Higgins boats, the first wave from the 3d Battalion of the 105th was to go ashore in LVTs (known as) "Alligators." In the months before the operation, members of the 3d Battalion received highly specialized training in operating these armored, amphibious landing vehicles. Initially, Alligators were hard to find in the Pacific Theater. Until October, only one Alligator was available to the 3d Battalion for training. By October 30, however, forty-eight Alligators were delivered to the 3d Battalion. They were quickly modified with machine-gun mounts stripped from other vehicles and loaded for the voyage. The Alligators could move through the water as well as cross reefs and land with fair speed. Soldiers from the 193d Tank Battalion were specially trained in their handling and became the assigned crews. The Alligators would prove critical not only during the assault phase, but afterward when they were shown to be the only craft capable of traversing the treacherous reefs with badly needed supplies.

Following a period of shore-based training, the regiment and its attached battalion conducted joint amphibious training on beaches in the Hawaiian Islands area with ships of Transport Division 20. Between October 4 and 18, the "Makin Expeditionary Force" went on a training cruise. On October 31, all transports were loaded, and Admiral Turner's Task Force 52, with the troops and equipment of the Northern Landing Force, proceeded from Pearl Harbor to the vicinity of Maalaca Bay, Maui. The next morning, rehearsals were held with simulated military gunfire and simulated naval gunfire and air support. All troops landed on the beach, but without equipment and supplies. This exercise was repeated on November 2, and at dawn on November 3, a full dress rehearsal was held off the coast of Kahoolawe Island employing actual gunfire and air support.

• • •

Makin Atoll, roughly triangular in shape, is an irregular formation of reefs and islands around a large lagoon near the equator about 2,000 miles southwest of Oahu. Its dominant land feature is Butaritari, or "Horse Island," as it became known to members of the American attacking force. It is a long, ribbon-shaped landmass fishtailing at its western end in a shallow curve. The average width between the ocean and the lagoon is only about eight-tenths of a mile and in some places much less. Off its eastern end, lies Kuma Island, separated by a coral reef three-quarters of a mile in length, which is dry at low tide. At high-water, it is six to eight feet deep with strong cross currents. The combined length of Butaritari and Kuma is thirteen miles.

Since the raid on Makin by the 2d Marine raiders under Lt. Col. Evans Carlson, on August 17, 1942, the Japanese had built two extensive tank barriers on the west and east, extending across the island of Butaritari. They consisted of large trenches reinforced with double-apron barbed wire, trip wires, and log antitank barricades. There were numerous gun emplacements and rifle pits and a few concrete pillboxes. The 3,000 yards between them was the most strongly defended area on the island and nicknamed "the Citadel." It was concentrated around three of the four piers that stretched out into the lagoon from the island's west center section. The Japanese had constructed their seaplane ramps at the end of King's Wharf. Of the 800 Japanese on the island, only about 300 were first-line troops from the Special Naval Landing Force.

On November 5, three slow-moving LSTs (landing ship, tanks)—carrying the three special landing groups (detachments X, Y, and Z) chosen from the 3d Battalion of the 105th—left Pearl Harbor for Makin Island, planning to arrive at the same time as the main force, which would leave Pearl Harbor five days later. Each special detachment contained eleven officers and approximately 130 enlisted men. On November 10, the main force—a convoy of five transports, each with a rifle battalion from the 165th augmented by troops from the 3d Battalion, 105th—departed for Makin Island.

Late on the afternoon of November 18, the three LSTs and their destroyer escort were spotted by an enemy plane. The next day, after dark, the LSTs were attacked by two planes, one of which attempted a suicide attack. Army gun crews manned the heavy machine guns of the Alligators on the deck of LST No. 31. The enemy plane began to burn as it veered in a slightly descending glide, and, like a flaming torch, headed toward LST No. 179. Swooping low over LST No. 179's bow, the plane plunged into the ocean, and burning oil lit up the sky casting a glow over the entire group of ships for several minutes. Soon afterward, the second enemy plane departed.

By the night of November 19, a vast armada of warships, transports, and cargo ships assembled off the coast of Butaritari. The assault the next morning opened with air strikes from the accompanying carriers at 0617. Enemy antiaircraft fire was extremely weak, and dive-bombers bombed and strafed the beaches while glide-bombers worked over the clearing at the west tank barrier. After the airplanes completed their missions, naval gunfire began at 0640 and kept up a steady rain of shells until 0825, just five minutes before the first troops hit the shore. After the landings, the commander of the division artillery, Brig. Gen. Redmond F. Kernan, stated that, in his opinion, "a high degree of neutralization was obtained." Admiral Turner's final conclusion was that "the effect of naval and air bombardment was highly satisfactory; and contributed materially in the reduction of hostile resistance." However, he added, "there was not enough of it."

The first troops to hit Makin came in two "Vs" of Alligators, each carrying the Special Landing Groups from the Apple-knockers of the 3d Battalion. Two destroyers moved into place on each flank of the long lines of boats and, with five-inch guns, directed a steady fire on the enemy positions on shore.

At approximately 0830, the Alligators approached the beaches, firing as they came. Rocket volleys fell short at first; rain and spray made some firing mechanisms useless. At 1,000 yards, the boats' .50-caliber machine guns opened up; 200 yards farther in they were joined by their .30-caliber brothers. About 100 yards offshore, the craft went over the coral reef and lumbered onto the shoulders of the beaches. The Apple-knockers scrambled over the sides and dropped to the ground seeking cover. Major Bradt later described his action: "I jumped down from my boat and stood straight up for two or three minutes, waiting for somebody to shoot me. Nobody shot! I saw many other soldiers doing the same thing." Some other Alligators, however, did not make it over the reef. Second Lieutenant John A. Lighthall of M Company, from Syracuse, New York, recalled: "I remember being hung up on a coral pinnacle and having to jump over the side into chest-deep water and walking into the beach through the surf."

After landing, the two special detachments moved to the left and right to mount defensive flank positions and protect the Higgins boats carrying the 1st and 2d Battalions of the 165th to the shore. Detachment Y, after debarking, cleared the immediate area near Red Beach 1, and then moved to the north clearing the area to Flink Point. Detachment X on Red Beach 2 replied to five minutes of weak Japanese sniping from the woods. When the firing ceased, it moved on to the right in the direction of Ukiangong Point. These actions created a corridor through which the larger units could attack the main defenses.

Around 1000, the 1st and 3d Battalion Landing Teams (BLTs) of the 165th reached the head lines of Red Beaches 1 and 2, about 1,300 yards inland. Although mostly unopposed, they were subject to adverse beach and landing conditions. There they halted. To fulfill previous plans, the 1st BLT then extended its line to cross the entire island, relieving the 3d BLT at 1055, so it could go into reserve for Tarawa if needed by the marines fighting there. The 3d BLT remained in this position behind the lines and was not recommitted to fighting on Makin for a period of 36 hours. Thus, within less than two and a half hours after the initial landing, Red Beaches 1 and 2 were secured to a line 1,300 yards inland, along with Ukiangong Point. Preparations were underway to make that area suitable for the establishment of artillery positions, which would support the main attack eastward against the tank barriers in the center of the island. By 1240, Flink Point on the north end of the island was also secured. Japanese resistance was minimal; only six Japanese marines had been killed and one Korean laborer captured. However, as the troops of the 1st Battalion, 165th and Special Detachments X and Y from the 3d Battalion began to move farther inland, they encountered increasing enemy sniper fire.

• • •

The initial assault on Yellow Beach, which lay between On Chong's Wharf and King's Wharf, on the northern (lagoon) side of Butaritari Island, was made by Detachment Z of the 105th Infantry on board sixteen Alligators brought to shore by members of Headquarters Company, 193d Tank Battalion. Detachment Z faced the most hazardous mission of the Yellow Beach landing force. It consisted of eleven officers and 122 enlisted men, under the command of Capt. William Ferns of Company M. Thirty-one men were from L Company, 3d Battalion; twelve from 3d Battalion Headquarters Company; and seventy-nine from M Company. Landing at 1041 hours, it incurred five killed and twelve wounded while securing the flanks for the follow-on infantry of the 165th.

At 1020 the Alligators carrying Detachment Z were halfway across the lagoon with 3,000 yards to go. At a distance of about 1,100 yards, they launched rockets to pulverize the enemy's beach positions. Then U.S. aircraft roared in, bombing and strafing the beach. About 500 yards from the beach, the men in the lead Alligators began to receive enemy fire from machine guns located to their left in an unidentified position near King's Wharf. For the last 250 yards, the men crouched low in their Alligators as a cross-fire of bullets whizzed over their heads. One boat ran up the seaplane ramp on King's Wharf, with both .50-caliber machine guns blazing. After disembarking, a squad from Company M crawled ashore on the seaplane side of the outer end of King's Wharf, avoiding fire from Japanese guns placed along the King's Wharf Causeway. Unable to bring their weapons to bear, the Japanese quickly fled and the pier was taken without further contest.

During this initial engagement, two officers from the other two battalions who had volunteered to serve with the 3d Battalion distinguished themselves. First Lieutenant Seymour P. Drovis, Company A, 1st Battalion, a platoon leader, had the initial mission of reducing all enemy resistance near King's Wharf, which was jeopardizing the flank of the beachhead. He landed at the end of the wharf in an Alligator, under heavy enemy machine-gun fire from the wharf and from the shore. Completely ignoring his personal safety, he swam and waded in the water along the wharf, leading his men under the enemy fire from the shore, until all enemy resistance on the flank had been reduced. For this heroic action, as well as others, First Lieutenant Drovis was awarded the Silver Star.

Second Lieutenant Arthur G. Hansen of Council Bluffs, Iowa, Company G, 2d Battalion came in on the first wave to land on Yellow Beach. More than fifty-four years later, he recalled: "When our LTV came ashore on the left flank of Yellow Beach we did not encounter any heavy resistance as we climbed over the sides. Our group spread out and advanced inland across what seemed to me to be a strange and alien environment." Suddenly, he saw "a Jap soldier rising up out of the underbrush and running off to my left in a crouch, carrying a rifle with bayonet in one hand and a pistol in the other. He had some sprigs of brush interlaced in the netting over his helmet for camouflage. Obviously, he did not see me, but I had my carbine at the ready as we were moving up, so I fired several rounds at him to be sure he went down." Second Lieutenant Hansen would later be awarded the Silver Star.

King's Wharf had already been taken by the left assault force of Detachment Z. The enemy protecting On Chong's Wharf, on the other hand, was putting up stiff resistance. Captain Ferns wasted no time in organizing the men of the right wing into small teams to root out the Japanese defenders from these shelters and bunkers. Within thirty minutes, ten shelters had been cleaned out with twenty Japanese dead and thirty-five captured, most of whom were Koreans who came running out with their hands up before any grenades were thrown. In one shelter, about 150 yards from the beach, a Japanese officer holding a sword appeared to want to surrender. As he approached Lt. John Campbell of M Company, from Amsterdam, he lunged with his sword, severely wounding Campbell in the hand and foot. The enemy officer was immediately killed by a soldier from the 3d Battalion. Private First Class Nicholas Johannes Timmens, five feet two inches tall and a native of Holland, entered the shelter and killed two more Japanese soldiers. Private First Class Timmens then killed two more Japanese soldiers near the shelter and two more who tried to escape. For his actions, Timmens would later receive a Silver Star.

Landings on Yellow Beach were initially held up because the planners had miscalculated the depth of the lagoon, causing the Higgins boats carrying the 2d Battalion of the 165th to go aground on the reef. The men had to cover the final 250 yards to the beach in waist-deep water under heavy machine-gun fire. The landings were further delayed more than an hour while carrier planes bombed and strafed two abandoned, half-sunk freighters in the lagoon, from which enemy troops were firing at landing ships. Two destroyers began firing shells at the abandoned hulks, some of which passed over the heads of the men of Detachment Z and landed among the assault waves of the 2d Battalion, 165th, as they pushed across the island toward the west tank barrier. Captain Ferns of Detachment Z pulled his men back 100 yards east onto On Chong's Wharf and immediately requested the cessation of all naval and aerial bombardment. By approximately 1257, the first phase of the assault on Yellow Beach was successfully completed with only minor casualties.

The main objective of the attacking forces on the first day of the invasion was the reduction of the enemy forces in the west tank barrier. To accomplish this, the west tank barrier was to be cut off from the rest of the island. From Yellow Beach, Company E of the 2d Battalion formed a line across the island facing east and advanced about 600 yards to the road that ran across the island from the base of King's Wharf. Company E's job was to protect the beachhead from counterattack by the Japanese in the east. Company F, supported by medium tanks, was to execute a similar movement to the right, with the support of Company G, and advance west toward the west tank barrier. The lagoon end of each line was to be held by a detail from Special Detachment Z. Detachment Z had been dug in at that location since it cleaned out the base of On Chong's Wharf. At the same time, the 1st Battalion advanced from the Red Beaches to the west, also supported by a platoon of light tanks. The west tank barrier would be completely enveloped by American forces and destroyed.

The westward movement was strengthened by tank support. With five tanks from the 193d Tank Battalion in support, Company F jumped off for the attack on the tank trap, which lay some 300 to 400 yards away. After encountering heavy opposition from an underground air-raid shelter, a medium tank advanced. It was accompanied by a demolition squad of two infantrymen and four combat engineers, including 1st Lt. Thomas B. Palliser, a platoon commander of Company C, 102d Engineers. First Lieutenant Palliser used a TNT pole charge to kill all of the Japanese personnel inside.

While the 2d Battalion was moving across the island from Yellow Beach and gradually wiping out resistance east of the west tank barrier, Colonel Kelley's 1st Battalion advanced toward the same objective from the Red Beaches. At 1130, he set up his command post at Rita Lake and began to direct the advance westward. Although there were a number of positions advantageous for resistance by the enemy, with the exception of some snipers, there was little or no opposition to the American attack. By 1400 the American troops had bypassed the various lakes between the Red Beaches and the west tank barrier with minimal casualties. At 1410 division headquarters sent the following message: "Continue your attack vigorously to effect a junction with McDonough without delay." By that time, the light tanks of Company C, 193d Tank Battalion, which had been delayed by a large shell hole, had joined the ground troops, and the advance was resumed.

While Company F, with elements of Company G attached, was moving across the island toward the west tank barrier, another force from the 2d Battalion moved to the left from Yellow Beach and took up a holding position facing the east tank barrier system. This force consisted of Company E, one-half of Detachment Z of the 105th Infantry, and, before the end of the day, a platoon of light tanks from the 193d Tank Battalion. Company E's three platoons moved toward the ocean and then turned east toward the east tank barrier on a line across the island. Although initially there was little or no enemy opposition as the 1st Platoon of Company E approached the ocean, it ran into a concrete pillbox with a machine-gun emplacement, flanked by rifle pits and double-apron barbed wire. A direct infantry assault with an assist from a medium tank's 75mm gun silenced the emplacement, and ten Japanese soldiers were killed.

By nightfall on November 20, 1943, the first objectives of the invasion of Makin had been accomplished. Command posts for the 165th Infantry Regiment and its 1st and 3d Battalions were established. By 1830, General Smith had come ashore and moved up to the forward echelons. Due to communications problems, division headquarters remained on board the attack transport *Leonard Wood* until the next day. Except for a small pocket of enemy resistance, the west tank barrier system had been neutralized and the likelihood of it being reinforced by Japanese soldiers from the eastern part of the island was reduced to a minimum by a lengthy artillery barrage and other defenses.

For most men, this was the first night that they'd spent on an enemy-occupied island in hostile territory. Although no major counterattacks were undertaken by the Japanese, there was a lot of energetic enemy activity that first night, particularly infiltrations. Before the night was over, the enemy set up at least seven new machine-gun positions to harass the advancing American troops the following morning. According to Captain Ferns, a few positions at the base of King's Wharf were reoccupied and new machine-gun emplacements constructed facing the American lines. One gun was placed in a wrecked seaplane lying in the lagoon off King's Wharf, another at the base of King's Wharf, and three more in buildings in the area immediately southward.

Second Lieutenant Arthur G. Hansen, Company G, 2d Battalion, recalled that first night on Butaritari:

It was a moonlit night with the night breezes ruffling the leaves of a big breadfruit tree close by. There was some sort of shed to our rear where the chickens decided to roost during the night, and you could hear them clucking and fluttering all night long. There was no discernable [*sic*] enemy activity in our immediate area, but the night sounds were rather eerie with the spasmodic sounds of rifle fire. At daylight, I was surprised to see a dead Jap across the parapet in front of an adjoining foxhole.

Although the Americans captured most of their objectives the first day, many Japanese still lurked in destroyed shelters and trees. This made the first night on Makin nightmarish for many GIs. As soon as darkness descended, the bypassed Japanese tried to escape. The men had been ordered to observe complete silence. When an armed Japanese came to a perimeter and called out: "Psst! Hey, Sarge!" he was immediately shot. There were other ruses to draw American fire. "Medics! Medics! Send a medic out here," some of the Japs called. Others cried out, "Hey, Charlie! Where's my buddy?" As daylight approached, the boldness of the Japanese soldiers increased. One crawled to the edge of a foxhole and blurted out: "Me no got gun." He was instantly shot. It turned out that he was in fact ready to fire when he'd been hit. Just before dawn, another foolhardy enemy soldier ran the whole length of Yellow Beach shouting: "Reveille, fellows! Get up! Reveille!" A weary GI shot him.

Much of the Japanese activity during the night of November 20 was organized. Enemy patrols tried to infiltrate the American positions near the perimeters of Companies A, B, C, and E, and thirty-eight Japanese soldiers were killed in these attempts. Captain Ferns recalled that in the sector assigned to Detachment Z, several enemies had infiltrated American positions. Three were killed and two wounded by rifle fire and grenades. One twelve-man patrol did manage to slip along the ocean shore and reach a point between Companies A and B. When dawn came the next morning, the patrol was discovered in prone positions only a few yards away; all its members were caught off guard and killed.

That first night there was a lot of undisciplined shooting by the Americans in the central part of the island at what turned out to be nonexistent targets. For most, this was their first night in combat and all were skittish. To make matters worse, just after daylight, a soldier from the 152d Engineers ran along the lagoon shore from the direction of On Chong's Wharf toward the 2d Battalion CP, shouting: "There's 150 Japs in the trees." A wave of shooting hysteria swept the area, and men started firing at bushes and trees until the place was ablaze with fire. Although the engineer later admitted that he had not seen any of the enemy, but had merely "heard firing," efforts to stop the firing proved to be difficult.

On the second day, the effort concentrated on the drive to the eastern end of Butaritari Island. Because the situation at Tarawa had prevented General Smith from moving the 3d Battalion, 165th Infantry to Kuma Island on the morning of November 21, he dispatched a small party from the Special Landing Group of the 105th Infantry under the command of Maj. Jacob H. Herzog from Albany, division assistant intelligence officer, with orders to investigate Kuma for the presence of Japanese forces. Upon arrival at dawn, his party found no evidence of the enemy and returned to the division headquarters.

The plan of attack for the second day provided that Company E, 2d Battalion, and attached elements, would push along the island toward the east tank barrier, while Company F remained in reserve near Yellow Beach. The 1st Battalion was to clean out the snipers near the west tank barrier and then move back toward the Red Beaches. The attack was delayed while Lieutenant Colonel McDonough waited for the tanks to be refueled. By 1110, the attack was in progress. Led by ten medium tanks, the 2d Battalion moved forward on the right. Detachment Z of the 105th (minus its Alligators, which were busy hauling cargo across Yellow Beach) moved up on the extreme left of the attack on the lagoon side. The line advanced steadily, albeit slowly, averaging about three yards a minute.

Lieutenant Arthur Hansen recalled the advance of Detachment Z:

Later that morning as our advance continued, we were held up while tanks and artillery were laying down fire in the area ahead of us. We noticed off to our right front a group of soldiers holed up in a depressed area directly under the line of fire, which was getting much too close to the area occupied by our own troops. I noticed that one of those entrapped held up his rifle with a white cloth attached to the muzzle trying to attract attention to their plight. No one seemed to be doing anything about it so it was at this point I moved forward to the front of the tank laying down fire and beat on the tank turret with the butt of my carbine, trying to signal a cease-fire to the operator. It continued, so I backed off to the front of the tank so they couldn't help but see me and continued to signal cease-fire, which eventually they did. This enabled the troops in the line of fire to withdraw to safety. I didn't think too much about what happened, except that somebody had better do some-thing.

For his actions in this incident, Lieutenant Hansen was later awarded a Silver Star.

The enemy opposition on the second day at Butaritari continued in the general area around the base of King's Wharf, where a machine gun covered a long stretch of beach and interdicted the road. Captain Ferns ordered up four medium tanks and directed them to fire into the fuselage of the wrecked seaplane. A half hour later, the plane exploded, and eighteen Japanese bodies were found in the wreckage. With this strongpoint demolished, Detachment Z moved in to mop up the King's Wharf area.

It moved steadily along the lagoon shore in the area where the Japanese had infiltrated the previous night, wiping out trenches and emplacements with the help of medium tanks. First Lieutenant Drovis of Company A, who had been assigned to Detachment Z's assault unit, moved forward with his platoon. Due to inadequate communications, he found it necessary to expose himself repeatedly to enemy fire by preceding the tank attached to his platoon and directing its fire toward the enemy. First Lieutenant Drovis was later awarded the Silver Star.

At 1730 the advance stopped, and the men began to dig in for the night. The line had reached a point 1,000 yards east of Yellow Beach, 200 yards short of Stone Pier. The east tank barrier was 450 yards away, and it was expected that it would be reduced the next day. Captain Ferns reported that Detachment Z had advanced from 600 to 700 yards east of King's Wharf, suffering only six casualties. Overall American casualties for the day were eighteen killed and twenty-six wounded. Proof that the end of the Makin battle was near came midway that afternoon. As Detachment Z passed through what had been the island air command post, the men came upon six Japanese officers in a foxhole. As the Americans came close, the officers proceeded to shoot each other in turn, the last one committing suicide.

That night, Detachment Z, which had dug in next to the lagoon shore in the center of the island, began to suffer from enemy grenade and mortar attacks. Private First Class Nicholas J. Timmens of Company M was in a foxhole with two other men from his company at about 2000, when a live enemy grenade landed among them. He remembered that he felt an extra-heavy piece of something hit his leg. He reached down and felt something hard and grilled. He didn't have to look at it to tell what it was; he knew it was an unexploded, hot grenade. Without hesitation, he immediately threw it out, saving the lives of his comrades as well as his own. Timmens also had earlier distinguished himself on the first day at Makin and was later awarded the Silver Star.

The object of the action on November 22, the third day at Makin, was to reduce the east tank barrier approximately 450 yards away from the American position and prevent the remaining Japanese from escaping to Kuma Island. When NTLF Headquarters gave General Smith permission to use the 3d Battalion, 165th Regiment, to attack the east tank barrier, the position became vulnerable and many enemy defenders began moving east toward Kuma. To cut them off, a detachment from Company A boarded six Alligators and made a three-mile run across the lagoon to the eastern end of Butaritari Island, effectively cutting off the retreating Japanese.

Another longer, amphibious move to Kuma Island off the eastern tip of Butaritari was made the same day by a detail from the 3d Battalion, under the command of Major (soon to be Lieutenant Colonel) Bradt. This group, in ten Alligators, was guided to Kuma by Major Herzog, who had reconnoitered the island the day before. The object was to block Japanese who might try to escape from Butaritari by way of Kuma. This detail from the 105th Infantry arrived on Kuma about 1400 on November 22.

Thus, at the close of day, November 22, the enemy was trapped between two forces. Major Bradt of the 3d Battalion was waiting for the Japanese on Kuma while Lieutenant Colonel Hart of the 3d Battalion of the 165th had pushed the Japanese back into the narrow eastern end of Butaritari. In the vernacular of the day, "push was coming to shove."

Tired after a long day in stifling heat, the "Shamrocks" of Hart's 3d Battalion dug in for the night of November 22 in three-man foxholes, stretching across the narrow eastern end of Butaritari Island. Confident that the fighting was over, the 1st and 2d Battalions of the 165th had already received orders to re-embark for Oahu the next day. Losses for the day had been light; the total of American casualties on the entire island were six dead and seventeen wounded. The 3d Battalion dug in for the night with less care than they might have shown had they known what lay before them. Because they had left their entrenching tools behind with their packs earlier that day, the foxholes were shallow, sometimes consisting of merely coconut logs arranged as a protective bulwark. Except for a small clearing surrounding the grass shack that had been chosen by Lieutenant Colonel Hart as his command post, the area was the usual tangle of underbrush and coconut trees, with the island's main road running through the left flank of the American defenses. At several points, the underbrush was thick enough to furnish considerable cover for infiltrating Japanese. The men had been instructed not to use their rifles except to repulse a direct enemy attack.

Night fell shortly before 1900. At 2030, the men heard a strange noise coming from the enemy lines, sounding like the thin, breathless wail of a baby crying and accompanied by women's voices. Then came the sound of many feet shuffling down the road toward the 3d Battalion's defenses. Out of the shadows, down the road from the east, came a group of twenty to thirty people, carrying their belongings. After answering a challenge, the group identified themselves as natives trying to get back to their village behind the American lines. For their safety, they were taken inside the perimeter and ordered to lie down on the ground until dawn.

At approximately 2040, a second group was spotted coming down the same path, imitating the cries of babies in an effort to pass themselves off as natives. This time they were Japanese soldiers, some dressed in their best uniforms and wearing medals. The Americans opened fire, killing approximately ten and scattering the rest into the brush. There were two American antitank guns guarding the approaches to the road. Suddenly, they became aware of activity to their front. The enemy kept moving back and forth in the brush, and jumping across the road, yelling such phrases as "Heil Hitler!" and "Blood for the Emperor!" Suddenly, three soldiers loomed out of the darkness and ran straight down the road. They were killed in hand-to-hand combat.

During the next four hours, the enemy remaining on the island made attack after attack against the positions held by the 3d Battalion, 165th Infantry. Barefoot Japanese ran up to gun positions, firing at almost point-blank range and jumped into a melee with the Americans, who killed them with knives and clubs in yelling, shouting struggles. Grenades sailed back and forth. Between attacks, the enemy crawled back to their own lines to drink sake. The clinking of glasses, amid sounds of drunken gaiety, could be heard by the isolated Americans. Some Japanese carried canteens of liquor, and one was found at daylight, standing beneath a tree, drinking out of his canteen and alternately shooting a few rounds and singing loudly. He was quickly dispatched with a single bullet by Sgt. Fred T. Proctor of the 3d Battalion, 165th Infantry.

What became known as "Sake Night" on Makin cost the 3d Battalion, 165th Infantry, three dead and twenty-five wounded. One-hundred and three enemy bodies lay in front of the perimeter, and another one hundred enemy bodies were later found in various parts of the jungle on the eastern part of the island. Most were either wounded soldiers who had dragged themselves off to the jungle to die or who had been dragged into the jungle by their comrades. "Sake Night" was the last concerted resistance by the desperate remnant of the original Japanese force on Makin.

Meanwhile on Kuma, Major Bradt had set up one platoon in a defensive line south of Keuea Village, another at the southwestern projection of the island, and a third on three small outcroppings of the reef to the southeast. Shortly before midnight on November 22, they heard a woman's voice scream, "Jap boy, Jap boy." At least ten Japanese soldiers tried to push across the reef to Kuma, using some as a screen. Machine guns opened up, killing the ten Japanese as well as the natives. Major Bradt recalled, "We opened fire and must have got all of them or we would have seen them retreat or heard them splashing in the water."

For his cool actions on Makin, Major Bradt was promoted to lieutenant colonel and was awarded a Bronze Star in addition to the Silver Star. Major Herzog was also awarded the Silver Star "for his coolness and efficiency in the presence of danger by first reconnoitering Kuma Island on November 21 and then, the next day, guiding Major Bradt's men to the objective."

By 1010 on November 23, the Shamrocks reached the end of Butaritari, mopped up the area, and then withdrew to set up a defense line. The Japanese who had been killed during the night of November 22 represented the bulk of the remaining Japanese soldiers on Butaritari Island. At 1030 on November 23, Maj. Gen. Ralph C. Smith reported to Admiral Turner, "Makin taken." At the end of the day, Admiral Turner announced the capture of Makin "though with minor resistance remaining" and congratulated General Smith and his troops.

Total battle casualties for the 27th Division on Makin were small, amounting to 218, of which 58 were killed in action and 8 died of wounds. Of the 152 wounded in action and the 35 who suffered non-battle casualties, 57 were returned to active duty while the action was still strong. At the end of the fighting, enemy casualties were estimated to be 550, including 105 prisoners of war, all but one of whom belonged to labor troops. By comparison, at Tarawa, American losses among the marine assault troops were much more severe: 913 killed and missing and 2,037 wounded.

Late on the afternoon of November 23, 1943, the 2d Battalion, 165th Infantry, under the command of Lt. Col. Joseph McDonough, began re-embarking over Red Beach 2. Entering the landing barges, they moved out to board the APA *Pierce* against four-foot swells; they were to spend the next ten days aboard the *Pierce* until they arrived back on Oahu. The next morning the 1st Battalion of the 165th went aboard the APA *Calvert* for re-embarkation. The 3d Battalion, 165th, under the command of Lieutenant Colonel Hart, remained behind on Makin with several supporting units to mop up the island until after Christmas of 1943.

The 3d Battalion troops returned from Kuma Island and began to board the APA *Leonard Wood*. Second Lieutenant Arthur Hansen recalls that the special landing force almost did not make it on time. He had been detailed to remain on Makin overnight awaiting a Higgins boat to pick up Major Bradt and the rest of his troops on the morning of November 24. When the boat arrived off Kuma, there was no sign of Bradt's troops. Hansen went "over the side to wade in water up to my armpits, hoping I wouldn't step into a shell-hole or other depression and go under, because I wasn't all that good a swimmer. I managed to locate the Colonel who didn't seem to be in any particular hurry until I impressed upon him the need to round up his men promptly, because the ship had to leave the lagoon at high tide in order to clear the entrance." At noon the detail from Kuma Island arrived just in time to board the APA *Leonard Wood*. Hansen recalled, "There were a number of prisoners on board (Korean labor used by the Japs to build fortifications), and there were quite a few survivors from Liscombe Bay, most of them badly burned. One lying on deck was completely swathed in bandages with only small openings for his eyes, nostrils, and mouth. He and several others died en route to Pearl Harbor and were buried at sea. Commitment services were held at shipside by Catholic, Protestant, and Jewish chaplains, and it was a sobering experience to witness the bodies slip over the side, wrapped in a weighted canvas shroud and disappearing forever into the deep." The *Leonard Wood* arrived back in Oahu on December 2, 1943.

On January 8, 1944, Lieutenant Colonel O'Brien, in a letter home, described the Makin operation as follows: "Yeah, the 27th landed at and took Makin and the newspapers told a much better story in some respects than my humble pen can do. You surely remember Ted Bradt. He used to play basketball against Company A vs. Company F in the old National Guard league! He was a major at Makin and now a lieutenant colonel in command of our 3d Battalion. So although the newscasts publicize the Frightened 69th, the Apple-knockers had to provide the interference for the 69th who were carrying the ball."

5 Return to Oahu

In early December 1943, the 165th Infantry (less the "Shamrock" Battalion) and the 3d Battalion of the 105th returned to Oahu from Makin. The 3d Battalion, 165th, plus supporting units, stayed behind to mop up the island. Five enemy soldiers were killed in late November, while trying to cross the reef to Kuma Island, and on December 13, 1943, nine more Japanese soldiers were killed on the eastern end of the island in a pitched battle with an American patrol of thirteen men. Among those killed was the top Japanese commander at Makin. Colonel Hart's 3d Battalion would not return to Oahu until January 1, 1944.

General George C. Marshall visited the 27th Division in Hawaii on December 19. On Oahu, he witnessed jungle-fighting maneuvers and told the assembled troops: "We have got the Japs beaten but we have to keep pushing. The Japs had jungle training long before the war and we didn't, but they're restricted and lack variation. Our great advantage is our enterprise and resourcefulness. Your training here is the best that can be given, and it is up to you to push the enemy through the jungle." He praised the resourcefulness and small-unit tactics the Germans had demonstrated in the Italian fighting. "You men have to do the same thing, and better. You have the initiative and leadership to do it."

After their return to Oahu, the men of the 165th and the 3d Battalion, 105th, shared their experiences with their comrades in the 27th Division. First Lieutenant Seymour P. Drovis, Company A, 1st Battalion, presented a critique of the Makin operation to the 105th at Schofield Barracks. On Makin, Japanese snipers concentrated their fire on officers with bars on their shoulders and whose khaki uniforms made them stand out from the enlisted men. He recommended that both officers and enlisted men wear the same uniforms and that all indications of rank be removed while in combat. Numbers on the back of helmets would be used to distinguish rank while in the field. For example, the number 8 designated an infantry staff sergeant. Such precautions undoubtedly saved the lives of many men.

Antitank Company, 105th Infantry, also benefited from the experiences shared by the men of the 105th. Second Lieutenant Robert D. Young from Pennsylvania had served as a rifle platoon leader with the 3d Battalion, 105th, on Makin. In late 1943, division headquarters ordered that army engineers construct an exercise on the west side of Oahu based on the firing techniques the Japanese had employed on Makin. Antitank Company and an engineer platoon worked hard on the assignment. Sergeant Taylor Hudson's platoon built a Japanese bunker like those Young had seen on Makin; it was a lot of work, because it had to be connected to "spider holes" by trenches. Hudson recalled, "We not only had to build the defensive network, patterned after the Japanese, but we fenced the entire area with barbed wire and posted warning signs."

As early as September 1943, the 106th Infantry Regiment had been told it would be assigned as a reserve for the invasion of the Marshall Islands in the Central Pacific. The Marshalls, north and west of the Gilberts, are a double chain of atolls, reefs, and islets, most rising only a few feet above sea level. Japan seized the Marshall Islands from Germany during World War I, retaining control under a League of Nations mandate. The most important of these were Majuro, Kwajalein, Roi-Namur, and Eniwetok. In December, the 106th learned that its mission was divided into two parts. Its 2d Battalion was assigned to capture Majuro, about 265 nautical miles southeast of Kwajalein Atoll. It contained a large lagoon, about twenty-six miles long and six miles wide. According to Admiral Nimitz, Majuro possessed the "finest lagoon in the Pacific." In American hands, Majuro could be transformed into a valuable forward naval base.

On January 31, 1944, the 2d Battalion landed on Majuro, but encountered no Japanese opposition. The island had been abandoned more than a year before; only one Japanese soldier was found there. The unit remained on Majuro until March 5, when it re-embarked for Oahu to prepare for the invasion of Saipan.

Meanwhile, the 1st and 3d Battalions of the 106th proceeded to Kwajalein where they became part of the reserve force supporting the assault on the island. When it became apparent that the reserve would not be needed, the 1st and 3d Battalions and the 22d Marine Regiment were assigned to capture Eniwetok, about 350 miles northwest of Kwajalein and a vital position to the Japanese. While it was in their hands, planes could be staged through it to the passed atolls to the east. In American hands, Eniwetok was a major threat to the main Japanese base at Truk. After four days of heavy fighting, the three islands comprising the Eniwetok Atoll—Engebi, Parry, and Eniwetok—were secured. Total American casualties suffered during the fighting on Eniwetok Atoll came to 1,096: 262 killed, 77 missing, and 757 wounded. Only 66 Japanese and Korean prisoners were taken; the rest were destroyed. The 106th remained on Eniwetok until late March, when it went back to Hawaii, arriving on April 13, in time to prepare for Saipan.

On January 15, Admiral Nimitz sent a plan to the joint chiefs of staff, outlining the 1944 campaign in the Pacific Theater, which was to close with the capture of the Mariana's and Palau Islands, including Truk in the Caroline Islands. The plan was approved on January 22, with some reservations about the time schedule. On March 13, Nimitz ordered that all planning to capture Truk cease and that the highest priority be assigned to the Marianas. "Operation Forager," as it became known, had a target date of June 15. In Nimitz's view, there was a threefold advantage to be gained by capturing the Marianas in the shortest possible time: (1) Truk, one of Japan's major bases in the Central Pacific, would be absolutely and irrevocably cut off; (2) the United States would be established in the enemy's intermediate defense line; and (3) the United States would have air bases within heavy-bomber range of Tokyo. Lieutenant General Robert C. Richardson, the U.S. Army's commander in the Central Pacific, concurred by saying, "This is where the serious phase of the war in the Pacific begins."

The operation involved the amphibious assault and seizure of three fortified islands located 1,200 miles from the nearest American base and 4,000 to 7,000 miles from the areas in which the invasion troops would be assembled for the attack. The units designated for the Marianas assault constituted the most powerful overall force ever to operate in the Central Pacific. The Fifth Fleet consisted of almost 800 ships, more than 100,000 foot soldiers, and nearly 25,000 sailors. It was by far the biggest amphibious operation ever undertaken in the Pacific Theater.

Admiral Raymond A. Spruance, USN, Commander Fifth Fleet, was designated to command all forces. Charged with command of the joint expeditionary force (JEF)—all organizations involved in amphibious operations there—was Adm. Kelly Turner, USN. Commanding general of the expeditionary troops was marine Lt. Gen. Holland M. Smith. The joint expeditionary force was divided into five major task forces, including the Northern Troop and Landing Force (NTLF), which consisted of the V Amphibious Corps, also under Lt. Gen. Holland M. Smith, and the Southern Troop and Landing Force (STLF), which consisted of the III Amphibious Corps under the command of Maj. Gen. Roy S. Geiger, USMC.

The troops assigned to the NTLF for the Saipan landings and for a shore-to-shore attack on nearby Tinian numbered about 77,000, including support troops. The combat units were the veteran 2d Marine Division under Maj. Gen. Thomas E. Watson and the relatively untested 4th Marine Division, under the command of Maj. Gen. Harry Schmidt. The STLF under the command of Major General Geiger had the 3d Marine Division and the 1st Provisional Marine Brigade assigned to it for the Guam landings. In Expeditionary Troop Reserve, prepared to land at either the northern or southern objective, was the 27th Infantry Division under Maj. Gen. Ralph C. Smith. The only maneuver units in the division that had not previously been in combat were the 1st and 2d Battalions, 105th Infantry, and the 2d Battalion, 106th Infantry. The Army's 77th Infantry Division was to be held in the Hawaiian Islands as a strategic reserve for the Guam attack and called into the Marianas area after D day plus 20.

The planning problems of the division staff for Forager were enormous, with weeks of preparation required. The original plan contemplated the use of the 27th Division as a complete assault unit, or as a floating reserve for Saipan, Tinian, and Guam, as required. This necessitated a careful study of the 27th's possible use on any of the three islands under varying conditions and on different landing beaches. Twenty-one separate plans were prepared, with sixteen in anticipation of Saipan landings. Because the division was to be the corps reserve, they had to plan for a number of contingencies. The three major ones were: (1) to support the marine landings on Saipan; (2) to support the marine landings on Guam; and (3) to launch an assault by itself on Tinian.

Around April 1, Col. Leonard E. Bishop learned that the 105th would participate in the operations. The regimental staff officers, and all battalion commanders, including Lieutenant Colonel O'Brien, were also notified immediately. Special training for the infantry was initiated on April 7, including operations with armor, engineers, and artillery. This training concentrated on advanced amphibious assaults, night perimeter exercises, field maneuvers for individual platoons, burned cane-field traversing, field firing exercises, BLT field maneuvers against fortified field positions, air-ground exercises, medical training (including malaria control), and shipboard training. From April 5 through April 15, the 105th conducted a training cruise off the coast of Oahu.

Individual training concentrated on weapons qualification for all personnel with assigned weapons, familiarization with all organic weapons, swimming 50 yards with and without clothing and equipment, physical conditioning in the form of a daily one-mile run, one hour per day of organized athletics, bayonet drill, and hand-to-hand combat. Scouting and patrolling emphasized small-unit leadership and night operations. Six of the nine infantry battalions participated in the Waiahole exercises, which integrated infantry, artillery, tank, engineer, and air corps operations as combined arms. The companies and platoons received further instruction in the proper organization of a perimeter defense to include the plan of fire and security. Advanced amphibious training was conducted May 18

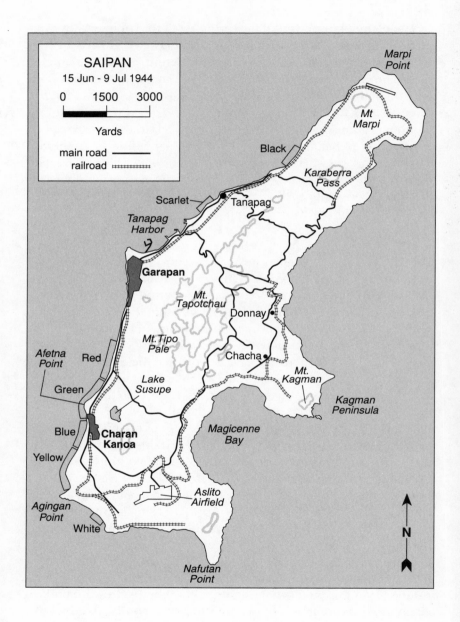

SAIPAN
15 Jun - 9 Jul 1944

0   1500   3000

Yards

main road ———
railroad ⊹⊹⊹⊹⊹⊹⊹⊹

Marpi
Point

Mt
Marpi

Black

Karaberra
Pass

Scarlet   Tanapag

Tanapag
Harbor

Garapan

Mt.
Tapotchau   Donnay

Mt.Tipo
Pale   Chacha

Afetna
Point   Red   Mt
Kagman

Green   Lake
Susupe   Kagman
Peninsula

Blue   Charan
Kanoa

Yellow   Magicenne
Bay

Agingan
Point   Aslito
Airfield

White

N

Nafutan
Point

through May 24, with ships that would carry the division to the Marianas. The troops did not practice embarkations in the landing craft, because there were limited amounts of this critical equipment and no replacements available should any be damaged. O'Brien even moved his battalion into huts near the firing range so that his men could have extra marksmanship training.

It was obvious to everyone in the 27th Division that something big was up, but that they did not know what. In the last letter O'Brien wrote to his brother on March 28, 1944, he referred to the fact that "we don't have much time to write—too much 'work' and not much increase in commissions, although we don't have any trouble getting orders." As for getting a leave to come back to the States, "Not a chance!" He then told his brother, "Never mind worrying, Bud, about getting into it. When they need you they'll reach out and take you, and I don't mind telling you that it's not so easy when you go over the 40 mark." Sergeant John Domanowski from New Hyde Park, New York, of Company B, recalled, "We painted our combat packs in camouflage colors and made sure our rifles and fighting gear were in good order. Trucks and jeeps had their exhaust pipes raised higher so they would be able to drive in deep water." The 105th didn't know where they were going. "Some thought that Japan was next. Yap Island and Truk were singled out. A few said Saipan. Truk was being bombed pretty heavy, and we thought it was the most likely to be invaded."

On May 14 the 105th began loading on transports that would take them to their unknown destination. On May 17, the 106th and 165th began loading. Between May 18 and May 24, 1944, the 27th Division conducted advanced amphibious training. Rehearsal exercises were conducted as follows: the 105th, including Antitank Company, landed in assault waves on Red Beach in Maui, early on May 21. All personnel and hand-carried equipment went ashore without any heavy impedimenta or vehicles. The units simulated the maneuver called for by the landing plan as they moved inland to capture successive objectives. At 0630 on May 22, the troops were re-embarked and critiques conducted aboard each ship during the balance of the day. On May 23, the 1st and 3d Battalions of the 105th Infantry assault waves participated in a rehearsal of the naval gunfire and air support plans using live ammunition on the island of Kahoolawe. The troops disembarked and approached the shore in wave formation but did not land. The next day the transports returned to Honolulu, where the troops were disembarked and moved back to their camps.

On May 31, the 105th Infantry Regiment, three and one-half years after it left Troy, New York, boarded the combat transports and was on its way to the biggest military challenge of its illustrious one-hundred-year history.

6 Target: Saipan

The Mariana Islands stretch for some 425 miles in a north-south arc, located 1,600 miles east of the Philippines and about 3,200 miles west of Hawaii. They form a vital link in an almost unbroken chain of islands extending 1,350 miles south from Tokyo. Many are small, rocky, and valueless from a military standpoint, but others are so located as to provide a series of mutually supporting airfields and bases. Like so many stepping stones—fifteen islands in all—they afforded protected lines of air and sea communications between the Japanese home islands and their island fortresses. At the north end is Farallon de Pajaros, 335 miles southeast of Iwo Jima. On the southern end is Guam, 250 miles north of the Caroline Islands, and the other larger islands, Saipan, Rota, and Tinian. Guam, the largest of the islands, has an area of more than 200 square miles. Saipan is fourteen and one-half miles long and six and one-half miles wide. Tinian, located about three and one-half miles off the southern coast of Saipan, measures about twelve and one-half miles in length and never more than five miles wide at any given point.

Guam, Saipan, and Tinian lay directly athwart of the advance of the American Central Pacific forces, from their westernmost base at Eniwetok to almost any part of Japanese-held territory in the Central Pacific. Thus, they were selected as the major targets of the Marianas campaign. Capture of these three islands would effectively cut enemy lines of communication and provide bases from which the United States could not only control sea areas farther west in the Pacific, but also provide springboards from which the United States could send long-range aircraft to bomb the home islands. Rota was eliminated by U.S. planners as a feasible target because of the inaccessibility of most of its coast line, its inadequate harbor facilities, and its general inferiority to the three other islands as naval and air bases for future operations against Japan. Saipan was set for attack first, with a target date of June 15, 1944.

Saipan is large and pistol-shaped about the length of Manhattan Island, but twice as wide. It contains a land area of approximately eighty-one square miles and can be technically described as a "limited land mass." Geologically, it is of coral-volcanic origin, composed of coral formations pushed upward by underwater volcanic activity. This made for rather rugged terrain: sharp ridges, fissure-like valleys, and numerous natural faults and caves. Unlike the jungles of the South Pacific, Saipan is semi-tropical, almost as far north as Hawaii and approximately 3,200 miles westward. Its climate is characterized by two seasons, the dry winter monsoon that begins in November and lasts through March, and the wet summer monsoon that starts in April and ends in late October or early November. Tanapag Harbor, on the west coast, was a fueling and supply station for ships en route to Japan in the years prior to World War II. Surface patrols for the Marianas shipping routes were based in Tanapag Harbor. There were two airfields and a seaplane base on Saipan, which served as stopover and refueling stations between Japan and destinations in the southern part of the Pacific.

For tactical planning purposes, Saipan was geographically divided into three sections. The southern third is relatively flat, with a series of terrace-like ridges that serve as gradual steps leading up from the beaches at Charan Kanoa on the west to the high cliffs and hills of Magicienne Bay and Nafutan Ridge on the eastern part of the island. About one mile from the south coast, the Japanese had built Aslito Airfield, the main runway on the island. At the time of the battle, the island was mostly cleared and planted with sugar cane, an industry that the Japanese had developed quite extensively. The middle third is a high, mountainous sector, dominated in the center by Mount Tapotchau, a 1,554-foot peak that seems higher because of its steep sides. The mountain, Saipan's key terrain feature, provided the Japanese excellent observation on whichever beachheads the Americans approached. This middle section of the island also contains Garapan, the principal city and capital of the Marianas, with a population of approximately 20,000 people. Foothills and buttress ridges led off in several directions from Mount Tapotchau creating what the American GIs would later call "Death Valley." The northern third of the island, the barrel of the pistol, resembles a hogback, some 700 to 1,000 feet in height, with a long coastal plain on the west averaging about 700 yards in width. This is the Tanapag Plain, which stretches from Tanapag Harbor and Flores Point to Makunsha on the road to Marpi Point. To the north there is a higher plateau, dropping away in a sheer cliff to a low shelf at the northern end. On this plateau, near the cliffs that marked its end on Marpi Point, a smaller airstrip was being built.

Saipan, a German possession since 1899, was seized by the Japanese in 1914 shortly after the outbreak of World War I. The League of Nations recognized the seizure and in 1920 mandated the Marianas, with the exception of Guam, to Japan. Saipan was colonized heavily in the 1920s and 1930s. By June 1944, there were about 30,000 civilians on the island, mostly of Japanese origin. There were also about 3,000 Chamorros, probably of Polynesian origin, who were the original inhabitants of the island. About 12,000 civilians lived in Garapan, and another, smaller group were in the village of Charan Kanoa. The remainder of the population was scattered in lesser villages and three main plantations, served by a fairly adequate network of roads and a narrow-gauge railway that nearly circled the island.

Saipan's military forces were commanded jointly by VAdm. Chuichi Nagumo and Lt. Gen. Yoshitsugu Saito. Nagumo, commander of the Central Pacific Fleet and 5th Base Force, was an illustrious officer, having established his fame on December 7, 1941, as commander of the forces that attacked Pearl Harbor. The senior army officer in the area, Lt. Gen. Hideyoshi Obata, commanding general of the 31st Army, was in the Palau Islands on an inspection trip at the time of the American invasion of Saipan. The on-site commander, therefore, was General Saito, commander of the Northern Marianas Army Group and the 43d Division (reinforced). The two basic Japanese army fighting units on Saipan were the 43d Division (reinforced), composed of three infantry regiments (the 118th, 135th [less 1st Battalion], and 136th), and additional units to perform transportation, medical, ordnance, and communication services. The other army unit on the island, the 47th Mixed Brigade, was made up of three independent infantry battalions (the 316th, 317th, and 318th), three battalions of artillery, and an engineer company. In addition, there was a tank regiment, an infantry battalion, an antiaircraft regiment, two regiments of engineers, and two transportation companies. Japanese army forces on Saipan totaled 22,702. Naval forces under Nagumo's command consisted of the 55th Naval Guard Force and the 1st Yokosuka Special Naval Landing Force of marines for a total of approximately 6,960, bringing the total of Japanese military forces on Saipan to 29,662.

From a ground defense standpoint, Saipan was divided into four defense sectors. The first included the northern third of the island, to the north of Flores Point, and extending to the east coast in a southeasterly direction. This included Marpi Airfield, which was still under construction. Defending the northern sector were two battalions of the 135th Infantry Regiment, commanded by Col. Eisuke Suzuki. The 3d Battalion was on Tinian. (The 43d Division, which was organized in 1943, had moved from Japan to Saipan in late May.)

The second sector was a naval defense area near the Flores Point Naval Base, to the south side of Garapan and east to Mount Tapotchau. Here was the naval base at Tanapag Harbor, Mutcho Point, the Garapan naval stores, and the Garapan landing beaches. This sector was defended by the Special Naval Landing Force (SNLF) and the 5th Base Force under RAdm. Takahisa Tsujimura. The 5th Base Force had been in command of the Marianas since before Pearl Harbor and continued to command naval shore forces and surface units within them. The largest single element of the naval forces was the 55th Naval Guard Force, about 2,000 officers and men, chiefly responsible for manning coast defense guns. Occupying the frontline beach defenses in the Navy Sector was the 1st Battalion of the 136th Infantry.

The Central Sector was the area from the southern edge of Garapan to Afetna Point and east to the central mountainous spine. It was directly south of the Navy Sector. This included the Oleai and Susupe

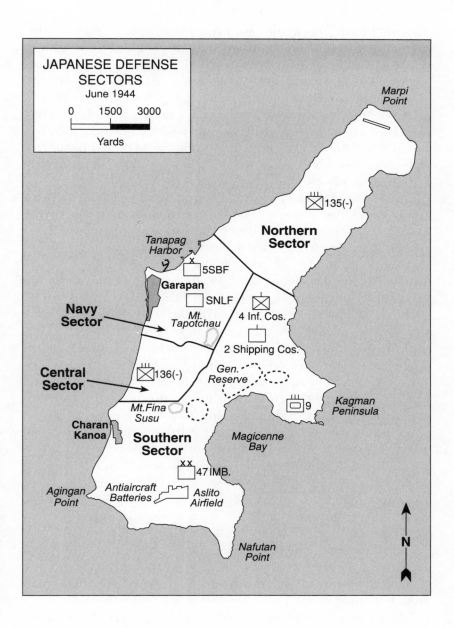

JAPANESE DEFENSE
SECTORS
June 1944

0   1500   3000

Yards

Marpi
Point

135(-)

Northern
Sector

Tanapag
Harbor

5SBF

Garapan

SNLF

Navy
Sector

Mt.
Tapotchau

4 Inf. Cos.

2 Shipping Cos.

Central
Sector

136(-)

Gen.
Reserve

Mt.Fina
Susu

Kagman
Peninsula

9

Charan
Kanoa

Southern
Sector

Magicenne
Bay

47 IMB.

Agingan
Point

Antiaircraft
Batteries

Aslito
Airfield

Nafutan
Point

N

Beaches (during the invasion the Red and Green Beaches) where the
2d Marine Division landed. Assigned to this critical place was one of
the best Japanese units on Saipan, the 136th Infantry Regiment. Commanded by Col. Yukimatsu Ogawa, it was at its full strength of 3,650
soldiers and had its full quota of equipment. Two companies of its 3d
Battalion were in reserve at Chacha on the eastern side of the island,
the 1st Battalion was in trenches in the naval sector, and the 2d Battalion (reinforced by the remaining company of the 3d Battalion),
defended the Oleai beaches, the site area where some of the fiercest
fighting took place in the initial stages of the invasion.

The Southern Sector, by far the largest, stretched along the west
coast from Afetna Point, around the entire south coast, and up the
east coast beyond Kagman Point to the boundary line of the North
Sector. This sector included potential western landing beaches
(Green, Blue, and Yellow) and the eastern shore landing beach of
Laulau Bay (or Magicienne Bay). Assigned to defend this sector was
the 47th Independent Mixed Brigade (IMB), commanded by Col.
Yoshiro Oka. Total strength of the 47th IMB at the time of the landing was about 2,600. Two companies of the 3d Battalion, 9th IMB,
and the 16th Shipping Engineers, commanded by Maj. Masaichi
Tsunekawa, were also stationed within the Southern Sector. The
Japanese had also concentrated all of their reserve troops (as well
as forty-eight tanks), their main artillery batteries, and the antiaircraft units clustered around Aslito Airfield in this sector.

In the Gilbert and Marshall Islands, Japanese defensive doctrine
stressed defense at the beaches with fortifications concentrated on
a thin line along the shores, but little defense in depth. If invading
forces succeeded in establishing a beachhead, Japanese tactics called
for counterattacks to push them back into the sea. The Marianas,
however, are volcanic islands, not coral atolls, and Saipan is much
larger in size than the Gilbert and Marshall Islands. Saipan's considerable elevation and rugged and mountainous terrain provided
favorable opportunities for defense in depth, but the Japanese commander's failure to employ defense in depth flawed their battle plan
from the outset.

The Japanese high command did not take advantage of the island's
mountainous terrain, which would have favored the defender. Gen-

eral Obata instead opted to create a linear defense on the beaches at the water's edge, just as the Japanese in the Gilberts and Marshalls had. If the enemy made it ashore, heavy counterattacks would be employed to drive the enemy into the sea. Saipan's thin linear defense, however, could not stand up to American firepower. Massive naval and air bombardment ripped apart the Japanese beach defenses and left the defenders dazed, disorganized, and ultimately forced to withdraw to the more defensible interior mountains.

An early question faced by the defenders was where the American invasion was likely to take place. Laulau Bay on the eastern shore of Saipan had been used as a harbor in the past. Consequently, General Obata had anticipated an American landing on the island's eastern side; so he assigned a high priority to its protection, including extensive trenchworks with supporting machine-gun positions, coastal defenses, and antiaircraft guns sited on the ridges to fire dual missions against low flying planes and land targets. The trenches had rifle pits and light machine-gun positions, and some of the trenches had barbed wire installations in front. They were especially strong at the mid-point of Laulau Bay, where they were tied to a four-gun blockhouse.

American planners had actually considered marine landings at Laulau Bay, but dropped those plans when they learned of the powerful defenses there. One plan proposed by the 27th Division planners had called for the 105th and 165th Infantry Regiments to land at the bay and drive northwestward across the island to the Flores Point Navy Base. This plan was dropped when the 27th Division was designated the floating reserve. To throw the Japanese off track, Laulau Bay actually received some preinvasion bombardment, but it was all a ruse. Had the 105th and 165th Infantry Regiments landed on these beaches, the casualties probably would have been enormous.

The first American troops left Pearl Harbor for Saipan on the morning of May 26, 1944. These were the amphibian battalions (assault troops, Alligators, and artillery) loaded aboard slow-moving LSTs. On May 28, the second echelon of amphibians left for the 3,200-mile journey. The transport ships carrying the 2d and 4th Marine Divisions (the main assault troops) departed Pearl Harbor on May 29 and May 30. The 27th Division completed loading on May 31 and sailed in three transports and four LSTs early on the morning of June 1. The division headquarters was split into two separate command and staff groups. Each boarded different ships both as a safety precaution and to deal with the possible separate employment of divisional units.

The 105th Infantry assembled at Schofield Barracks on May 31 and proceeded to the docking area where they boarded the USS *Cavalier*. To get to the troop ships from Schofield Barracks, some of the men were crammed into little gondolas or railroad cars that had previously been used to haul sugar cane to refineries. Private First Class Samuel Di Nova from Troy, New York, of Company D, recalled that the cars were uncomfortable, but necessary to avoid being observed by Japanese spies who were thought to be everywhere. Sergeant John Domanowski from New Hyde Park, New York, Company B, recalled that "We were packed like sardines in a can." At Pearl Harbor, the men boarded the waiting ships.

The 1st Battalion, commanded by Lieutenant Colonel O'Brien, was the first unit of the 105th Infantry to board the *Cavalier* at 1730. By 2114 the 2d Battalion had also boarded the transport. Private First Class Seymour M. Krawetz from Skokie, Illinois, Company F, recalled years later, "We boarded our troop ship at Pearl Harbor, climbing up cargo nets to get aboard ship." The 3d Battalion did not go on board the *Cavalier* until the next morning. The ship got underway at 0645 on June 1, and by 0800 had cleared the channel. Krawetz recalled the departure: "We were all impressed by the sight of the battleship *Oklahoma*, which had been sunk on December 7, 1941, and had just been raised. We could read her name plainly on the fantail and her big guns were all in plain sight."

Once the ship was at sea, Colonel Bishop informed the men that their destination was Saipan. Sergeant John Domanowski recalled that shortly thereafter O'Brien's voice came over the loudspeaker. "Now hear this. This is Colonel O'Brien." Although his message was considerably longer, Sergeant Domanowski clearly remembered that O'Brien said with a great deal of emphasis: "Target Saipan." Like most men, Sergeant Domanowski had never heard of Saipan. Other men said that they did not learn that their destination was Saipan until they had been at sea for several days.

En route to the objective, the members of the 105th were briefed extensively on the invasion by Maj. Philip E. Smith of Troy, New York (Regimental S-3); Maj. Kenneth J. Dolan of Watervliet, New York, Assistant Plans and Training Officer; and Maj. Malcolm M. Jameson, Schenectady, New York (Regimental G-2). Schools and staff exercises were conducted; lectures given; and maps, relief maps, terrain models, charts, and photographs prepared, studied, and put on display. The various tactical plans were explained by unit commanders, as were abandon-ship and debarkation drills. Physical exercise was conducted to maintain a high degree of physical condition. Krawetz recalled that the men were briefed on the geography of the island so well that when they went ashore "we felt as though we had been there before."

Although the training was laudatory, the conditions on board for physical training were extremely poor, because the transports were incredibly crowded. The men slept five deep in bunks and had to keep their barracks bags with them at all times. The duration of the voyage, more than two weeks, resulted in a noticeable deterioration in the men's physical condition. The shortage of space also limited the extent to which battalion and company officers could prepare the men for the formations they should take for the assault.

At 1435 on June 4, Maj. Gen. Ralph C. Smith, 27th Division commander, informed Colonel Bishop, "I am considering study of landing our division in assault on Tinian, two regiments on Green Beaches and one over Blue Beach. Suggest you begin studying ship-to-shore movement plan. Will hold conference on Kwajalein Island." The convoy sighted Kwajalein Atoll at 0900 on June 9, and the next day at 1500 a conference was held on board the *Fremont* by Major General Smith for his three regimental commanders. This meeting added three more alternate plans to the nineteen already under consideration for the invasion of the Marianas. At the Kwajalein meeting, practically all planning for Saipan centered around the 105th and 165th Infantry Regiments. The 27th Division's third regiment, the 106th, had just returned from heavy combat at Eniwetok and was counted upon as the division reserve in all planning for the

Marianas. Just before the Saipan battle, however, the 106th was detached from the division at the express request of Maj. Gen. Thomas Watson, USMC, and attached to STLF with the mission of seizing Orote Peninsula on Guam when that island was to be invaded. By the time the division arrived off the coast of Saipan on June 16, the 106th Infantry was also being considered as a possibility to capture Tinian.

On June 11, 1944, favorable weather conditions permitted VAdm. Marc Mitscher's Task Force 58 to begin intense bombardment of the islands of Saipan, Tinian, Guam, Rota, and Pagan. At 1300, June 11, the sixteen fast carriers of Task Force 58, located approximately 192 miles northeast of Guam and 225 miles southeast of Saipan and Tinian, launched a 225-plane fighter sweep that completely surprised the Japanese. The carrier-based attack destroyed 150 Japanese planes on the ground and in the air. This crippling blow reduced the Japanese air strength by about one-third, and thereafter prevented the enemy from reacting in strength. "Control of the air," reported Admiral Nimitz, "had been effected by the original fighter sweep on 11 June." The American air advantage, once gained, was never lost, and it was a pivotal factor in the success of the Marianas campaign. Only twelve American planes were lost in the attack.

The impact of the June 11 air attack on Saipan was devastating. A member of the Japanese 9th Tank Regiment wrote in his diary, "At a little after 1300, I was awakened by the air raid alarm and immediately led all men into the trench. Scores of enemy Grumman fighters began strafing and bombing Aslito Airfield and Garapan. For about two hours, the enemy planes ran amuck and finally left leisurely amidst the unparalleled, inaccurate antiaircraft fire. All we could do was watch helplessly."

For the next three days, from June 12 to June 14, the planes attacked and bombed enemy airfields and installations again and again to ensure that the Japanese had no air capability to counter the coming invasion. Surface ships began bombarding Saipan on June 13, firing their main and secondary batteries for nearly seven hours into the Japanese installations on the western coast of Saipan and Tinian, turning the impact areas into scenes of desolation.

On June 14, fire support ships of the Northern and Southern Attack Forces under the command of Adm. Jesse B. Olendorf arrived off Saipan and joined Task Force 58 in a blasting bombardment of the landing beaches and inland defensive positions. The men of the 47th Independent Mixed Brigade on Afetna Point came under especially intense naval and air bombardment. Several gun positions were destroyed with corresponding personnel casualties. The defenders of Nafutan Point were in their cave shelters for eight hours as U.S. warships shelled the peninsula. American underwater demolition teams (UDTs) were also observed on June 14 landing on the western beaches to clear them of deadly obstacles. Japanese beach defenders fired on the UDT teams, killing four and wounding fifteen. Very few obstacles or mines were encountered.

The preinvasion air and naval bombardment had a devastating impact upon the morale of the Japanese soldiers on Saipan. One soldier's captured diary tells the story of the three or four days before the actual invasion took place on June 11: "Second air raid since landing on Saipan Island. The enemy bombing was carried out in large pattern bombing and received terrific bombardment right after noon and toward the evening. Although our AA put up a terrific barrage and our planes intercepted them, it seems that the damage was considerable. Charan Kanoa and Tinian area was burning terrifically." Again on June 13: "In the afternoon, enemy fleets appeared off shore and commenced furious naval bombardment. Seems as if the bombardment was concentrated around Charan Kanoa and Garapan." On June 14, the day before the actual invasion by American forces, the Japanese diarist (Tarao Kawaguchi) wrote, "Toward the latter part of the day, naval bombardment and bombing was prevalent. Today we transferred to the air raid shelters on the left side of the valley. . . . On this day the enemy landed and the time has come at last."

7 The Marines Hit the Beaches

The attack on Saipan's western beaches in the early morning hours of June 15 achieved strategic surprise, to a greater degree, perhaps, than the American planners had dared to hope. It was not until the intensive two-day, prelanding naval bombardment was well underway that the Japanese high command became convinced that Saipan was the true objective of American forces. With dozens of islands to consider, their elaborately planned defenses were not scheduled for completion until November. As a result, on June 15, some beaches and reefs were unmined, heavy coastal defense guns lay unmounted beside their half-finished emplacements, permanent defense positions were negligible, and there was no organized, cohesive system of defense on the island.

At approximately 0400 on June 15, UDTs (underwater demolition teams) reported that the reef off the western coast of Saipan offered no natural or artificial obstacles to a crossing by amphibious vehicles. The depth of the water in the lagoon was a little greater than had been expected; no mines had been found in the reef or in the lagoon; although a path to the beach was undetermined, tanks could be landed on the reef; the beach was organized throughout the landing area with an occasional pillbox and many trenches; and mobile artillery was observed moving into position. One complicating factor, however, which was not reported by the UDTs, was the presence of mortar and artillery registration flags on the reef and in the lagoon. These markers, which enabled the enemy to place accurate fire on the assault waves, could be plainly seen on the morning of June 15 even from ships thousands of yards offshore.

At 0520 on June 15, transports carrying portions of the 2d and 4th Marine Divisions moved into position in the transport area 18,000 yards offshore of Charan Kanoa. Aboard the *Rocky Mount*, Admiral Turner's flagship, was marine Lt. Gen. Holland M. Smith and his staff. At 0545 the naval bombardment of Saipan resumed. At 0700, air strikes pounded the Japanese positions demonstrating beyond question that the United States had achieved complete naval and air superiority. The landings originally scheduled for 0745 were postponed until 0841.

The two-division landing front on the morning of June 15 was composed of the 2d Marine Division on the left and the 4th Marine Division on the right as they attacked the western side of the island, extending from Agingan Point at the southwestern tip, northward some 10,000 yards to a short distance below Garapan. Upon landing, the 2d Marine Division was to pivot to the left, swing to the north, and seize Mount Tapotchau in the center of the island. Its sector began some 500 yards north of Charan Kanoa, with the 8th Marine Regiment on the right, the 6th on the left, and the 2d in reserve. The Southern Sector was assigned to the 4th Marine Division, the 25th Regiment on the right, the 23d on the left, and the 24th remaining afloat as reserve. The 4th Division was to drive straight across the island to the east, capture Aslito Airfield, clean up Nafutan Point, and then swing to the north, taking up a position on the right of the 2d Division. The 27th Infantry Division was to serve as a floating reserve, which would be deployed on the beaches when and where needed.

Shortly after 0700, the thirty-four LSTs carrying the assault battalions moved into position and dropped anchor about one-half mile off the line of departure. The line of departure, the starting point from which the assault landing craft would take off, was located about 4,000 yards offshore, about twenty-seven minutes from the beaches. Bow doors swung open, ramps lowered, and hundreds of amphibian tractors and amphibian tanks crawled into the water and commenced to circle. In all, 719 of these craft were employed in the operation. For the next thirty minutes, all ships' fires ceased while navy aircraft conducted an area bombing attack.

• • •

While the first landing wave, a line of amphibian tanks of the 2d Marine Division, was approaching the Susupe (Green) Beaches 1 and 2 north of Afetna Point, other marine landing craft from the same division headed north toward Tanapag Harbor and the Black Beaches off the town of Garapan. This was the demonstration group consisting of the 2d Marines; 1st Battalion; 29th Marines; and the 24th Marines. Boats were lowered, troops embarked, and standard waves were formed and went in as far as 5,000 yards off the beach. There they circled for ten minutes without receiving any fire and returned to their mother ships. It had been a successful feint to hold the Japanese 135th Infantry Regiment guarding that sector in place while the real attack hit the beach farther south.

Meanwhile, the first wave of amphibian tanks, comprising the 2d Armored Amphibian Battalion on the left, and the army's 708th Amphibian Tractor Battalion on the right, began firing their weapons at the enemy about 300 yards from the beach. Though some of the Alligators were hit in the water, most were able to move inland. At about 0843, the men of the 6th, 8th, 23d, and 25th Marines hit the beach and immediately came under intense mortar and artillery fire. All units suffered heavily. Nevertheless, the attack moved forward and the marines were able to land 700 Alligators and 8,000 troops on the beaches in the first twenty minutes. Many leaders were hit, but their responsibilities were rapidly assumed by immediate subordinates as enemy shells showered upon them.

Confusion on the part of the navy guide boats, however, resulted in the assault waves of the 2d Marine Division veering too far to the left off course on the Red Beaches. The entire right flank of the leading waves veered to the left, causing a northerly shift along the entire line and considerable crowding in the center. The resulting mix-up delayed the landings significantly. In particular, the amphibian tanks and troop-carrying tractors broke down because of terrain features, man-made obstacles, burning ammo dumps, narrow streets, and swamps. Commanders ordered their men overboard to assault the objective on foot. On the Red Beaches, the 2d and 3d Battalions of the 6th Marines encountered stiff resistance and suffered heavy losses in personnel and equipment. The 6th Marines faced serious opposition and much heavy fighting from 0950 until 1650. By the end of the first day, they had only reached the ridge about one mile inland.

Over on the right, near Green Beach and Afetna Point, the Japanese fought tenaciously to hold their lines so that elements of the 8th Marines were unable to reach their objective by the end of the day. The enemy's Afetna Point defenses behind the Green Beaches held out longer, causing heavy casualties from a fierce concentration of fire that enfiladed the landing beaches. These defenses were not neutralized until they were attacked from behind by elements of the 4th Division on D day plus 1. Seizure of Afetna Point was important for another reason: Its possession would make Green Beach 3 available for the landing of tanks to support both the 2d and 4th Divisions. By the end of D day, the stench of dead bodies on Red and Green Beaches was overwhelming, and some assault units had suffered 35 percent casualties.

In the meantime, the 4th Division landings on Blue and Yellow Beaches near Agingan Point were having their own share of trouble. The first wave landing consisted of sixty-eight amphibian tanks, formed abreast from the army's 708th Amphibian Tank Battalion. All commenced to fire 75mm howitzers or 37mm guns about 400 yards from the shore after mounting the reef. Astern in four successive waves came the assault troops boated in the Alligators of the Marine 10th Amphibian Tractor Battalion. From the line of departure to the reef, the first waves moved in good order and met only moderate enemy gunfire. Once the vehicles were on the reef, however, the Japanese opened up with automatic weapons, anti-boat guns, and mortar barrages as the successive waves of assault troops came over the reef. Of the sixty-eight tanks in the first wave, all but three arrived safely; of the 196 troop-carrying tractors, only two failed to land their passengers. Between 0843 and 0907 all leading waves, with 8,000 marines, were ashore.

Though two assault regiments of the 4th Marine Division had placed elements along the 0-1 line, meeting the first day's objective, by 1040 there were small groups of bypassed Japanese soldiers that continued to harass the attacking troops. Locating the hiding Japanese was a difficult job. The Japanese would remain concealed in spider holes until the marines passed by. Then the lids of the holes opened and rifle or light machine-gun fire was directed at the marines' rear. Artillery fire from the Japanese-occupied Nafutan Peninsula area interdicted every approach. On the extreme right of Yellow Beach, the 1st Battalion of the 25th Marine Regiment encountered bitter opposition from Japanese dug in with machine guns and anti-boat guns on Agingan Point. It was a honeycomb of installations, originally constructed for firing out to sea, but capable of bringing flanking fire to bear against troops on shore. By 1000, the 1st Battalion of the 25th had achieved a beachhead of only twelve yards in depth. On Blue Beach, the 3d Battalion of the 23d's advance through the village of Charan Kanoa had met with only sporadic opposition, and the battalion pushed through the town without encountering serious difficulty. Once the 3d Battalion reached the 0-1 line, however, direct Japanese artillery, mortar, and machine-gun fire kept the battalion pinned down.

By evening on D day, the marines had pushed the 10,000-yard wide beachhead inland to a maximum depth of 1,500 yards, but they were still short of their goals. Artillery was firing, and tanks and the Marine Division Command Posts were ashore and operating. The beachhead line had been established roughly along a front, running in a long arc from the middle of Red Beach 1 on the extreme left, around Lake Susupe, along the reverse slopes of Fina-Susu Ridge almost to Agingan Point, where it dropped back sharply to Yellow Beach 3. Because contact had not been established between the two divisions in the area between Afetna Point and Lake Susupe, it was necessary to give careful attention to protecting their respective flanks, as conditions on the beaches were chaotic. Sergeant Frank C. Cimaszewski, 106th Field Artillery, landed on one of the beaches in the early evening of D day to support the attack. He saw the mess and predicament in which the marines found themselves. He recalled: "All we heard was bad news from a marine officer. To save our howitzer from falling into enemy hands, the officer told us to get back on the boat."

The Japanese, moreover, still held the dominating heights in front of the marines as well as the skillfully camouflaged ridgeline and mountain artillery positions missed by the American bombardment. The dominating ridgeline, which ran parallel to the western beaches, allowed the Japanese to observe the marines digging in and to place fires wherever they pleased. The fact that these enemy fires did not cause even heavier marine casualties than they did was directly attributable to the enemy's inability to mass artillery fire. Nevertheless, casualties on the island by the end of the first day amounted to approximately 2,500, almost 10 percent of the total invasion force. In the 2d Division alone, there were 238 killed, 1,022 wounded, and 315 missing. These casualties and the tremendously wide frontage, coupled with strong enemy counterattacks, stalemated all attempts to extend the beachhead or to advance farther that first day. For more than twenty hours, from 1430 on June 15 until shortly before noon on June 16, the lines of the two opposing forces remained virtually stationary.

After the marines landed, American naval and air bombardments continued with unrelenting force. Tarao Kawaguchi's diary describes in vivid detail how the Japanese tried to survive and protect wounded comrades during the maelstrom of the barrage. He wrote: "During the evening, the unit commander and a large part of the NCOs departed for the Saipan shrine for the treatment of patients. First Lieutenant Kunieda performed bravely and courageously treating the patients under terrific naval barrage, and he should be considered as an ideal model for the medics section. We administered medical aid to one patient and it was the first time we carried out medical aid since landing on Saipan Island. Under terrific naval bombardment, an impressive ceremony for our country was carried out at the Saipan Shrine. During the night transferred the paitents [sic] to the 3d company on top of the hill. Upon returning immediately departed for the rocks."

The Japanese defenders did not wait long in launching a number of counterattacks against marine lines. About 2200, June 15, a company-sized infantry force launched a probing attack along the coastal road against the left flank of the 2d Division, looking for weaknesses for future exploitation. Finding none, they withdrew, but probing actions of this nature continued throughout the night. At 0300 on June 16, the enemy launched their final, major effort of the night. A bugler sounded a loud, clear call that resonated in the tense night air, and with a waving of flags, loud screams, and a brandishing of swords, they counterattacked the 2d Division down the beach road leading from Garapan. Three destroyers, responding to the 6th Marines' shouts for flares, fired five-inch star shells, which turned night into day on the beaches, clearly revealing the attackers. These soldiers, attacking in an upright position, were cut down by automatic and rifle fire, as well as five-inch shells from the USS *California*. Daylight revealed that at least 700 enemy soldiers, possibly a battalion of the 135th Regiment, died in this fanatical counterattack.

The pattern of counterattacks the first night was similar in the 4th Division zone. A series of local attacks against the center of the marines' line on Yellow Beach just south of Charan Kanoa, at 0330 and 0430, was unsuccessful. The attack at 0430, however, was preceded by a heavy enemy artillery and mortar barrage. As a ruse, the Japanese put many civilians, including women and children, at the front of the attacking force to create the impression that a surrender was taking place. The marines were frustrated by having to hold their fire, but once they detected the ruse they annihilated the attackers quickly. The 25th Marines, nevertheless, were forced back nearly 400 yards by the Japanese attack, but were able to recover the lost ground the next day. There were also heavy infiltration attempts throughout the night in the Susupe swamp area, where some 200 Japanese slipped through a gap between the 2d and 4th Marine Divisions in order to join comrades who broke out of the pocket left behind at Afetna Point. Their mission was to disrupt the beach unloading process and to kill marine shore parties. This infiltration was repulsed by the marines with heavy Japanese losses.

On the night of June 15, Admiral Spruance received two reports from submarines saying that the Japanese fleet, for the first time since the naval battles around Guadalcanal in late 1942, was coming out to do battle. Many enemy carriers, battleships, cruisers, and destroyers were observed moving from their anchorage at Tawi Tawi in the Southern Philippines toward the Marianas at a speed that would enable them to attack the American fleet by June 17, D day plus 2. On the morning of June 16, Spruance announced several decisions, at least two of which would have an impact on the 27th Division. First, the tentative date for the Guam landing (June 18) was cancelled and the designation of a new date would await further clarification of the situation. The 106th Infantry, which had been assigned to the STLF for the Guam operation, was now available for use on Saipan if circumstances warranted. Second, he ordered that unloading at Saipan would continue through daylight of June 17, and at dark, all transports and LSTs not required for immediate unloading would withdraw to eastward of Saipan and not return the next day. This decision immediately raised the question of if, and when, the 27th Division would come ashore in support of the two embattled marine divisions.

The landing forces commander, marine Lt. Gen. Holland M. Smith, decided to land the 27th Division as soon as possible, for two reasons: First, a long, vicious fight was in prospect, and it was already apparent that more troops would be required. Second, according to Smith, "It is always better to get them [the reserves] on the beach rather than having them sitting out at sea on ships." Brigadier General Merritt A. Edson, assistant division commander of the 2d Division and a Medal of Honor recipient on Guadalcanal, was reported to have said: "Will we have to call in the 27th Division? Sure we will, and we may need the Guam force, too, before this thing is over." The marine planners of Operation Forager had clearly underestimated the strength of the Japanese resistance on Saipan.

The transports carrying the division arrived off the northwest coast of Saipan at about 0530 on June 16. At 0600, the two transport divisions bearing the 105th and the 165th RCTs, plus 27th Division headquarters and headquarters units, were within sight of the island, about twenty miles from the beaches. The message that successful landings had been made by the marines on Red, Green, Blue, and Yellow Beaches reached the men of the 105th Infantry on June 16 via the ship's public address system. It also stated that the marines were under heavy mortar fire and casualties were heavy. While this announcement was being made, some men from the 105th saw Japanese troops in an assault boat trying to sneak in behind the beachhead to attack the marines on the beach. A U.S. destroyer, however, spotted the Japanese attack and "blew them out of the water." Private First Class Samuel Di Nova recalled that from his vantage point on the deck of the transport, he could see "the big flashes" of the guns pounding Saipan. At one point, he saw an ammunition dump blow up. "It looked like an atom bomb blew up half of the island." Private First Class Seymour Krawetz recalled watching a battleship firing on the island. "They must have hit the aviation fuel dump because it blew up and a flame shot up that dwarfed Mt. Tapotchau, the tallest point on the island at more than 1,500 feet. It was then followed by a shorter blast."

On the morning of June 16, 1944, from the decks of the *Cavalier*, 1st Lt. George O'Donnell of Troy, New York, Company G, 2d Battalion, also witnessed the battleships' attack on Japanese installations. In a letter to his parents written shortly after the Saipan battle, he said:

> My first glimpse of Saipan was early in the morning, before dawn; I saw star shells casting off their illumination, with silhouetting of the island ahead of us. Then, almost over the horizon, we saw gun flashes, followed by explosions and the burning of something between Saipan and the island to the north. Much later, we saw that they were Japanese supply boats, sneaking in supplies: They were being hit and were burning. That was when I saw my first group of Jap soldiers afloat over the waters.

That night First Lieutenant O'Donnell witnessed some more extraordinary fireworks. He wrote: "It was the huge explosion of a Jap aviation gas dump. The flames seemed to leap about 10,000 feet in the air, and to burn instantaneously. About ten seconds later we heard the report; it almost knocked us off our feet." Sergeant Hudson, of the Antitank Company, was also watching the Japanese gas dump explode. Sergeant Domanowski recalled that "Navy guns are

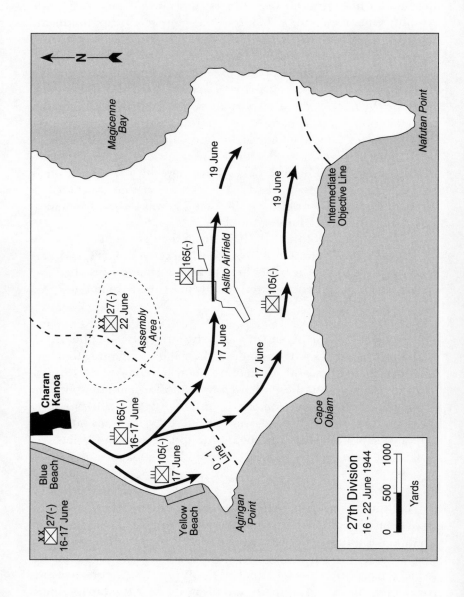

27th Division
16 - 22 June 1944

in action softening up the island. It looks like a hundred rockets going off. When a shell hit an ammo dump, the whole sky would light up. It was beautiful to see the tracer trail that the shells left in their flight to the target."

Sergeant Felix Giuffre, of Company A, recalled what it was like when he first saw Saipan. "It was at night. I am leaning on the railing and looking over the railing at Saipan. You could see explosions." Two recruits came up to him and said, "Hey sergeant, the way they are bombing that island chances are there will be no Japs waiting for us." Sergeant Giuffre immediately responded, "No, don't kid yourself. They are waiting for us to come in. I told them that the marines had just gone in during the day. We'll probably be called in tomorrow. The place was on fire. How in heavens name can anyone survive?"

Shortly after noon on June 16, Maj. Gen. Ralph C. Smith received a warning order from NTLF: "Be prepared to land your unit (less RCT 106) on order upon arrival. Report on board USS *Cambria* for conference." Upon reaching the anchorage around 1630, he and his key staff members met with RAdm. Harry W. Hill and Brig. Gen. Graves B. Erskine, USMC, chief of staff for Lt. Gen. Holland M. Smith. At the meeting, Maj. Gen. Ralph C. Smith was informed that the 27th Division Artillery was to land as soon as possible to support the 2d and 4th Divisions against enemy positions in the Mount Tapotchau and Nafutan Point areas. In addition, the 165th Infantry Regiment was to land immediately and move to the 4th Marine Division's right flank to support the next day's attack. The remaining 27th Division troops were to land as rapidly as possible with the exception of the 106th Infantry, which was to remain afloat in reserve. Once ashore, the 105th was to unite with the 165th and relieve the 4th Division on the right zone, which included Aslito Airfield. Upon receipt of these conflicting orders from NTLF, there was much confusion among the staff officers of the 27th Division. On extremely short notice, the division had been ordered to land almost 20,000 men on a hostile shore with utmost speed, but there were no details accompanying the order on mission assignments, or what the troops were supposed to do once they were on the beaches. Further, darkness was fast approaching as the transports entered the debarkation areas about 6,000 yards west of the Blue Beaches.

At about 1700 on June 16, Colonel Bishop received a warning order from Major General Smith on board the *Fremont* that the 105th should be prepared to land on the Blue Beaches beginning on June 17. On receiving that order, the staffs of the combat battalions met on the ship to discuss their assignments after the landing. Lieutenant Colonel O'Brien immediately convened a meeting of his battalion staff on board the *Cavalier* to discuss their movements once the battalion hit the beach.

Major General Ralph C. Smith returned to the *Fremont* from the *Cambria* at about 1930 on June 16, where Brig. Gen. Ogden J. Ross, assistant division commander, and Col. Gerard W. Kelley, commander of the 165th, were awaiting his orders. Kelley had already sent a message at 1830 to Lt. Col. Joseph T. Hart, executive officer of the 165th Infantry, to land the 165th over Blue Beach 1, immediately south of the Charan Kanoa pier in a column of battalions with 2d Battalion leading, followed by the 1st and 3d Battalions. There the battalions of the 165th would find marine guides to lead them to the right flank of the 4th Division line. Brigadier General Ross and Colonel Kelley were then to go ashore and establish contact with the 4th Division. At about the same time, Colonel Bishop was informed that the 105th Infantry would land on Blue Beaches 1 and 2 the following morning and then move to assembly areas to the south in the vicinity of Yellow Beach 3.

8 The 27th Division Comes Ashore

At 1930 on June 16, amid much confusion, elements of the 165th RCT were lowered into boats for the trip to Blue Beaches 1 and 2, some 6,000 yards away. It soon became dark, and the landing craft were forced to circle around the transports. At 2040, the 1st and 2d Battalions began the trip in almost total darkness, the only illumination provided by gun flashes from naval support ships standing off shore. Within a few minutes, after the columns of boats started for the shore, organization was lost. Ducking in and out among the ships, dodging other landing craft moving from the beach to ships farther removed from shore, and stopping for directions at various ships, the flotilla of landing craft carrying the 165th shoreward became a hopelessly separated and uncoordinated mass of boats. From 2230 to 0200 the following morning, units landed at various locations all the way from Green Beach in the north to Yellow Beach in the south. Following the landing, the 165th's lead battalions nevertheless managed to assemble their widely dispersed men. They then moved to an area in the rear of the 24th Marines on the extreme right flank, with orders to pass through that unit and extend the right flank the following morning.

At 2100 hours on June 16, Brig. Gen. Ogden J. Ross, and Col. Gerard W. Kelley, departed for shore in Ross's landing barge. The coxswain lost his way, and, after much fumbling in the dark and many futile inquiries among other landing craft, the party finally located a guide boat to steer them through the channel to Blue Beach 2, where they waded ashore at about 0130. Kelley reported that "Great

difficulty was encountered in entering Blue Beach, initially in finding the proper direction to the channel entering Charan Kanoa."
After locating the command post of the 23d Marine Regiment, about
300 yards south of the point where they landed, Colonel Kelley contacted the marine guide, Lt. Col. Lewis Rock, who took them to the
4th Division headquarters. Rock had previously located Lt. Col.
Joseph T. Hart, executive officer of the 165th, after searching up and
down the beach all evening. After talking to Kelley by telephone,
Hart led the two battalions of the 165th to 4th Division Headquarters near Yellow Beach 2, arriving at approximately 0500. Preparations were then made for an attack against the Aslito Airfield at 0730
on June 17.

Also landing on the Blue Beaches that night, at the express orders of the landing forces commander, Lt. Gen. Holland M. Smith,
were three of the four artillery battalions of the 27th Division's artillery under Brig. Gen. Redmond Kernan. The 105th Field Artillery
Battalion landed at Blue Beach 1 at 0515 on June 17, and by 1055
was in position and ready to fire. The other two artillery battalions,
the 106th and the 249th supporting the 105th Infantry, came ashore
somewhat later, but were registered and ready to fire by the same
time as the 105th. The 104th Field Artillery remained afloat and detached from division artillery until June 19 (D day plus 4) when it
was brought ashore.

All during the day on June 16, 1944, the transports carrying the
105th Infantry stood off the northwest coast of Saipan awaiting orders to land. That evening an advance detachment from the 105th
disembarked from the *Cavalier* and made its way to the shore. Major Kenneth J. Dolan, assistant plans and training officer, recalled the
landing that night in remarks made to the 27th Division Association,
Inc., upon his return to Troy in December 1944:

> My first glimpse of Saipan occurred at daybreak on the
> morning of June 16, when we arrived off the northwest coast.
> All that day we watched the navy shell the island and the dive
> bombers plant their eggs. Later that night the first elements of
> the division began their disembarking. On the morning of the

17th, I received orders to go ashore with Lt. Col. George H. Hopkins of Whitehall, New York, executive officer of the 105th. In the landing boat with me were Johnny Baker of Troy, captain of Regimental Headquarters Co.; Walt Sluzas of Hoosick Falls, the regimental communications officer; several additional specialist officers; and about 25 enlisted men—technicians, radio operators, etc.—many of them being local boys.

Our mission was to get ashore, establish an advanced command post and coordinate the arrival of our battalions. Things went fairly well—the sea was not too rough—but the area adjacent to the landing beaches was cluttered with all types of craft imaginable. We had gotten into the small channel and were heading for the beach when the boat grounded, started to take in water, and soon was listing about forty-five degrees to starboard. The water had risen to waist high so we began to get out, over the side. We were about 200 yards from shore, and the water was about chest deep at that point, so we began wading ashore. After many minutes we reached the shore. Men who had been carrying heavy radios had a terrible time trying to walk, but came through in fine shape. Not a piece of equipment had been damaged. The beach was known as Beach Blue, and what had once been the proud little town of Charan Kanoa was nothing but a shambles with twisted wreckage everywhere. There were plenty of dead Japs all around and the odor of the dead was beyond description. We started walking to the south. After a while, we came to the 4th Marine Division CP where we met a very welcome individual, our assistant division commander (Brigadier General Ross). He had been ashore all the previous night, gathering information from the marine commanders. He showed us our assigned assembly area on the map, so we proceeded along the beach, and, after a lengthy trip, arrived at our destination. Radios were set up and soon we were in communication with the rear echelon still aboard ship. Shortly thereafter, our battalions began arriving.

On the night of June 16, Japanese troops, under Lieutenant General Saito, launched a counterattack designed to recapture the

Saipan radio station, located about 400 yards behind the 6th Regiment's lines (near Lake Susupe). The objective was a revision to Saito's pre–D day policy to "destroy the enemy during the night, at the water's edge." Even if captured, the radio station was 500–600 yards from the beaches. Nevertheless, the attack force under the personal command of Vice Admiral Nagumo, moved down the coast road from the Garapan area in a joint operation with approximately forty-four tanks from the 9th Tank Regiment. The objective was to "annihilate the enemy's front line and advance towards Oreai [Charan Kanoa] Airfield." It was to be the first major tank attack on a marine unit in the Pacific War. After some delay, on June 17, the attack began at 0330 with approximately 1,000 men and thirty-seven of the forty-four tanks in action. The attack continued until almost 0700 and was decisively repulsed by marine artillery, machine-gun, mortar, bazooka, and rifle fire. Daylight revealed between twenty-four and thirty-one smoldering or burning enemy tanks and large numbers of enemy casualties.

Once ashore, the 165th RCT was ordered to take over the right of the 4th Division line, replacing the 3d Battalion, 24th Marines, and elements of the 1st Battalion, 25th Marines. An attack was scheduled for 0730 on June 17 with the objective the 0-2 line, which included Aslito Airfield in the southern portion of the island. The 165th would be attached to the 4th Marine Division until such time as the 27th Division could establish itself and assume responsibility for the right flank. At this time, the 165th Infantry had only two rifle battalions instead of three. The 2d Battalion was largely intact, but the 1st Battalion under Maj. James Mahoney was minus C Company and still wandering on the beaches. It did not assemble until 1130, four hours after the attack jumped off. The 3d Battalion did not reach the shore until 0945 on June 17 and did not participate in the attack until almost 1200 that day. The 3d Battalion, 24th Marines, stayed in the area until the 3d Battalion of the 165th Infantry arrived.

By 0900 on June 17, elements of the 165th Infantry had advanced 800–1,200 yards against relatively light opposition. By 1400, the 2d Battalion under Lt. Col. John McDonough on the left of the line was on the southwest edge of Aslito Airfield, halfway across the island. Meanwhile, the 1st Battalion under Major Mahoney, became involved in a serious battle for a dominating ridgeline, later named Ryan's Ridge, which extended from the airfield's southwest corner to near Cape Obiam. This proved to be the key to the defenses of the airfield. As long as it remained in Japanese hands, the airfield itself could not be captured safely or supplied. The 1st Battalion's attack at 1130 was unsuccessful. After fifteen minutes of artillery preparation, a second attack at 1230 also failed. The problem was twofold: First, the artillery fire did not damage the enemy position on the high ground, and second, the support fire did not keep the Japanese underground long enough for the infantry to reach and destroy them. Colonel Kelley decided to increase the firepower aimed at the ridge. From shortly after 1230 until 1415, artillery and naval gunfire pounded the ridge and Nafutan Point. Beginning at 1415, the final assault on the ridge by the 1st Battalion commenced with both Company A and Company B reaching the ridgeline and beginning to dig in. The Japanese immediately counterattacked. By 1700 the fighting had become continuous and heavy all along the crest of the ridge, and by 1800, with darkness fast approaching, the two assault companies of the 1st Battalion of the 165th were forced to withdraw to their point of departure. There they dug in for the night.

At 0605 on June 17, Colonel Bishop received orders to land the 105th RCT on Blue Beaches 1 and 2 as soon as boats were available. They were then to move to assembly areas to the south of Yellow Beach 3. By 0845 the 1st Battalion was loaded and headed for the beach; the other two battalions did not land until later in the morning due to low tide and heavy congestion in and around the Charan Kanoa channel. The 105th CP landed ashore at 1210. By 1900, all three rifle battalions of the 105th were ashore on Blue and Yellow Beaches. Once ashore, the 2d Battalion was attached to NTLF as a separate reserve. It moved to an assembly area behind the 4th Marine Division in the early evening to provide greater depth in case a strong counterattack developed. At about 1930, the 1st Battalion was attached to the 165th Infantry and moved to an assembly area just west of Aslito Airfield. The 3d Battalion of the 105th Infantry remained in bivouac in the area of Yellow Beach 3 during the night of June 17.

The 105th Infantry made several false starts before they actually began to head for the Saipan beaches. Sergeant Giuffre of Company A recalled that first, "We were told that we were going to land on the Magicienne Bay (or east side of the island). . . . We got on the Higgins boat, came down the cargo nets. . . . We were going around in circles. . . . They pulled us back into the landing ships. We went up the cargo nets and we laid around until we were called again for another steak dinner, about 7 o'clock in the morning [on June 17]." After that meal, the men went down the cargo nets, reboarded the boats, and headed for the beach. Giuffre said, "This time they told us we are not going to Magicienne Bay, but we were going in between the 2d and 4th Marine Divisions on the Blue and Yellow beaches." Private First Class Nick Rregilo, Company B, recalled that the evening before, they had left the ship and were on the way to the beach. But then, "It was determined that it would soon be dark, and we had to go back up the nets and spend another night on board. . . . Next day we went in. I recall a Jap shell going over our heads and not exploding. I was thankful it was a dud."

At 0845 on June 17, Lieutenant Colonel O'Brien reported to regimental headquarters that the 1st Battalion was on the way to the beach, expecting to land at about 0900. Unfortunately, the 1st Battalion's tank and antitank support units were still on the transports. The 3d Battalion, under Lieutenant Colonel Bradt, reported that by 1008 about 60 percent of its men were loaded onto the landing boats and on the way to the shore. At about the same time, the 2d Battalion, under Lt. Col. Leslie M. Jensen, reported that some of its units had disembarked for the beach, but they did not have orders and had been recalled. Sy Krawetz recalled that, "For some reason we were not permitted to land and kept going around in circles. Around noon the ship lowered sandwiches to us, but by then we were all so sea sick that we could not eat." When some boats finally came near shore, the men disembarked and waded in from the reef to the shore.

Sergeant Domanowski recalled what it was like to board the landing boats. "We climbed down at least forty feet over rope ladders into the landing craft. They were pitching and weaving, but we made it with no one getting wet. I will never forget the smell of diesel fuel as the air was pretty heavy with it, as the landing craft were circling and circling to get into position and make the dash to the beach." As the landing craft approached the beach, the stench of death was in the air. Some units were waved off by the marines on the shore because of the heavy enemy opposition.

When the 1st Battalion hit Blue and Yellow Beaches, their first sight was that of dead bodies, marines and Japanese, floating in the surf and lying on the beach. Private Frank Standarski of Cohoes, New York, who landed at Yellow Beach 2 with Company A, recalled that the men "had to push the bodies aside." Sergeant Giuffre recalled that when his company hit the beach, "There were bodies floating around in the water. Some of them were Japanese and some were marines and they were being evacuated from the beach. There was a stink around there, and some of the bodies were covered with maggots." Corporal Charles Beaudoin from Troy, New York, of the 105th's Medical Detachment, recalled that when he hit the beach he noticed stacks of dead marines piled five or six high. "The water was still full of them," he recalled. "The marines had taken a terrible beating." Sergeant Ernest L. Pettit from Wynantskill, New York, was with Company D. When his landing craft dropped its front gate, the first thing he saw "was a whole bunch of dead marines." They were lined up on the beach and medics were moving among them placing tags on their toes. An exhausted marine sitting on the beach near the dead bodies exclaimed, "Boy! Are we glad to see you guys."

By 1052 on June 17, the Intelligence and Reconnaissance (I & R) platoon of the 1st Battalion landed on Blue Beach 1, followed at 1200 by the 1st Battalion Headquarters contingent, including Lieutenant Colonel O'Brien, Captain Catlin (S-3), 1st Lt. Luther C. Hammond (S-2), and 1st Lt. Francois V. Albanese (S-4). Hammond described the trip into the beach as a nightmare. "The first dead Jap to come before my eyes was seen floating off the island, before we landed, evidently a victim of a sunken ship. When we landed, we assembled in an area where many Japs had been killed. The odor was terrible—

so bad that it was absorbed into the C rations we ate that evening, leaving a bad taste in the mouth." All that Albanese saw on the beach were dead and wounded marines. Once ashore, Hammond noticed that "The beach was alive with people, vehicles, etc. Someone was being given blood plasma, and a small Jap child was lying on a stretcher eyeing us unafraid. A marine smiled, [and] said 'It's alright now Mac.'"

Once he hit the beach, O'Brien was a bundle of energy. Sergeant Domanowski recalled, "I will never forget the way he walked to the front lines—sure of himself, very cocky, and unafraid. His radioman, (Sgt. Ronald L. Johnson from Hoosick Falls, New York), was constantly at his side and always had words of encouragement. I recall that Colonel O'Brien always carried his pistol, his helmet hardly ever secured, and always had a brisk walk."

The 2d Battalion also hit the Blue Beaches near Charan Kanoa on the morning of June 17. First Lieutenant Donald G. Speiring from Beaverton, Oregon, executive officer, Company G, recalled what it was like: "The beach was so cluttered with gasoline drums, ammunition, and supplies that landing craft couldn't go in a straight line to their destination. They had to land wherever they could find a spot on the beach. Some landed on the sugar dock, a pier jutting out from the sugar mill that had been demolished at Charan Kanoa." Once on the beach, G Company assembled on the main road that went through the town. Just as it began to get dark, "A Japanese Tojo, a fighter plane, came down and strafed the beach. It was so close that one could see the pilot." Machine guns loaded with tracers fired at the plane. "There were so many tracers in the air they seemed to light up the sun on the plane's wings." Nonetheless, the Japanese plane flew away untouched.

When it got dark, G Company received orders to move out. This was risky because the American soldiers and marines had a policy that anyone seen moving after dark would be shot, adopted because the Japanese frequently attempted to infiltrate the American positions at night. The assumption, therefore, was that anyone moving after dark must be the enemy. While the column from G Company was moving forward that first night, someone in the rear of the ranks panicked and made a sudden move. Within a few seconds, the whole company scattered off the road every which way, and shots were fired by marines guarding the beach. Two men from Company G were killed instantly—2d. Lt. Donald I. Gunn and Pfc. Maynard J. Rogg were the first combat casualties suffered by the 2d Battalion on Saipan. Private Frederick F. Neubauer of Company G recalled, "We disarmed the marine with the help of a marine sergeant who explained that the marine had just killed a half dozen Japs and was still trigger happy, and in addition, 'Why the hell are you moving at night? No one moves at night!'"

All throughout the morning of June 17, other units of the division came ashore, including the 3d Battalion, 165th Infantry, elements of the 105th, the 249th Field Artillery (FA) Battalion in support of the 105th, and some parts of the 762d Provisional Tank Battalion. These landed near Agingan Point on the extreme southwest coast. The 249 FA's reconnaissance party left LST 272 on June 16 at 2200 and arrived on Blue Beach 2 early on the morning of June 17, where it met with Col. Harold G. Browne, division artillery executive officer. Reconnaissance was made that night for a landing area, Yellow Beach 3. By 1000, the 249th Field Artillery Battalion came ashore and took a position to support the 105th Infantry.

The landings were slow and complicated because of the narrow approaches to the beaches, and heavy congestion soon developed among the landing boats waiting to come in. As a consequence, the navy beachmaster in charge of the landings ordered that no additional landing boats be allowed into the Blue Beaches until later that afternoon when the tide changed. This decision had a devastating impact on the 105th. Most of its organizational equipment, including practically all of its vitally important communications equipment, vehicles, and many headquarters personnel, were left aboard the USS *Cavalier*. Due to impending naval action in the Philippine Sea, all transports were ordered to weigh anchor and put to sea. None of the ships were allowed to return to Saipan until June 25. During this eight-day period, the 105th was forced to operate in combat with almost no signal communications and without most of its headquarters personnel. This later proved to be a distinct handicap as acknowledged by Ralph Smith.

The sudden order to lift anchor and put to sea on the evening of June 17 affected the whole division, as there was a serious shortage of trucks, supplies, and other basic equipment for that eight-day period. Only the 105th Infantry, however, was affected operationally. Sergeant W. Taylor Hudson recalled that Antitank Company, 105th Infantry, "sailed around for a couple of days before we returned to Saipan" on June 19. The beach was so covered with supplies of all kinds it was difficult to see the sand. Sergeant Julius Kovalaski, of Regimental Headquarters Company, recalled that after the troops landed, "Most of the equipment of the 105th Infantry was still aboard the transport—practically all the regimental communications equipment vehicles and the personnel to man them." Most of Headquarters Detachment, 1st Battalion, stayed aboard ship and did not land on Saipan until about a week later, after the Battle of the Philippine Sea.

On the morning of June 18, the soldiers on the beach were astonished to see that most of the naval ships had left Saipan. The first reaction was that they had been abandoned. How were they going to receive supplies and ammunition to support them in the impending battle? Later they learned that the naval ships had left to engage in a huge naval battle with the Japanese fleet that became known as the "Great Marianas Turkey Shoot," a decisive American naval victory that destroyed what was left of the once vaunted Japanese fleet. In two days of heavy air combat, June 19–20, 1944, the Japanese fleet suffered horrendous losses, losing a total of 395 carrier-based planes (out of an original strength of 476). Thirty-one Japanese float planes based on battleships and cruisers as artillery spotters, scouts, search and rescue, and antisubmarine patrol aircraft were also destroyed. About 455 Japanese aviators were lost. United States losses were 130 planes (eighty of which were forced to ditch in the ocean during the night recovery on June 20) and seventy-six air-crews members.

After the 1st Battalion reached the beach, O'Brien huddled with his staff and then detailed First Lieutenant Hammond and two of his men to walk down the beach and locate the 105th's regimental CP. He was to learn from Lieutenant Colonel Hopkins, the regimental executive officer, where the 1st Battalion was to be positioned. Hammond took two men from his S-2 squad as guides: Pfc. Charles P. Skene Jr. and Private Valdez. He first found the division CP and after conferring with Maj. Jacob G. Herzog, assistant division G-2, he located Hopkins at the regimental CP on the Yellow Beach road. Hammond then sent a message to O'Brien conveying the required information. While at regiment, Hammond gave Brigadier General Ross and Colonel Bishop a full report on the status of the 1st Battalion and placed his two men as guides to help the battalion find its assigned position. After some confusion, the units of the 1st Battalion reached their assigned positions inside the perimeter.

By the time the battalion was positioned, it was late in the afternoon of June 17. A Japanese sniper opened up and "people hit the deck." Booby traps and land mines had to be cleared out, and dead Japanese had to be buried. Hammond recalled that "The stink [of dead bodies] was terrible." He and some of his S-2 squad members picked up some enemy weapons, books, and documents off the beach and brought them to the 105th Headquarters for review. Shortly thereafter, O'Brien and Capt. Emmett C. Catlin, S-3, arrived. They went forward in a jeep to reconnoiter the front lines, and returned shortly with an order that the battalion should prepare to move out. Major Philip E. Smith, 105th regimental intelligence officer, informed them that the 1st Battalion of the 165th had been driven from the ridgeline near Aslito Airfield and O'Brien's battalion was to be attached to the 165th for action the next day. O'Brien and Catlin said that they would meet the battalion farther up the line.

Captain Albert A. Butkas from Hoosick Falls, New York, executive officer of the 1st Battalion, assembled the company commanders and told them that the battalion was moving that night to a position where it could support the 165th Infantry's attack the next day. Though it was already dark, the battalion moved up the hill to join the 165th Infantry. Many comments were made by the men about the battalion moving in the darkness, in spite of a standing order that the men were to remain in their foxholes at night. When the 1st Battalion arrived at the top of the hill, O'Brien and Catlin came down from the front to meet them. Catlin laughed and said that he and O'Brien had already been to the top and had been fired upon by Japanese snipers while reconnoitering. The message was clear: The enemy was near, but the 105th could prevail when it attacked the next day. The men dug in for the night as best they could in the hard coral rock and pouring rain.

9 The 105th Joins the Attack

The NTLF Operations Order for June 18 (D day plus 3) called for an attack by all three divisions; the two Marine divisions at 1000 and the 27th at 1200, giving time to move the 105th Infantry into position on the right flank along the south coast of the island. In the division's zone, the morning of June 18 found the enemy drawn up behind the ridgeline southwest of Aslito Airfield, which had been given up by the 1st Battalion, 165th, the previous day. At 0550 the 165th had been restored to division control. With the 3d Battalion of the 165th now in the line, the two battalions of the 165th, with four tanks preceding them, easily recaptured the ridge with very little fighting and few casualties. Large numbers of Japanese were reported withdrawing in the direction of Nafutan Point. The capture of the ridge opened the way for the easy capture of Aslito Airfield by the 2d Battalion of the 165th. The airfield's broad, hard-surfaced runways had hardly been touched. Its huge frame hangar had been partly wrecked, but the Japanese planes inside and outside had not been touched. Also discovered and put to good use was an oxygen plant, a power plant, a million-gallon reservoir, and several shelters and warehouses with steel-reinforced concrete walls. That afternoon, when Ralph Smith arrived at the 165th CP, the airfield was officially renamed Conroy Field in honor of Col. Gardiner J. Conroy, former regimental commander of the 165th, who had been killed at Makin. Later, on June 30, 1944, the airfield was renamed in honor of a naval aviator, Comdr. Robert H. Isely, who on June 12 had been shot down and killed over Saipan while leading an attack on the field.

The 27th Division was ordered by NTLF to assume responsibility for the extreme right zone of action relieving the 4th Marine Division. It was then to launch an attack across the island at 1200 toward Magicienne Bay on the east coast of the island. At the same time, the 105th (less the 2d Battalion) was to be inserted on the right in the zone previously held by the two right battalions of the 165th. The 3d Battalion of the 165th would hold the ridgeline until relieved by the 105th and then revert to regimental reserve. By 1700 on June 18, the whole of the 165th Infantry's line had moved forward until it reached a point just short of the beach fronting on Magicienne Bay. The enemy, who had been driven back into Nafutan Point, was cut off from the main Japanese forces farther to the north by this advance. Because it was well ahead of the 105th, the 165th had to make some adjustments to protect its flanks that evening.

At 0805 on June 18, 1944, division headquarters contacted Colonel Kelley of the 165th by radio: "Where is O'Brien's battalion? What is it doing? Has it been in action?" Kelley responded at 0810: "O'Brien's battalion has not been in action. Last night his assembly area was 118 I. This morning he was directed to proceed to original assembly area in 119 P as soon as possible to await your orders." Under O'Brien's orders, Hammond brought the 1st Battalion of the 105th Infantry to the designated assembly area on the ridge. Shortly before noon, Capt. Walter G. Gallagher of Headquarters Company ran up with orders from regiment to attack at 1200, supported on the right by the 3d Battalion, 105th Infantry. O'Brien ordered Hammond to move forward, contact the 165th Infantry, and set up a battalion Operations Post (OP). Enemy artillery had already begun to pummel the ridge.

Suddenly, the 1st Battalion OP came under heavy enemy artillery fire. Hammond described it as the 105th's "Baptism of Fire." He recalled the following: "Moore [S-2 Squad] and I are looking through the telescope . . . 'bang!' . . . scramble for shell holes . . . heart beat faster . . . frightened as hell . . . finally could raise my head between shots . . . I would hear the report then I would duck in time . . . Spotted the gun." O'Brien then came up and took Private Valdez back for medical help. Hammond located the enemy gun and then moved back to give the artillery coordinates to Capt. Bernard A. "Bernie" Toft, of the 249th FA Battalion. The battalion fired a concentration of shells, but the enemy artillery did not let up. Toft fired a second time and Hammond noted that this time the Japanese artillery had moved from its original position. Although some members of the fire direction center wanted to continue the shelling, the decision was made to suspend the fire due to ammunition limitations. Naval gunfire support also did not materialize.

First Lieutenant Hammond was terrified during the Japanese bombardment: "I was lying prone on a ridge scanning enemy territory. Suddenly, a shell whistled overhead and exploded a few yards to the rear. I scrambled into a shell hole nearby and compressed myself as low as possible. The shells kept coming over every few seconds. You could hear the Jap howitzer fire, and then the shell whistle by and an almost immediate explosion. I wanted to spot the flash of the gun if possible so that we could get our own artillery on it, so I would stick my head up to scan the ridge about 1,500 yards away, and duck down after I heard the report of the gun. I had time enough to get down, and I spotted the flash of the weapon too."

At 1245 on June 18, the 105th assumed responsibility for the right half of the division front. On the extreme right, the 3d Battalion of the 105th relieved the 3d Battalion of the 165th, which then went into division reserve. About the same time, the 1st Battalion of the 105th relieved the 1st Battalion of the 165th, which was then shifted to the left flank of the division line to close the gap between the 4th Marine Division and the 2d Battalion, 165th, occupying Aslito Airfield. According to the division historian, Capt. Edmond G. Love, "The 1st Battalion, 105th Infantry, was destined to become, before the close of the battle on Saipan, both the most colorful and the busiest unit in the 27th Division. On the morning of July 7, its members were to stand in the face of the greatest single enemy Banzai raid of the Pacific War. They were to die almost to a man in one of the more courageous struggles of American military history." Captain Love goes on to say, "Much of the credit for the record of this fine battalion must be given to its commander, Lt. Col. William J. O'Brien. A cocky little rooster of a man who couldn't stand still, O'Brien's characteristics were mirrored in his battalion."

The 1st Battalion's mission on June 18 was to push to Magicienne Bay on the eastern side of the island. After being subjected to thirty minutes of artillery fire from the Nafutan Point area, by 1600 it had reached a point even with the east end of the airfield. Facing much more difficult terrain than that confronting the 165th, the 105th Infantry made much slower progress and had to dig in for the night well to the rear of the 165th line. To maintain contact with its sister regiment, the 165th Infantry also dug in, delaying its attempt to reach the east coast until the following day. The line soldiers in the 105th "had to wade through a matted jungle of small trees that hid a virtual forest of jagged coral pinnacles." One soldier from the 105th, "his hands cut and bleeding, his trousers torn right off his legs, and suffering from heat exhaustion, confessed that he had fought in this area for three days without seeing an enemy soldier." He went on to say, "Hell, I wouldn't have been able to do anything about it if I had seen one. I've been so damned busy playing mountain goat since we came into the line that I haven't had time for war."

During its advance eastward, the 1st Battalion had encountered only minor enemy resistance, along with artillery and mortar fire. But it was friendly fire that took its toll. First Lieutenant Norman C. Arnold from Sergeant Bluff, Iowa, Company B, and two other soldiers were killed instantly by a barrage of friendly fire late on the afternoon of June 18. Arnold's "head was sliced in half as if an ax fell on it. He knew that his time was up and told Captain Ryan about the feeling he had." Hammond, a close friend of Arnold's, was distraught over the loss. Private First Class William F. Erbach from Chicago, Illinois, was one of the enlisted men from Company B killed in that same barrage. "His stomach was torn up and his last words were 'Shirley, Shirley.'"

At about 1800, the 1st Battalion dug in on both sides of Aslito Airfield. While Hammond and his S-2 squad, along with Sgt. Thomas A. Baker, Company A, were moving back through a cane field toward the airfield, he recalled "We heard planes overhead. I noticed a flight of ours [two U.S. carrier planes] and then two or three Jap planes flying in formation. We all stopped and looked up. The planes were east of Magicienne Bay. The two flights passed each other." Then suddenly there was a dog fight. Planes were zooming and twisting in every direction. After only a few seconds passed, one of the planes started to go down in a steep dive, and someone reported seeing a parachute floating down. One of the enemy planes left the dog fight and headed straight toward First Lieutenant Hammond's squad in the cane field. "Over it went, at a couple of hundred feet and I looked at the big rising sun under the wing. A hail of AA fire poured at him. I imagine some riflemen even fired. The 90mm batteries shot to [sic] low, for some reason; they [the battery rounds] landed on the ridge along the road ahead of us."

Nick Rregilo remembers the air battle: "Later we arrived at the bunkers [near the airfield] and witnessed our first dog fight by navy planes and Zeros. One of ours was shot down and I saw the pilot parachute from the plane. A Jap Zero was hit badly and I marveled at the skill of the pilot as he brought the plane down right over us and onto a runway. The plane, which was engulfed in flames, rolled a few hundred feet and finally tipped on its nose, and the pilot jumped out and was rescued."

By the end of June 18, the 4th Marine Division had penetrated to Magicienne Bay and cut the island of Saipan in two. Lieutenant General Holland Smith's plans for the next phase of the operation called for a change in direction of the main attack from east to north across the breadth of the island. The 2d Marine Division would hold and consolidate its positions south of Garapan and would constitute the pivot of a wheeling movement. The outer end of the wheel spoke would be the right flank of the 4th Marine Division resting on Magicienne Bay. When the turn had been completed, the two divisions would be abreast and ready to launch their northerly drive against the main enemy defense line, which now stretched across the island in a southeasterly direction from the outskirts of Garapan to Magicienne Bay.

Nafutan Point and the approaches to it along the south coast of Saipan remained occupied by Japanese troops that had to be cleared out before Aslito Airfield could be considered safe from Japanese counterattack and infiltration. Nafutan is a short peninsula—a southward extension of the east coast of Saipan. Dominating most of the peninsula is a high, cragged ridge running in a north-south direction not far inland from the east coast. This is Mount Nafutan, whose highest point is approximately 407 feet. Its northern and western faces are almost sheer cliffs. About 400 yards west of the northern part of Mount Nafutan lies a ridge about 300 feet in height. Although the exact number never became known, there were well over 1,000 Japanese military personnel isolated in the Nafutan Point area. Initially, two regiments of the 27th Infantry Division, the 165th and the 105th, were assigned to eliminate this hotbed of Japanese opposition. Eventually only one battalion of the 105th Infantry (the 2d Battalion) had to deal with this problem.

D day plus 3 definitely marked the conclusion of the initial phase of the Saipan operation. The 4th Marine Division had reached the eastern shore of Magicienne Bay cutting off the southeastern segment of the island and arriving in position for the sweep northward across its entire width. With the swinging of the main drive by the marines to the north, the southeastern corner of the island was assigned to the 27th Division. The 165th Infantry, having secured Aslito Airfield on D day plus 3, drove on to the eastern shore. Here they wheeled southward, with the 105th Infantry on the right, gradually driving the enemy back to the narrow confines of Nafutan Point. By then even the Japanese must have known that their defense of the island was futile. Far from driving the invaders into the sea, the Japanese themselves had been driven back from their strong positions and forced back all along the line. Their communications had become so disrupted that they lacked the means to organize major counterattacks with any hope of success.

Since coming ashore on June 17, 1944, the 2d Battalion, which had been assigned to the 4th Marine Division for operational purposes, remained in bivouac in the vicinity of Yellow Beach 3. When 1st Lt. George H. Williams, 2d Battalion S-2, wanted information about what was going on up in the front, Pvt. Frederick O. "Fritz" Neubauer, a scout for G Company, volunteered to scout ahead and report back to Captain Olander, the G Company commander. In a recent memoir, Neubauer recalled that on June 18 he "joined up with some marines and the sergeant that helped us the night before. Snipers everywhere, a marine got nailed by a sniper while riding a bicycle in front of us. While exploring some caves in a side gully, I found a marine demolition team that got ambushed—all bullet holes in the back. . . . Reported back to the marine sergeant, and we got comp C explosives from the dead marines, and I crawled up and blew up the sniper's hole while the marines covered me. Then we blew up the rest." Neubauer further recalled that he "got some valuable information from a Jap Major that we blew out of one cave—a picture of him and his men waving a flag with coastal guns in the background. According to our S-2, Lieutenant Williams, we were up against the veteran 43d Division that took Singapore and Hong Kong."

Tarao Kawaguchi of the Japanese 43d Division Hospital Unit recalled the events of June 18 on Saipan in his diary: "The patients are coming in ever increasing numbers. During the evening, transported some medical supplies to the pharmicists [*sic*] section. Today, the strafing by enemy planes was terrific."

Although by June 18, the Japanese air fleet in the Marianas had been all but destroyed by the U.S. Navy and there was only token resistance in the air, at about 1900 until the end of the Saipan battle, the American troops on the line could expect a visit from "Bed Check Charlie," or, as some called the Japanese airmen, "Washing Machine Charlie." Militarily, "Charlie's" nightly attacks were ineffectual, but they "were disruptive and kept the men awake at night."

At 0730 on June 19, the 27th Division continued its attack eastward toward Nafutan Point. The 165th Infantry reached the eastern shore of the island near Magicienne Bay with its 1st and 2d Battalions positioned to the north of Nafutan Point. It maintained contact with the 4th Marine Division on the left. The 1st and 3d Battalions of the 105th continued their advance from the west toward Nafutan Point. On the extreme right, the 3d Battalion had initially met little opposition, but soon encountered heavy resistance along the rugged southern coast. Enemy soldiers occupied strong positions in caves along the face of the cliffs, slowing progress on the right flank. At approximately 1600, the 3d Battalion of the 105th reported, "Coast line filled with cover containing enemy. Movement on right will be slower than contemplated." By nightfall, it had advanced only 1,800 yards in its zone. That night a group of twenty to thirty civilians, who had been hiding in caves along the southern coast, stumbled into the perimeter of Company L, 3d Battalion, and all were killed.

At 0805 on June 19, the 105th radioed the 1st Battalion that air reconnaissance reported that "Jap tanks [were] approaching area." At about 1030 Companies A and B ran into heavy Japanese opposition near Ridge 300 ("Bloody Ridge"), a ridge that flanks Mount Nafutan to the northwest. Here the terrain looked like a giant ramp tilting upward into the rugged hills and valleys of the Nafutan Peninsula. On June 18, the 165th had bypassed this area without incident on its way to Magicienne Bay. The 1st Battalion's left flank was at the base of the upslope; with the right flank at the spot where the upslope met the high ground. Both assault companies from the 1st Battalion began receiving heavy Japanese small-arms and automatic-weapons fire as they approached the ridge from the west. C Company was at this time in battalion reserve.

Under strong covering fire, the leading elements of the assault companies reached the top of the ridge without trouble, but as they went over the crest to a stretch of level ground they were pinned down by a heavy concentration of fire from pillboxes to their immediate front. The Japanese had waited for most of the men to start down the reverse slope of the ridge and then let loose with mortars and machine guns. The machine guns seemed to be concentrated in a series of six or seven camouflaged pillboxes, which looked like little more than low mounds of earth about 100 yards away. The whole area was filled with big coral rocks and concrete emplacements. "We didn't even see the Jap pillboxes until a little later," said Pvt. Merril E. Bethel, of Fruitvale, Idaho. Captains Ackerman and Ryan, after a brief conference, placed their men in a semicircle around the area and began to pour fire into it.

Protected by that fire, several combat engineers made a sortie to blow up the Japanese pillboxes. The engineers made headway, but very slowly. One of them, with a satchel charge of dynamite in his arms, got to his knees and started for the nearest pillbox at a low crouch. Everyone in the rifle companies gave him protective fire. A few yards from the pillbox, he was blown up in the air, probably by a land mine, and landed like a rag doll, misshapen and unmoving. The rest of the engineers were pinned down by the enemy fire.

After Company A's attempt to flank the enemy gun emplacements from the right rear was unsuccessful, Captain Ryan of Company B ordered Lt. Martin A. Olsen from St. Albans, Long Island, to flank the enemy pillbox from the left. Lieutenant Olsen selected a squad under SSgt. William D. Stanczak from Cohoes to lead the attack. Staff Sergeant Stephen P. Chinnici from Brooklyn came along to "see if he could be of any help." The squad began crawling through the short grass toward the objective about forty yards away. Chinnici reached a good firing position and launched four rifle grenades into the enemy pillbox position before he fell wounded.

After crawling about ten yards, Olsen noticed that there was a deep tank trap directly in front of the pillbox. He told Stanczak and Pvt. William L. Stahl from Hightstown, New Jersey, to run with him and jump into the tank trap. Two squads of four men each were directed to encircle the pillbox from the left and the right. Olsen and Stanczak made it to the tank trap without difficulty, but Stahl dropped to the ground just before the tank trap and was crawling toward it when a Japanese soldier inside the pillbox dropped a grenade into the trap. The explosion killed Stanczak instantly, but not before he tossed three grenades through the firing slit of the pillbox. Stahl was wounded in the explosion, and the concussion blew Olsen out of the trap, cut and bleeding and with most of his clothes and equipment torn apart. The Japanese in the pillbox began throwing grenades at the four men on the left led by Sgt. William N. Gilkes from Oceanside and Staff Sergeant Chinnici, Pfc. Harrell L. Weaver from Cohoes, and Pfc. Ralph Skalac from Lockport, Illinois. All four men were wounded. Private First Class Weaver had one grenade go off twelve inches from his face, but by some miracle he escaped with only minor injuries.

A medic, Pfc. William Schuerpf, made his way to Olsen's group in the tank trap. As he was examining Stahl's wound, a Japanese threw another grenade, blowing Stahl's leg off, killing him instantly. Schuerpf was badly hit by fragments, but Olsen was revived by the explosion, retrieved his carbine, and killed three Japanese who tried to throw grenades out of the pillbox at the wounded men.

When Olsen ran out of ammunition, a fourth Japanese soldier trying to get at him was killed by Schuerpf who calmly pulled a pistol out of the inside pocket of his fatigue jacket and shot the man. Protected from the enemy from other positions by Company B's covering fire, Olsen ordered the survivors of his patrol to fall back from the enemy's pillbox to B Company's protected position on the perimeter.

Private First Class Nick Rregillo, a machine-gunner with Company B, recalled the pillbox incident well: "A rifle squad had assaulted a pillbox that was located in an open area. A couple of men were killed, including the leader, Sgt. William Stanczak. We were called upon to place fire on the pillbox while the wounded were taken to safety. The gun jammed while firing and it was a few minutes before our ammunition carrier, [Pfc.] Nunzio R. Tarentino of San Francisco, California, was contacted and we got the ruptured cartridge out and resumed our firing." Shortly thereafter, he recalled: "A volley of mortar shells fell around us. One threw dirt and rock on us. Finally, we heard shouting behind us and it was Corporal Savage telling us to get out of there and pull back to safety. It was then we learned that we were the only two remaining there." While pulling back, Rregillo recalled, "That after the first barrage, while retreating with the gun that another one followed and I threw it and hit the ground. The hot barrel slightly burned my arm. After returning to his company, Howard reported that he had unbuckled his belt while firing the gun and left his pack, kit, belt, and .45 pistol there."

Approximately ten minutes after Lieutenant Olsen returned to Company B's position, the whole crest of Ridge 300 was swept with a hail of bullets from Japanese machine guns and small arms of all types firing from the pillbox positions. Both companies were pinned down by this fire and were unable to neutralize the enemy. First Lieutenant Van M. Crocker, commanding the Weapons Platoon of Company A, was wounded in this exchange of fire. About this time 2d Lt. Albert D. Brockett of Company A volunteered to crawl to attack the hidden positions that were protecting the main Japanese pillbox. Sergeant Floyd J. Wilson of Company A, 102d Engineers, carrying a demolition charge, and Pfc. Herman L. Burks, who had loaded himself up with grenades, volunteered to go with Second Lieutenant

Brockett. The three crawled forty yards through the grass under constant enemy fire. When they reached the pillbox, Wilson fixed the fuse on the demolition charge but was killed by an enemy rifleman before he could throw it. Second Lieutenant Brockett grabbed the charge and, as he was trying to fix the fuse, he was shot and mortally wounded. Burks was seriously wounded by an enemy grenade but was able to get back to the company and report to Captain Ackerman regarding the location of several of the enemy positions. In a valiant try to save Brockett, four litter-bearers from the 1st Battalion CP tried to bring him to safety. They were in the field when an American tank appeared up over the crest of the ridge, causing an enemy dual-purpose gun to open up. One litter-bearer was killed; the other three, though wounded, were able to bring Second Lieutenant Brockett in, but he died a short time later before he had a chance to report to Captain Ackerman.

The heavy concentration of enemy fire from Ridge 300 forced Company A to pull back to the reverse slope of the ridge and reorganize. Company B, however, was pinned down by the enemy fire and out of communication with everyone. When it became clear that it could not withdraw without taking serious casualties, Lieutenant Colonel O'Brien ordered up a self-propelled gun from the Cannon Company under Lt. Clarence S. Pearson to the ridge. When required to pull back due to enemy fire, Ackerman ordered battalion and company mortars to fire close to the company lines. This allowed the company to align itself with Company A on the other side of the ridge.

Learning of the situation, regiment ordered the 1st Battalion to reform and come up with a new plan of attack. After meeting with his company commanders shortly after 1300 on June 19, O'Brien called regiment and advised that he did not think another frontal assault on the Japanese position was feasible. Instead, he requested permission to turn his battalion around so that it faced south. By attacking up the ramp of Ridge 300, he could bring tanks into the action and perhaps outflank the enemy. Tank support had already been requested by the 1st Battalion OP manned by Lieutenant Hammond. Permission was granted by division headquarters to proceed with the attack. Starting at 1530, a fifteen-minute air strike with rockets, bombs, and strafing was delivered on the enemy positions, followed by a thirty-minute artillery concentration and constant mortar fire from Company D.

At 1610 the 1st Battalion jumped off on the attack accompanied by several tanks and almost immediately ran into trouble. B Company, on the left, had to climb the ridge a considerable distance from the enemy's positions in order to execute the flanking movement. A tank fired a round that hit an enemy ammunition dump, thus disrupting the attack and forcing it to move well to the right to avoid the danger of exploding ammunition. The force of the explosion was so great that 1st Lt. George O'Donnell of Company G felt it at the 2d Battalion CP about a mile away. O'Donnell recalled, "It was a much bigger dump than expected, and rocks and debris fell all around us. . . . I got most of myself underneath a building." No sooner had Company B reached the top of the ridge at about 1730 than the Japanese opened fire with dual-purpose guns forcing Company B to halt its advance for the day.

Company A's advance on the right was also held up by heavy enemy automatic and small-arms fire almost at the outset. Sergeant Thomas A. Baker, Company A, volunteered to slip along Ridge 300 where he observed the location of several enemy gun positions. He borrowed a bazooka from one of his comrades and under heavy enemy fire walked boldly about 100 yards into the fields that covered the ramp and calmly knelt down and fired his weapon single-handedly into one of the Japanese dual-purpose gun positions, knocking it out with his second shot. He then got up and walked back to his company with bullets striking the ground all around him. This heroic action, among others, resulted in his receiving the Medal of Honor posthumously in May 1945.

The Japanese tanks, which had been previously spotted by aerial reconnaissance, appeared in front of the 1st Battalion's position near Ridge 300. Fortunately, army engineers had buried live enemy shells in the road. When a tank hit the buried shells, it blew up and the other two enemy tanks withdrew. At or about the same time, Sgt. Dominick M. Dioguardo from A Company ran into the middle of the road waving a Samurai sword and yelling "Banzai! Banzai!" The men from Company A withheld fire when they saw that the man with the sword was one of their own.

10 The Attack on Nafutan Point

The NTLF attack orders for June 20 again involved a pivoting movement to the north on the part of the marine divisions that were to attack toward objective Line 0-4. The 27th Division was to complete the seizure of objective 0-3, including all of Nafutan Point at the southernmost part of the island. After viewing the terrain and conferring with his regimental commanders, Maj. Gen. Ralph Smith ordered the 165th Infantry, located along Magicienne Bay, to attack Nafutan Point from the north and northwest on the morning of June 20. In view of communications problems experienced by the 105th, it was decided to attach the 1st Battalion for this operation. Colonel Kelley of the 165th had established his command post atop the control tower at Aslito Airfield, a useful location for directing his troops' movements. The 3d Battalion, meanwhile, was ordered to move east along the southern coast to trap the enemy on the southern tip of the island.

At 0800 on June 20, Maj. Gen. Ralph Smith called a conference of unit commanders most concerned with the new plan of attack, including Lieutenant Colonel O'Brien. Following the conference, Smith issued Field Message No. 1 calling for a coordinated attack at 1000 by the 165th Infantry from the north with three battalions abreast—the 2d and 3d Battalions of the 165th, and the 1st Battalion of the 105th. The 1st Battalion of the 165th was to remain behind to hold the Magicienne Bay area and maintain contact with the 4th Division moving north along the east coast. The 3d Battalion, 105th, was to continue to drive eastward on the southern coast of the island, along the Saipan Channel to close the noose around the Japanese remaining on Nafutan Point.

Before the coordinated attack got underway as scheduled at 1000, the 1st Battalion, 105th, came under heavy enemy artillery fire from across Magicienne Bay. At 0945, O'Brien radioed seeking assistance, "Send vehicles to 1st Battalion to evacuate casualties." About thirty minutes later, he again reported that they were "under Jap artillery fire." Although the original jump-off hour had been set at 1000, Major General Smith postponed it until 1200 to allow the 1st Battalion to get into position. At 1145, division artillery fired along the entire front. By 1155, having advanced 600 yards to get into position, the 1st Battalion reported that it was in place to attack. At 1200 the troops jumped off, supported by tanks and automatic weapons. The 2d and 3d Battalions, 165th, met with varying degrees of success in attacking Ridge 300, because the terrain was wide open country that sloped gradually uphill to their front until it reached the high ground of Nafutan Point itself. By 1630, these two battalions launched a concerted attack against the hills north of Mount Nafutan. By 1730 no further progress seemed possible before nightfall, so all units were ordered to dig in.

On the right of the attacking line, because the terrain was less favorable, the 1st Battalion had to struggle to keep abreast of the other two battalions. Plagued by enemy machine-gun and heavy-weapons fire from its left front and flank, from the time they moved out at 1200, its two assault companies had to hold up. C Company on the right, which had received heavy enemy fire from some buildings on its boundary line with the 3d Battalion, 165th, decided to dig in. The whole line stopped. O'Brien came forward and after identifying the buildings as the source of the enemy fire, he ordered them burned down; thus, forcing the enemy snipers to either flee or be burned alive. Tanks, self-propelled weapons, antitank guns, and flame throwers joined in the destruction of the Japanese positions.

At 1550 on June 20, regiment received a report from a marine unit that the "enemy has come forth displaying white with rifles and light machine guns [MGs)] strapped to their backs and then opened fire on our troops." The Japanese were masters of deception and tried all manner of ruses to infiltrate the American positions. Private First Class Arthur Herzog, Antitank Company, recalled that the "Japanese had taken the marine uniforms—you know—that had been killed. . . . They were trying to get to the rear and raise hell with the beach party." The phony marines were intercepted, and about 150 of them were killed by the American soldiers.

Later that afternoon, Sgt. Charles Mazzarella from Leonardo, New York, assigned to the 102d Medical Battalion stationed near Aslito Airfield, saw a jeep carrying three men drive into his aid station. One of them was a wounded Japanese soldier seated in the rear. When the jeep stopped, the Japanese soldier jumped out and began hopping about on one foot; the heel of his other foot had been shot away. He, nevertheless, declined medical assistance. Another passenger approached the medic, showing him his forearms. They were covered with small puncture-like holes caused by shrapnel. According to Mazzarella, "He said that he only wanted me to put something on them to clean them up. . . . While I was attending him, he kept saying what a hard time his men were having, and that he had to get back to them." The wounded man was Lieutenant Colonel O'Brien. His "attitude and concern for his men really impressed me," Mazzarella recalled many years later.

By nightfall on June 20, the 1st Battalion had advanced about 500 yards along relatively level ground. They dug in near the foot of Ridge 300 where the original assault had been made the day before, in a position to flank the ridge the next day. The 2d Battalion, 165th, was almost directly in front of the nose of Mount Nafutan, while the 3d Battalion was facing Ridge 300 from the north, forcing the enemy back into its final defensive positions. The June 20 attacks had carried the whole American line directly into the strong points of the main enemy position on Nafutan Point.

Around 2130 there was a lot of enemy activity in front of the 1st Battalion. One Japanese soldier ran out in front of Company A, shouting at the top of his lungs: "Shoot me! Shoot me!" It was all a ruse to get the Americans to reveal their positions, but it didn't work. The troops lay silent in their foxholes listening to the Japanese jabbering only a few yards away. Shortly before 2200, an enemy dual-purpose gun, dubbed "Saipan Sam" by the Americans, began to open up not more than 150 yards from the fronts of the 105th Infantry. The Japanese gun overshot the 3d Battalion's position, but some rounds fell on the 1st Battalion, killing one man and wounding three in Company

A. At 0840 June 21, the 1st Battalion reported to the regimental S-2 that "Companies A and C received harassing fire from enemy last night consisting of grenades, small arms, and knee mortars."

While the 1st Battalion was advancing toward Ridge 300, the 3d Battalion was pushing eastward along the rugged southern shore of Saipan. Little infantry opposition was encountered by the assault companies, although they did receive scattered artillery fire at different times during the day. The principal problem they faced was the presence of many civilians in caves along the coast. Using loudspeakers mounted on tanks, about 335 civilians were persuaded to surrender. The majority, however, persisted in firing at the Americans from caves and other defensive positions.

The caves had to be assaulted and the occupants destroyed; in some cases, they were sealed in the caves by using explosives. By nightfall, the 3d Battalion had reached a point only 100 yards short of tying in with the attack coming down the Nafutan Peninsula. The division, therefore, presented a solid front that hemmed the Japanese defenders into an ever tightening pocket.

On June 20, 1944, the 106th Infantry Regiment, which had remained afloat in Joint Expeditionary Troop Reserve, landed on Saipan's Yellow Beaches and was assigned as NTLF corps reserve. The 1st Battalion was placed in the rear of the 2d Division and the remainder behind the 4th Division. As soon as the 106th was ashore, the 2d Battalion, 105th, commanded by Lt. Col. Leslie M. Jensen, was released from NTLF reserve and moved to an area near Aslito Airfield in division reserve. One company of the 2d Battalion, 105th, was dispatched to Magicienne Bay to bolster the outposts there. Colonel Kelley of the 165th Infantry requested that the 2d Battalion be attached to the 165th for the attack against the Nafutan ridges the next day and that the 2d Battalion, 165th Infantry, be relieved of any assignments in the Nafutan area. This request was granted by division at 0600 on June 21, and the 2d Battalion, 105th, was ordered to relieve the 2d Battalion, 165th, by 0730 that day.

The decision to land the 106th Infantry was not made without a great deal of thought and consideration. On the evening of June 18, Lt. Gen. Holland M. Smith formally recommended to Adm. Kelly

Turner that the 106th be landed "in order to maintain the continuity of the offensive." On June 19, Turner requested that Smith reconsider the matter, because landing the 106th on Saipan would postpone the Guam attack. Shortly after noon on June 19, Lieutenant General Smith sent another message to Admiral Turner stating that there was an urgent need for the 106th Infantry ashore and renewed his recommendation that it be landed. This time Turner concurred, stipulating, however, that the 106th land as little equipment and material as possible so that it could be re-embarked on short notice.

Divisional plans for June 21 called for a continuance of the attack to the south on Nafutan Ridge with four battalions abreast. Under an order issued at 0615 on June 21, the attack was to jump off at 0930 after a thirty-minute artillery preparation. Upon reaching the first phase line, the 3d Battalion, 165th Infantry, was to be pinched out and replaced by the 105th Infantry. Command of the attack southward was to be assumed by Colonel Bishop. His forces were aligned as follows: on the right Companies I and L of the 3d Battalion; in the center Companies A and C of the 1st Battalion; and on the extreme left Companies F and G of the newly arrived 2d Battalion.

At 0930 the 1st Battalion jumped off, initially encountering little or no opposition. Company A's attack was delayed for approximately two hours while cane fields to its front were burned to remove the possibility of enemy infiltration. At approximately 1255, Company A was hit by a heavy mortar concentration coupled with sweeping small-arms and automatic-weapons fire. Three men were wounded almost at once. Caught out in the open field with no cover, Captain Ackerman ordered his men back into the foxholes they had occupied the night before and radioed battalion headquarters for tank support.

On the right of the 1st Battalion line, Company C, commanded by 1st Lt. Bernard A. Tougaw, had escaped the Japanese mortar barrage, but now faced a Japanese counterattack. Just as the counterattack hit, O'Brien arrived with three tanks that quickly broke up the Japanese attack. He then moved the tanks to the left to A Company. Shortly before 1500, O'Brien organized a coordinated attack along the whole front of the 1st Battalion supported by the three tanks. After a brief artillery preparation, the battalion jumped off. First Lieutenant Hammond, from his vantage point in the OP, described the attack, "I witnessed an old-time mass attack by C Company. Colonel O'Brien was there. They fired like hell advancing in mass."

The tanks, which were buttoned up, moved out ahead of the line of infantrymen spraying the area ahead with machine-gun fire. A few yards from the line of departure, the tanks veered to the left and within a few minutes had completely reversed course and headed back toward the advancing infantrymen of Companies A and C of the 1st Battalion, firing as they came. The two rifle companies were completely pinned down and there were some casualties. When First Lieutenant Hammond came up a little later, he recalled, "I saw a dead corporal of A Company—later I learn killed by our own tanks."

Lieutenant Colonel O'Brien, who was up on the line with the assault troops at the time, tried frantically to reach the tankers by radio, but could not get through. With complete disregard for his own safety, he ran out in the midst of deadly fire and crawled up on the turret of the lead tank. He banged on the turret with the butt of his pistol until he got the driver's attention and told him to stop firing. The tank then contacted the other two tanks by radio and the firing stopped. O'Brien turned the vehicles around and sat atop the lead tank's turret and ordered the advance to proceed. The whole battalion jumped off in a rapid push that carried it across the open ground. He remained on top of the tank throughout the whole movement, alternately firing his pistol, giving directions to the men inside with his pistol butt, and shouting encouragement to the infantrymen, who were advancing at a dogtrot behind the tanks and keeping up a steady fire against the enemy positions to the front. When the advance was halted to reestablish contact with the 3d Battalion, 165th, on the left, O'Brien got down from the tank, holstered his .45, walked back to a man who had been mortally wounded, picked him up, and carried him back out of range of the enemy's fire. He was posthumously awarded the Medal of Honor for his heroic actions.

Recognizing that as a result of the rapid advance behind the tanks, there was a gap of approximately 500 yards between A Company and L Company of the 3d Battalion, 165th, O'Brien ordered a reserve platoon from B Company to establish contact with L Company, out of sight above the ridge. The platoon reported that the Japanese had set up a machine-gun position at the crest of the ridge between the two battalions and that the only way to establish contact was to knock it out. O'Brien ordered that mortar fire be placed on the position and then assaulted. The platoon attacked at 1615, but was immediately pinned down by enemy fire that killed two men and wounded three others. When O'Brien learned that mortar fire from his battalion was hitting L Company, he called off the assault on the west side of the ridge. The two battalions, therefore, dug in for the night even though physical contact had not been established.

On the extreme left of the division line, the heretofore untested 2d Battalion was inserted into the line. Its commander, Lt. Col. Leslie Jensen, placed Company G, commanded by Capt. Frank H. Olander on the right of the line facing the nose of Mount Nafutan. Company F, under Capt. Earl L. White, was placed on the left of the line close to the ocean shore with orders to proceed through the overgrown coral area and clean it out and then scale Mount Nafutan at its south end. Company E, under the command of Capt. Clinton E. Smith, was left facing Magicienne Bay as battalion reserve, ready to move against Nafutan Point.

The terrain to the immediate front of the 2d Battalion was extremely difficult. The most prominent feature was the nose of Mount Nafutan, a sheer cliff splitting the battalion front like the bow of a ship. The cliff was not more than thirty feet high, but the approach to it was up a steep slope through the stubble of a cane field that offered no cover. The brunt of the fighting by the battalion on June 21 was borne by Company G. Its mission was to neutralize the nose of Mount Nafutan and advance along the right, seizing all the ground between Mount Nafutan and Ridge 300. At 0800, 1st Lt. Donald G. Spiering, executive officer of G Company, received a message, "Be ready to attack at 1000." The company moved out at 0930 in a skirmish line with two platoons abreast. Before it had gone twenty-five yards, it was immediately met with terrific small-arms, machine-gun, and mortar fire. Two men were killed and three wounded in this first attempt. A second attempt moments later left three more men dead and four more wounded. Finally, after ten minutes of rifle and mortar fire, the whole line reached cover in a small wooded area, overgrown with shrubs.

Private Fritz Neubauer of the 2d Battalion I & R Platoon was with Captain Olander, First Lieutenant O'Donnell, and Pvt. Steve Behil in that attack, "when all hell broke loose." As Private Neubauer recalled, it was "all small-arms fire. I saw Sergeant Mikerowski and two others go down, all grazing fire, and they were shelling the cliff. Sergeant Pete Sanzen of Amsterdam, New York, barely made it back while putting out the front line panel, but later got it." Private Neubauer made it back to the company CP and reported what had happened. While attempting to reach the artillery forward observer on the other side of a burned-out cane field, Private Neubauer was severely wounded in the elbow by a Japanese sniper and almost lost his arm.

The 1st Platoon of G Company, under the command of 1st Lt. Don F. Lee Jr., was on the left of the line about seventy-five yards from the base of the cliff. From there, he could see an enemy machine gun on the top of the nose. It commanded all of the open ground behind his platoon, so he and SSgt. Joseph Ochal's squad scaled the cliff in an attempt to knock it out. The rest of the 1st Platoon under TSgt. John F. Polikowski gave covering fire from under the cliff. Ochal and his men reached the top of the nose without any trouble, killing one Japanese soldier as they came across the crest of the cliff. However, the men found themselves blocked by dense undergrowth and virtually impassable terrain formations. After nearly thirty minutes, First Lieutenant Lee ordered the men to return to the low ground below the base of the cliffs.

The 2d Platoon of G Company, under 2d Lt. Arthur G. Hansen from Council Bluffs, Iowa, farther to the right of the base of Mount Nafutan, did not fare much better than the 1st Platoon. When one of his squads became separated by a strip of open ground, he crawled to the edge of the clearing and shouted to the squad leader to bring the men across. Three men were killed and one wounded in the attempt. Two men decided not to attempt it. When Hansen discovered that the squad had not reported to him, he ordered his platoon sergeant, TSgt. Max J. Tracz, to see what had happened.

Tracz crawled to the clearing and called across. When he did not receive an answer, he walked into the clearing and was immediately wounded four times by enemy fire. Hansen and his runner, Pfc. Harry R. Pritchard, spotted another wounded man on the other side of the clearing. With the aid of two men remaining from the missing squad, the four men began to carry him to safety. At that moment, a Japanese machine gun opened up, cutting the wounded man in two, and wounding Pritchard and another man. All four men, however, reached safety as did Tracz, who managed to crawl out of the clearing. Hansen tried to reach Captain Olander by radio to inform him of his platoon's situation, but was unsuccessful. He then decided to stay where he was until he received further orders.

Captain Olander, in the meantime, had taken personal command of the 3d Platoon of Company G and was trying to move forward to the base of the cliff to relieve the 1st Platoon. After a series of efforts, he also was pinned down by enemy fire after suffering three men killed and three wounded. The 3d Platoon had reached the base of the cliff but were now to the left of the 1st Platoon instead of the right. Olander called the battalion and asked Jensen for help, particularly for the wounded men. There were now about fifteen men from G Company lying about who desperately needed medical care; some would later die from their wounds. Around 1200 a jeep carrying medical supplies arrived but was hit by enemy fire and the aid man wounded. For the time being, there would be no medical help for the wounded men of G Company.

Desperate to obtain help and unable to communicate by radio, Olander made his way to the 2d Battalion CP to request more aid, even though it meant running the full length of an open field through intense enemy fire. He explained the situation to Jensen and actually took him out to reconnoiter the enemy positions. After observing the situation, Jensen immediately ordered two self-propelled mounted guns (SPMs) from the 165th Infantry's Cannon Company to come forward. The SPMs were loaded up with medical supplies, water, rations, and ammunition and sent forward to find the three platoons of G Company. Meanwhile, the 1st Platoon of G Company under First Lieutenant Lee and the 2d Platoon under Second Lieutenant Hansen had jointly dug in to establish a perimeter defense at the base of the cliff. Using the radios on the SPM, the two lieutenants contacted Olander, who ordered them to dig in for the night where they were, just short of the high ground under assault. Although historian Edmund G. Love states that "both platoon leaders agreed," Hansen disagrees, stating that he returned to the area after evacuating some of the wounded from his platoon and asked Olander, "Who in hell gave orders to dig in here? Can't you hear them [the enemy] setting [*sic*] up on top of the bluff? Come daylight it will be like shooting fish in a barrel." Olander responded, "Battalion said not to give any ground."

Second Lieutenant Hansen could see that Olander had some misgivings about the company's position. Concerned about his wounded men, during the night, Olander gave Second Lieutenant Hansen the radio and went back to the battalion commander to see what he thought about the situation. The next morning after daylight, he called Hansen and told him to start withdrawing the men one at a time. According to Hansen, "The Japs opened up with machine-gun fire when the first few men crawled out of their foxholes. One of them was riddled by machine-gun fire and fell draped over a stack of ration boxes still alive and calling for help. Another was badly wounded and was calling to 1st Sgt. Jack Falkenstein to shoot him and put him out of his agony." Hansen told the rest of the men to stay where they were under cover because anyone who moved would be dead.

Although the division artillery was initially reluctant to fire on the nose of the ridge or anywhere near G Company's advanced position, on June 21, Battery B, 104th Field Artillery Battalion, was moved forward at 1535 to fire directly on the nose of Mount Nafutan. Under cover of this fire, Company G was withdrawn to the positions in the rear that it had occupied earlier that morning. Olander used the SPMs that had arrived earlier to evacuate G Company's wounded to the rear.

On the extreme left of the 2d Battalion line, Company F, under Capt. Earl White, had achieved some success reaching Mount Nafutan from the rear by working through the dense jungle near the coral fringe along the shore. By 1100, his 2d Platoon had worked its way up the cliff and established a small toehold near the top. There it was greeted by a burst of enemy machine-gun fire that killed one man and wounded two others. By 1700, the 2d Platoon found the top of the ridge unoccupied. White ordered the 2d Platoon to return to its starting point. When warned that friendly artillery fire was about to be placed on the nose of Mount Nafutan, he ordered F Company to withdraw to the point of departure and dig in alongside of G Company. The 2d Battalion, therefore, finished the day on June 21, 1944, essentially where it had started that morning.

On the extreme right, on June 21, the 3d Battalion was still pushing its way eastward along the southern coast of Saipan, when it met serious enemy opposition for the first time. Shortly before noon, the right platoon of Company I, operating along the seashore, crossed the face of a cave in the ridge. A Japanese machine gun opened up, placing enfilade fire along the platoon line and stopping the advance at once. As requested by the company commander, Capt. Ashley W. Brown, the division dispatched a platoon of tanks to assist. In the meantime, Lieutenant Colonel Bradt, commander of the 3d Battalion, sent forward a self-propelled mount from Cannon Company. The vehicle fired throughout the area but failed to get close enough to the cave to deliver direct fire into the mouth. Shortly after 1500, the tanks arrived and immediately knocked out the position with their machine guns and 37mm guns. At about 1700, the 3d Battalion line pushed forward to a point about 600 yards from the morning line of departure and dug in for the night.

Thus, by the close of fighting on June 21, 1944, the 27th Division units had made insignificant progress on either flank of the attack down Nafutan Point. The 2d and 3d Battalions of the 105th on the left and right, respectively, were basically where they had started that morning. In the center, the 1st Battalion of the 105th had made some progress, but the advance was still 500–1,000 yards away from the intermediate objective line. The nose of Mount Nafutan, which had been reached by elements of Companies F and G of the 2d Battalion, 105th, had been relinquished, and the mountain itself still had to be scaled before the southeastern tip of the island could be secured. Sergeant Julius Kovalaski, Headquarters Company, 105th, recalled that the action of June 21 was "severely disappointing. Only the 1st Battalion 105th showed any gains that day. The 2d battalion of the 105th, after a bitter experience, was right back where we started from in the morning."

By June 21, the 2d and 4th Marine Divisions, after some bitter fighting at Hill 500, completed their pivoting movements to the north and Lt. Gen. Holland M. Smith decided to launch a general attack on the morning of June 22 toward the main line of Japanese resistance in the area of Mount Tapotchau. In drawing up his plans for this major effort, he decided he would need the bulk of the 27th Division as NTLF reserve. Accordingly, he proposed to reduce the number of 27th Division troops committed to the Nafutan Point operation and to move most of the division units to the reserve area behind the marine front lines to the north. In large part, Smith's plan was based on the optimistic figure presented by the NTLF G-2 report, which claimed that, as of June 21, only 300 Japanese were left in the Southern Sector of Nafutan Point. This estimate proved to be woefully low. At the conclusion of the Nafutan campaign, it was determined that there were almost 1,500 enemy troops on the Nafutan Peninsula at that time.

At approximately 1215 on June 21, while the 27th Division was heavily engaged in the attack on Nafutan Point, NTLF issued Operations Order 9-44 directing the division, less one battalion and one light tank platoon, to assemble northwest of Aslito Airfield in NTLF reserve. Paragraph 3(e) of this order stated: "One Infantry battalion, 27th Infantry Division (to be designated) will operate in the garrison area . . . (Nafutan Point). It will mop up remaining enemy detachments. . . ." The order was delivered to the 27th Division CP on June 21 at 1215. Under the order, control of the 27th Division Artillery was to pass to the XXIV Corps Artillery.

In view of the enemy's stubborn opposition on June 21, and the breadth of the front to be covered on the Nafutan Peninsula (more than 2,500 yards), Maj. Gen. Ralph C. Smith believed that one rifle battalion could not handle the frontage in the Nafutan area, which was then covered by four rifle battalions. Accordingly, on June 21 at

1430, Col. Albert K. Stebbins, the 27th Division Chief of Staff, contacted Col. R. C. Hogaboom, USMC, the G-3 of the NTLF, and advised that at least two battalions were needed to push the enemy back at Nafutan the next day. At 1700, after consideration of NTLF Operations Order 9-44, Maj. Gen. Ralph Smith telephoned Lt. Gen. Holland M. Smith and recommended that the entire 105th Infantry Regiment be assigned the task of cleaning up the Japanese on Nafutan Point. He stated that with the entire regiment at his disposal, the job could be completed in a couple of days. Lieutenant General Holland M. Smith granted this request provided that Colonel Bishop use only two of his battalions for the attack; the third battalion was to be held in reserve near the Aslito Airfield, ready for immediate use elsewhere if needed. This modification of Operations Order 9-44 was delivered via mailbrief to 27th Division Headquarters on June 22 at 0830.

At 2000 on June 21, based on his earlier telephone conversation with Lt. Gen. Holland M. Smith, but before he had received the mail brief containing the modification of Operations Order 9-44, Maj. Gen. Ralph Smith issued 27th Division Field Order No. 45A, which provided, in pertinent part, for the following: (1) RCT 105 will hold present front line facing Nafutan Point with two battalions on the line and one in regimental reserve; (2) elements of RCT 165, then on the present front line, will be relieved by RCT 105 by 0630 the next morning; (3) the reserve battalion will not be committed to action without authority of the division commander; and (4) reorganization of the present front lines facing Nafutan Point was to be effected not later than 1100 on June 22, and offensive operations against the enemy were to be continued.

On June 22, the two marine divisions continued their attack north to the 0-5 line, which included the village of Laulau, at the southwestern base of Kagman Peninsula on the right, Mount Tapotchau in the center, and the western coast approximately 1,000 yards south of Garapan. The 27th Division (in NTLF reserve) was ordered to reconnoiter possible routes to the zones of the two marine divisions for possible commitment. The 105th Infantry (under NTLF control) was ordered to continue its assigned mission of clearing Nafutan Point of Japanese defenders.

The 105th Infantry spent much of the day on June 22 reorganizing its front lines. On the right, the 3d Battalion was ordered to hold its line and spread out to the left to relieve the 1st Battalion, which had been assigned to corps reserve. The 3d Battalion, although it had been in combat at Makin, had not seen much combat on Saipan since it went on the line on June 18. For four days, it had struggled through the most difficult terrain on Saipan to reach Nafutan Point. A combination of illness, fatigue, and rugged terrain had reduced its effective strength to about one-third its normal complement of sixty-six officers and 1,294 enlisted men. Nevertheless, under the leadership of Lieutenant Colonel Bradt, it accomplished its mission of relieving the 1st Battalion on the morning of June 22.

On the left flank, the 2d Battalion was assigned to hold the line facing Mount Nafutan and then to move to the right to relieve the 3d Battalion, 165th Infantry, a difficult task. The night before Companies F and G of the 2d Battalion had tried to dig in for the night on the open ground facing the nose of Mount Nafutan. The coral-studded ground made digging foxholes impossible; so the troops resorted to building rock shelters for protection from enemy fire. They were out on the open ground "like pins in a bowling alley." During the night, it became evident that the Japanese were reinforcing their positions on the nose of Mount Nafutan, and all night long there was much jabbering, grunting, and digging, plainly discernible to the men in foxholes below Mount Nafutan.

When the sounds of enemy activity grew louder an hour before dawn, Captain Olander of Company G tried to reach Lieutenant Colonel Jensen for permission to pull back. When he found his radio out of order, he ran back to the battalion CP to Lieutenant Colonel Jensen who then gave permission to withdraw. Runners were sent to G Company, with orders to pull back. At daybreak on June 22, Companies F and G lost no time in moving back. F Company lost only one man in the withdrawal, but G Company was hit harder. Within a matter of minutes, Company G suffered six men killed or mortally wounded and twenty-one other casualties. The rest of the men were pinned down by enemy fire all over the area—behind rocks, in shallow holes, and in furrows between rows of cane stubble. First Lieutenant O'Donnell, G Company, executive officer, recalled that incident later in a letter to his parents: "The 'buggers' had, off and on, been pestering me all day. One time I had to make a dive behind a boulder, the only one around close by, while a sniper chipped bits of rock off the top of it. Then, to complicate matters, a knee mortar opened up too; but, their shots were falling at least twenty yards away, and never came any closer. One of the boys finally spotted the sniper near us, and, of all places, he was up a tree! However, not for long." Captain Olander brought up three self-propelled guns and their concentrated fire dispersed the enemy and allowed the wounded from G Company to be evacuated. E Company commanded by Captain Smith was brought up from reserve to replace G Company and to protect against any enemy breakthrough. Because his company was seriously understrength, Olander had to place his men some twenty yards apart in the line protecting his perimeter.

Around 1515 on June 22, Army Maj. Gen. Ralph C. Smith visited NTLF headquarters and talked with marine Lt. Gen. Holland M. Smith. The latter expressed concern about the slowness of the advance by the 105th Infantry on Nafutan Point. Ralph Smith pointed out: ". . . difficult terrain and Jap positions in caves and said rapid advance was impracticable if undue losses were to be avoided and if Japs were to be really cleaned out." He thought that Nafutan Point could be cleaned up "in a couple of days." He then conferred with Brig. Gen. Graves B. Erskine, USMC, the corps chief of staff, who informed him that the 27th Division was committed to the line in the north the next day (June 23), and that only one battalion from the 27th Division was to be left to clean up Nafutan Point. Though Ralph Smith vigorously protested, his pleas were ignored by the marine high command.

On June 22, the 1st Battalion was relieved by the 3d Battalion and began moving into an area near Magicienne Bay to become part of NTLF reserve. When O'Brien learned from a division ordnance officer, Lt. Col. Armand C. Feichtmeier, that a sizable Japanese ammunition dump in the coral rocks of the beach jungle was going to be blown up, he frantically tried to reach the 105th Regimental CP by radio to warn them of the impending explosion. Finally, at 1420 he got through with this message, "Large amount of bombs and ammunition in caves in the vicinity of 132 QMRV. . . . A squad from Division now destroying caves."

The Japanese ammunition dump was blown up about 1520 on the afternoon of June 22. It was a tremendous explosion that could be heard and felt for miles around. Corporal Charles "Eddie" Beaudoin, 105th Medical Attachment, said, "It sounded like the whole island blew up." Just about that time, the 2d Battalion of the 105th Infantry was preparing to attack the Nafutan ridges. Because it had not been possible to communicate with the 2d Battalion CP due to a lack of equipment, the explosion of the ammunition dump caught the 2d Battalion completely by surprise. Its CP was almost completely destroyed, vehicles were damaged, what radios there were did not function, and a number of personnel were injured by fragments and flying rocks. Several members of the ship's party for the badly depleted G Company who had just reported to the 2d Battalion CP were wounded and out of action before they were actually assigned.

To make matters worse, Capt. Earl White of Company F had called on a navy destroyer, lying offshore in Magicienne Bay, to deliver fire on the seaward side of the Nafutan nose. By mistake, the naval gunfire struck the 2d Battalion CP, killing eight men and wounding thirty-two, including some key communications personnel. One of those wounded was Lt. George P. Schongar of Troy, New York, who served with Headquarters Detachment.

Though he disagreed with Holland M. Smith's plan to reduce the force on Nafutan to one battalion, Ralph Smith returned to 27th Division Headquarters, and at 2130 issued Field Order No. 46, which stated: "2d Battalion, 105th Infantry (1 platoon light tanks attached) continue operations to mop up remaining enemy detachments in the Nafutan Point area. On completion of this mission revert to Corps control as Corps reserve at TA 130 D." Just one-half hour later, or at 2200, NTLF issued Operations Order 10-44, which was received by the 27th Division Headquarters at 2330, two hours after the 27th Division FO 46 had been sent to all subordinate commands. Operations Order 10-44 referred to Nafutan as follows: "2d Bn. 105th Inf (with one platoon light tanks attchd) continue opns at daylight to mop up remaining detachments in Nafutan Point area. . . ." The "at daylight" reference was added after 27th Division Order No. 46 had been issued. Nevertheless, the failure to include the daylight attack order in the 27th Division Order of 2130 was later cited by marine General Smith as disobedience of orders by army Maj. Gen. Ralph C. Smith. This omission, plus marine General Smith's contention that the 2d Battalion was no longer under the tactical control of the 27th Division when Field Order No. 46 was issued, were the major reasons cited in support of the decision to relieve army Major General Smith from command of the 27th Division on June 24.

11 Second Battalion, 105th: Alone on Nafutan

From June 22 until July 3, the 2d Battalion, already understrength due to previous combat, had the unfortunate task of being assigned to secure the Nafutan Peninsula; an almost impossible assignment. One rifle battalion, composed of approximately 650 officers and men, with no supporting artillery, had the job of covering a front of almost 3,000 yards in rugged terrain against a force estimated to be between 300 and 1,200 Japanese soldiers, many of whom so well concealed that American front line soldiers seldom saw a live enemy soldier. To alleviate somewhat the lack of artillery support, Colonel Bishop attached to the 2d Battalion one platoon from the 105th's Cannon Company armed with self-propelled howitzers. Also, the 2d Platoon of the 105th's Antitank Company was moved up to join the 2d Battalion at mid-afternoon on June 22, but was withdrawn to the 105th's Regimental Headquarters the next day. Sergeant W. Taylor Hudson described that movement as follows: "Getting our supplies, we proceeded to the position of the 2d Battalion, arriving just before dark. They had left us a space in their defense perimeter and we were told to dig in. This was an old field with a thin (very thin) layer of dirt over some very tough coral rock. We were forced to pile up loose rock to simulate holes, since it was impossible to dig. A long night followed, much noise and many flares, but the Japanese did not hit our positions. Next morning we had hardly finished our breakfast of C rations before we were ordered back to Regimental HQ."

The difficult terrain on the Nafutan Peninsula was described as follows:

The ground there was so rocky that digging holes was impossible, so we picked up hunks of coral to protect us. We also learned to memorize the location of every rock and tree stump near us, because we kept sending up flares all night to prevent Jap infiltrators. The terrain was loaded with huge boulders, from five-feet to six-feet high and wide and horribly dense brush; and the Japs used these to set up their strong points. The only way to knock them out was to call our Cannon Company, and with their assistance we were able to knock out these positions.

The morning of June 23 was spent readjusting the lines so they stretched clear across the peninsula. All three rifle companies were allotted a portion of the frontage. A platoon leader in F Company told the 27th Division historian that by standing on a high hill and looking through his field glasses, he was able to see the next platoon in his company working through the brush 600 yards away. Captain Olander of G Company placed every man in his company on the line, including radio operators, and found that he could cover only half his frontage with a twenty-yard gap between men. He made riflemen out of his weapons platoon, leaving only skeleton crews to man the weapons. The battalion was clearly stretched thin on Nafutan.

By 1230 on June 23, Companies E and G were in position and ready to attack the Nafutan ridges with E on the right and G in the center. F Company on the left under Capt. Earl White was assigned to flank Mount Nafutan from the south or rear by moving through the brush along Magicienne Bay. F Company's 2d Platoon, commanded by 1st Lt. John E. Titterington of Green Island, New York, reached the top of Mount Nafutan at approximately 1700 by skirting it to the left through the brush just inland of the east coast and coming up to the top from the rear. The men encountered no Japanese along the way. The 3d Platoon under Lt. Cecil A. Greenwell, twenty-eight, from Louisville, Kentucky, took up positions along the inner slopes east of Ridge 300 to protect the right flank of the attacking force, which included three light tanks. His mission was to knock out any enemy position that could bring fire to bear on the valley.

The 1st Platoon under Lt. Charles C. Magyar, twenty-six, from Cleveland, Ohio, was advancing up the valley between Ridge 300 and Mount Nafutan and ran into heavy fire from the ridge. The 1st Platoon had to halt until Greenwell's platoon came up to eliminate the Japanese opposition. When Magyar learned that Greenwell's men could not reach the enemy position, he sent out a patrol with a self-propelled gun to attack from below. A separate patrol from the 1st Platoon also came under enemy machine-gun fire from a small group of farm buildings, wounding TSgt. Raymond Levesque from Schenectady, New York, Magyar's platoon sergeant, and one other man. Before sending out his patrols, Magyar said to his men: "You fellows know what we're up against. We got kicked off that ridge once, but this time we're going to hold it. There are lots of foxholes up there—make sure you use them. We must advance in squad rushes, a couple of men at a time, from foxhole to foxhole. We've got to get up there today. We've got to walk in and hold that ground. Brownie," he said, turning to the platoon medical aid man, Cpl. James A. Brown, twenty-five, of Troy, New York, "you'd better take a lot of stuff with you—you know what I mean. We've got litter bearers behind us. I don't want to bring this up at all, but hell, all of you know what I mean. Any questions? Well, let's get ready. We kick off in five minutes."

Private First Class Seymour Krawetz, who served in Greenwell's 3d Platoon, recalled the action that day on Ridge 300: "Our first action was on Nafutan Ridge, which was very rough terrain. Heavy dense brush and huge boulders made for tough strong points that were hard to breach. The rocks and brush made it impossible to get into except through narrow openings that were easily covered by automatic weapons. At one such position, Lieutenant Greenwell ordered up an SPM and stood in front of it directing fire at the enemy. A Japanese machine gun opened up and wounded the machine gunner in the SPM through a gun port in the armament. Incredibly, Lieutenant Greenwell was left without a scratch." Greenwell's heroics were numerous. Krawetz recalled another time when his platoon was attacked by a Japanese unit that killed and wounded injured men in their foxholes. Greenwell stood on the top of a boulder and calmly shot it out with the Japanese soldiers. Once again, he did not suffer a scratch. Krawetz said: "My platoon commander, Lt. Cecil Greenwell, was the bravest man I ever saw. When a fire fight started we would all make as small a target out of ourselves as we could. He would stand up erect and out in the open, very sure and calm and seemingly in contempt of the enemy. What a guy!"

On June 23, as G Company under Captain Olander from Amsterdam, New York, moved up the slope of Mount Nafutan, one of its advance patrols under SSgt. Joseph Ochal stumbled on a Japanese machine-gun position, surprising its crew and killing all five of its members within a few moments. The noise of the skirmish, however, alerted the whole Japanese position. Soon the northern slope of Ridge 300 was blanketed by heavy mortar and machine-gun fire. Within fifteen minutes, four heavy machine-gun positions had been located and Captain Olander ordered up his last mortar in an effort to knock them out. Japanese units as large as platoons launched three separate counterattacks against G Company's position, but all three were beaten off. First Lieutenant George O'Donnell, Company G's executive officer, tried to bring three tanks up to bring fire to bear on the enemy positions, but the tanks could not negotiate the rough and rocky coral terrain. When the enemy counterattacks continued in force, Olander withdrew his men to already prepared positions at the north base of the slope and dug in for the night. Greenwell's platoon dug in alongside G Company.

Captain Clinton E. Smith's E Company on the right flank had a frontage of about 1,000 yards to cover facing Nafutan Point. Its 1st Platoon was ordered to move down the right flank through the coral jungle protecting the company's flank as it went forward. The 3d Platoon, under TSgt. Oscar L. Knight from Tampa, Florida, supported G Company against the Japanese counterattacks starting at about 1500. Knight's platoon had to hang on to the steep hillside and fight throughout the afternoon. When G Company withdrew for the night, Knight's platoon returned to the E Company position and dug in for the night.

The 2d Battalion had accomplished little on the first day at Nafutan. Except for one platoon atop Mount Nafutan, because of stubborn enemy resistance, the battalion had withdrawn to approximately the same positions it occupied at the beginning of the day's advance. The terrain consisted of steep ridges, deep gulches with cliffs, ground broken with coral pinnacles, and thick jungle-type underbrush that impeded progress and made observation impossible. The only tangible result was the development of a rather well-defined position on Ridge 300. Although heavy firing had been encountered in some areas, most of the men had yet to see a live Japanese soldier.

At daybreak on June 23, the 1st Battalion, which reported thirty-six officers and 840 enlisted men present or accounted for that morning, as part of 27th Division reserve, moved north to its assembly area east of Mount Tapotchau toward the center of the island. First Lieutenant "Luke" Hammond recalled that Lieutenant Colonel O'Brien was on the scene directing the rifle companies to their locations. He sent Hammond forward to tell C Company to "keep moving and stop holding up the movement." The battalion CP was set up near a marine CP, and B Company was located to the east of the 1st Battalion CP. First Sergeant Charles J. Stephani recalled that at 0800 on June 23, the company moved out from a position near Magicienne Bay and marched three and one-half miles over hard, rugged terrain to relieve a marine outfit on the other side of the bay. At 1500 the company was hit with a Japanese counterattack led by several tanks. By 2000, the tanks had all been knocked out, and B Company dug in for the night. The 3d Battalion with sixty-seven officers and 1,199 enlisted men also moved north to the 27th Division assembly area, arriving there on June 23 in the late afternoon. Two rifle companies were assigned to anti-sniper patrol for the night of June 23, as well as protection of the division artillery headquarters.

The division's progress on June 23 was disappointing to Lt. Gen. Holland M. Smith. The NTLF operations order for June 23 set 1000 as the attack hour, yet the 106th and 165th Infantry Regiments, which were to attack up the center of the island, did not jump off until 1055. Moreover, the gains achieved for the day were negligible as compared to the 2d and 4th Marine Divisions moving on the flanks against relatively light opposition. Following a mid-afternoon staff conference, Lt. Gen. Smith called in Maj. Gen. Sanderford Jarman, USA, Saipan garrison force commander, to discuss the situation, including the relief of Maj. Gen. Ralph Smith. Lieutenant General Holland M. Smith was also disappointed with the progress of the 2d Battalion, 105th Infantry, on June 23. This unit, which had been placed under NTLF control on June 22 without Major General Smith's knowledge of the division commander, failed to attack Nafutan Point at daylight on June 23 in compliance with an NTLF order issued at 2200 on June 22. It did not attack until 1330 on June 23. This unit, removed from the 27th Division to operate directly under NTLF control, was to attack Nafutan Point at daylight on June 23. The battalion did not commence its attack until 1330, and then only minor actions were conducted. In Lieutenant General Smith's view, the day's progress was negligible.

The night of June 23 was a relatively quiet one for the three rifle companies of the 2d Battalion. In the E Company sector on the extreme right flank, however, a lone soldier attacked its positions early in the morning with hand grenades. One grenade landed in a foxhole and SSgt. Max Yusselman from Schenectady, New York, was seriously wounded trying to get the grenade out of the foxhole. As soon as the sun came up that morning, the Japanese placed a heavy fusillade of fire on the company positions, wounding Pfc. George C. Gracyalana.

On June 24, the 2d Battalion was ordered by NTLF to continue operations at daylight to mop up the remaining enemy detachments on the peninsula. At 0800, after a period of readjusting its overextended lines and trying to establish contact with its various units, it moved out on the attack. On the extreme right flank, the 1st and 2d Platoons of Company E encountered little or no opposition, although the 1st Platoon did kill four enemy soldiers found hiding in the undergrowth. By nightfall, the two platoons had reached a point about 100 yards beyond that previously gained. Knight's 3d platoon, however, working along the slopes of Ridge 300, ran into considerable Japanese opposition. By 1100, the 3d Platoon had moved along the slopes of the ridge to a point where the steep bluffs gave way to a more gradual rise in the ground. They were about 400 yards ahead on the left of G Company, with whom they had reestablished contact. Coming upon a group of farm buildings on the plain, Knight ordered SSgt. Angelo D. Nicoletti, twenty-four, of Brooklyn, New

York, to take a patrol of fifteen men to investigate the buildings before the platoon ventured out into the open ground above them. He and the rest of the platoon stayed on the slopes to cover the patrol.

After killing one Japanese soldier with rifle fire, Nicoletti's patrol sprinted across the open ground at a dead run. As they reached the buildings, they came under heavy rifle and machine-gun fire from the hills behind them. Private First Class Clifford W. McCallum was seriously wounded, forcing Nicoletti to order his patrol to take cover under the buildings. By mid-afternoon, the fire had increased and Nicoletti was concerned that the Japanese were preparing an attack. Private First Class Herman L. Militante of Honolulu, Hawaii, volunteered to go back to the E Company CP and to bring up reinforcements and medical help for McCallum, whose condition was worsening. About forty-five minutes before dark, a relief party under 2d Lt. Claude M. Gregory, twenty-three, from Hobbs, New Mexico, of H Company, 2d Battalion, began to move up with litter bearers and ammunition. The patrol was pinned down by enemy fire, and Gregory was wounded. Staff Sergeant Nicoletti then decided to move back to the E Company CP as soon as it became dark.

Knight tried to help Nicoletti in his precarious position near the farm buildings. He brought up two light mortars and laid mortar fire on the suspected Japanese position, but failed to knock it out. He also sent a three-man patrol to G Company on the left for help, but none was forthcoming. So Knight decided to attack hoping to take pressure off Nicoletti. After moving ahead for about 100 yards under heavy fire, his men were pinned down. At approximately 1500, the Japanese counterattacked through the gap between E and G Companies. A group of from fifty to seventy-five Japanese rose out of the ground higher up the slope and came charging down the hill at the twenty men in Knight's detachment. For thirty minutes, Knight and his men fought off the attack, killing many of the enemy. At 1630, when it appeared that the Japanese might surround the position, Knight withdrew to the American lines. It was after dark before he reported to Captain Smith at the E Company CP.

Captain Smith had also been trying to rescue Nicoletti and his men from their predicament after Gregory's party ran into trouble. He sent another, larger patrol forward, equipped with a self-propelled gun. Heavy enemy mortar fire disabled the gun and the patrol was pinned down. Nicoletti, however, had already left the position at the farm buildings. As he retired, the Japanese attacked his former position with a force of approximately 100 soldiers. After burning the buildings, the Japanese broke up into smaller patrols and began to work toward Aslito Airfield. E Company rallied and blocked the enemy's escape from the plateau. In a pitched battle that lasted all night, the Japanese were forced to retire to Ridge 300, leaving behind twenty dead. E Company finished the day with no registered gain of ground against the enemy and occupied the perimeter of the night before.

On June 24, over in the center of the line, Olander's plan for attacking the Japanese positions atop Ridge 300 was to assemble tanks and SP guns and to take the enemy's strong points under direct fire. Moving the tanks forward was extremely difficult, because they had to pick their way through the rough terrain, guided by infantrymen from G Company. After they jumped off to the attack around 1200, they immediately ran into heavy enemy rifle and machine-gun fire and were pinned down before they advanced fifty yards. As soon as the first Japanese gun position was located by Staff Sergeant Ochal, Olander crawled back to one of the SP guns and went inside. He ordered the crew to open fire, and they immediately scored a direct hit on the enemy gun position, sending Japanese bodies flying in all directions. But when G Company tried to move up to take advantage of the situation, it was hit immediately by renewed fire. For the next two hours, a full-scale battle raged near the crest of Ridge 300. Company G tried to advance twice, each time pinned down by enemy fire from prepared positions. The Japanese attempted counterattacks, only to be stopped by the mass fire of SP guns and automatic weapons of G Company.

Throughout all of this, Olander remained inside one of the SP guns and methodically eliminated four enemy machine guns located in the rocks, killing all the crews. At about 1630, he ordered TSgt. John F. Polikowski to take a squad of eight men and rush the Japanese position in the rocks with fixed bayonets. Upon reaching the position without casualties, a Japanese grenade exploded wounding two men, including Staff Sergeant Ochal. Within a few minutes, the rest of G Company swarmed into the rocks and all Japanese opposition effectively ended. It was nearly dark on the night of June 24.

On the left, the 2d Platoon of F Company, which had spent the night on Mount Nafutan, was ordered to form a skirmish line and comb the nose of the ridge until the 1st Platoon of F Company could come up on its right. The 1st Platoon, however, ran into scattered Japanese fire and was stopped in its tracks. Meanwhile, on the right, Greenwell's 3d Platoon had worked its way through dense underbrush up the side of Ridge 300. About fifty yards beyond where G Company was held up, Greenwell's lead platoon scout, Pfc. Wesley F. Walker, discovered a path that led uphill toward the crest of the ridge. Moving up the path, he came upon a large clearing with rocks on one end of it marking the Japanese main defensive line. He began to crawl into the open space using tall grass for concealment, but a machine gun hidden in the rocks opened up killing him instantly. A shower of grenades into the open area followed and the balance of the platoon, which had just begun to move into the open area, moved back under the cover of some trees. No one had any idea where the machine gun was located or where the grenades had come from.

Staff Sergeant Edward Bleau, twenty-three, from Schenectady, New York, volunteered to crawl into the opening to locate the machine gun by drawing its fire. He had moved fifty yards into the open without being seen, when two Japanese soldiers emerged from behind the rocks and walked boldly down the path toward Walker's body. Bleau waited until they were almost beside him, then killed them both with two shots from his rifle. Another machine gun opened up on him, but he found a hole to roll into and escaped injury. He then went back to report to Greenwell.

In the meantime, an SP gun from the 105th's Cannon Company, commanded by 1st Lt. Raymond E. Agee from Farmington, Montana, came up. Around 1300, after maneuvering the gun into the open, Agee fired two rounds into the position, demolishing it and killing the crew. A second machine gun opened up, however, wounding one of Agee's men and forcing the gun to withdraw. Efforts to flank the second enemy machine gun were thwarted when a third enemy machine gun opened up wounding Agee in the shoulder. By the time Greenwell had reassembled his platoon for a further advance, it was 1530 on June 24. As no further progress seemed likely, Captain White of E Company ordered his men, including the platoon on top of Mount Nafutan, to withdraw to the G Company perimeter of the night before.

Greenwell went over to Company G on his right and borrowed two tanks to aid in his assault on the machine-gun positions. He ordered the lead tank to move out to the clearing, keeping well to the right and ordered his men to stay to the right of the tank to shield themselves from the enemy gunfire. But when the tank and the men got into the open area, another Japanese gun to the right of the tank opened up, wounding SSgt. Ralph Deshazo, the squad leader. At about 1600, Greenwell, after placing punishing tank and mortar fire on the Japanese positions, was preparing another assault. He was about to begin his attack when G Company on the right broke through the right flank of the enemy's line and began mopping up the Japanese machine-gun positions in front of his platoon. G Company's move was accomplished quickly. Within twenty yards after they had moved off, G Company completely surprised a force of fifty Japanese. For ten minutes, the fighting was almost hand-to-hand, the men loading and firing at point-blank range. The Japanese ran in all directions, some of them charging into G Company's ranks where they were bayoneted by the American soldiers. By the time the last enemy soldier was killed, it was completely dark and G Company was totally disorganized. Second Lieutenant Arthur Hansen from Council Bluffs, Iowa, though wounded in the shoulder by a grenade during the abortive counterattack, took temporary command of G Company and ordered his men to withdraw from the area to reorganize and establish a night perimeter.

Hansen later recalled it was not until nightfall, while they were digging in, that he became aware that he was wounded. He explained what had happened: "Earlier, following the over-running of the strong point on the edge of the cane field, a Jap came out of concealment and lobbed a potato-masher–type grenade at me and one of my men. We both hit the ground and the grenade exploded fairly close to me; the shrapnel must have grazed my back and side, because someone called attention to the fact that my jacket had been shredded and was bloody. I was taken back to the aid station where one of the attendants probed around and picked out a few small bits of shrapnel, bandaged it, and sent me back to my unit. After the war was over I found I still had a piece of shrapnel embedded in the flesh between my ribs, and it always shows up in my chest X-rays. I still have my plastic case of maps, which I carried inside my jacket, with smears of blood and a half-inch hole through several folds of the maps."

By nightfall on June 24, though some progress had been made, the 2d Battalion occupied positions in practically the same places in which it had dug in the previous night. With no night supporting fires, the men had to dig in securely, a most difficult task with coral rock lying only two or three inches below the surface. As a result, any gains achieved during the day had to be sacrificed in order to safeguard against enemy attacks. Although Mount Nafutan had all but been abandoned by the enemy, Lieutenant Colonel Jensen had no idea how many Japanese were left on the Nafutan Peninsula. The terrain was ideal for hiding and for camouflaging positions, and for the most part, the enemy stayed in their cleverly devised strong points and avoided detection.

Early on the morning of June 24, Lt. Gen. Holland M. Smith messaged Maj. Gen. Ralph Smith expressing extreme dissatisfaction with the failure of the division to advance sufficiently the previous day. At 0630, Ralph Smith and his assistant division commander, Brig. Gen. Ogden J. Ross, went up to the front lines and planned a strategy to outflank the Japanese stronghold in the center of the island. No one from marine headquarters was present when Ralph Smith went over the ground with his front-line companies. At 0909 he issued the following statement, "This division is advancing against a determined enemy that must be destroyed. You can destroy them. This must be done immediately. Upon capturing a position, never give it up, hold and send for reinforcements. I know I can depend on every member of the 27th to get into the fight with everything he has. Good hunting to every man."

Before Ralph Smith had a chance to present his plan to marine headquarters, Holland M. Smith had already visited Admiral Turner's flagship at 1130 to ask for authority to relieve Ralph Smith of command of the 27th. Holland M. Smith and Turner then went to Admiral Spruance's flagship. Based solely on the unsubstantiated allegations of Holland M. Smith, Spruance authorized Ralph Smith's relief. Orders relieving him were delivered to him by courier at 1500 while he was at his front-line post. He was told to turn his command over to Maj. Gen. Sanderford Jarman, USA, the Saipan garrison commander, and to report for transportation to Pearl Harbor. Upon reading the orders, he went over his plans with his regimental commanders and at 1700 returned to division headquarters where he met with Jarman, formerly of the coast artillery. He was a 1908 graduate of the U.S. Military Academy, fifty-nine years old, and had been selected to be the garrison commander once the island was secured. After briefing him, Ralph Smith was ordered to leave Saipan via seaplane at 0530 the next morning, accompanied by one aide, very few of his personal belongings, and no records.

At 1800 on June 24, Holland M. Smith, also dissatisfied with the progress of the 2d Battalion, 105th Infantry, on the Nafutan Peninsula relieved Lt. Col. Leslie M. Jensen from command and replaced him with Col. Jeffrey M. O'Connell, USA, acting commander of the Saipan garrison force in the absence of Major General Jarman. O'Connell's assigned mission was to eliminate Japanese resistance on the Nafutan Peninsula.

Early on the morning of June 25, O'Connell visited the 2d Battalion Headquarters and met with Jensen to go over the ground facing the American forces. His first move was to attach two batteries of the 751st AAA Gun Battalion armed with four 90mm guns to support the 2d Battalion on Nafutan. Four 40mm antiaircraft guns from another battalion were moved forward and placed just behind the 2d Battalion CP to deliver direct fire against caves and located enemy strong points on Nafutan. The guns from the 751st were to fire air-bursts into the tree tops, approximately twelve feet above ground level, from their fixed positions south of Aslito Airfield. Air bursts were particularly effective in the type of terrain facing the 2d Battalion. The 40mm guns were accurate in hitting cave entrances as small as four feet in diameter from an average range of 2,000 yards. Sergeant Edwin Luck of Company G recalled that these guns lowered their elevations and totally disrupted the Japanese positions on the peninsula.

By 1000 on June 25, the 2d Battalion resumed its attack on Ridge 300 with Greenwell's 3d Platoon leading the way. Shortly after jumping off and moving up about 150 yards, Greenwell discovered that during the night the Japanese had mined the approaches to the rock line and had moved new machine guns into position. Engineers were brought up to dispose of the mines and by 1230, with the aid of two tanks, the two enemy machine-gun nests had been destroyed. Greenwell sent SSgt. Thomas L. Wilson and his squad out to investigate. As soon as the men stepped into the clearing, two new machine guns opened up and the men were pinned down. At about 1500 his platoon, aided by two tanks, attacked the new Japanese line under a terrific concentration of canister and machine-gun fire, crushing all opposition. The men found six machine guns, seventeen mortars, two wrecked dual-purpose guns, grenades, and ammunition in large quantities. In and around the area lay the bodies of more than one hundred Japanese, dead only a few hours.

On the right flank, E Company under Capt. Clinton E. Smith had been moving up steadily. By 1030 on June 25, its 1st and 2d Platoons had swung left and established contact with G Company. At about 1130, after an advance of 150 yards, the 1st Platoon suddenly began receiving enfilade fire from its left flank and was pinned down. Smith sent out a three-man patrol under the command of Sgt. Eugene C. McCandless to investigate the situation. About twenty yards in front, McCandless killed two Japanese soldiers hiding in the undergrowth. Captain Smith then sent out a squad under TSgt. Karl H. Enstad to reinforce McCandless. Enstad's patrol was ambushed and Enstad and another man were wounded. Second Lieutenant Chester W. Sillman, the 3d Platoon leader, sent out another squad under the command of SSgt. Broadus L. Albertson to outflank the position. Albertson spotted an enemy in the rocks below. He fired his rifle, but missed, a costly mistake, because the Japanese soldier fired back, killing him instantly.

Sillman then called up some tanks, but they became entangled in the undergrowth and coral rocks and proved to be of no assistance.

Shortly after 1700, Captain Smith ordered his platoon to withdraw, and for the first time air bursts from the antiaircraft artillery batteries located near Aslito were called in. This fire effectively cleaned out the enemy rifle and machine-gun positions in the area. Because it was getting dark, Captain Smith ordered E Company to dig in for the night and tied in with G Company on the left. G Company had encountered little or no enemy opposition on June 25, and shortly after 1600 Captain Olander decided to pull his men back to the demolished enemy stronghold and dig in for the night.

By the end of the day on June 25, the Japanese defensive positions on Ridge 300 (which, a few days before, had defied the assault of three full-rifle battalions for one week) were significantly reduced. During the day, the 2d Battalion of the 105th knocked out and overran the main defensive line of Japanese positions guarding the approach to Nafutan Point. Ridge 300 had proven to be heavily fortified. Originally, it had contained more than twenty machine guns, fifty mortars, and ten 5-inch dual-purpose guns. With the fall of this position, the abandonment of Mount Nafutan, and the lack of any defenses on the western plain, the whole Nafutan garrison was weakened significantly. Captured enemy documents revealed that on June 25 the Japanese commander on Nafutan had lost all his remaining heavy and automatic weapons, ammunition was low, and food and water supplies were dwindling rapidly. Morale of the remaining Japanese troops was also sinking.

At 0845 on June 25, 1944, the 1st Battalion of the 105th was attached to the 165th Infantry Regiment and was in division reserve near Chacha Village on the east coast of the island. The arrival of the naval transports that day, which had been sent out to sea on June 17 with vital communications vehicles and supplies, rejuvenated the 105th Regiment's communications and combat capabilities. When Colonel Kelley learned that the left flank of the 4th Marine Division had moved past Chacha Village on the east side of the island and was advancing north with little or no enemy opposition, he ordered the 3d Battalion, 165th Infantry, to move up and fill the gap between the marines and the 1st Battalion, 106th Infantry. To plug the gap between the left flank of the 4th Division and the right flank of the

165th's 3d Battalion, Kelley brought up the 1st Battalion, 105th Infantry, under O'Brien from division reserve. It was already en route to the north by way of the Chacha Road and thus was in a good position to close the gap. First Sergeant Charles Stephani of Company B recalled that they moved out at about 1200, contacted the 105th regimental CP at about 1400, and moved through Chacha Village at about 1500. At approximately 1700, they established a night position north of the S road, about 1,400 yards north of Chacha Village.

Plans for the 2d Battalion on June 26 on the Nafutan Peninsula were the same as the previous day, except that the 1st and 2d Platoons of Company F were to leave the northern mouth of Nafutan Valley and take a position on the left flank of the battalion line. At 0645, to prepare for the day's attack, the 81mm mortars commenced softening up fires. From 0750 to 0800, the 90mm guns of Batteries A and B of the 751st joined in the artillery preparation, using air bursts to attack the enemy. Further support was provided by three destroyers whose guns were trained on the west side of the peninsula's cliff line. At 0800 elements of the 2d Battalion, spearheaded by the light tanks of Company D, 762d Tank Battalion, began an attack down Ridge 300 to the juncture of Mount Nafutan and Ridge 300. By 0900, Greenwell's platoon on the left flank encountered a large cave on the eastern slopes, where it received rifle and mortar fire, as well as a few grenades. Engineers came forward with TNT charges and threw them into the cave, destroying the position instantly. More than twenty dead Japanese soldiers were found inside with maps and papers outlining the whole defensive system of the peninsula. By 1700, F Company reached the southern end of Mount Nafutan, 1,000 yards from the tip of the peninsula.

On the right flank, E Company commanded by Captain Smith moved slowly forward, fighting the terrain and the underbrush. It encountered determined Japanese opposition in a series of craters along the mountainside, but by 1400 it had worked clear of them without suffering any casualties. At approximately 1500, a burst of machine-gun fire from directly ahead pinned the company down. Sergeant Walter E. Ghedozzi of the left platoon was first wounded in the neck, then mortally wounded, when he tried to run away to safety. Staff Sergeant Edward Orzechowski and Pfc. Kenneth E. Durst were both hit in the burst of machine-gun fire that killed Ghedozzi. Smith then brought forward his SP guns to knock out the enemy machine gun, but the guns could not be brought to bear. Finally, after G Company had come up on the left of E Company at about 1630, Captain Olander sent a squad from his extreme left flank to move around and attack the enemy machine gun from the rear. The plan worked. Private First Class Frederick Workman, a Browning automatic rifle (BAR) man from G Company, calmly stood a few yards away and killed the enemy crew.

The right platoon of E Company also ran into heavy Japanese opposition as it moved into a depression toward its front. A shot rang out and SSgt. William H. Allen, twenty-four, from Athens, Ohio, one of the squad leaders, was hit in the head. He shouted for his second in command, Sgt. Everett J. Barrett, to take over the squad, but as Barrett moved forward, he was hit in the hip by a rifle shot that came from the bottom of the depression and was left lying in an extremely exposed position. Two privates, John M. Purcell, twenty-two, of Schenectady, New York, and Edward E. Widman, twenty-four, of Baker, Oregon, tried to pull him back out of the line of fire, but he was killed by a second shot. The right platoon began to move up and started firing into the depression. In the ensuing firefight, two more men from E Company were hit: Pfc. Fred H. Johnson, a BAR man, was killed and Sgt. Eugene C. McCandless was wounded.

On June 26, as F and G Companies (and later joined by E Company) moved southward toward the tip of Nafutan Point from the juncture of Mount Nafutan and Ridge 300, an entirely new and different kind of terrain was encountered. There were deep gulches from which coral pinnacles jutted and over which a deep, thick tangle of jungle undergrowth had spread. As they proceeded, the companies began to receive heavy enemy fire from the gulches below. It became increasingly evident as the fighting progressed that the enemy force below them was by far the biggest concentration of enemy troops yet encountered at Nafutan. Later accounts show that there were approximately 500 Japanese still left as of June 26. The strength of the Battalion by the night of June 26 had shrunk to 556 officers and men. Around 1800, the company commanders of the three rifle companies conferred and decided to take up a strong defensive position atop Ridge 300 with good communications to the rear and a means of resupply. There the three rifle companies of the 2d Battalion dug in for the night in five separate perimeters, prepared to move anywhere on the peninsula in the event of a Japanese counterattack. Flanking the main position were a series of listening posts across the open ground, with scattered patrols on the edge of the coral jungle. The men were in small groups, spaced as close together as the number of men would allow—in some cases, at fifty-yard intervals. This line was commanded by Maj. Edward McCarthy, 2d Battalion executive officer, who had established a forward CP near the mouth of Nafutan Valley. The last night position was that of the 2d Battalion CP, located behind the main line and the outposted positions. There were serious gaps on the right of the line.

Life had not been pleasant for the Japanese defenders of the Nafutan Peninsula either. From seaward, destroyers pounded the rocks and caves unmercifully; from land, a monotonously heavy volume of fire was maintained by 40mm and 90mm antiaircraft guns, and 81mm and 60mm mortars, as well as the light tank platoons, self-propelled mounts, and small-arms fire. Movement on the peninsula was difficult, and the shortage of food and water became acute. Captain Sasaki, commanding the 317th Independent Infantry Battalion of the 47th Independent Mixed Brigade, was determined to move his battalion out of the Nafutan trap and join other Japanese forces that he believed to be in the vicinity of Hill 500, approximately 6,000 yards to the north. The troops composing Sasaki's command, around 500, consisted of remnants of his command that had escaped to Nafutan as well as scattered army and navy men from other units, including the service and antiaircraft troops formerly stationed at Aslito Airfield. On June 26, he issued the following order for the breakout and raids en route to the 47th Independent Mixed Brigade's former headquarters at Hill 500:

> The Battalion will carry out an attack at midnight tonight. After causing confusion at the airfield, we will advance to Brigade Headquarters in the Field (Hill 500). The C.O. of the

Ikeda Company will command the first attack unit. Under his command will be: 3d Company, the Hira Company, and the Murone Platoon. C.O. of the Koshiro Company will have under his command the Inoue unit, the engineers, the remaining naval units. Units will assemble at 1930 in areas to be designated separately. You must carry out the attack from the designated places. Casualties will remain in their present positions and defend Mount Nafutan. Those who cannot participate in combat must commit suicide. We will carry the maximum of weapons and supplies. The password for tonight will be "Schichi sei hokoku" ("Seven lives for one's country").

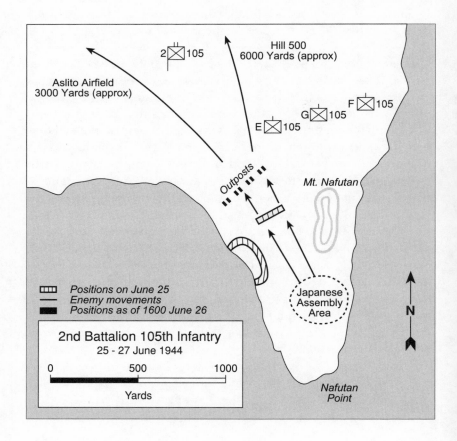

Shortly before midnight on June 26, Sasaki moved his columns out by three carefully selected routes to Aslito Airfield. One was the coral jungle area that ran along Saipan Channel, west of Ridge 300. Another used the tangle of undergrowth along the beaches next to Magicienne Bay. The third column made its way down Nafutan Valley and slipped through the American lines somewhere near the nose of Mount Nafutan. None of the three columns was discovered by 2d Battalion outposts, although Sergeant Nicoletti of E Company's 3d Platoon (who had earlier discovered Captain Sasaki's headquarters) did investigate mysterious sounds of activity in the dense brush near his outpost on the shore, but did not find anything.

At about 0200 on June 27, an extremely large group attacked the main CP of the 2d Battalion, 105th Infantry, east of Aslito Airfield and approximately 1,500 yards in the rear of the front lines. In a sharp encounter, four Americans were killed and twenty wounded; twenty-seven dead Japanese were found the next morning in and around the 2d Battalion CP. At 0230 another large force attacked the eastern end of Aslito Airfield, but were repulsed by service troops after they destroyed a P-47 parked on the runway and damaged three others. They then moved on to Hill 500 where they were destroyed by the 25th Marines. At 0500 large groups began attacking American defensive perimeters near the airfield to break through to their front lines in the north. Elements of the 25th Marines, 14th Marine Artillery Regiment, 27th Division Artillery, and 3d Battalion, 105th Infantry, eliminated these forces. By the end of the day, the Sasaki raids were defeated and 500 dead Japanese lay on the ground of Aslito Airfield, Hill 500, and the 14th Marines camp.

The Japanese breakout from Nafutan Point was the climax of the campaign there. At about mid-morning on June 27, the three line companies of the 2d Battalion (unaware of the breakout until the next morning) formed a skirmish line, and by 1800 had swept to the end of the peninsula. Not one live Japanese soldier was encountered. At 1840 on June 27, Lieutenant Colonel Jensen notified Colonel O'-Connell that the Nafutan Peninsula was secure. Mop-up squads investigating ravines and other out-of-the-way places found a cave containing more than 200 Japanese bodies, neatly stacked—proof that the enemy had been removing their dead. Contrary to earlier reports that only a handful of Japanese were concentrated on the Nafutan Peninsula, figures compiled by the Saipan garrison force commander and submitted to the War Department on July 12 estimated the total Japanese strength as being 1,250 on June 23, 1944, when the 2d Battalion had taken Nafutan Point.

Once the Nafutan Peninsula was declared secure, G Company of the 2d Battalion spent most of its time counting Japanese dead and rounding up Japanese civilians and soldiers. The battalion subsequently reported counting 850 bodies on Nafutan Point, not including the 500 or so killed in the breakout on the night of June 26. From June 27 to July 3, the 2d Battalion captured 175 Japanese soldiers and eighty-nine armed civilians. Eighteen others who refused to surrender were killed. The battalion was decimated by the Nafutan campaign. Out of 186 officers and men in G Company at the start of the campaign, only eighty were left. On July 1, the 2d Battalion was assigned the mission of providing local security to Aslito Airfield on the south and east sides. The 2d Battalion remained in the Nafutan area until July 3 when it reverted to 105th regimental control and joined the rest of the troops on the Tanapag Plain for the final decisive battle on Saipan.

12 The Fight for Central Saipan

While the 2d Battalion was struggling on the Nafutan Peninsula, the balance of the 27th Division moved to its assembly area north of Aslito Airfield to support the 2d and 4th Marine Divisions in their attacks northward. By June 22, the 2d Division was attacking up the west side of the island toward Mount Tapotchau and the 4th Division was on the east side of the island toward Hill 600 and Chacha Village. The 27th Division (less the 105th RCT, which was kept in reserve) attacked up the center of the island through what became known as Death Valley. At about 1530 on June 22, the 4th Division ran into increasingly heavy enemy opposition. It was decided by NTLF at the time that, tired and weakened by heavy casualties, it would be relieved on the line by the 27th Division, which was fresher and at relatively full strength. After further discussion with NTLF, it was decided that the 27th would pass through the two left regiments of the 4th Division up on the line, and its right flank would be protected by one regiment from the 4th Division after the capture of Kagman Point.

On June 23, the corps switched its attack to the north, with the 2d Marine Division on the left, the 27th Division (less the 2d Battalion, 105th Infantry) in the center, and the 23d Regiment of the 4th Division on the right. In the 27th Division's sector, the 106th attacked on the left, the 165th on the right, and the remainder of the 105th (the 1st and 3d Battalions) stayed in 27th Division reserve. For the next fourteen days, the 27th's attack continued northward with shifts of the three regiments and various battalions as required by the tactical situation. The progress was slow, particularly on the left of the division sector where the terrain was extremely difficult.

Wooded hills and valleys, honeycombed with caves, provided extraordinarily strong defensive positions, which had been well developed by the Japanese. The eastern slopes of Mount Tapotchau leading down to Death Valley, Purple Heart Ridge, Hill "King," Hill "Able," and a number of other wooded hills provided a network of defenses that the men of the 106th and 165th would never forget. Lieutenant Colonel A. A. Vandergrift Jr., a battalion commander in the 4th Division, told Colonel Kelley of the 165th that, "He was up against the strongest position yet encountered on Saipan."

For the next several days, the rugged terrain and the strength of the enemy in the 27th Division front made it extremely difficult for the assigned line companies of the 106th and the 165th to advance. On both sides of Death Valley were cliffs containing caves in which the Japanese had hidden men with arsenals of weapons. Units of the division moving through Death Valley, in particular the 106th, were subject to intense enemy fire every step of the way. The soldiers had to advance through wooded areas at the opening of a plateau onto a flat plain where the Japanese held the high ground on both sides; it was a virtual death trap. Unknown to the American command, the Japanese selected the Death Valley area as one of its main defensive positions and carefully prepared artillery, mortar, machine-gun, and even a few 75mm positions on the cliffs that controlled the entire area. Brush was laid in the front of the firing ports, hiding the gun positions from observation. One writer described the Japanese defenses of Death Valley as "awesome."

Some of the best Japanese troops left on the island were also placed in the caves above Death Valley by Lieutenant General Saito. One full regiment of infantry (the 135th) reinforced by the 9th Tank Regiment and also the headquarters troops of the Thirty-first Army were positioned to cover Death Valley; about 4,000 Japanese crack troops guarded the plateau. General Saito placed his CP in a deep ravine later known as the How Position, just east of Hill Able. One observer noted that the tactical situation faced by the Americans was roughly comparable to that faced by the Light Brigade when it charged against the Russians at Balaclava during the Crimean War almost a century before: "Cannon to right of them, Cannon to left of them."

Thus far, the 105th Infantry had not been involved in the combat actions near Mount Tapotchau, Death Valley, or at Purple Heart Ridge. Apart from the 2d Battalion at Nafutan, the 105th had remained in division reserve since June 22. By 1700 on June 25, however, its 1st Battalion, acting under orders from Col. Kelley, had moved up from division reserve to cover the left flank of the 3d Battalion, 165th, under Major Dennis Claire to the north of the S road. The whole movement by O'Brien's battalion that day had taken place with the loss of one man wounded and one killed. The only enemy opposition had come from the hills in front of Lt. Col. Cornett's battalion in the form of long-range flanking fire. In view of the lack of enemy opposition in front, confirmed by a reconnaissance in force by the 27th Division Reconnaissance Troop on the night of June 25–26, Col. Kelly decided to make a long, rapid movement to the north the next morning. O'Brien's 1st Battalion was assigned to the 165th Infantry for that assault.

By the end of June 25, it had become increasingly obvious to the Japanese high command that the situation was desperate. A message from Thirty-first Army headquarters to the 29th Division on Guam stated that the ten-day battle had reduced the armed strength of the line forces to approximately 2,000 men and only three tanks. There were additional units, but they lacked weapons and fighting ability. Many units faced serious water and food shortages. The despair faced by the Japanese high command is summarized in a lengthy message sent from Thirty-first Army Headquarters on Saipan to the 29th Division on Guam around June 25:

The fight on Saipan as things stand now is progressing one-sidedly since, along with the tremendous power of his barrages, the enemy holds control of sea and air. Even in daytime the deployment of units is very difficult, and at night the enemy can make out our movements with ease by using illumination shells. Moreover, our communications are becoming disrupted, and liaison is becoming increasingly difficult. Due to our serious lack of weapons and equipment, activity and control is hindered considerably. Moreover, we are menaced by brazenly low-flying planes, and the enemy blasts at us from all sides with fierce naval and artillery cross-fire. As a result even if we move units from the front lines and send them to the rear, their fighting strength is cut down every day. Also the enemy attacks with fierce concentration of bombs and artillery. Step by step he comes toward us and concentrates his fire on us as we withdraw, so that wherever we go we're quickly surrounded by fire.

At 0610 on June 26, orders were issued by the 165th Regiment for an attack to the north to seize the 0-5 line in the area just beyond Purple Heart Ridge. Three battalions would attack in echelon with the 3d Battalion, 165th, on the right, the 1st Battalion, 105th, in the center, and the 1st Battalion, 165th, on the left. The 2d Battalion, 165th, was assigned to mop up and clean out any of the enemy in the rear of the 0-5 line. After a ten-minute artillery barrage, Major Claire's 3d Battalion, 165th, jumped off and advanced about 400 yards against little opposition. It then halted to allow adjustment of the lines on each of its flanks. On the right of the 3d Battalion, the 23d Marines had been slow in re-forming their lines, and on its left, the 1st Battalion of the 105th had run into difficult terrain, which slowed them down considerably. Instead of the relatively flat, eastern coastal plain over which the 3d Battalion had been advancing, the 1st Battalion had to push through the foothills of the extension of Purple Heart Ridge, badly cut-up country. Its B Company, the right flank unit, was forced to split up into small patrols to investigate a maze of deep ravines occupied by enemy soldiers. One of its patrols led by Lt. George B. Dolliver from Battle Creek, Michigan, and a BAR man, Pvt. William C. Callahan from New Haven, Connecticut, knocked out two machine guns in one cave; several other enemy snipers were cornered in the narrow ravines and killed. B Company then established contact with the 1st Battalion of the 165th Infantry on its left.

C Company, 105th Infantry, under 1st Lt. Bernard G. Tougaw, was lost in the maze of corridors and had swung too far to the left, ending on the top of the ridge next to the Aslito-Tanapag Highway. As its left platoon came to the ridge, two individuals came out of the woods about 200 yards to the front dressed in marine fatigue uniforms and wearing cloth-covered, marine camouflaged helmets. They waved their arms and whistled. The platoon sergeant, TSgt. Raymond J. Toomey, answered them with a shout. They then ran back into the woods and almost immediately the platoon was hit by machine-gun fire and shells from a high-velocity weapon. Private First Class Lawrence D. Flynn of C Company was killed and nine other men, including Technical Sergeant Toomey, were wounded. After reporting this incident to the 165th, the 1st Battalion received the following message at 1530: "Give me more information on enemy opposing you. Your msg. stated they were dressed in marine helmets and jackets. Can you secure identification?"

Following the enemy attack, the platoon broke for the cover of a nearby grove of trees. As they started to move, a navy plane flew low over them. When the men reached the trees, the navy plane circled back and let go with a rocket barrage that killed another man. According to First Lieutenant Hammond, O'Brien "was raising hell with C Company" because it was all bunched up. In O'Brien's view, this was a quick way for a military unit to get killed. Later that afternoon, the 165th S-2 asked the 1st Battalion to provide the "following information on the plane that caused casualties in your unit. Type of plane, time, direction, number of planes and TA." Hammond recalled that O'Brien personally questioned a number of men from C Company about the navy TBF attack.

Companies B and C of the 1st Battalion, commanded by Capt. Richard F. Ryan and 1st Lt. Bernard G. Tougaw, were then reorganized, and at 1400 a line was established ready to move out to the north abreast of the 3d Battalion, 165th. During this movement, four men from the 1st Battalion were wounded by enemy fire from How Position, now almost 1,500 yards to the rear. Before digging in for the night, both the 1st Battalion, 165th, and the 1st Battalion, 105th, moved to the right to have their left flank rest on Purple Heart Ridge. The 1st Battalion, 165th, dug in to the left rear of the 1st Battalion, 105th. The 3d Battalion, 165th, had already dug in at 1700 to the right of the 1st Battalion, 105th, astride the main coastal highway that led toward Donnay. As night fell on June 26, the 165th faced north with three battalions abreast. Late in the afternoon, elements of the 4th Division came abreast of Claire's 3d Battalion, establishing a solid line from the Tapotchau Corridor to the sea. At 1800, the 1st Battalion, 105th, was informed by 165th headquarters, "It is imperative that you submit casualty reports as of 1300 and 1800 each day by any means available at that time." That night the enemy was active along Purple Heart Ridge. Sergeant Julius Kovalaski of Torrington, Connecticut, who served with Headquarters Company, 105th, recalled that, "Several parties of as large as twenty men were killed while trying to infiltrate through the American lines."

When the 106th Infantry, under Col. Russell G. Ayers, failed to launch its attack by 1000 on June 26, and an investigation showed that the regiment "was somewhat demoralized," Major General Jarman, the new division commander, decided to relieve Ayers. Jarman was already unhappy with Ayers for allowing his regiment to swing too wide in making a flanking maneuver the previous day. He replaced him with Col. Albert K. Stebbins, chief of staff of the division. Stebbins, forty-three, was a graduate of the U.S. Military Academy and the Command and General Staff School. Brigadier General Ogden J. Ross, assistant commander of the division, was assigned additional duties as chief of staff.

At 1815 on the afternoon of June 26, the 165th received word that it was attached to the 4th Division for an attack on the 0-6 line within its zone of action scheduled for the next day. The 4th Marine Division had under its control a total of nine infantry battalions—three each from the 23d and 24th Marines, two from the 165th (less the 2d Battalion), and the 1st Battalion, 105th. The timing of the attack on June 27 was set for 0630, but due to the transfer of control of the 165th to the 4th Marine Division, the jump-off did not take place until 0900. In the interim, messages flashed back and forth between the 165th Regimental Headquarters and the 1st Battalion, 105th:

0703 Report Immediately when Mar. FO and artillery LN report to your units.
0732 Tanks for 1st Battalion of 105th Infantry and 1st Battalion of 165th Infantry sent forward. Meet guide at 197-H.
0734 Did you jump off following arty. preparation at 0730

0815 1st Battalion, 105th, reports that they have advanced 100 yards from LD and are abreast of 3d Bn., 165th.

By June 27, a firm and well-integrated line had been established by the Americans across the full width of Saipan, firmly securing Mount Tapotchau and somewhat more than the entire southern half of the island. The 2d Division had advanced to the lower edge of Garapan, where they dug in to await straightening of the whole front line. On the extreme right, the 4th Division completed mopping up the Kagman Peninsula and anchored their flank firmly on the shore. In the center, the 27th Division was in the final process of straightening out the line and its units were mopping up the Japanese in Death Valley and on Purple Heart Ridge. More than 4,000 Japanese were dead and the road to Tanapag Harbor was clear. Even Lt. Gen. Holland M. Smith, viewing the scene from the top of Mount Tapotchau, sent a personal message of congratulations to the men of the 27th Division who had fought in this difficult area.

The naval shelling of Mount Tapotchau was unrelenting during the time American forces were slowly driving the Japanese back into the northern half of the island. Lieutenant General Saito had moved his command post several times because of the constant shelling. Major Takashi Hiragushi, the 43d Division intelligence officer, agreed that what he feared most was the constant shelling by the American navy. A captured Japanese lieutenant stated that the greatest single factor of the American success on Saipan was naval gunfire. Saito himself recognized this when he wrote on June 27, "If there were no naval gunfire, we feel with determination that we could fight it out with the enemy in a decisive battle." Because of the constant shelling, he once again moved his CP from Mount Tapotchau to a new cave command post, in an overgrown depression about 2,200 yards north of Mount Tapotchau. There a third and final defense line would be drawn along the narrow waist of the island from Tanapag on the west coast, through Hill 221 and Taraho to the east coast, cutting across the base of the island's northern tip.

At 0900 on June 27 the coordinated attack by the 1st and 3d Battalions of the 165th and the 1st Battalion of the 105th, jumped off and moved rapidly northward without opposition, especially on the right flank where the 3d Battalion, 165th, was moving across flat, open country. About thirty minutes after his battalion had moved off, Major Claire reported that they had moved forward approximately 1,600 yards. After an hour delay while an air support mission was flown over the ground ahead, the 3d Battalion, 165th, moved forward again covering another 1,500 yards to the north by 1400. The 1st Battalion of the 105th Infantry, though moving through rougher terrain, was able to reach RJ (road junction) 547 by 1400. With two hours of daylight left, and having encountered no opposition, Lieutenant Colonel O'Brien ordered B and C Companies to take the ridge in front of the 1st Battalion before nightfall. A Company was held in battalion reserve. Following artillery fire called in shortly after 1400, the assault companies led by a platoon of light tanks reached the crest of the rise. As the assault companies broke over the rise, they encountered heavy enemy fire from one high-velocity gun and several automatic weapons. In B Company two men were wounded, and in C Company one man was killed and six men wounded. A Company, which was following the assault, suffered eight men wounded. O'Brien ordered his men to pull back and at 1630 he ordered the 1st Battalion to dig in just north of RJ 547. At 1724, 165th Headquarters advised the 3d Battalion, 165th, and the 1st Battalion, 105th, to "establish strong perimeter defense in your areas tying into units on right and left. Patrols will be coordinated with harassing arty. fire in areas not patrolled and during hours patrols are not operating." During the period the 1st Battalion, 105th, was attached to the 165th, the 3d Battalion, 105th, remained in an assembly area near Hill Able as 27th Division reserve, awaiting orders.

In his diary for June 27, Tarao Kawaguchi reported, "Slept good because of the saki we took last night. Upon being awaked by Captain Watanbe, immediately departed for Donnay. Proceeded to Donnay under terrific artillery fire. We received heavy casualties due to the concentrated fire by land units and tanks and took refuge on top of mountain. Was ordered by hospital commander to be prepared to attack the enemy with rifles, hand grenades, or bayonets attached to sticks. I was ordered by 2d Lt. Yamaguchi to burn medical supplies.

Because of the furious fire by our troops one enemy tank was knocked out and the enemy withdrew. It was decided that the severely wounded be evacuated to Tara-Hoko by way of the mountain pass. On the way we were separated from 2d Lt. Yamaguchi and lost our way and came out near the sea coast."

During the night of June 27, 1944, the 1st Battalion,105th, which had dug in just north of RJ 547, was harassed by a Japanese field piece and several machine guns on a ridge near RJ 547 in the vicinity of Donnay. At 0645 on June 28, O'Brien reported to his regimental headquarters that his battalion had run into "a small Kasserine Pass situation at RJ 547," and that it will "attempt to outflank with assistance of the 3d Battalion, 165th." When daylight came on the morning of June 28, the 1st Battalion came under heavy enemy machine-gun fire from the heavily defended ridge in front of them. At 0830 Maj. Kenneth Dolan from Watervliet, New York, the 105th's assistant plans and training officer, arrived at O'Brien's CP and reported back to regimental headquarters that the 1st Battalion was also under enemy mortar fire from the ridge and that two battalions of the 165th were "helping O'Brien to reduce resistance encountered." At 1000, O'Brien decided to outflank the ridge by a double envelopment rather than take it frontally. Two combat patrols were formed, one consisting of a platoon from B Company led by 1st Lt. John F. Mulhern from Portland, Maine, and the other a platoon from A Company, under 1st Lt. Kendrick R. ("Fig") Newton from Greenville, Alabama.

While maneuvering into position, the patrols came upon an abandoned Japanese field hospital filled with dead and dying Japanese soldiers. This open-air cemetery contained more than 400 Japanese bodies. The Japanese military had moved out the day before, telling every wounded soldier who had been able to move to shift for himself. Those who could not move were given grenades and told to commit suicide. The problem of what to do with those still in the hospital occupied O'Brien for most of the rest of the day. The men in the hospital refused to surrender and began blowing themselves up with grenades. From time to time, an enemy soldier emerged from a cave and ran around through the hospital killing off the wounded soldiers. First Sergeant Charles J. Stephani of B Company recalled that some American soldiers began shooting the wounded Japanese, but this was immediately halted. While the patrols were occupied with the hospital, Japanese artillery pieces on the ridge continued to pound the American positions. One of these rounds had already scored a lucky hit on the 165th's CP, seriously wounding Colonel Kelley and forcing Lieutenant Colonel Hart to take command of the 165th. When the patrols resumed their movement to the ridge line, the B Company patrol was held up by heavy enemy fire. O'Brien ran 1,200 yards through sniper-infested underbrush to take personal charge. Leaving some men to contain the enemy, he selected four soldiers to go with him and search out the enemy guns. Two riflemen from B Company were on the point: Pfc. Ralph J. Carpenter from Farmington, Michigan, and Pvt. Charles D. Smith from Baton Rouge, Louisiana. Close behind them were TSgt. Raymond D. "Lefty" Lefebvre from Cohoes, New York, First Lieutenant Mulhern, and O'Brien. The rest of the patrol was strung out behind them.

Due to the difficulty of the terrain, the progress was agonizingly slow. Suddenly, Smith and Carpenter came around a rock and found themselves not five feet away from the muzzle of a 77mm field piece. Nearby were several machine guns and approximately thirty or forty enemy soldiers. They were momentarily startled and did not fire right away. Lefebvre came up and began to open fire followed by Mulhern and O'Brien. All of the Japanese were either killed instantly or ran away and were chased by the rest of the patrol. The field piece and five machine guns were captured. O'Brien radioed for reinforcements and by nightfall all of "Obie's Ridge," as it came to be called, was in American hands. The 1st Battalion held the position all through the night and the next day, June 29, against numerous counterattacks. O'Brien's heroic conduct on June 28 was one of the actions mentioned in the citation posthumously awarding him the Medal of Honor.

One of O'Brien's colleagues, Major Dolan, referred to this incident in his remarks before the 27th Division Association in December 1944, just after he returned to the United States, "The morning of July 5 arrived and Col. Les Jensen and myself moved forward on a reconnaissance preparatory to the displacement of the regimental command post, also to meet the various battalion commanders for plans to continue the attack. Eventually, we arrived at our rendezvous. Of course, Bill O'Brien was right on top—the old nonchalant O'Bie, talking a mile a minute with a cigarette dangling from his lips. O'Bie, with his battalion and through the great effort of his officers and men, had just completed one of those very daring maneuvers which, when successful, go down with the great deeds of history."

At 1030 on the morning of June 28, 1944, Maj. Gen. George W. Griner, from Whitesburg, Georgia, took command of the division, having flown to Saipan from the Hawaiian Islands the day before. He had formerly commanded the 98th Infantry Division in Hawaii, which was subsequently turned over to Maj. Gen. Ralph C. Smith who had been so humiliatingly relieved of command only four days before. Griner, forty-nine, was a 1917 graduate of Southern Methodist University and a veteran of World War I. He had graduated from the Army's Command and General Staff School in 1933 and from the Army War College in 1939. He arrived on Saipan late in the evening of June 27 and spent the night at NTLF Headquarters with Lt. Gen. Holland M. Smith. Smith reportedly told Major General Griner that the 27th Division had been "a dismal failure as a fighting division prior to that time." With this ringing endorsement in his ears, Griner took command. He requested Brig. Gen. Ogden Ross to continue on his staff in his dual capacity as chief of staff and assistant division commander.

Later that evening, General Griner discovered that he had only five out of nine battalions under his control. The 2d Battalion, 105th, was attached to the island's garrison force for mopping up operations on Nafutan Point. The 1st Battalion, 105th, and the 1st and 3d Battalions, 165th Infantry, were attached to the 4th Division. Of the battalions he did command, the 3d Battalion, 106th Infantry, had been so badly cut up in the Death Valley combat that it was no longer considered an effective fighting unit. Griner, therefore, ordered that the 1st Battalion, 106th Infantry, relieve the 3d Battalion, and that the 3d Battalion, 105th, which had not seen action since its withdrawal from Nafutan Point, be ordered onto the right of the division line with the responsibility of seizing Hill Able. When Griner asked NTLF Headquarters to have his full battalion strength returned to him, he was told that the other battalions would be put back under his command as soon as the division "demonstrated that it could fight."

On the afternoon of June 28, Griner ordered Col. Leonard Bishop of the 105th to take over the right flank of the division line and move forward to the north as rapidly as possible. The only combat battalion Bishop had available was the 3d Battalion, 105th, under Lieutenant Colonel Bradt, then in position near Hill Love. Bradt was ordered to march into position at daylight on June 29 for the attack north. Ironically, around 1200 on June 28, Bishop and Maj. Philip E. Smith, 105th Regimental S-2, while en route to 165th Headquarters, were ambushed by enemy snipers and sustained coral cuts around their knees. Smith had to be evacuated from the island due to the severity of the cuts and did not return.

In his diary for June 28, Tarao Kawaguchi recorded the following: "We found the main strength of the company and [were] relieved to hear that Lt. Yamaguchi was safe. Suddenly we received a terrific bombardment as we were resting near the 'Y' junction. We immediately hit the dirt and were covered by dirt and sand. I received a slight wound across the forehead. When the barrage subsided, there were cries of pain and help all around the area. Took to the forest, assembled, and waited. During the night, we received another barrage. Quenched our thirst with rain water."

As the Death Valley campaign ended on the morning of June 29, Bradt's 3d Battalion moved into position to take over the right flank of the 27th Division line at Purple Heart Ridge. At 0630, its K Company, the leading company, was met at Hill X-Ray–Yoke by guides from the 2d Battalion, 106th. It then moved along the inside of Purple Heart Ridge as far as Hill Oboe where it ran into the rear elements of the 2d Battalion, 165th. One of its guides wanted to enter Death Valley to avoid congestion, but the other preferred to stay on Purple

Heart Ridge where the foliage offered some concealment from the enemy fire coming from Hill Able. The more protected route seemed safer to Capt. Alexander C. Bouchard from Gloversville, New York, the commander of K Company, so he decided to use it.

As the men moved along the ridge following the protected route, they began to receive rifle fire from the top of Hill King. Bouchard sent a squad under SSgt. Carl A. Neidt to circle the hill and clean out the snipers. As the squad moved out, friendly fire began to land on Hill King. The first fifteen shells landed squarely in the middle of K Company, wounding nineteen men. Bouchard ordered them to charge the crest of Hill King and seek shelter on the reverse slope to avoid the artillery fire. Unexpectedly, they landed in the Japanese foxholes on the reverse slope just as they were hunkering down to wait out the American artillery fire. In the next few minutes, K Company engaged in a battle royal, killing enemy soldiers as fast as they could shoot. With the aid of E Company, 2d Battalion, 165th, they succeeded in killing all of the Japanese on Hill King. More than 125 Japanese bodies were counted. Over at Hill Able just north of Hill King, the 1st Battalion, 105th Infantry, also killed several Japanese.

On June 29, after stopping to reorganize at 1300, K Company moved into line to the right of I Company and closed the line across Death Valley. The attack began as soon they were in position. At 1400, almost immediately after the attack started, K Company ran into heavy fire from the Japanese on Hill Able as it crossed the open ground. Enemy machine guns also began to open up on K Company from the front. One was destroyed by SSgt. Allen D. Parsley, K Company, from Glens Falls, New York, who picked off the crew of four, one by one, from a distance of 200 yards. Bouchard kept his men moving ahead by laying down a cover of mortar and machine-gun fire, but as the company reached the center of the open ground, the enemy fire increased in intensity and gradually the whole company was pinned down. Within minutes four men were wounded. First Lieutenant William H. Morton, commanding the right flank platoon of Company K, worked his way forward and contacted Bouchard by radio, informing him that either tanks or artillery would be needed to destroy the enemy position. Because artillery support was out of the question, the decision was made to pull the two platoons of K Company back to the road junction until tanks could be brought forward from the Death Valley entrance.

I Company of the 3d Battalion, 105th, led by Capt. Ashley W. Brown from Poultney, Vermont, also had its attack delayed by a lack of supporting tanks. Like K Company, Brown formed two platoons for the assault. His right platoon had just pushed across the road when a soldier stood up from behind what looked like a brush pile and threw a grenade that wounded the two leading I Company scouts. One man, Pfc. Miner F. Gardner, took umbrage at this and tried to kill the man. After he threw his grenades into an opening of a concrete pillbox with no effect, the same soldier jumped up and threw another grenade at him. Gardner did a little dance and the grenade exploded harmlessly in a ditch behind him. By then he was bleeding badly from his wounds, and so he rejoined his platoon and received medical attention.

On the left, 2d Lt. Frederick C. Spreeman's platoon of I Company was also receiving enemy fire from the position on the ridge. He sent two squads from his platoon to silence the enemy gun position. Despite heavy enfilade fire, the two squads negotiated the slope without causalities. They were a few yards from the top of the ridge when Pfc. Robert M. Stevens, on the extreme left flank, spotted a Japanese tank not more than twenty feet away. It was expertly camouflaged to look like a bush on the skyline. Although Stevens gave a warning, his words were too late. The tank opened up and three Company I men were killed instantly. At the same time, four men of G Company, 106th, under cover next to Spreeman, were killed and fourteen wounded. As the tank traversed the area, a Japanese soldier popped out of the bushes and began laughing and throwing grenades. Spreeman's men were so close to the Japanese tank that one of them, SSgt. Francis A. Garcaeu, dove under the tank and remained there, safe from the tank's fire. Under heavy machine-gun fire, the tank retreated up the Aslito-Tanapag Highway to the north, but was destroyed by an American tank commandeered by TSgt. Frederick N. Martin, Spreeman's platoon sergeant. The same tank destroyed a second Japanese tank concealed in a straw stack on the forward slopes of the hill.

Captain Brown then sent out his reserve platoon led by Lt. James M. Braley in an attack on the pillbox. The platoon suffered several casualties, including Pfc. Edward L. Stevening, who was killed as he sprinted up the slope. Sergeant Conrad Steen, a rifle grenadier, and Pvt. George Kovocavich, a bazooka man, both tried to fire on the pillbox, but before they could get their first rounds off, Steen was killed and Kovocavich was seriously wounded. A moment or two later, Pfc. Boyce O. Broome and Pfc. Joseph F. Kratky, a medic, were both killed trying to pull Kovocavich out of the enemy's line of fire. Lieutenant Braley was wounded when he tried to help Kratky. Brown then brought up a self-propelled gun from Cannon Company, whose single round finished off the Japanese in the pillbox. At 1700, I Company dug in for the night, after tying in with K Company on the right and the 106th on the left.

During the afternoon of June 29, Capt. Paul G. Brunet, Catholic chaplain of the 105th, was wounded while trying to locate men who had been hit in action. Father Brunet, who had been a member of the 105th before he entered the priesthood, accompanied a detail of litter bearers up the hillside to reach the wounded men, wanting to give them last rites. The detail came under enemy sniper fire and the chaplain was struck in the right ankle. A man who accompanied him, Pfc. Cornelius R. Abbott of Troy, New York, and a member of the 105th's medical detachment, was wounded and later died of his wounds.

During the night of June 29, the Japanese gave every appearance of withdrawing from their strong points in the center of the island. The 3d Battalion, 105th, captured the heights near Purple Heart Ridge and this seemed to spark the retreat. The road leading to the northern part of the island was filled with enemy soldiers moving to the rear. The retreating men were taken under mortar and artillery fire by the 165th Infantry from the American positions on Hill 700 and Charan Danshii Mountain. They had a field day, killing more than 400 frantic enemy soldiers. It was the beginning of the end of the Battle for Saipan. All in all, it had been a good day for the 27th Division. At last Holland M. Smith could find some good things to say. That morning he and Maj. Gen. Harry Schmidt, USMC, visited the 165th's CP. As they left, each remarked, "Tell the regiment they are doing a swell job." Holland M. Smith is also reported to have said, "The 105th and 106th gained a couple of thousand yards." By this time, fighting in areas assigned to the 2d and 4th Marine Divisions had almost ceased and the 27th Division had caught up with the marine positions along the eastern slopes of Mount Tapotchau.

By the end of the day on June 29, the defense of Death Valley was over with the exception of Hill Able. During the night, however, the Japanese defenders pulled out, leaving only a small delaying force that easily succumbed the next day to the 105th Infantry. General Saito wanted to pull back, shorten his line, and regroup his forces. On June 30, mortar shells falling near his headquarters convinced him to set up a new command post in a cave in Paradise Valley, about 1,000 yards east of Makunsha Village. This would be Saito's last command post.

The despair felt by the Japanese defenders of Saipan is clearly reflected in Tarao Kawaguchi's diary entry for June 29: "Dug foxhole due to scare of previous night. Stayed in this area until the afternoon and again received terrific bombardment. When the firing was over, everything was desolated. Took up our duty of treating patients again. During the night orders were received to proceed to Tara-Hoko, but the trip was hampered by a terrific rain. Under the flare lighted road, continued to Tara-Hoko. When we reached the 'Y' junction again, there was a feeling of sadness, pity, and anger, and we resolved to gain revenge for the dead."

13 The Drive to Tanapag

The last day of June witnessed the end of the long and bitter struggle of the 27th Division to capture Death Valley and Purple Heart Ridge in central Saipan. Marine Lieutenant General Harry Schmidt later stated, "No one had any tougher job to do." The 2d Battalion, 165th, captured Hill Able by 0940 on June 30, 1944, and spent the rest of the day consolidating its positions. Also, on June 30, the 1st Battalion, 105th, was relieved of its assignment to the 4th Marine Division advancing up the east coast of the island and was ordered to join the 3d Battalion, 105th, in its attack on the enemy near RJ 482. These two battalions encountered only slight Japanese opposition as they moved forward on the right of the division line. Shortly after noon, Lieutenant Colonel Bradt ordered a platoon from L Company, 3d Battalion, to mop up a number of enemy-occupied caves and ravines that dotted the ridges in the area. Many dead and wounded enemy soldiers were found in these caves, and there was slight enemy resistance, which was easily overcome. Late in the afternoon, I Company of the 3d Battalion ran into serious enemy opposition near Hill Uncle-Victor. Rather than trying to knock out the enemy position with only one hour of daylight remaining, the two battalions of the 105th dug in for the night on a ridge just south of Hill Uncle. From there, the enemy could be observed and harassed with rifle and machine-gun fire during the night.

First Sergeant Charles J. Stephani from East Patchogue, New York, Company B, 1st Battalion, recalled that after Hill Able had been taken, B Company dug in on an adjacent hill next to a pass. Patrols were sent out and there was some enemy sniper fire. About 2000 on June 30, B

Company received a visit from "Washing Machine Charlie," also known as "Bed Check Charlie." As usual, a bomb or two was dropped that had no physical impact on the men, but it did keep the men awake at night and disrupted planned operations. The bombs were typically dropped "every place but . . . where they were intended."

At 2250 on June 30, the 165th received the following message from division: "The following officers were reported to have distinguished themselves in combat over the past several days: Lt. Col. [John F.] McDonough, 2d Battalion, 165th Infantry; Major [James H.] Mahoney, 1st Battalion, 165th Infantry; Major [Dennis E.] Claire, 3d Battalion, 165th Infantry; Major [Martin] Foery, 3d Battalion, 165th Infantry; 1st Lieutenant O'Brien, I & R Platoon; Capt. Herman M. Lutz, S-4, 2d Battalion, 165th Infantry; Lt. Col. Nicholas D. Lamorte, 105th Field Artillery; Lt. Col. William J. O'Brien, 1st Battalion, 105th Infantry; the late Captain Paul E. Ryan, Company C, 1st Battalion, 165th Infantry; the late 2d Lt. Merritt L. Pequeen, Company C, 1st Battalion, 165th Infantry; 1st Lt. George E. Martin, Company A, 1st Battalion, 165th Infantry; and 1st Lt. Edward L. Cloyd, Company C, 1st Battalion, 165th Infantry."

With the close of action on June 30, 1944, the battle for central Saipan ended on a successful note, but it came at a high cost. Total American casualties were estimated at 3,987. Of these, the 4th Marine Division suffered 1,506; the 2d Marine Division 1,016; and the 27th Infantry Division 1,465. The officer corps of the 27th Division was especially hard hit. The 165th lost its commander, Colonel Kelley, who was wounded in action on June 28 by an exploding mortar shell; his place was taken by Lt. Col. Joseph T. Hart, the 165th's executive officer. Lieutenant Colonel John F. McDonough, commander of the 2d Battalion, 165th, was also wounded and evacuated; his successor, Major Brusseau was wounded and later died. Colonel Harold I. Mizony of the 3d Battalion, 106th Infantry, was killed in action. In addition, a total of twenty-two company commanders of the 165th and 106th Infantry Regiments were either killed or wounded in action during the period. In the 105th, Lt. Col. George H. Hopkins, executive officer, had been wounded on June 22, 1944, and his place taken by Lt. Col. Leslie M. Jensen. Regimental S-3, Maj. Philip E. Smith had been wounded on June 28, 1944, and evacuated from the island. Several platoon leaders in the various rifle companies of the 105th Infantry had already been either killed or wounded by this time.

Things went from bad to worse for the Japanese defenders. Tarao Kawaguchi recorded in his diary for June 30, "Toward the morning we reached the Tara-Hoko area. Immediately started on construction of an air raid shelter and received a rain of bombs from the enemy planes while constructing. Stayed in shelter all afternoon. Toward the evening, did my duty as a medic. Ate rice for the first time since the 25th and regained strength. Felt like stamping the ground and tears came to my eyes. On this day the hospital received concentrated fire and numerous casualties occurred. I received a slight wound on the left thigh."

On July 1, the division continued its drive to the north and west of the island against little or no enemy opposition. At 0700, the 3d Battalion, 105th, began its move forward with the 2d Battalion, 165th, in reserve and mopping up the rear area as the advance proceeded. Enemy resistance increased and the assault elements were subjected to flanking fire from the caves in the hills above. The 3d Battalion by passed an enemy strongpoint on Hill Uncle leaving the reduction of that position to K Company. Hill Uncle was a little cone-shaped knob that rose out of the floor of the corridor like a giant haystack. Captain Alexander C. Bouchard from Gloversville, New York, in command of K Company, believed that during the night the Japanese had reinforced Hill Uncle with a machine gun and several mortars. He detailed a platoon from K Company led by SSgt. James L. Webb to take the Japanese position while the rest of the company moved around Hill Uncle to the north. Thinking that the Japanese might try to escape, Bouchard sent 1st Lt. William H. Morton of K Company to the north slope to intercept the Japanese as they clambered back over the summit. By the time Morton's men had gotten into position, however, Webb's men had destroyed the Japanese on Hill Uncle and successfully occupied the position. Morton, unfortunately, was wounded by rifle fire during that engagement.

While the reduction of Hill Uncle had been fairly simple, other elements of K Company had a tougher time. By noon on July 1, the company was still working in and around the caves and ravines at the road-pass through the ridge. More than thirty enemy soldiers were killed there, but each one had to be literally dug out of a separate hiding place and eliminated one by one. The rest of the 3d Battalion, however, continued to move forward until it reached a point just south of Papako where it dug in for the night approximately 400 yards north of RJ 482.

At about 0800 on July 1, 1944, the 1st Battalion, 105th, which had spent the night on a hill adjacent to Hill Able, was relieved by the 1st Battalion, 165th, and moved into a rest area for a few hours. At 0910 Lieutenant Colonel O'Brien reported to the 105th CP, "We are moving back into assembly area. CO 1st Battalion will get in touch with CO as soon as possible." By 1000 the 1st Battalion, now under division control, moved down the coastal road to Chacha Village where it went into reserve. That night it moved to a forward assembly area in the rear of the 3d Battalion, 105th, near 187 J in preparation for a movement the next day to Tanapag. Colonel Bishop planned to use O'Brien's battalion as a mop-up force behind the 3d Battalion as it moved out of the valley toward Tanapag Harbor.

The action on July 1 ended another phase of the division's role on Saipan. From the morning of June 29 until the end of July 2, the division with three battalions abreast had slugged its way north through the upper reaches of the Death Valley corridor against determined but weakening enemy opposition. Effective July 3, the division was to attack north and west across the island toward Tanapag Harbor eventually pinching out the 2d Division, which was fighting its way through the city of Garapan. The 2d Division was then to be pulled out of the line to rest for the forthcoming assault on Tinian. The 4th Division, also attacking to the northwest, would reach the west coast above Tanapag Village. As it moved in that direction, it would peel units off to face the northeast, effectively confining the enemy to the narrow, mountainous extension of the island that stretches to Marpi Point.

In his diary for July 1, Tarao Kawaguchi reported as follows: "While working, everybody seemed to regain their strength and upon seeing this, I felt greatly relieved. Stayed in air raid shelter all morning due to concentrated fire. During the let-up rice was cooked with the lid sealed with paraffin. The taste of rice was indescribable. After eating, fixed the dugout and attended medical supplies."

The morning of July 2 was dark and rainy. The 4th Division, which had spent most of its time during the past days resting and patrolling, moved forward for about 1,500 yards suffering only one casualty. At 0830, the 3d Battalion, 165th, which had been at Hill 700 since the morning of June 28, and which now had returned to division control, moved out on the attack at the same pace. Within half an hour, it was moving around Charan Danshii Mountain to the west when it came under fire from enemy artillery batteries on Radar Hill. The battalion commander, Maj. Martin Foery, decided to move the 3d Battalion around the mountain to the east. After a brief firefight in which about fifty Japanese soldiers were killed, the battalion pushed out across the rolling hills. By noon, with little or no opposition, the advance had moved 1,700 yards, well in advance of the 3d Battalion, 105th, in its left rear. This battalion had been held up by intense enemy rifle and machine-gun fire coming from an enemy strongpoint near Papako. At 1400, Major General Griner (concerned that a gap had been created in the lines by the rapid advance of the 165th and the delay of the 3d Battalion, 105th) ordered the 165th Regiment to halt its advance and to dig in for the night.

With the left flank of the 3d Battalion, 165th, uncovered, Griner ordered Colonel Bishop to move the 1st Battalion, 105th, close behind the 3d Battalion, 105th, now positioned near the Charan Danshii Mountain in the center of the island. Once it made contact, the 1st Battalion, 105th, was ordered to move north through the 3d Battalion, 105th, until it reached the left flank of the 165th Infantry. After facing left and digging in, the 1st Battalion was to tie in with the right flank of the 106th Infantry. The movement that late in the afternoon was considered extremely hazardous, because it required an advance in daylight over 1,700 yards of open ground that had not been completely cleared of Japanese forces. It was a virtual nest of hornets, and there was a very real chance that the soldiers of the 1st Battalion would dig in for the night and the next morning find themselves surrounded by the Japanese. At 1430 Griner informed the commanding officer of the 165th that the 1st Battalion, 105th, would tie in with the 165th's left flank at 221 K.

At 1440 on July 2 when he received his orders to move up, O'Brien's battalion was 800 yards south of the Charan Danshii road junction. By the time he got his men moving it was 1515 and Bradt's 3d Battalion had already reached the junction, but had halted to eliminate a Japanese machine-gun emplacement that had fired on them. While the 3d Battalion waited for this action to be completed, 1st Battalion moved up the Aslito-Tanapag Highway and passed through the 3d Battalion's lines at the Charan Danshii road junction. At 1545, O'Brien reported to 105th Regiment, "Leading elements pinned down by enemy MG fire." Colonel Bishop responded at 1730 that the 1st Battalion was ordered to occupy line 221 K to 230 L and to "Fight your way to it if it takes all night." In view of this order, O'Brien instructed his men to waste no time in moving forward. If opposition was encountered, it was to be bypassed. The men broke into a dogtrot as soon as they passed the 3d Battalion lines. By 1650 1st Lt. Bernard A. Tougaw, in command of C Company, 1st Battalion, reported to Lieutenant Colonel O'Brien that he had reached the 165th's flank and was digging in. By 1800 all companies of the 105th were in line and had dug in for the night on the left flank of the 165th. The division presented a solid front facing west.

That night, recognizing that the 1st Battalion, 105th, was vulnerable to an attack from the rear by enemy soldiers who had concealed themselves during the battalion's headlong dash that day, Sgt. Thomas A. Baker of Company A went to Capt. Louis F. Ackerman, his company commander, and requested permission to go out that night and wipe out as many of the Japanese who had been bypassed as possible. After Ackerman granted his request, he asked three of his good friends, SSgt. Cleo B. Dickey, SSgt. Harold M. Rehm, and Pfc. Charles I. Keniry to join him that night. The three volunteers covered him while he methodically worked his way through the open fields through which the 1st Battalion of the 105th had passed that day. In more than an hour, Baker personally killed eighteen Japanese soldiers. At one point, he walked directly into a concrete pillbox and killed four Japanese soldiers with one burst of fire before they could get off a single shot. For these efforts, as well as others on Saipan, Baker was posthumously awarded the Medal of Honor.

After 2d Lt. Thomas J. Donnelly's patrol from L Company, 3d Battalion, 105th, had completed mopping up the enemy position on Charan Danshii Mountain, the battalion continued its push north encountering along the way three stubborn enemy positions, each containing five to fifteen soldiers. These positions were cleared out at a cost of two wounded men from L Company. Nightfall found the 3d Battalion's right flank about 400 yards north of Charan Danshii Mountain. During the night many Japanese who had been bypassed by the 1st Battalion, 105th, the previous day, and who had not been killed by Sergeant Baker's group, tried to escape to the north; most were killed. Along the rear of O'Brien's line, more than thirty Japanese were killed in hand-to-hand fighting. In B Company, 1st Battalion, five men were wounded by grenades or were bayoneted, and in A Company three men were hit.

Tarao Kawaguchi's diary for July 2 started off on a somber note: "At dawn visited the place where my friend lay dead with a bayonet wound in his head. Covered him with grass and leaves. Upon returning, ate a meal of hardtack and pickled prunes for breakfast. Suddenly while eating, heard gunfire, and orders were issued for security disposition. However, no attack was received so returned to shelter. During the evening, took care of medical supplies and fixed shelter."

Late on the afternoon of July 2, the direction of the attack by the 27th Division the next day was changed to the northwest. In a turning movement designed to assist the 2d Marine Division on the left, whose progress at the time in the town of Garapan was being stubbornly resisted by the enemy, the new objective of the 105th Infantry would be the seacoast near the Flores Point Seaplane base north of Tanapag Harbor. It was contemplated that the 1st Battalion, 105th, would attack in that direction from its night position on July 3, and that the 3d Battalion in the vicinity of Papako would continue to the north, destroying the men in the enemy strong point in the area that had been bypassed earlier that day. The attack was scheduled for

0830 the next morning. In order to keep the advance even, an intermediate objective was designated by General Griner along the high ground, just before the descent to the coastal plain began.

When the sun came up on the morning of July 3, it was discovered that during the night the Japanese had placed a number of machine guns along the crest of the hill just beyond where the 1st Battalion, 105th, had dug in for the night. As soon as the men began to move around, these guns opened up. In C Company, 1st Battalion, two men were killed and five wounded. Artillery fire was called in that eliminated most of the machine-gun positions. First Lieutenant Bernard A. Tougaw, in command of C Company, sent out a small party to observe the effects of the artillery fire on the Japanese positions on the next hill. The first man to reach the summit was amazed to see, on a rock about 100 yards over the hill, a nude woman calmly combing her hair. Nearby in a dugout were several other civilians. Within ten minutes, practically all of Company C came forward to view this bizarre spectacle as well as most of the men of Company A. Fearing that the woman's presence was a trick to get the men to gather, the company commanders ordered the men back down to the bottom of the hill. Eventually, the woman and the other civilians were persuaded to come into Company C's position where they were placed in a holding facility. According to the division historian, the naked woman continued to run around the island as late as August 1944.

The 105th's attack on the morning of July 3 was further delayed when the 4th Division on the right decided to relieve one of its front line regiments with the 25th Marines. The relief took until 1000, at which time the attack jumped off encountering negligible opposition. The advance was conducted with artillery support, a novel experience for the division so far in the battle for Saipan. By 1410, the 1st Battalion, 105th, had reached its objective line for the day, the high ground 2,000 yards east of Tanapag Harbor overlooking the plains of Tanapag that stretched to the sea. It was at this point that the battalion encountered its most serious opposition that day. Company A halted its forward movement just behind a secondary road that ran along the rim of the high ground at the point where the ground sloped to the sea. After one of his men was wounded by enemy fire, Captain Ackerman went forward and discovered a well-camouflaged Japanese pillbox located about thirty yards across the secondary road. To deal with this problem, he first ordered his company to fire at the openings of this strong point. Second, he ordered TSgt. Harry E. Okonczak, Sgt. Thomas L. King, and Pfc. Rueben Aiperspach to move forward and attack the pillbox. Not a shot was fired until the three reached the pillbox and looked inside. At that point, the soldiers inside opened fire, wounding Aiperspach and killing King. Technical Sergeant Okonczak was able to throw a number of grenades into the openings of the pillbox killing several Japanese inside. Three soldiers ran out of the pillbox and were cut down immediately by rifle fire. Okonczak got to his feet to see if there were any more Japanese in the pillbox and was immediately shot in the stomach; he survived the wound and the battle.

Ackerman then ordered up an SP gun to knock out the pillbox, but because of the elevation, the attempt was unsuccessful. Corporal Wilfred MacIntrye, of the 102d Engineers, crawled forward and blew up the pillbox with a demolition charge. Three more Japanese gun emplacements, flanked by forty or fifty spider holes hiding enemy soldiers, were discovered and wiped out by the 105th and 106th. More than forty enemy were killed and ten Americans wounded. It was not until after 1600 on July 3 that the last enemy resistance was terminated. At that time, the elements of the division in the area were ordered to dig in for the night and prepare to move down to the sea early next morning.

Private First Class Frank Standarski from Cohoes, New York, who served with Company A, 1st Battalion, recalled the fighting on July 3: "We had made a 1,000-yard gain the night before and were dug in on a defensive perimeter in T-type trenches, each big enough for three men," he related. "The Japs and our artillery were dueling. It was raining pitchforks and dark enough for the favorite Jap tactic of sending out small raiding parties." He went on, "A party of four got close enough to toss a grenade into my trench and wound me in the right leg, but one of the other men in the trench opened up with his Browning Automatic rifle and not only got the four in the party but got seven more who were marching up behind in close order."

Private First Class Warren F. Garrett from Troy, New York, D Company, 1st Battalion, 105th Infantry, recalls the fighting that day. Garrett, and Cpl. Joseph Mariano of Troy, New York, were carrying Company D's supplies of ammunition and rations to the frontline troops on the heights. They rode in a jeep called *Lucky Linda*, which by July was as full of bullet holes as a sieve, but had never been hit in a vital part. To reach the men, the jeep had to travel over a hill. The men knew when they started up the hill because the jeep would begin to roar and the Japanese machine-gun fire would sputter. If the jeep kept on roaring, the men knew that they had made one more lucky trip. Garrett said, "Company D never had any kick over transportation of supplies. . . . If they needed so much as a button, we got it there. Even mail."

July 3 was the last trip of the *Lucky Linda* with Garrett driving and Mariano and another soldier from Company D aboard as passengers. The night before the three had slept on the front lines with Company D and by 1100 on July 3 had made four trips up and down Purple Heart Road. The fifth trip was with 120 rounds of mortar ammunition aboard. Mariano said to Garrett, "This is our last trip." Garrett replied, "Pipe down or it will be." Suddenly, Garrett felt a stinging sensation in his right arm and found that a bullet had gone clean through it, just above the wrist. "I hollered," he said, "and we dove out of the jeep and ran for cover. There we were sweating it out with the [Japanese] machine gun trying to find us when down the road came another jeep with Joe Baron of Hoosick Falls, New York [Headquarters Detachment, 1st Battalion], driving. I held up my arm to indicate I was hurt and he took us aboard. That took courage."

As of 1300 on July 3, the 2d Battalion, 105th, which since June 22 had been operating under NTLF and Saipan garrison force control, reverted to the division and began moving forward to join the rest of the regiment on the hills overlooking the Tanapag Plain. Sergeant Edwin L. Luck from Amsterdam, New York, a member of Company G, recalled that it was dark by the time the battalion linked up with the 1st Battalion on the hills above the plain. First Lieutenant George H. O'Donnell from Troy, New York, recalled that G Company arrived after dark, "with a moon out bright enough to give us considerable light." After digging in, he heard a sentry from G Company issue a challenge. "Halt! Who Goes There?" When the soldier on guard received no reply, he determined that the trespasser was a Japanese soldier and let out a yell. First Lieutenant O'Donnell described what happened next: "All those not already in their foxholes made a dive for them. One of the boys who had been out answering a 'call' [of nature] came back sans trousers, and never retrieved them till next morning. What a time *he* had with the mosquitoes! Well, this Jap was about fifty yards away from me when he had first been discovered. At the time I was eating a K-ration and sitting up in my foxhole. There was a road about five yards below me, and to my front. All of a sudden I saw a figure running there. I was so surprised, but yelled 'Halt!' dropped my canteen, and reached for my carbine when the Jap started to run right into our perimeter. I was afraid of hitting one of my own men, so yelled to the men, and they finished him off in short order."

In his diary entry for July 3, Tarao Kawaguchi wrote: "At daybreak, the sound of enemy artillery and rifle fire echoes throughout the valley. Immediately took up security disposition. The rifle reports seemed nearer and more terrific than yesterday. However, the situation cannot be comprehended. If the enemy approaches, the whole unit will repulse them with every weapon at hand. Toward the end of the day, took refuge in the dugout with Lt. Yamaguchi due to attack and fire of land units. Later, tried to transport rations under command of Lt. Yamaguchi but failed due to enemy fire and action. Today the casualities were three in the pharmacists."

In the early morning hours of July 4, a large group of Japanese, trying to escape to the north to join General Saito, stumbled into the command post of the 165th on the high ground overlooking Tanapag Plain. After a brisk fire fight, twenty-seven of the enemy were killed, including a number of officers, one of whom proved to be Colonel Ogawa, commanding officer of the 136th Infantry Regiment. On his body, he carried Saito's withdrawal order of July 2 and many other documents and maps that revealed the enemy's final plans for defending the island. One of these contained detailed instructions relative to the establishment of new defensive areas to the north. Ogawa himself ordered the remnants of his own regiment, now bypassed by the Americans, to commence their withdrawal north at 2200 on the night of July 3.

Independence Day, July 4, on Saipan started out rainy and dark, although morale was high. In the division, the catchphrase was, "We'll spend the 4th on the beaches at Tanapag." At 0800 the division began to move down the sharp, slippery slopes to the sea in a heavy rain storm. By 1000 the men were drenched to the skin and the steep slopes had become difficult to negotiate. Sharp gullies, box canyons, and ledges that dropped abruptly twenty or thirty feet slowed up the advance and caused gaps in the advancing line. Only on the extreme left, where two battalions of the 106th were advancing down a long gradual slope, was any significant progress made. The 106th moved rapidly downhill to the sea, far outstripping the other regiments. By 1322 the 1st Battalion reached the beach, captured part of the great Japanese naval base at Tanapag Harbor, and was mopping up the northern half of the destroyed naval base, including the wreckage of the seaplane station at Flores Point.

The rapid push to the sea, cutting the island in half, forced large numbers of Japanese to move north along the coastal plain in a totally unorganized fashion. There seemed to be no exercise of command, nor did they move in any military type of formation. Some merely ran out in the open as far and as fast as they could go; some moved from cover to cover; others hid waiting for darkness to give them an opportunity to escape. Most of them were armed, and some set up positions from which they could fire on the Americans coming down from the heights above them. Some positions were in the open; others were set up in bushes or clumps of trees. Wherever they were, the Japanese were inviting targets for the men of the division on the ridge overlooking the Tanapag Plain. The 1st Battalion, 165th, atop the ridge spent most of the afternoon taking pot shots at the enemy soldiers milling in the coastal plain below.

In the center of the 27th Division line, the 1st Battalion, 105th, did not make significant progress down the slopes. Companies A and B, led by Capt. Albert A. Butkas, thirty, of Hoosick Falls, New York, the battalion executive officer, started their drive to the beach at

0730. As he later said: "We advanced on a front of about 500 yards, north of the Tanapag installations. We had no sooner started down the ridge slope than we dropped into a gulch about 280 feet deep. We knew there was a gully at that point because our map showed one, but that little gully turned out to be a deep canyon with sheer walls." The men were compelled to climb down hand-over-hand from ledge to ledge, all the while keeping an eagle eye out for the enemy. A few caves were flushed out with rifle fire and grenades on the way down.

Captain Louis F. Ackerman, thirty, of Brooklyn, New York, in command of Company A, later said: "We were lucky there was no heavy fire from the Japs in that gulch. We'd have been dead ducks if the Japs had played it smart and put in heavy emplacements to cover that gulch. First, we climbed down to clean out one wall of the canyon, and then we had to climb back up again on the other side. In one cave we found about 20 Chamorros, whom we took to safety."

At about 1220, the 1st Battalion units reorganized below the bluffs and began a quick movement toward the beach, through patches of banana trees and small cane fields. A Company immediately came upon a small village of squatter shacks near the coast. Finding that there were a number of Japanese stragglers there, Ackerman divided his men down into several small squads and began a systematic mop up of the village. The Japanese tried to flee the houses, but were cut down by Company A. More than 200 Japanese were killed in two hours, the company suffering no casualties.

By 1400 Ackerman moved his men past the settlement of small houses into a lumberyard containing several large piles of boards, where the enemy was hiding. Over the next hour, the men played a macabre game of hide and seek with Japanese fanatics. The enemy ran up and down the piles of lumber, with Americans chasing them, trying to get in a shot. Finally, a large group of Japanese, hidden in a clump of trees and underbrush near the north edge of the lumberyard, were flushed and began to run to the north in one big howling mob. The 1st Battalion, 165th, on the high ground overlooking the ocean, blasted them with rifle and machine-gun fire and reported most of them killed.

At 1620 on July 4, O'Brien reported that Company A had reached the beach, but that there was much enemy resistance. Technical

Sergeant John J. McLoughlin, twenty-four, of Troy, New York, noted, "The Japs all ran from us and seemed to head for the narrow strip between that road and the beach. I wondered why they all headed for one particular spot, until we reached that spot. It was lousy with dugouts and trenches." The drive ended up in the northern extremities of the Flores Point seaplane base where the enemy had constructed a series of dugouts, pillboxes, and firing trenches as defenses against beach landings in that area. The dugouts, barricaded with palm trunks, lumber, and earth, were in a grove of fir trees in which visibility was a bare ten feet.

Artillery fire was called in and self-propelled cannon mounts brought up to blast the emplacements. Under cover of the fire, Company A moved up to attack. Two of its leading scouts, Pvt. Andrew Sandoval and Pfc. Leo Lund, approached the dugouts. Sandoval noticed some movement in one of the firing trenches. When he went to investigate, a Japanese rifleman popped up in front of him and shot him in the stomach; he later died of his wounds. Private First Class Lund shot and killed the enemy soldier, but was then killed himself. For the next thirty minutes, Ackerman and his men crawled along the ground dropping grenades and firing into every ditch and concrete emplacement. Forty dead Japanese were counted in the area after the battle.

Private First Class Charles Nevay, twenty-six, of Stamford, Connecticut, and Pfc. David Boynton, twenty-one, of Honolulu, Hawaii, advanced under covering fire to call to the men in the dugouts to surrender. They were answered with a couple of grenades, which wounded two Americans. Sergeant Philip W. Dominque, twenty-eight, Toledo, Ohio, stood up and, still under Japanese fire, fired a rifle grenade into the dugout to eliminate further enemy fire. Before another dugout, Sgts. Everett DeWitt, twenty-five, of Springfield, Ohio, and Anthony Auzis, twenty-six, of Waukegan, Illinois, went ahead of Company A's firing line to drag back a wounded man who was near the mouth of the Japanese position.

As the mopping up proceeded, a group of Japanese broke out of one of the positions and made for the beach. First Sergeant Mario Occhienero, twenty-six, of Rome, New York, later said, "I guess they figured they could swim to Yokohama; they didn't make it." Private

First Class Leon B. Pittman, twenty-seven, Valdosta, Georgia, picked up a light machine gun, fired it from the hip at the running Japanese soldiers, and killed them all with the help of some riflemen. Five soldiers in one dugout committed suicide just as a squad of Americans under TSgt. Ralph N. Gannaway, twenty-seven, of Fort Worth, Texas, brought it under fire. The men heard a muffled explosion of several grenades inside, met no resistance as they advanced, and looked into the dugout to see the remains of the dead Japanese defenders.

Staff Sergeant Louis S. Doddo, twenty-seven, of Norwalk, Connecticut, tossed a grenade into a trench; then as the smoke and debris fell away, saw a lone Japanese stagger out. The man stumbled up to him and said in broken English that he was Comdr. Jiro Saito, a member of the staff of RAdm. Takeshita Tsujimura, commander of the landing party on Saipan. He was the sole survivor of the unit in the dugout and came out with his hands up. "He asked for a knife or any other weapon to commit hara-kiri," Sergeant Doddo said. "But I figured he'd have some information for us. He didn't insist too much, either." Commander Saito, who had been left behind in the sector north of Tanapag to head the Japanese defense, was then taken to the rear for interrogation by 1st Lt. Francois V. Albanese, twenty-nine, of Jackson Heights, New York, the Battalion S-4.

Company B, 1st Battalion, 105th, had a much harder time with the terrain and Japanese opposition as it made its way down the slopes to the Tanapag Beach. By 1220, when Company A was forming up below the bluffs that faced the plain, B Company had just begun its descent. It did not reach the Tanapag Plain until 1500. Under orders from O'Brien, Capt. Richard F. Ryan, commanding Company B, immediately reorganized the unit. When B Company reached the small settlement of squatter houses that A Company had reached earlier, it began mopping up the remaining enemy hiding there. Technical Sergeant Michael J. Mele, twenty-four, of Albany, New York, led a platoon in the advance. "The Japs fired at us from most of the houses, and we tried to take care about shooting back because we'd found some Chamorros in some of the shacks," said Mele. "We didn't have too much trouble with the Japs, though,

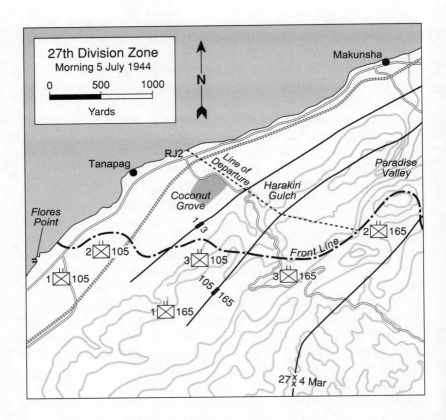

because their spirit seemed to have been broken, in that sector any-way. As soon as we'd get up close, they'd try to get away." Private First Class Floyd E. Cox, twenty-four, of Greenwood, Missouri, and Pfc. Charles A. Reeves, twenty-five, of Dayton, Kentucky, both machine gunners, had a field day as they set up their guns on the ridge and fired at Japanese soldiers scurrying from foxhole to foxhole in the fields below.

After about an hour, the houses were cleaned up, and Ryan be-gan reorganizing his men for the push to the beach. Shots from the rear, however, killed two of his men and wounded two others. Al-though he wanted to turn around and clean up the enemy in the rear, O'Brien ordered him to push on to the beach. Captain Ryan decided to leave a small patrol under Sgt. John A. Sidur from Cohoes, New York, to finish the mop up of the enemy stragglers. Sidur recalled that his men killed one enemy soldier and found a lot of enemy wounded, moaning, groaning, and begging to be killed.

Company B soon came to the same lumberyard through which Company A had passed earlier that day. O'Brien came up and met with Ryan, and they decided that B Company would move directly north and then move to the beach from a point 100 yards above the lumberyard. While they were meeting on the high ground above the battle scene, a machine gun opened up, narrowly missing O'Brien and Ryan. The bullets threw up spurts of dust at their feet, between them, and then went up the hillside to kill a sergeant ten feet away. O'Brien later said, "That sergeant was one of my best men. . . . He led a whole platoon for more than two weeks after it was left without officers." He was TSgt. Altergio Colangelo, of Astoria, New York, who commanded the lead platoon of Company B in several actions on Saipan after 1st Lt. Norman Arnold had been killed. Ironically, twenty minutes before Colangelo was killed, he confided to Sgt. John Domanowski of Company B that he was not going to make it through the forthcoming battle. Colangelo was subsequently posthumously awarded the Silver Star.

By late afternoon on July 4, the Japanese Naval Air Base at Flores Point was secured by the division. Several hill positions east of the Tanapag Plain were also captured by the marines, including Hills 721, 767, and Fourth of July Hill. At 1300 that day, Lt. Gen. Holland M. Smith ordered the 27th Division to be ready to swing to the north for the attack the next day. The entire northern part of the island remained to be seized, including the important Marpi Point area. This demanded a swing of the axis of attack to the northeast. Lieutenant General Holland M. Smith, therefore, split the unconquered portion of the island in half, assigning the left zone of action to the 27th Division and the right zone to the 4th Division.

Major General Griner immediately divided the 27th Division area into two regimental zones, assigning the left zone along the beach to the 105th and the right zone facing the beach to the 165th, stationed on the high ground. The 106th was in reserve near Tanapag Harbor. Later that day, the 105th was joined by its 2d Battalion, which had been committed at Nafutan Point in the southern part of the island since late June. The 3d Battalion, which had been in regimental reserve, was brought up and ordered to take over a position on the right flank of the 165th Infantry. The 105th was now a complete fighting unit. With the release of the 2d Battalion, 165th from corps control, Major General Griner had control of all nine of the 27th Division's rifle battalions for the first time since he took command. The joint attack the next day was to jump off at noon on July 5.

In the 105th's zone of action, the 2d Battalion was assigned to attack on the left, along the beach, while the 3d Battalion was on the right flank on the cliffs above the coastal plain near the 165th. By 1745 on July 4, it was apparent that these two battalions had to finish mopping up the territory between the hills and the beach before they could attack the next morning. To accomplish this without creating a gap between the 1st Battalion of the 165th, and O'Brien's battalion on the beach, the 2d Battalion, 105th, was ordered to take up a position on the plain below the hills and the 3d Battalion was moved in on the right of the 1st Battalion, 165th. The 1st Battalion had already reached the beach near the Flores Point seaplane base and was waiting for orders to attack the next day.

By nightfall on July 4, the 105th and 106th were drawn up facing the direction of their new attack to the north. The terrain would prove to be difficult. From the west, a flat coastal plain stretched inland for 400–800 yards, giving way to a gradual slope that carried up into the central hogback of the island. Farther to the north, this ascent was replaced by abrupt cliffs rising almost perpendicular out of the coastal plain. Ravines, gulches, and cone-like hills dotted the landscape, and vegetation, except on the plain, was plentiful. A coastal road ran along the shore, paralleled closely by a sugar cane railroad. From the main coastal highway, there were two cross-island roads, one of which reached the eastern shore of the island.

Lt. Col. William J. O'Brien (left) and battalion staff aboard troopship *Cavalier* bound for Saipan on June 16, 1944. (U.S. Army Signal Corps)

Aboard an LCVP heading for Saipan on June 17, 1944. From left, Brig. Gen. Redmond F. Kernan, Commander of the 27th Division Artillery, Maj. Gen. Ralph C. Smith, Commander of the 27th Division, and Col. Albert K. Stebbins, Chief of Staff, 27th Division. (U.S. Army Signal Corps)

Lt. Col. O'Brien at the front as his battalion relieves another battalion on June 18, 1944. From left, 1st Lt. Kendrick R. "Fig" Newton, Company A, 1st Battalion, Lt. Col. O'Brien, and 2d Lt. Albert D. Brockett, Company A, 1st Battalion. (U.S. Army Signal Corps)

Lt. Col. O'Brien and his company commanders plan an attack on the Japanese positions on Nafutan Ridge on June 19, 1944. (U.S. Army Signal Corps)

Soldiers of the 105th Infantry move across a field to attack Japanese positions on Nafutan Ridge on June 20, 1944. (U.S. Army Signal Corps)

Three members of Headquarters Company, 105th Infantry, crouch behind a rock pile on one of the hills near Nafutan Ridge overlooking a canefield on June 21, 1944. (U.S. Army Signal Corps)

Explosion of Japanese ammunition dump on June 23, 1944. (U.S. Army Signal Corps)

Japanese prisoner of war guarded by SSgt. Louis S. Doddo, Company C, 105th Infantry, who captured him on July 4, 1944, as the Japanese walked out of a dugout into which Doddo had tossed a hand grenade. The prisoner proved to be Comdr. Jiro Saito, member of the staff of RAdm. Takeshita Tsujimura, commander of the landing party on Saipan. (U.S. Army Signal Corps)

SSgt. William H. Allen, points to the bullet hole in his helmet he received on July 6, 1944. His three comrades from E Company are, from left, Pvt. Mitchell Rabinowitz, Pvt. Edward Wardman and Pvt. John Purcell. (U.S. Army Signal Corps)

Lt. Col. William J. O'Brien issues orders to his battalion staff and company commanders at his command post near the Flores Point seaplane base on the afternoon of July 6, 1944, prior to the drive north up the Tanapag Plain along the beach. (U.S. Army Signal Corps)

General view of the Tanapag Harbor area during the battle. (U.S. Army Signal Corps)

During the Japanese counterattack on the Tanapag Plain on the morning of July 7, 1944, the attacking Japanese became so confused that they bayoneted their own troops hiding in foxholes in the path of the attack. (U.S. Army Signal Corps)

Dead Japanese soldiers line the beach at Tanapag Harbor after their disastrous counterattack on army positions on July 6–7, 1944. (U.S. Army Signal Corps)

Capt. John C. Baker, Headquarters Company, 105th Infantry, awarded the Silver Star for heroism during the Japanese counterattack on July 7, 1944. He would later become a major general in command of the New York State National Guard. (U.S. Army Signal Corps)

Lt. Col. William J. O'Brien, commanding officer, 1st Battalion, 105th Infantry, was posthumously awarded the Medal of Honor for refusing evacuation after he was seriously wounded during the Tanapag Plain banzai attack. He continued the fight and manned a jeep-mounted .50-caliber machine gun until his death. (U.S. Army Signal Corps)

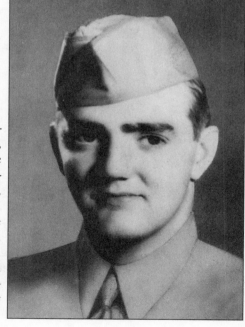

Sgt. Thomas A. Baker, Company A, 105th Infantry, posthumously awarded the Medal of Honor for refusing, even though wounded, to leave the lines of battle. He carried the fight alone as long as he could. Later, when his body was found, his weapon was empty, and eight Japanese lay dead before him. (U.S. Army Signal Corps)

27th Division soldier kneeling at grave of buddy killed on Saipan, 27th Division cemetery, Saipan. July 1944. (U.S. Army Signal Corps)

Dead Japanese soldier killed by American flame throwers. (U.S. Army Signal Corps)

Dead Japanese soldiers in stream cut down by fire of soldiers of 105th Infantry near Tanapag Harbor. (U.S. Army Signal Corps)

Members of Company C, 1st Battalion, 105th Infantry, display flags, weapons and swords captured on Saipan the day after the banzai attack. (U.S. Army Signal Corps)

Pfc. Joseph Vega of Newark, New Jersey, Company E, 2d Battalion, 105th Infantry, takes cover by a road bank and looks out for Japanese snipers. (U.S. Army Signal Corps)

TSgt. Bob Hoichi Kubo, an interpreter with 27th Division G-2, tries to console a Japanese child found in a field of U.S. infantrymen. Sgt. Hoichi Kobo would later win the Distinguished Service Cross for his acts of bravery on Saipan. (U.S. Army Signal Corps)

Maj. Gen. Ralph C. Smith, left, commander of the 27th Division, congratulates Colonel Gerard Kelley, commander of the 165th Infantry, after the capture of Aslito Airfield on June 18, 1944. Brig. Gen. Ogden J. Ross looks on. (U.S. Army Signal Corps)

Lt. Gen. Robert C. Richardson, commanding general of the Pacific area of operations, speaks to staff officers of the 27th Division, including Brig. Gen. Ogden J. Ross, during his tour of inspection of Saipan in late July 1944. (U.S. Army Signal Corps)

Men of the 27th Tank Battalion who were credited with knocking out the most Japanese tanks during the Saipan battle. From left, bottom, Pvt. John Coakley, bow gunner; Tech. 4 Jesus Tyerina, driver; Lt. James A. Bullock, tank commander; and Pfc. Louis Tocci. (U.S. Army Signal Corps)

Pallbearers carry Lt. Col. O'Brien's casket out of St. Augustine's Church. Major Emmett T. Catlin, left, and Maj. William H. Whalen. (personal collection, Francis A. O'Brien)

Lt. Col. O'Brien's body is interred at St. Peter's Cemetery, Troy, New York, on May 13, 1949. Officer members of the 105th Infantry who served with Lt. Col. O'Brien on Saipan present a salute. Members of Col. O'Brien's family look on. (personal collection, Francis A. O'Brien)

A firing squad commanded by Capt. Vincent E. Busone of men from Company A, 1st Battalion, 105th Infantry, who left Troy in October, 1940, with Lt. Col. O'Brien, who served with him on Saipan, honors the fallen hero with a volley of fire. (personal collection, Francis A. O'Brien)

14 The Final Battle for Saipan

At the end of the day on July 4, American intelligence estimated that out of an original garrison of about 30,000 Japanese, there were between 4,000 and 10,000 remaining on Saipan. Most of the remaining troops were either from the 5th Naval Base Force or the 47th Independent Mixed Brigade. The 5th Naval Base Force was the naval garrison before the invasion. Its principal element was a Special Naval Landing Force of about 1,500 men, which was still virtually intact. There were also about 1,000 civilian construction laborers attached, but they were of doubtful military value. The 47th Independent Mixed Brigade had seen some action earlier against the marines on Hill 500 on June 21–22, but it had been withdrawn from the line before that stronghold had fallen and had not seen much action since. It was composed of four infantry battalions from crack Japanese divisions and was a relatively fresh and strong unit. The 43d Division, which had largely been destroyed in combat by this time, still had many soldiers roaming the hills of northern Saipan. These remnants could be rounded up, given competent leadership, and added to the enemy force. One artillery battalion remained, but it had little ammunition. About ten tanks were left to support the Japanese defenses.

These forces were thought to be concentrated in three principal places. One was at Marpi Point and the airfield at the northern tip of Saipan where VAdm. Chuichi Nagumo had concentrated his naval forces. A second was in a deep and winding mountain canyon some 500 yards south and east of the village of Makunsha. It was called "Paradise Valley" by the Americans and "The Valley of Hell" by the Japanese. This was the headquarters and final defensive position of General Saito. In and around Paradise Valley, he had gathered the bulk of his remaining organized troops. The third remaining enemy stronghold was the so-called Tanapag Line, a southern outpost area near the Paradise Valley position. The key to this line was another difficult and treacherous mountain canyon called "Hara-Kiri Gulch" by the American soldiers. Both the Paradise Valley and Hara-Kiri Gulch positions were within the 27th Division's zone of action.

The morale of the Japanese forces on Saipan was at a low ebb by the end of July 4. Every indication supported the belief that the enemy soldiers remaining in the island's upper end were ill-equipped, ill-supplied, and, in many cases, ill. Communications had broken down, and there were serious shortages of food, water, hospital facilities, small arms, and ammunition. Many remaining combat units were disorganized because they'd lost their officers, and all commanders of the infantry regiments on Saipan had been killed. Field hospitals had been forced to move back constantly. Each time there was a move, the seriously wounded were killed and the less seriously wounded were released to wander the hills either to be killed or captured by the Americans. Further, a captured Japanese officer said, "General Saito was feeling very poorly, because for several days he has neither eaten nor slept well and was overstrained. He was wearing a long beard and was a pitiful sight."

July 4 was a bad day all around for the Japanese defenders. The 165th Infantry had attacked Paradise Valley and a fierce naval bombardment hit the command post area, wounding Saito. His defense line was disintegrating. After conferring with his subordinates, he concluded that he had only two options: (1) retreat to the northern tip of the island and fight to the end (VAdm. Chuichi Nagumo, the highest ranking naval officer on the island and the man who had led the infamous attack on Pearl Harbor favored this option since he still believed that a Japanese fleet might yet appear) or (2) stage an all-out counterattack in which all who participated would die in battle with the enemy. This *Gyokusai* attack would be similar to the one at Attu in the Aleutian Islands on May 29, 1943, when 1,000 Japanese soldiers attacked the American forces instead of surrendering. Literally translated, *Gyokusai* means "die in honor" and is a Japanese army tradition whereby upon order of the emperor, each Japanese soldier attacks the enemy knowing that he will die. Saito concluded on July 4 that the most honorable and heroic option was a *Gyokusai* counterattack. The battle cry used on Saipan in the *Gyokusai* attack, "Seven lives for the emperor!" was characteristic. Each Japanese soldier on Saipan was to die, and in dying was to take seven American lives with him. Since it would take time to assemble the available men and arm them (many Japanese soldiers were weaponless at this time) with whatever weapons were available (spears, bayonets tied to poles or sticks, etc.), it was decided that the counterattack would take place on the night of July 6. Army troops would assemble in the Makunsha area 900 yards north of Paradise Valley. Navy troops would assemble at Matoisu on the northwest approach to Mount Petosukara.

The final great battle of Saipan began on the morning of July 5, 1944. On the right half of the corps line, the 4th Marine Division advanced steadily against very little resistance and by 1630 had reached its objective for the day, which was about 1,200 yards from the line of departure. On the left or western half of the front, the 27th Division with two regiments abreast moved off on the attack in a zone about one and a half miles wide. On the division's left, the 105th Infantry advanced along an 800-yard strip of relatively low-level coastal plain, flat or slightly rolling between the beach and the hills that ran parallel to it. The most important landmark on the plain was a large coconut grove about 600 yards east of Tanapag Village. The main coastal road ran along the beach and was paralleled by a small sugarcane railroad. On the division's right, the 165th Infantry advanced into the rugged hills in the interior of the island that paralleled the coastal plain of Tanapag, which included Hara-Kiri Gulch. The 106th Infantry Regiment had been pinched out of the attack the previous day and was now in division reserve near Tanapag Harbor.

Early on the morning of July 5, mop-up operations in the Flores Point seaplane base area were conducted by the 105th. The 2d and 3d Battalions, with the 2d on the left and the 3d on the right, moved cautiously ahead, against light opposition, cleaning out pillboxes and farmhouses along the beach as they moved. The 1st Battalion, under Lieutenant Colonel O'Brien, remained in regimental reserve near the Flores Point seaplane base. Major Edward A. McCarthy, forty-three, from Schenectady, New York, who had replaced Lt. Col. Leslie Jensen as commander of the 2d Battalion, inched the battalion along the beach, investigating extensive defensive installations built by the Japanese long before to repel an anticipated American landing on the northwest coast. Although virtually no opposition was encountered, each position had to be explored carefully. Shortly after 1430, the 2d Battalion had progressed about 1,500 yards and was at RJ 2, north of the village of Tanapag, about to traverse the cross-island road. A few scattered Japanese had been encountered and an exploding ammunition dump held up the advance. First Lieutenant George H. O'Donnell from Troy, New York, a member of G Company, 2d Battalion, remembered the explosion. "In the afternoon, I happened to be crossing an open field on the run, when there was a big explosion about 400 yards away. It knocked me off of my feet and onto my stomach."

At 1600, after reorganizing south of the cross-island road, the 2d Battalion moved on to the north, working along the coastal plain with E and F Companies abreast, hoping to reach Makunsha by nightfall. Thirty yards north of RJ 2, the two lead companies—Company E, commanded by Capt. Clinton E. Smith, Schenectady, New York, and Company F, under 1st Lt. John E. Titterington, Green Island, New York—were hit with a fusillade of heavy enemy machine-gun fire from an unknown location. Although some of the fire was coming from the cliffs to the right front, it was determined by patrols that most of it was coming from the beached hulk of a Japanese landing barge about 600 yards to the north, along the coastal road.

Smith ordered two tanks to run up the coastal road and to dispose of these machine guns. They blasted the hulk with canister and machine-gun fire, which seemed to silence the enemy. Once this was accomplished, the tanks turned around to go back to E Company. One pulled off the road and started across an open field toward the E Company CP where the sugar-cane railroad crossed the branch highway. It made it safely across the open field, but the second tank hit a mine and was completely demolished. Private First Class Jack

Levine of E Company had tried to warn the tanks about the mine-field, but he was too late. He was only fifteen feet from the tank when it exploded. Levine lost an eye, but he was able to drag himself back to E Company's lines without any assistance. Sergeant Jesus Tejerina, thirty, Charlotte, Texas, and Private First Class Sudovich from the first tank crawled out and brought back the lone survivor of the blast. The demolition of the tank in the minefield was the starting point for the Japanese defense of the Tanapag line. Enemy fire erupted along the whole front stopping any further advance by the 2d Battalion. At ap-proximately 1700, Companies E and F dug in along the road that ran from RJ 2 into the hills. The front now extended from the beach to the coconut grove where it bent back toward K Company of the 3d Battalion.

Lieutenant Colonel Bradt's 3d Battalion, 105th, had moved for-ward slowly throughout the day, doing little more than routine mopping-up until late in the afternoon. Its zone included the es-carpment that edged the coastal plain; therefore, its units moved northeast straddling the plain and the rugged hills that closely fringed it. L Company, commanded by Capt. Robert J. Spaulding, thirty, of Laconia, New Hampshire, moved along the rugged hillside keeping abreast of K Company as far as Hara-Kiri Gulch. Toward the middle of the morning, when L Company's men reached the crest looking down into the gulch, they began receiving heavy fire from Japanese in the cliff positions on the far side of the ravine. L Com-pany, along with the 3d Battalion, 165th, on its right, could advance no farther that day and were forced to dig in for the night.

To the left of L Company, K Company under Captain Bouchard advanced along the flat ground until 1500 without incident, but as it entered the southeast corner of the coconut grove about 800 yards east of Tanapag Village, it encountered heavy enemy machine-gun fire from the grove and from the hills to the right. Tanks of the 762d Tank Battalion worked through the trees without finding any enemy positions, and K Company made no further progress. Just at the end of that action, Bouchard, while trying to direct tanks against a Japa-nese machine gun he had located, was mortally wounded by fire from the hills on the right. He died on July 7. The new commander, 1st Lt. Roger P. Peyre of New York, ordered a withdrawal and had the company dig in for the night in a drainage ditch just south of the coconut grove.

Although the 105th had registered gains of almost 2,000 yards that day, cleaning out most of the enemy's northern beach positions, its units were still 1,500 yards in the rear of the 2d Battalion, 165th, which was in contact with the 4th Marine Division. Furthermore, except on the right flank, the 105th had not yet determined the extent and strength of the enemy's positions in its front. Although it was known that Hara-Kiri Gulch was strongly held, no one had yet realized how much this would affect its advance along the coastal plain the next day; a serious lapse of intelligence. At 1800 on July 5, General Griner ordered the 105th and the left battalion of the 165th to move out on July 6 at 0700 and advance their lines to Makunsha, in elongation of the line held by the right battalion of the 165th. This was to be accomplished by 0900 so that the division could attack with units abreast. Griner's message stated: "It is imperative that the left of the division line be advanced to be abreast of the other units for the coordinated attack at 0900. The early advances will be pushed aggressively."

At about 2100 that evening, the Japanese (about forty strong) made a Banzai charge against the right side of the 2d Battalion, 105th Infantry, which had dug in for the night behind the coconut grove. The enemy was repelled by perimeter and artillery fire provided by the 249th Field Artillery Battalion. Eleven dead Japanese soldiers were found in front of the 2d Battalion positions the next morning, and there were most likely many more dead in the rear areas. In the 3d Battalion, 105th sector, the enemy mounted harassing patrols throughout the night, leaving approximately seven dead within the 3d Battalion, 105th's, perimeter position.

While the 2d and 3d Battalions of the 105th were moving up along the coast, the 1st Battalion remained in regimental reserve on July 5 near the Flores Point seaplane base. First Lieutenant Luther "Luke" Hammond, 1st Battalion, S-2, recalled that he had some mechanics assigned to the battalion fix up a Japanese pick-up truck that had been captured a day or so before. When they had the two-cylin-

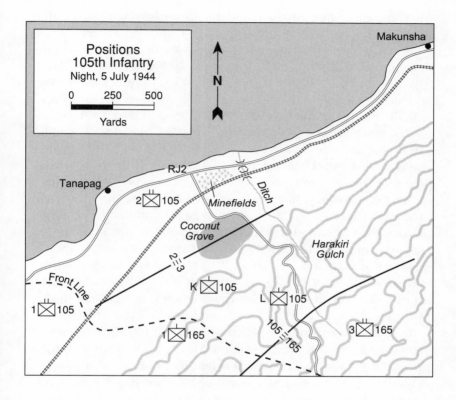

der, air-cooled engine running smoothly, he got behind the steering wheel on the right side, shifted gears with his left hand, and took off down the road. He remembered, "It was so light, it bounced over the road, but it ran good. It would be just the thing for my section. One of my men used it to haul up a load of Jap beer and sake from a storehouse they had discovered in a rear area. After that, when my pick-up was seen back in the rear, the guys wanted to know if we were hauling more beer." That afternoon, the 1st Battalion received a visit from "Washing Machine Charlie." One or two Japanese planes flew over, but no one was hurt.

In his diary entry for July 5, 1944, Tarao Kawaguchi recorded:

1st Lt. Matsumi came to our dugout saying, "As long as I'm going to die, I want to die with the pharmacists section." He joined us. Also, "If this is going to be our grave, let's make it clean." So after reveille, we attended to cleaning up the area. While waiting in the hole after finishing breakfast, the furious assault of the enemy commenced. The 2d Co. under the command of Lt. Matsumi formed into three squads and took up positions on top of the mountain. Seeing that we were surrounded in the front and rear, we approached the enemy with the determination of annihilating them. We fired at the enemy in the rear but there was no effect. The enemy was advancing rapidly along the road. We drank milk, coffee, and sake while awaiting further orders. The order was issued that each company will carry out night attacks. 2d Lt Yamaguchi went to work with Lt. Col. Takeda. 1st Lt. Omura and the pharmacist section bid farewell among themselves and awaited the commencement of the movement. Two men committed suicide due to severe wounds. The Lt. and the pharmacists section bid farewell and promised to meet at the Yasukumi Shrine after death. I along with 2d Lt. Yamaguchi was absorbed into command of Capt. Watanabe. The weaponless unit commenced night attack. As the units commenced movements, communications between the units could not be taken.

On the morning of July 6, the 27th Infantry Division was still on the near side of Hara-Kiri Gulch, short of its line of departure on the plain north of Tanapag Village. On the line from right to left were Major Claire's 2d Battalion, 165th; Major Mahoney's 1st Battalion; Lieutenant Colonel Bradt's 3d Battalion, 105th; and Maj. Edward A. McCarthy's 2d Battalion, 105th. Plans for the morning of July 6 called for the 27th Division's two assault regiments, the 105th and the 165th, at 0730 to press the attack toward Makunsha, which had begun the day before. The objective was to bring the 105th Infantry's line abreast of the 165th Infantry's in the hills by 0900, at which time the coordinated attack was scheduled to begin.

At daybreak on July 6, Major McCarthy had Companies E and F of the 2d Battalion in a tight perimeter around RJ 2. Directly ahead athwart his line of advance was the minefield, about one hundred yards deep. He'd discovered the minefield that ran from the coastal road to the railroad the day before. It consisted of about 150 Japanese bombs set in the ground in four rows, noses up; only about one hundred of which had been fused. A little beyond the minefield was a deep ditch running from the base of the cliffs at the western mouth of Hara-Kiri Gulch to the sea. It provided perfect cover for enemy movements and was also a potential tank trap. To the right (east) of the minefield, toward the coconut grove, there was a wide expanse of open, slightly rolling ground, covered by Japanese small-arms and automatic-weapons fire from the cliffs still farther to the east.

Major McCarthy decided the best opportunity for a rapid advance was the narrow strip between the beach and the road, a sandy piece of ground about fifty yards wide. Accordingly, he ordered F Company to move to the left on the morning of July 6 and attack through this narrow corridor to avoid the minefield. Company E would follow in column and then fan out north of the minefield to cover the zone between the highway and the railroad, an area about 100 yards wide. The open plain between the railroad track and the cliffs where the 3d Battalion, 105th, was located (a distance of about 800 yards) would be covered by fire, but not by troops. McCarthy did not believe that physical possession of that ground was necessary.

Promptly at 0700, July 6, Company F, led by 1st Lt. John E. Titterington, moved forward through the narrow gap between the beach and the road under cover of an old-fashioned, fifteen-minute, rolling artillery barrage provided by the 249th Field Artillery Battalion. The barrage was intended to keep the Japanese in the prepared beach defenses in their holes while the 2d Battalion advanced. Company E, commanded by Captain Smith, followed behind Company F and once past the minefield began to deploy in a three-platoon front along a line running east of the coastal road. A three-man patrol from E Company led by Sgt. Carlos A. Harris was sent across the open plain to locate Company K, 3d Battalion, which was pushing through the coconut grove. Once the minefield was bypassed, E Company could then hook up with K Company. Company

G, under the command of Captain Olander, was in reserve, and began mopping up whatever enemy forces had infiltrated into the area the night before.

Within a few minutes after the jump off, F Company had moved about one hundred yards past the northern edge of the minefield, and E Company had begun to deploy beyond the minefield about 150 yards short of the ditch that crossed the coastal plain. When the artillery barrage moved away from the ditch, the two companies were immediately hit with concentrated, heavy enemy fire coming from the ditch. First Lieutenant Ferdinando Savastono of F Company was seriously wounded. The men hit the dirt, but there was no cover other than foot-high grass, which offered little concealment. McCarthy, who was with Company E at the time, moved up and down the line yelling, "Up and at 'em! Up and at 'em!" but to no avail. The first two men from Company E who tried to get up were killed instantly. Twenty minutes after the jump off, the attack of the 2d Battalion had stalled; it would not resume until later on the afternoon of July 6.

Between 0730 and 1000, while his battalion was bogged down just beyond the minefield, McCarthy undertook several steps to alleviate his position. First, he maneuvered Company E into a position with a three-platoon front to fight off any Japanese counterattack from the ditch area. Secondly, at 0900 he withdrew Company F from its cramped position between the beach and the road and moved it around to the right between E Company and Company K of the 3d Platoon, 105th Infantry. This took about an hour, but it closed the gap between the 2d and 3d Battalions of the 105th. Thirdly, he brought up 1st Lt. Richard M. "Tiger" Hughes, twenty-seven, of Schenectady, New York, from the 102d Combat Engineer Battalion, with a platoon from Company A of that unit, to survey the minefield and to remove the mines. This was dangerous and tedious work because the men had to lay flat on their stomachs to remove the mines, all while under enemy fire. Hughes' men worked all morning to deactivate the minefield. According to one reporter, "Tiger Hughes, a combat engineer lieutenant with old eyes peering out of a reddish bearded young face, is one of those characters you don't really forget. He and his inseparable tommy-gun. . . . What a team! When he wasn't blazing away with the tommy-gun, he'd take what he called a breather to defuse a few land mines or blast some Jap-filled cave with satchel charges of explosives."

Unable to move forward, Major McCarthy decided to bring up tanks and SPMs to lay down direct supporting fire for the attacking infantry units along the front of the 2d Battalion. Unfortunately, his radio communications were out, so he had to send a runner back to Tanapag Village to order up the vehicles. At 1000, five medium tanks came rumbling up to Road Junction 2 under Lt. Dudley A. Williams of the 762d Tank Battalion. Rather then send them down the road, which was almost certainly mined, McCarthy ordered the tanks to move forward in single file along the thin roadbed under the railroad track at twenty-yard intervals (Tiger Hughes had already determined that the railroad track had not been mined). When the lead tank became disabled by snarling its tread in one of the steel rails, a second tank tried to come to its rescue. Suddenly, both tanks were hit by heavy artillery fire from the cliffs above to the right. Williams hooked cables to the two vehicles and hauled them loose of the tracks. McCarthy then ordered the tanks to withdraw. The crews of the two tanks hit by enemy fire, although not put out of action, reported that they "could see daylight through their tanks."

It was now 1100 on July 6 and the attack of the 2d Battalion, 105th, had shown little or no progress. Shortly after 1100, Pfc. Edwin J. Kula, twenty-four, of Chicago, Illinois, assigned to the 3d Platoon, E Company, who had been crawling forward, noticed the ditch to his front and located at least one Japanese machine gun firing from that position and probably more. He told his platoon leader, SSgt. Angelo Nicoletti, about his discovery. He crawled back to the road junction at RJ 2, and commandeered an SPM from the 105th's Cannon Company. However, the Japanese artillery on the cliffs opened up, forcing the SPM to withdraw. For the next two hours, Nicoletti tried to move his platoon forward, but was finally pinned down about fifty yards from the ditch containing the enemy machine-gun positions. At this point, SSgt. William H. Allen, twenty-four, of Athens, Ohio, assigned to E Company's 3d Platoon, rushed the ditch with his squad. When the Japanese opened up, all of the men in the squad except Staff Sergeant Allen dove for cover. In one blind dive, Allen landed in the middle of eight enemy soldiers. He shot two of the Japanese with his weapon and bayoneted a third. Incredibly, he was wounded four times by a Japanese bullet, which passed through four different parts of his body. After being hit, he decided to crawl back to his platoon, with bullets kicking up the dirt all around him. Although he wanted to go back to the ditch and wipe out the rest of the Japanese there, McCarthy ordered him to stay behind. It was now approaching 1300, and the 2d Battalion still had not been able to get moving.

Meanwhile, on July 6, over on the right flank, K Company, 3d Battalion, under 1st Lt. Roger Peyre, jumped off on the attack at 0700 from its position behind the coconut grove. It was accompanied by a platoon of light tanks, commanded by 2d Lt. Willis K. Dorey, twenty-two, of Newton, Kansas. K Company moved along a deep gully that circled the southwest corner of the coconut grove, making use of the cover and concealment it offered. As the men left the gully, they came under heavy enemy fire from at least two Japanese machine guns concealed deep within the grove, pinning down the entire unit. When the patrol from E Company blundered into the coconut grove from the 2d Battalion's position near the beach, a Japanese machine gun opened up on them. Sergeant Harris was wounded in the back. Private First Class John Lopez elected to stay with him while Pvt. Keith M. Jarrell went back to the E company CP for help. While he waited with Harris, Lopez was able to spot and mark the enemy's machine-gun positions in the coconut grove. Then, at considerable risk to himself, he made his way by short rushes to a point where he could guide Second Lieutenant Dorey's tanks to the front. Ten minutes later they wiped out the two machine guns. By 0815, K Company had reached the northern limits of the grove and faced the open ground of the plain to the north beyond the cross-island road.

For the next three hours, K Company remained in the coconut grove under heavy fire from enemy positions located along the cliffs on the right overlooking the Tanapag Plain. The Japanese fire swept the open ground over which K Company had to advance; most of it from cave positions that the Japanese had constructed in the sheer bluffs overlooking the open ground north of Hara-Kiri Gulch. The 3d Platoon of K Company was ordered by First Lieutenant Peyre to keep in contact with Company L, 3d Battalion, 105th, in the hills south of Hara-Kiri Gulch. To maintain that contact, the 3d Platoon had to move into the open ground just south of the coconut grove and almost beneath the cliffs. Heavy enemy fire from their positions along the cliffs near Hara-Kiri Gulch pinned the 3d Platoon down. Dorey's tanks came up and neutralized the enemy's fire. When the tanks were firing, K Company could move about the coconut grove and the 3d Platoon was protected. But when they stopped firing, the Japanese would go back to their guns and rain fire down. At about 1000, Dorey informed First Lieutenant Peyre that he was almost out of ammunition and had to go back to the supply dump to replenish his tanks.

During the morning of July 6, L Company, 3d Battalion, under Capt. Robert J. Spaulding, renewed its effort to cross the lower end of Hara-Kiri Gulch. He planned to make two separate attempts. He ordered his 1st Platoon, on the right, under the veteran TSgt. Seigbert S. Heidelberger, to crawl down into a small tributary draw that branched off from the main gulch in a southwesterly direction. The platoon was to work down the draw to its mouth and there set up machine guns that could cover enemy positions on the floor of the gulch and fire into the caves on the opposite side. Under cover of this support, Spaulding sent his 2d Platoon over the near walls of the canyon, across the floor of the gulch, and up the opposite side. To aid the attack, he had at his disposal four light tanks under the command of Lt. Ginio Gano, which he planned to send up the gulch along the trail that entered it from the east.

At 0700 on July 6, Sergeant Heidelberger's platoon crawled up over the ridge and down into the tributary ravine without drawing fire. Moving stealthily in single file along this narrow corridor, the platoon escaped detection and reached the corridor's mouth. There the men set up two light machine guns and began firing at the caves in the face of the opposite wall. Their position exposed, Heidelberger's men began to receive heavy return fire from a disabled American tank that had been left in the gulch the day before and was now in the hands of the Japanese. For thirty minutes, his men, using bazookas and hand grenades, tried to knock out the Japanese guns in the tank, but to no avail. Unable to move forward, his platoon was ordered to withdraw.

Spaulding's attempt to bring tank support into the attack on the lower end of Hara-Kiri Gulch was also unsuccessful. The four light tanks in Ganio's platoon arrived at about 1000, and he ordered them to work up the trail that ran through the middle of the gulch. Under the guidance of Pfc. James R. Boyles of L Company, who had volunteered to man the intercom phone at the rear of the buttoned-up lead tank, Ganio managed to get well into the ravine. Boyles, however, was almost immediately killed by the enemy; leaving the tanks blind without a means of communicating with the infantrymen. Lieutenant Ganio first withdrew his tanks from the gulch, but after being fired upon by the turret guns of the disabled American tank, he returned and destroyed it, killing several enemy soldiers. While maneuvering in the gulch, three enemy soldiers carrying magnetic mines disabled one of his tanks. The crew from this tank had to be evacuated and Ganio decided to withdraw once again.

Shortly after 0900 on the morning of July 6, NTLF Headquarters decided to change the direction of the attack northward. On July 5, the 4th Marine Division on the right, encountering little or no opposition, had made advances of 3,000 yards or more along the east coast of the island. The 27th Division, however, had encountered fierce enemy opposition. At approximately 0900, Lieutenant General Smith called Major General Griner and informed him that the mission of the 27th Division was to be changed. Instead of attacking to the northeast, along the axis of the island, the 27th Division would swing more to the north, meaning that its right flank would reach the sea at the village of Makunsha. There it would be pinched out by the 4th Division, which would continue to Marpi Point to secure the rest of the island. This move would not only enable the 27th Division to properly mop up the Tanapag/Makunsha/Hara-Kiri Gulch area, but might also cut off enemy retirement to the northern tip of the island. Upon completion of these tasks, the 27th Division would revert to reserve.

As a result of the decision by corps to change divisional zones and to redirect the attack from northeast to north by midday on July 6, changes had to be made in the disposition of the various units of the 105th. Whereas the focus of the attack had been on the left along the beach, the emphasis was now shifted to the right where Bradt's 3d Battalion had been ordered to force a passage through the lower

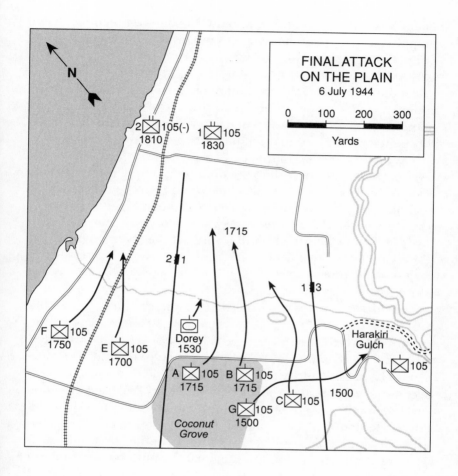

end of Hara-Kiri Gulch. To strengthen his force, Bradt requested permission to withdraw K Company from the coconut grove and place it in 3d Battalion reserve. This request was granted, and K Company moved off the coastal plain and into battalion reserve near the 3d Battalion CP at about 1400. With the emphasis of the attack changing from the left to the right, the 2d Battalion, 105th, was to assume responsibility for all of the ground below the cliffs on the Tanapag

Plain. McCarthy, therefore, ordered Company G, which had been mopping up in the rear, to relieve Company K in the coconut grove at 1200.

Pending relief by G Company at noon, First Lieutenant Peyre, in command of K Company, decided to advance to a small hill in front of the coconut grove, about a hundred yards away, where there were three enemy machine-gun positions. To interdict these positions, as well as the enemy guns on the cliffs to the right, Peyre brought his own machine guns forward to the north edge of the coconut grove and prepared to attack the small hill. When Dorey's tanks returned at about 1030, Peyre and he conferred and developed their plans. The right or 3d Platoon was given the task of taking the hill while the left platoon remained on the fringe of the coconut grove, delivering covering fire. Dorey's tanks were to move up the cross-island road, take the trail up to Hara-Kiri Gulch, and neutralize enemy fire coming from the cliffs around it.

The 3d Platoon was ordered to cover the ground between the grove and the small hill as rapidly as possible. At about 1045, the signal was given and the men jumped up from behind the road and ran at full speed across the open ground toward the hill. The Japanese in Hara-Kiri Gulch and on the cliffs above were apparently expecting an attack, so they opened up with a hail of rifle and machine-gun fire, forcing all but one man of K Company to hit the ground. Private Herman C. Patron, who kept on running, managed to get to the crest of the little knoll before being hit in the chest with a bullet. Sergeant John A. Monaco immediately got to his feet and ran out to where the wounded man lay; a moment later he was joined by TSgt. Arthur A. Gilman. The two sergeants were able to drag Patron back behind the rest of the platoon. While they were waiting for an aid man, Monaco was killed by an enemy bullet.

With the 3d Platoon of K Company stalled in front of the hill, Peyre ordered his left platoon to make a try for the hill, accompanied by some light and heavy machine guns from M Company. Just as these men were moving out of the coconut grove, the Japanese counterattacked down the cliffs and along the paths behind the small hill. Technical Sergeant Arthur A. Gilman looked up to see two

Japanese soldiers running toward him at full speed. Suddenly, there was a tremendous blasting, a crashing explosion rent the air, hurling Japanese in all directions. Gilman saw the leading two Japanese soldiers fly up in the air amid a tremendous geyser of dirt and debris. Before he was knocked down by the concussion, Gilman swears he saw parts of the first Japanese soldier's body flying at least one hundred feet in the air. Apparently, the first Japanese soldier had stepped on a large embedded mine that had been placed years before. The detonation of the one mine set off a number of others, and the effects of the explosions were devastating, creating havoc within the Japanese lines. Japanese gun crews were literally blown off their weapons dooming the counterattack before it started.

Enemy firing virtually ceased for about an hour. Many dazed enemy soldiers were observed walking back up the cliffs. In K Company virtually every man was blown off his feet and almost everyone in the company was shaken by the force of the blast. By the time the men had recovered, G Company came up to relieve them. Even the men in Second Lieutenant Dorey's tanks, moving toward Hara-Kiri Gulch, were shaken up quite severely by the blast. As they were trying to get their bearings, two Japanese soldiers ran out of the mouth of Hara-Kiri Gulch, attached a magnetic mine to the lead tank, and threw a Molotov cocktail at another. Both tanks were put out of action, forcing Dorey to withdraw his remaining tanks. The crews of the disabled vehicles got out and ran for it.

15 The Afternoon Attack on July 6

By mid-afternoon on July 6, the 2d Battalion, 105th, was bogged down in its attack up the Tanapag Plain. Company G was at the north edge of the coconut grove, having just relieved Company K, 3d Battalion, 105th, which had moved into 3d Battalion reserve. Company F was on the open ground to the left of the coconut grove, and Company E was just south of the railroad tracks. Both companies still faced the ditch running across their front, strongly held by the enemy. This was the core of the whole Tanapag line. Both companies were inching their way forward on their stomachs to get close enough to make a direct assault. At about 1530, however, the cavalry arrived to save them. Three tanks under Second Lieutenant Dorey refueled and resupplied, moved through the now cleared minefield at twenty-yard intervals to the lower end of the ditch, and began attacking the enemy. For more than half an hour, his tanks moved up and down the ditch, as far east as the cliffs, driving the enemy into corners and then slaughtering them with canister and machine-gun fire. Dorey even dropped grenades out of the turret of his tank on the Japanese defenders. At one point, he chased a Japanese officer up the ditch with his tank, firing all the way. The Japanese officer finally stopped and committed suicide by falling on his sword. Enemy opposition was for the most part ineffective, although one of Dorey's tanks was destroyed by a magnetic mine and its crew killed. At 1700, when Companies E and F of the 2d Battalion moved out on the attack, they found the ditch littered with 100–150 dead Japanese. In one bold strike, Dorey had wiped out enemy opposition on the west end of the Tanapag line, which had held up the advance of the 105th

Infantry for almost twenty-four hours. Following this massacre, the 2d Battalion advanced without difficulty.

While the 2d Battalion was moving forward, the 1st Battalion remained in reserve at Flores Point. Sergeant Ronald L. Johnson recalled, "At the navy base there were a number of stores and supplies that the Japanese obviously had captured from the British either at Hong Kong or Singapore or some place like that, and among these stores were cases of Scotch whiskey. A number of us sat around there drinking this Scotch whiskey and kind of looking things over and estimating how long the battle would continue and also feeling greatly relieved that we had been able to come this far and to have fared as well as we did." Johnson's best friend, T4g. Ervin D. "Dale" Deadmond, however, was pessimistic and convinced that he was going to get killed. Forty years later, Johnson remembered, "I can see him clearly now, just as though it were yesterday. He's sitting on a box and I'm down on the ground, and he has a mess cup with Scotch whiskey in it. He's drinking and we're talking, and I say to him, 'Well, Dale, how do you feel now? You know the worst is over. We're just about at the end of the island. It's only a matter of another few days and it's over. . . . Don't you feel you're going to make it?'" According to Johnson, Dale "kinda laughed, smiled" and said, "I don't think I'm going to make it." The next day he was killed during the Japanese Banzai attack.

At 1520 on July 6, Major General Griner telephoned Colonel Bishop and directed him to commit his reserve battalion, the 1st Battalion, 105th Infantry, on the line with the 2d Battalion, 105th Infantry. The two battalions were to bypass Hara-Kiri Gulch, which would be contained by the 3d Battalion, 105th, and move to the beach approximately 1,200 yards past RJ 2. G Company, 2d Battalion, in the coconut grove ready to attack, would be attached to the 3d Battalion, 105th, move to the right, and throw a blocking line across the mouth of Hara-Kiri Gulch to prevent the Japanese from attacking the two assault battalions as they moved north. Bishop objected to committing his reserves at such a late hour and argued that the two battalions would not have time to prepare a proper perimeter defense. His objection was overruled and O'Brien received orders to report to the 105th Regimental CP at 1530. Before going to the CP, he alerted his battalion to prepare for a movement to the front about 2,000 yards away.

At 105th Regimental Headquarters, O'Brien was told to move into the line with all three rifle companies abreast, but with C Company on the right, echeloned to the rear. Company A on the left and Company B in the center were to move straight to the objective, the beach about 1,200 yards south of Makunsha, bypassing the enemy strongpoint at Hara-Kiri Gulch. C Company was to cover this advance by attacking the cliffs north of the gulch with the objective of diverting as much fire as possible from the main attack on the plain. To make room for the 1st Battalion on the plain, the 2d Battalion of the 105th would move Company F back around the rear of Company E to the left of the regimental line, where it would again take up a position between the railroad tracks and the beach. Company G in the coconut grove, under the command of Captain Olander, would be attached to the 3d Battalion, 105th. G Company's assignment was to swing on its right flank across the western mouth of Hara-Kiri Gulch, pivot to its right, and contain the enemy in the gulch, thereby protecting the rear of the 1st Battalion's advance. The next morning the 3d Battalion of the 105th would mop up the enemy isolated in Hara-Kiri Gulch.

When O'Brien returned from regimental headquarters to the 1st Battalion CP, his face was grim. First Lieutenant Francois V. Albanese, his S-4, and a close friend, was there waiting for him. He had a look on his face "that I will never forget," Albanese said. He could tell that O'Brien was not happy with the order to move up, because darkness was approaching and it would be dangerous and difficult to make such a movement at night. Nevertheless, because the order had been initiated by division, O'Brien knew he had to comply or be relieved of his command. Albanese offered to move his supply vehicles up to the front lines with the rifle companies, but O'Brien said no. It would simply add to the confusion. He was ordered to stay about 1,000 yards behind the front lines, ready to bring up supplies and ammunition when needed. The supply officer then provided the 1st Battalion troops with enough ammunition, food, and water to handle a normal combat situation. No one had any idea at the time that the Japanese were about to launch the biggest Banzai attack ever mounted against American troops in the Pacific campaign.

Bill O'Brien was an aggressive officer and had twice led his battalion in rapid and important advances during the Saipan battle. On the afternoon of July 6, he had his battalion up and moving even before he knew its mission. As he briefed his staff and company commanders about the forthcoming attack, his apprehension over the role that had been assigned to his battalion was apparent. Captain Ackerman, of Company A recalled that "Obie was nervous and restless, as usual. He drew a picture for us and told Dick [Capt. Ryan of Company B] and I that no matter what else happened, we were to keep going. 'It's the old end run all over again. Whenever they get a job nobody else can do, we have to do it. Sooner or later we're going to get caught and this may be it,'" said O'Brien. He further ordered, "Disregard any enemy fire you encounter. We must reach our objective before dark." Sergeant John Domanowski of B Company remembers O'Brien talking to Captain Ryan, "Whatever you do, don't stop—keep moving, keep moving! I can still see the colonel's radioman with him at his side." Sergeant John A. Sidur of Company B recalls hearing Lieutenant Colonel O'Brien say, "Anyone would be lucky to get back alive."

By 1645 on July 6, each of the rifle companies of the 1st Battalion was in line. After spending approximately thirty minutes resupplying and reorganizing, the 1st Battalion moved off at 1715 in a coordinated attack. Company A, under Captain Ackerman, was the 1st Battalion's left wing. It moved out rapidly with two platoons abreast from the road in front of the coconut grove. The attack progressed rapidly for the first 150–200 yards against relatively light opposition. The men were running across the open ground even though Ackerman had ordered them to move by leaps and bounds from one point of shelter to another. At the ditch in front of the coconut grove, which had caused so much trouble all day, A Company's right platoon encountered a nest of fifteen to twenty Japanese. Some were wounded and others were trying to hide from Dorey's tank fire by hugging the walls of the trench on the near side. Ackerman's men waded into the ditch with bayonets and knives. For twenty minutes, a sharp hand-to-hand fight took place, wiping out the Japanese defenders. No prisoners were taken.

Company A moved forward across the ditch and on a diagonal toward the beach for a distance of 500 yards. In spite of increasingly heavy Japanese machine-gun fire from the cliffs on the right, Ackerman urged his men to keep moving ahead. Members of the 165th OP on Hill 721 were close enough to see the men of the 105th in a long skirmish line pushing along the level ground. Lieutenant Colonel Lewis R. Rock of the 4th Division, who was attached to the 165th Infantry as liaison officer, remarked to his superiors, "The 105th has broken through. They're going a mile a minute up the island and they will be in Makunsha in about twenty minutes. They're all over the place. This looks like the end."

Corporal Eddie Beaudoin of Troy, New York, assigned to the Medical Detachment, 105th, moved up that day along the Tanapag Plain with the 1st Battalion, 105th Headquarters Detachment. He remembers that the enemy machine-gun fire was heavy: "The machine-gun fire went by my ear; it sounded like a bee's nest." They moved up three or four hundred yards until enemy fire forced them to stop. Corporal Beaudoin recalled that O'Brien was running right in front of him as they moved up the plain, and that he had two bottles of scotch in his back pocket from the cache Sergeant Johnson found at Flores Point.

After advancing 500 yards beyond the ditch, Company A began receiving enemy fire from the front. Ackerman halted his men to see where the fire was coming from. Directly ahead there was a small house and a little stone building that might have been a stable filled with Japanese snipers. He sent two Pfc's from Sergeant Giuffre's squad, Joseph S. Jarosewicz and Frank N. Saetes, to investigate the situation, while the rest of the company waited. Saetes (known as "Greek") fired his BAR into the bottom part of the house while Jarosewicz crept forward and slipped a grenade under the floor. While Saetes was trying to light the straw of the roof with a match, the grenade came flying back and landed at his feet where it exploded, wounding him severely. He later died of wounds to his legs. Ackerman then ordered two more men forward to attack the house. Staff Sergeant Cleo B. Dickey walked boldly into the front door of the house and, with his rifle, killed one of the snipers and wounded another. Technical Sergeant E. Hermans, a cook assigned to A Company, then set the house on fire, driving out the remaining Japanese who were then killed by Company A riflemen. It was now almost 1800, less than an hour until darkness.

Company B, 105th Infantry, commanded by Captain Ryan, then came up on the right of Company A and sought cover from the enemy machine-gun fire coming from the cliffs on the right. He had moved his men forward by short leaps and bounds, but had kept well abreast of A Company. Sergeant John Domanowski of Company B remembered the advance that day: "A Company and C Company are on our flanks and we are moving forward at a pretty good pace—almost double time. The attack is on. A lot of firing is going on and we have the Japs on the run." The Japanese were retreating as their line was broken. After Company A was held up, Ryan ordered his 1st Platoon to set up two light machine guns on the right flank to keep the Japanese guns on the cliffs occupied. This only increased the rate of the Japanese fire, causing additional casualties to Companies A and B.

While Ackerman and Ryan were deciding what to do next, Capt. Emmett Catlin, the S-3, came running up from the coconut grove to find out what was holding up the advance. Rather than authorizing a patrol to deal with the enemy machine-gun emplacements, he emphasized that Lieutenant Colonel O'Brien wanted the whole battalion to move forward as quickly as possible. Just as Catlin gave this order, a shot rang out hitting Ryan in the head and killing him instantly. Ryan's death was a tremendous blow to O'Brien. In the years they had served together, he and Ryan had developed a close personal and professional relationship. Upon his death, command of Company B passed to 1st Lt. Hugh P. King from Hewlett, Long Island, who would be killed the next day in the Japanese *Gyokusai* attack.

During its advance, Company C of the 1st Battalion, under the command of First Lieutenant Tougaw, had been subject to direct, heavy enemy machine-gun fire from the cliffs above the plain, as well as from the Japanese machine guns atop the little knoll north of the coconut grove (the location that had previously held up K Company of the 165th, and G Company of the 2d Battalion). Mindful of O'Brien's instructions to continue moving forward, Tougaw ordered his men to keep going in spite of the enemy fire. Up on the cliffs, the Japanese had cleverly set up two machine guns about ten yards apart at the mouth of a cave near the entrance to Hara-Kiri Gulch. The two guns interdicted a stretch of open ground over which C Company had to advance. To minimize the effect of American fire on the position, the Japanese had formed relays consisting of thirty men that served the two machine guns at the mouth of the cave. Japanese soldiers would run pell-mell out of the cave, perform a baseball-type hook slide under the machine gun, fire off a few bursts at C Company, and then roll down into the shelter of a little ditch out of sight. Each man would then crawl back into the shelter of the cave and take his place at the end of the line ready to repeat the process. The system was arranged so that the two guns were not fired in any particular order; it was impossible to tell which gun would be fired first.

Technical Sergeant Ralph N. Gannaway, twenty-seven, of Fort Worth, Texas, in command of the 1st Platoon, C Company, 105th, figured out a way to solve the problem. He ordered his men to lie prone on the ground. One-half of the platoon would watch one gun; the other half, the other. Every time a Japanese soldier popped over the horizon, one of Gannaway's men picked him off. He later said that the Japanese "just couldn't seem to realize what was happening. They kept right on coming at the guns until they were all dead." Lieutenant Colonel O'Brien, who at the time was in the coconut grove not far from the Company C position, sent up an SPM to deal with the two machine guns. After the SPM fired one round, which scored a direct hit on one of the Japanese coming out to man the guns, the SPM vehicle moved off up the plain toward where A and B Companies of the 1st Battalion, 105th, had advanced.

When the Japanese stopped running out to the two machine guns, Sergeant Gannaway decided to assault the position. Three riflemen from the 1st Platoon of Company C—Pfc. Irvin A. George (who was killed the next day), Pvt. Harold L. Peterson, and Pfc. Robert J. Jones—volunteered. They reached the top of the knoll where they could look down into the trench, almost at the point where it entered the cave. There the three men encountered several Japanese hiding in the ditch. A fierce firefight at point-blank range ensued for the next two to three minutes. The three Americans were out-numbered, and after Jones was wounded in the face, Gannaway ordered the men to withdraw out of range. Gannaway left SSgt. Raymond C. Norder to hold the position while he went back to the battalion CP to bring up an SPM. (Norder would be killed the following day during the *Gyokusai* attack.)

First Lieutenant Bernard Tougaw, with C Company's 3d Platoon, the Weapons Platoon, and the Headquarters Detachment, continued to move forward pursuant to O'Brien's orders. In Gannaway's absence, First Lieutenant Tougaw contacted Norder and asked why the 1st and 2d Platoons had not moved forward pursuant to O'Brien's instructions. Tougaw was upset since it was now near 1830 and the rest of the battalion had already started to dig in for the night—darkness was only a half hour away. He ordered Norder to bring the 2d Platoon forward, and Gannaway's 1st Platoon moved up as soon as it cleaned out the pockets of enemy soldiers in the ditch.

The 1st Platoon, meanwhile, became engaged in a heavy, forty-five-minute firefight with the Japanese in a trench not thirty yards away. Darkness came and the fight continued, with both sides using every possible weapon—grenades, rifles, and machine guns. Three Americans were hit: Pfc. Emil S. Zimandel was shot in the head and killed and two other men were hit by grenade fragments, including Pvt. Max O. French, an acting staff sergeant and one of Gannaway's acting squad leaders. French was knocked unconscious, making it difficult to evacuate him to the 1st Battalion perimeter. A few minutes after dark, an SPM that Gannaway had ordered came upon the scene and proceeded to pour howitzer shells from forty yards away, eventually wiping out the enemy's position. While Gannaway was on a patrol looking for Tougaw, SSgt. Frederick A. Westlake, who had been left in charge of the 1st Platoon, received a radio message from Tougaw ordering him to bring the 1st Platoon, C Company, forward to join the rest of the company immediately. He stated that he would do so, but that he first had to evacuate the platoon's wounded to the aid station, which had just been moved from the coconut grove to the new battalion perimeter. Westlake and one of his men carried

Private French to the coconut grove, where he was put aboard a jeep and transported to the aid station. Westlake then ordered the 1st Platoon to move forward in the darkness to join the rest of C Company. By moving to the railroad tracks and following them north, he was able to locate the C Company position on the perimeter by 2100.

At 1715 the 2d Battalion, 105th (with the exception of G Company, which had been assigned to block the mouth of Hara-Kiri Gulch), moved forward in the assault with the 1st Battalion, 105th, under O'Brien. Joining Companies E and F in the advance were most of H Company, the heavy weapons company, and Headquarters Company. Major McCarthy placed Company F on the 2d Battalion left, between the beach and the road. Company E's line was extended from there to the railroad tracks. Due to the effective work of Dorey's tanks in front of the battalion position just thirty minutes before, E Company had an easy time advancing forward to the new perimeter position. Staff Sergeant Angelo Nicoletti recalled: "We had to walk across that ditch on dead Japs. There were so many of them you couldn't find the ground. I must have stepped on about ten of them myself." By 1800, E Company was at its objective and waited for the 1st Battalion, 105th, on the right and F Company on its left, to come up to the front line.

F Company, 2d Battalion, 105th, arrived at the perimeter objective about ten minutes later, having been held up by a series of pillboxes and dugouts that dotted the beach. Each had to be checked out. Just before reaching the objective, the 3d Platoon, moving up next to the road, encountered a shelter occupied by three Japanese soldiers. Technical Sergeant John W. Kuder, twenty-four, of Schenectady, New York, and one other man were wounded by a grenade they had thrown into the shelter that the Japanese had thrown back. Though it appeared that Kuder was not wounded seriously, he died on July 6. Other soldiers dispatched the enemy in the shelter.

Late in the afternoon of July 6, the 2d Platoon of the Antitank Company, attached to the 2d Battalion, commanded by 2d Lt. Robert D. Young, was ordered to move up from the vicinity of the 105th CP to support the 2d Battalion on the perimeter. Sergeant W. Taylor Hudson from Louisville, Kentucky, recalled where Major

McCarthy placed the Antitank Platoon that night: "Since the base units had already established their perimeter for night defense, we were told to dig in about fifty yards to the rear of one of the rifle companies. This meant we would be unable to fire to our front since our own troops were forward of us. Lieutenant Young spread the guns out in a line separated by several yards and had each squad establish its own defense positions." The 1st Squad, under SSgt. John H. Schlagenhauf was on the left and the 3d Squad, led by SSgt. Robert Hott, was on the right. The platoon headquarters was placed in the rear of 2d Squad, commanded by SSgt. Richard C. Horn. Lieutenant Young, Staff Sergeant Hudson, and Staff Sergeant Horn shared a foxhole slightly behind the gun itself, manned by three men, with the rest of the squad on either side of the gun. Hudson recalled, "All were securely dug in, the ground here being deeper and softer than most of our previous locations. After a cold meal of C rations and water, we tried to get some sleep."

While the 1st and 2d Battalions of the 105th were moving up along the plain, G Company, 2d Battalion, was positioned on the right flank of the coastal plain at the edge of the coconut grove. Captain Frank Olander began moving the company to the mouth of Hara-Kiri Gulch to prevent the Japanese from attacking the rear and right flank of the advancing 1st and 2d Battalions. After moving his men out of the coconut grove, Olander assembled them just south of RJ 64, the cross-island highway that ran from the beach area to the ridge where Company L, 3d Battalion, 105th, was located. Olander, accompanied by his radioman and a single rifleman, then set out on a personal reconnaissance of the area into which G Company was to move. He moved along a deep ditch on the side of the road. Twenty yards from where he started, Olander came across a burned-out American tank destroyed that morning by the enemy. Finding no enemy in the vicinity, he shouted back to his radioman to order the 1st Platoon forward, which moved out immediately down the road. Halfway to the burned-out tank, the Japanese, hidden in the bushes alongside the road, opened up with rifle and machine-gun fire from both sides of the road, hitting two men and pinning down the platoon. Olander, who was not affected by the enemy fire, used his radio to order his 2d and 3d Platoons to move up to support the advance. The 2d Platoon was to move to the high ground, while the 3d Platoon was to go into the area below the hairpin turn.

While moving up with the 2d Platoon to the high ground, 2d Lt. Arthur Hansen of Council Bluffs, Iowa, was crawling alongside of 1st Lt. George H. O'Donnell when a burst of enemy machine-gun fire almost blew his rear end off and riddled his canteen. O'Donnell remembered, "About 1700 we were trying to clean out a particularly bad hilly and rocky place, so that we could get set for the night. Our tanks had been fighting up the draw just below us. It was here that I had my closest call. We had just killed a Jap inside a large hollow stump, and I moved around it, to make doubly sure that he was out of the picture—when I spotted two other suspicious places, about ten yards away. I put about four shots into the one, when the other one opened up on me with a machine gun! Needless to say, I moved fast, and ducked behind the hollow stump. But, before I reached this spot, one bullet had hit the inside part of my canteen [left side] and a second one had gone right through it! I lost a half canteen of water, and decided to drink the remainder so I wouldn't lose it all. But first, I sat, watching this particular spot for half an hour, and no sooner had I started to drink, than a Jap took off, on the run! By the time I had gotten a bead on him, however, he had dropped over the bank and down into the draw. Well, I still have the canteen since it was the one that I was issued back in Troy in 1940, and am keeping it as one of my souvenirs."

Staff Sergeant Edward J. Wojcicki, platoon sergeant for the 3d Platoon, G Company, 2d Battalion, had been working his men forward along the ditch below the road that led to Hara-Kiri Gulch. He was halfway to where Olander was located when he ordered the platoon to come forward through the brush to his position on the double. As soon as they left the ditch, they ran into a large Japanese patrol hiding in the bushes. Machine guns opened up, grenades began exploding, and men began running off in all directions. A brisk hand-to-hand fight ensued. Olander, a short distance away from the action, fired his carbine, then used it as a club against the enemy until it broke. He then picked up a saber, which he also put to good use on the enemy. In the furious melee that raged for the next fifteen minutes, two of Wojcicki's men—Pfc. James Messer and Pfc. Vernon Bugg—were killed. Sergeant Benjamin J. Drenzek was wounded four different times. On three separate occasions, his men killed the Japanese soldiers who were trying to carry Drenzek away. After the last attempt to kidnap the wounded man, Olander ordered Wojcicki to withdraw, and all the platoons of G Company were pulled back to the west along the road to the point from which they had started earlier in the day.

After advising Lieutenant Colonel Bradt that he did not think that it was possible for G Company to build up a line across the mouth of Hara-Kiri Gulch, Olander was given permission to dig in for the night on the high ground overlooking RJ 64. From there, he hoped to be able to interdict enemy movement from the mouth of the gulch. During the establishment of its perimeter that evening, G Company was constantly harassed by enemy machine-gun fire from across Hara-Kiri Gulch. Olander spotted the gun in a cave on the opposite wall and called up a volunteer, Pvt. Joseph F. Kinyone, to fire a bazooka round at this position. Although 1st Lt. Donald P. Spiering, twenty-six, of Beaverton, Oregon, told Kinyone to keep his head down, he wanted to take one more shot with the bazooka. As soon as he rose up to fire, he was killed by an enemy rifle bullet.

16 Prelude to Gyokusai

By 1810 on July 6, the 2d Battalion, 105th (less Company G), had taken up night positions between the coast road and the sugar cane railroad about 1,200 yards south of Makunsha and about 1,200 yards northeast of where RJ 2 met the coast road. The faulty maps Major McCarthy and Captain Smith used incorrectly showed that the battalion had reached its objective. The 2d Battalion was almost 200 yards beyond its original objective. Nevertheless, after conferring with his company commanders, McCarthy gave the order to dig in for the night between the coast road and the railroad tracks. Although the local maps showed the coast road and the railroad to be quite close together, the road actually was forty to fifty yards in from the beach and the railroad was fifty yards or so inland from the road.

The defensive perimeter prepared by the 2d Battalion was a good one. To the front was a small swale extending some seventy-five yards out and traversed the whole area from the sea to the cliffs. The swale did not exceed five feet in depth at any one place and there was no vegetation of any kind. On the opposite side to the north, there was a thick tangle of small bush-like trees four to five feet in height. This wooded belt extended all across the front of this position. McCarthy had picked the best available terrain feature for the battalion's defense. To attack, any enemy coming from the north had to emerge from the wooded area and cross seventy-five yards of low, open ground. The terrain behind the perimeter, over which the 2d Battalion had advanced, was a rolling plain, offering little cover or concealment. At the point where F Company's advance stopped, there was a huge clump of bushes that filled the space between the coast road and the beach.

The battalion's perimeter was oblong in shape and tightly drawn, occupying the fifty-yard space between the railroad right of way and the coast road. McCarthy decided not to extend the perimeter to the beach, which was only about fifty yards away. Instead, he posted two men from Headquarters Company armed with carbines to take a camouflaged position in the bushes, filling the space between the road and the beach. They had orders to report any signs of enemy movement along the beach. Company E's 1st and 2d Platoons were dug in across the front or north side of the perimeter and the 3d Platoon of E Company was bent back along the railroad track, forming one half of the east side of the perimeter. F Company's 2d Platoon occupied the other half of the perimeter's east side; the back or south side was held by the two other platoons of F Company; and the west or coastal side was held by Headquarters Company. The mortars of both rifle companies as well as those of H Company occupied the center of the perimeter along with 2d Battalion Headquarters and most of the battalion's vehicles. Private First Class Seymour Krawetz from Skokie, Illinois, a member of F Company, recalled: "It was just before sunset July 6 when we dug into our night defensive position. A little after it turned dark we were told that the 3d Battalion was under a counterattack. Since they were on a hill, the attackers had to come up a slope and were repelled."

McCarthy placed two of the battalion's three antitank guns on the north side of the perimeter—one bearing on the road to Makunsha and one covering the plains to the east toward Paradise Valley—assuming that the main enemy threat would come down either the road or railroad from the north, or across the plains from Paradise Valley. At the time he was devising the defenses of the perimeter, it was assumed that the 1st Battalion, 105th, would drive to the beach north of the 2d Battalion's position and thus be able to intercept any enemy thrust from the north. His concern, therefore, was to protect the open side of the perimeter on the east. With this in mind, a third antitank gun was placed on the southeast corner of the perimeter also covering the plain in the direction of Paradise Valley. All three antitank guns were positioned about fifty yards to the rear of the entrenched rifle companies. The two forward antitank guns were flanked on each side by E and F Companies' light machine guns. The third antitank gun facing southeast was flanked by two heavy machine guns from H Company. McCarthy also ordered that all BAR gunners be positioned on the north or east side of the perimeter.

Meanwhile, the 1st Battalion, 105th Infantry, arrived at the front about 1830. After a short conference with his company commanders, O'Brien ordered the battalion to advance another one hundred yards, moving diagonally across the front of 2d Battalion's perimeter toward the beach and on the other side of the swale. O'Brien with the frontline companies, ordered the advance halted about 150 yards from the beach. He did not want to advance any farther until patrols investigated the trees to the front. Although they did not locate any enemy, he nevertheless was concerned that digging in on the beach in the midst of thick tree growth would deprive his men of clear fields of fire. Accordingly, after consulting with Major McCarthy, he decided to pull his battalion back from the tree line and tie in for the night with the 2d Battalion's perimeter on the south side of the swale. The next morning the 1st Battalion could move up the beach toward Makunsha as planned.

O'Brien's battalion occupied the ground on the east side of the railroad tracks. No attempt was made to tie in with G Company located on high ground 500–600 yards to the right. Both battalion commanders did not consider it feasible to extend the line that far. Instead of oblong-shaped, the 1st Battalion's perimeter was more rainbow-shaped. Company A dug in on flat ground on the north side of the perimeter, tying in with the 3d Platoon, E Company, 2d Battalion, along the railroad tracks and extending 100 yards to the east. B Company was next to A Company along the center of the perimeter to the right of the railroad tracks. The men dug three-men–square foxholes, in which one man took turns standing guard while the other two slept.

C Company was late in arriving at the perimeter. The 1st Platoon was still fighting near Hara-Kiri Gulch and did not arrive until 2100. When it finally got into position, digging in well after dark, its line extended well south of where it was supposed to be and missed tying in with F Company, 2d Battalion, by about fifty yards. C Company did, however, anchor its position along the railroad tracks. Nevertheless, the rear elements of C Company were dug in almost

100 yards behind the 1st Battalion's front lines. This had severe consequences the next morning, when some men were caught asleep in their foxholes. They were so far behind the front lines that the sentries on duty were not able to give adequate warnings until the Japa-nese had broken through. By that time, it was too late; many C Company men were either killed in their foxholes or forced to withdraw.

The 1st Battalion CP was set up inside the perimeter approximately in the middle. Those present included: O'Brien; Capt. Butkas, executive officer; Capt. Emmett Catlin, S-3; Sgt. Robert Smith, liaison from the 249th Field Artillery Battalion; Sgt. Ronald Johnson, communications sergeant; Cpl. Joseph O'Keefe, medic; and Corporal Beaudoin, another medic. First Lieutenant Luke Hammond, S-2, dug his foxhole next to a concrete cistern (probably used as a watering point for trains) next to the sugar cane railroad track.

To cover the approximately 500-yard gap between the 1st Battalion on the left and G Company, 2d Battalion, in the hills to the right, O'Brien moved the 1st Battalion's three antitank guns to the front of the perimeter facing north and east. The guns were located just a little behind the front lines and about twenty-five yards in front of the 1st Battalion CP. They were aimed at the cliffs just north of Hara-Kiri Gulch. All four of D Company's heavy machine guns were also placed along this section of the perimeter. A Company's two light machine guns faced north—one covering the railroad track and another in the ruins of a little concrete building covering the swale to the front. B Company's two light machine guns were placed on the arc, one facing Paradise Valley and the other facing the cliffs. C Company's light machine guns were not put into place until after dark, but the consensus of the men interviewed by Captain Love was that they most likely faced east.

In retrospect, the combined perimeter defense did present problems for the two battalions. First, two rifle platoons from the 2d Battalion, one from Company E and one from Company F, were now inside the combined perimeter, losing firepower. Second, one of 2d Battalion's antitank guns and H Company's heavy machine guns were now inside the combined perimeter; their fear of hitting friendly forces inhibited their ability to fire. Company A, 1st Battalion, in particular, was pinned down each time the H Company guns opened fire. Later in the evening, when word was received that a counterattack was expected, the heavy machine guns were moved up onto the railroad tracks.

Behind the combined perimeter, there were several other military units that would be affected by the *Gyokusai* attack the next morning. The 105th Infantry CP was located approximately 2,000 yards behind the front lines, positioned between the highway and the beach in a clump of trees overlooking an open field to the north. Colonel Bishop's CP was in a concrete shelter that once served as a Japanese air raid dugout as part of the Tanapag Harbor defenses. The field was devoid of grass and literally cut to pieces with trench systems, foxholes, and spider holes. The field was low lying and often covered by water, and on July 6, it was a sea of thick, heavy mud. There was nothing behind the Headquarters Company position except thick brush and bushes.

The north end of the field in front of the Regimental CP dipped into a creek that later became known as "Bloody Run." The creek was between ten and fifteen yards wide at the water's edge and ran inland for 300–400 yards. The coast road crossed the stream on a concrete bridge about twelve feet wide and seventy-five yards from the beach. On both sides, east and west of the road, there were several large trees. The distance from the 105th Regimental CP to Bloody Run was about 400 yards. The town of Tanapag, still largely intact, was 800 yards north of the 105th CP and about 1,400 yards south of the combined perimeter. By 2100 on July 6, telephone lines connecting the two battalions and the 105th Regimental CP were functioning. Private First Class George F. Herman of Headquarters Company from Chicago, Illinois, repaired a break in the wire that ran to 1st Battalion. He remembered, "Nobody worried about who, what, or where. It was a twenty-four-hour-a-day job. We laid wire, repaired wire, and checked areas around the CP." The single, narrow road that supplied the two entrenched battalions was extremely congested by vehicles moving to and from to supply their respective units.

At 1700 on July 6, the 3d and 4th Battalions from the 10th Marine Artillery Regiment came up on the coast road from the direction of Garapan and set up a position about 1,200 yards south of the entrenched 1st and 2d Battalions, 105th. The two marine battalions were to support the 4th Division, which was then mopping up the enemy from Makunsha north to Marpi Point. No one from these marine units notified 27th Division Headquarters or the 105th of their position, nor did they obtain permission from the army units to fire so close to the army's front lines or use the already congested single supply road providing the three battalions of the 105th with supplies and ammunition. No one in the 27th Division or in the batteries were warned by marine higher headquarters that a Japanese counterattack was imminent.

The 4th Marine Battalion moved into a position along the road directly south of the 105th CP. Their constant firing to support the 4th Division mop-up operations directly interfered with the 105th's operation and communications efforts. Colonel Bishop said later, "The muzzles were hanging right out in the road." All traffic up and down the main supply highway had to stop each time the guns fired, and the congestion along the road became so severe that Bishop was finally forced to order the 4th FA Battalion commander to move away from the road.

The 3d FA Battalion, positioned to the right of the coastal road, about 1,400 yards behind the front line battalions of the 105th Infantry, did not bother to dig in for the night. They set up their howitzers in the trees just across Bloody Run, directly behind the 500–600 yard gap between the right flank of the 1st Battalion, and Company G, 2d Battalion. The three 3d Battalion batteries were on the front lines, and although their guns were registered on various points across the island, there is no evidence that they ever fired again that night or the next morning. Nor did they make any effort to register their guns to protect the large gap between the right flank of the 1st Battalion and G Company. Instead of digging foxholes, the marines set up tents, lit campfires, and slept in cots.

Although there was a good deal of firing on both sides after darkness fell on the evening of July 6, there also was a sense of euphoria among the American troops. Many believed that the main body of the Japanese on Saipan had been destroyed and that only mop-up operations remained to be completed. Forward artillery observers on the heights above the plain where the 1st and 2d Battalions, 105th, had dug in for the night had noticed earlier that the marine infantry battalions that had been moving north toward Makunsha began to withdraw, leaving the area open to enemy infiltration. Sergeant Frank C. Cimaszewski from New York, a forward observer for the 106th Field Artillery, which fired 155mm howitzers, was assigned to provide supporting fire for the marines. He recalled that "Before the Banzai charge, we got a report that all that was left was mop-up operations; the marines pulled their infantry from the line and left it up to the 27th to carry the main thrust, to so called, mop-up operations. . . . We were located on a high hill or mountain, when the charge overran the line, so we had a grandstand view of the Banzai charge. When we requested infantry support, who came up was two machine guns manned by armed personnel from the 27th. I never saw a marine during the charge." It was widely believed that the marine units were withdrawn by Lt. Gen. Holland M. Smith so they would be rested for other invasions.

Even the staff officers at the 105th CP believed that remaining enemy resistance would be minimal the next day. Sergeant Ronald Johnson recalled that "The intelligence which they [1st Battalion, 105th Infantry] had [the] day before [the] Banzai attack was that [the] Japanese had been reduced to a small force incapable of withstanding an attack. [We were] led to believe it was only a matter of two or three days of mopping up, . . . so I think at that point our guard was down, so to speak, because we believed that the force we were facing was not very formidable. And as a matter of fact, our intelligence was wrong, because the next morning they hit us with far more than we realized were there." Long after the Saipan battle, Johnson remembered another factor that he thought indicated overconfidence on the part of the American high command. He recalled: "This was the first night that I can remember that we did not have overnight artillery fire all night long. Prior to this time, we had artillery fire—particularly we had the star bursts/star shells that would light up the landscape so that the front lines were always fairly well lighted. But this particular night, aside from the fact that it was raining and dark in the earlier part of the evening, we had no such support. Again I attribute that to this overconfidence, this underestimating the forces that remained."

The night before the fatal Japanese attack was quite uncomfortable for the men of the 105th up on the front lines. Rain fell in torrents. Foxholes, which had been dug under the fire of Japanese guns, were flooded. Sleep was impossible. But there was time for reverie. When Lieutenant Colonel O'Brien and Sergeant Johnson finished digging their slit trenches that evening, Johnson recalled that O'Brien, "sat down on the lip of his slit trench and reached across the front of his fatigues and took his wallet out of his front pocket. He opened it up, and he looked at it for some time. I'm still digging, but I'm aware of what he's doing. And then, quite unexpectedly, he hands his wallet to me and says, 'That is what I am fighting for.' I look in his wallet, and there is a picture of his wife and young son."

Though the Americans on Saipan called the mass Japanese counterattack on the morning of July 7 a *Banzai Raid* or *Sake Attack,* it is more properly described as a *Gyokusai* attack. General Saito knew that only the emperor could order a *Gyokusai* attack, so it's generally believed he fabricated a story about a Japanese plane dropping a personal note from the emperor.

The decision to launch a *Gyokusai* attack was decided upon on the evening of July 5 at a ceremonial dinner held in Saito's cave headquarters in Paradise Valley. Vice Admiral Chuichi Nagumo, Saipan's naval commander, attended the dinner, which lasted all night. At 0800 on the morning of July 6, Lieutenant General Saito assembled all his staff officers and read his final message addressed to all men defending Saipan. Among other things, the message stated: "For more than twenty days since the American Devils attacked, the officers, men, and civilian employees of the Imperial Army and Navy on this island have fought well and bravely. . . . We have not been able to utilize fully the terrain. We have fought in unison up to the present time but now we have no materials with which to fight and our artillery for attack has been completely destroyed. . . . Despite the bitterness of defeat, we pledge, 'Seven lives to repay our country. . . .'" General Saito went on, "The barbarous attack of the enemy is being continued. We are dying without avail under the violent shelling and bombing. Whether we attack or whether we stay here where we are, there is only death. . . . I will advance with those who remain to deliver still another blow to the American Devils, and leave my bones on Saipan as a bulwark of the Pacific. . . . Follow me!"

He then called in messengers and dispatched them to all parts of the island with copies of his farewell message. On the evening of July 6, all troops were to assemble in Makunsha, Marpi Point, Paradise Valley, and Hara-Kiri Gulch, beginning at 1800. From those places, they were to form one large group at Makunsha and then launch the all-out attack on the American lines at 2200. Saito and Nagumo planned a three-pronged attack that would carry as far south as Aslito Airfield. One prong was to go through Paradise Valley, across the island, and then down the east coast. Another prong was to go over the mountains in the vicinity of the coconut grove to Charan Kanoa. The third group was to move down the beach along the Tanapag Plain. As it turned out, most Japanese attackers came in one huge mob along the railroad tracks down the west coast toward Tanapag Harbor.

In spite of his claim that he would "advance with those who remain to deliver still another blow to the American Devils," Saito was too feeble and too sick to lead the charge in person. After issuing the attack orders, he and Nagumo retired to their quarters and at 1000 on July 6, long before the attack was to take place, they both committed suicide in the traditional manner: First, they opened their stomachs with their ceremonial swords, and then their aides killed them with pistol shots to the head. Their bodies were then burned, although only partially, and then interred. American authorities later discovered the remains and took them to Charan Kanoa where they were buried with full military honors.

Shortly after dark on July 6, the Japanese began to assemble for the attack in the hills above Makunsha. The attacking force was drawn from almost every conceivable Japanese unit that had served on the island. Specific identifications of units made from Japanese dead included the 118th, 135th, and 136th Infantry Regiments, 43d Division Headquarters, 43d Field Hospital, 3d Independent Mountain Artillery Regiment, 16th Shipping Engineer Regiment, 9th Tank Regiment, 55th Naval Guard Force, 1st Yokusuka Special Naval Landing Force, and various other remnants. Some civilians, including one female whose body was found later, also joined the *Gyoku-sai* attack. All wounded soldiers who were not able to walk were either killed or, by order of the Japanese commanders, committed suicide using grenades. Japanese soldiers who were able to walk were armed with whatever weapons were available. There were not enough rifles, grenades, or machine guns, so many were given daggers or hunting knives. Japanese officers gave away their pistols and kept only their sabers. When these gave out, the men cut down bamboo poles and either sharpened the edges or attached pieces of metal to them to be used as spears. Evidence discovered after the attack showed that many of the attackers, in particular the Japanese civilian construction workers, had consumed large quantities of sake and beer before launching the attack and were drunk when they died.

The Japanese Naval Force left Marpi Point shortly after dark and made their way, in one long column, to rendezvous near Makunsha by 2200. As they passed along the road in a column three- or four-men wide, other and smaller groups joined them. It was estimated that when the head of the column approached Makunsha, the rear was just leaving Marpi Point. Although the Japanese enforced no march discipline whatsoever, their presence was never detected by 4th Division units that had responsibility for the area north of Makunsha. The 105th Infantry Operational Report for the evening of July 6 noted that "the additional regiment of marines who had been given the mission of closing the corridor to the North of Makunsha" had been unable to advance in its zone and reach its objective.

The *Gyokusai* attack was commanded by Col. Takuji Suzuki of the 135th Infantry Regiment, who most likely was one of the last high-ranking Japanese officers on the island. One of his first actions was to send out reconnaissance patrols to probe the American lines for weaknesses and gaps. They were at first composed of six or seven men, but later grew to as many as twenty. The patrols quickly discovered the large gap between the 1st Battalion of the 105th's right flank and G Company's position in the hills to the right. Once the attack was underway, Suzuki directed some of his units to move through the gap and make a rush for Tanapag Village. Other units were ordered to use the gap to get in behind the entrenched 1st and 2d Battalions, 105th. Probes of the combined perimeter of the 1st and 2d Battalions by Japanese patrols were frequent and their tactics maddening. Part of a patrol would creep up to the very edge of the bushes on the north side of the swale and, hidden from view, create a big commotion, yelling, singing, and running through the bushes to distract the entrenched Americans.

The 1st and 2d Battalions, dug in along the railroad tracks, and the 3d Battalion, dug in on the adjacent hills, were not aware of the Japanese preparations for attack, although there was a general sense of uneasiness as they probed the outer limits of the combined perimeter. To make matters worse, a heavy tropical downpour began. Sergeant Ronald Johnson recalled, "I was ill-prepared for this. I was full of misery from the scotch or maybe my diet or something, but anyway I was just miserable. . . . But the rain came down. And at this point the colonel said to me, 'Do you have a poncho?' . . . And I said, 'No. I don't. But I think there are a couple in the trailer on the jeep.' And he said, 'Do you think you could get one?' So I said, 'Well I don't know, but I'll try.'" Johnson went to the jeep fully aware that he was taking his life in his own hands. Luckily, Johnson safely retrieved the ponchos from the jeep and gave one to O'Brien.

At 2000, an hour after dark on Thursday, July 6, in the full moonlight, the 3d Battalion CP was startled to find a Japanese seaman of the 55th Naval Guard Force sleeping near the road where it was bivouacked. He was immediately captured and interrogated for half an hour. At 2030 the following message was passed on to 105th Headquarters: "Prisoner says that his unit has been ordered to attack at 2000 tonight. That all men alive at 1500 on July 7 must commit suicide." Upon receipt of this message, Maj. Malcolm M. Jameson, twenty-five, of Rockland County, New York, the S-2, ordered that the prisoner be taken by a detail from the 3d Battalion to the 27th Division POW collection point at Garapan for further interrogation. There the prisoner was questioned by intelligence officers, including

Lt. Benjamin Hazard, the 27th Division language officer, for several hours. The prisoner stated that he was a member of the 55th Naval Guard Force, and that on July 6 at 2000, there was to be an all-out counterattack on the American positions by all Japanese troops able to bear arms. The attack was to start from a road junction in the vicinity of the town of Matansa. It was then about 2100 on July 6. Brigadier General Ogden J. Ross, assistant division commander and acting chief of staff, received notification of the attack by Lt. Col. William M. Van Antwerp, forty-two, of Albany, New York, 27th Division G-2. Ross immediately notified 27th Division Artillery and each of the infantry rifle regiments, specifically ordering them to alert their battalions to be prepared to defend against an enemy counterattack.

Based on increased enemy activity to their front, the 1st and 2d Battalions already in the front lines knew that something was happening. In the area of the 3d Battalion near Hara-Kiri Gulch, numerous small Japanese counterattacks had been probing the American lines all through the night. At approximately 2000, while the 1st Battalion of the 105th was still digging in, Maj. Edward McCarthy, commander of the 2d Battalion, noticed a good deal of enemy activity ahead of his position in the town of Makunsha. He ordered his artillery, which had previously registered on the Makunsha area, to break up the enemy troop concentrations with heavy, persistent rounds of artillery fire. The effort was successful: The bombardment disorganized the enemy's forces and delayed the enemy's attack for several hours.

Shortly after 2100, O'Brien and McCarthy received a message from Brig. Gen. Ogden Ross stating they needed to be ready to repel a Japanese counterattack. The battalion commanders conferred and decided to shift the 2d Battalion's machine guns into a firing position atop the railroad tracks. The individual company commanders were then notified to prepare to repel a counterattack. Captain Ackerman went to the 1st Battalion CP and asked O'Brien if some of Company D's heavy machine guns could be shifted to a point where they could be brought to bear on the railroad track to the north. O'Brien told Ackerman to wait and immediately asked Lieutenant Colonel Jensen, the regimental executive officer, if there was any chance that additional forces could be brought forward to cover the gap between his right flank and G Company. Jensen responded that there were no additional troops available and that O'Brien would have to cover the gap with what he had. O'Brien then told Ackerman that he could not move any of Company D's guns at that time, but if any help came up in the meantime he would do so.

When Ackerman returned from his conference with Lieutenant Colonel O'Brien, it was sometime between 2115 and 2130. This was about the same time that the Japanese began assembling in the town of Makunsha, about 1,000 yards ahead of the front-line positions of the two battalions. First Sergeant Mario Occhienero, twenty-six, of Rome, New York, Company A, 1st Battalion, described what happened next:

> Captain Ackerman came back from seeing Colonel O'Brien, and he had just started to tell me about the machine guns. While he was talking, we began to hear this buzz. It was the damnedest noise I ever heard. I think you could describe it as a great big hive of bees. It kept getting louder and louder and then it began to sound like I guess the old Indian war dances did, sort of like a chant. All at once a couple of Japs busted out of the bushes to our front. Somebody shot them. That's when things got going in earnest.

Another member of the 105th, Pfc. Samuel Di Nova of Troy, New York, Company D, 1st Battalion, recalled hearing a big "commotion" in front of their machine-gun positions on the perimeter. Sergeant John Domanowski, of Company B, 1st Battalion, remembers talking that night with Sgt. Jay B. Hollifield from Blowing Rock, North Carolina, about Company B's exposed position. "We were told to dig in and stay where we were. Jay and I dug in and stood guard over the men while they slept. There was a lot of rumbling and it sounded like bees in a hive." Sergeant John Sidur of Cohoes, New York, with Company B on the front lines that night, also heard the buzz of the enemy forming to attack.

The noise and enemy activity to the front began to increase. Ackerman called in Capt. Bernard A. Toft, 1st Battalion forward observer

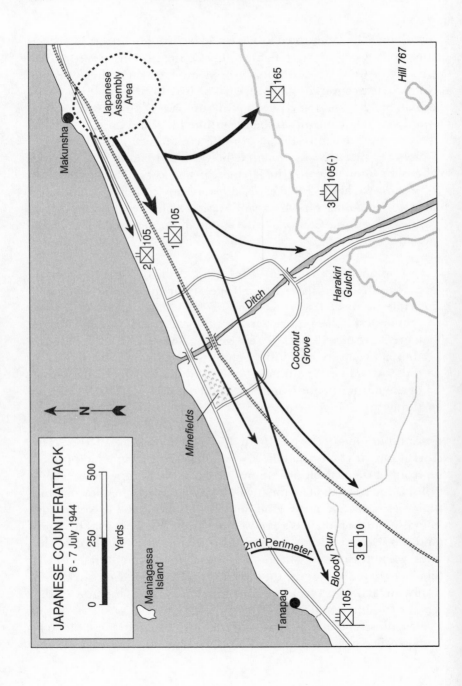

for the 249th Field Artillery Battalion, and together they charted interdiction fires along the railroad and coastal road in and above the Makunsha area to disrupt the enemy concentrations. Major McCarthy, who had previously registered the 2d Battalion's artillery in the same area, also ordered his guns to concentrate in the Makunsha area. Beginning at 2200 and ending shortly after 0700 the next morning, 27th Division Artillery fired 2,666 rounds of ammunition in the area immediately in front of the 1st and 2d Battalions. The 249th FA itself reported firing almost 2,000 rounds during approximately the same period. The fire was incessant and effective in delaying the Japanese attack from 2200 that evening until 0400 the next morning. Captured Japanese later stated that the artillery barrage completely disorganized the advancing column. Every few steps, the Japanese had to disperse and dive for cover. Nevertheless, the artillery did not stop the counterattack.

Starting at about 0300 on July 7, American artillery fire was directed at the area immediately in front of the defending two battalions of the 105th Infantry. When the Japanese attack began in earnest, Captain Toft who was with O'Brien, called in artillery fire to within 200 yards of the combined perimeter. Private First Class Charles McCullough of C Company, 1st Battalion, O'Brien's runner during most of the first part of the attack, said that Toft spent the first twenty minutes of the attack with O'Brien, adjusting fire on the incoming enemy hordes. Ackerman later said that fifteen minutes after his company was hit by the first wave of the attack, he called the 1st Battalion CP on his radio and talked with Toft. "For God's sake, Bernie, get that artillery in closer," he said. Toft replied that he already was within 150 yards of the line. Ackerman told him to pull it in to seventy-five yards of the company line. Toft made the adjustment, but then communications with the front ceased. The Japanese juggernaut just kept coming.

Sergeant Robert W. Smith, 249th Field Artillery Battalion, was the Liaison One sergeant at the 1st Battalion CP that fateful night. He recalls: "To start from the beginning, the Japs started to move and make a lot of noise on our front while it was still dark. Captain Toft called for battalion fire and after a short period of firing I felt the effect was good. It was shortly after this the Japs started to overrun our position. At this point Captain Toft became separated from us. Corporal Cotter, our radioman, was still with me. I called for our artillery to fall on us. I remember calling fifty over fire for effect. This means drop fifty feet and fire the battalion for effect. I also remember Colonel O'Brien was within twenty feet of our foxholes before our withdrawal. It was always necessary for our artillery section to stay close to Colonel O'Brien in case he wanted artillery fire on any special target."

The whole scene became a surrealistic nightmare. For the first time in the battle for Saipan, the Japanese began to use tracer and incendiary bullets. The men of the 105th who survived the battle stated afterward that the sky seemed to be filled with red, green, and yellow trails. Sometimes the pattern of colors showed white phosphorescence; other times a peculiar blue-colored bullet came sailing over now and then. For the men who witnessed and lived through it, the spectacle was probably the biggest and best fireworks display they had ever seen. Sam Di Nova of Company D recalled that at about 0400 a big flare went off in the area and "lit up the whole mountain."

17 Day of Hell

On July 7, held up by the American artillery fire, the main body of the Japanese force launched its attack from Makunsha at 0400. The entire Japanese force started south, following three general routes of advance. The main force went down the railroad tracks and spread out on each side for about twenty-five yards, hitting the 1st and 2d Battalions of the 105th with overwhelming force. A second sizable column went along the base of the cliffs at the edge of the plain through the gap between the 1st Battalion, 105th, and G Company of the 2d Battalion, and hit the elements of the 165th Infantry and the 3d Battalion of the 105th Infantry on the high ground above the plain. The third column, which was much smaller, came straight down the beach right at the water's edge, skirting the positions of the 2d Battalion. Once the combined perimeter of the 1st and 2d Battalions of the 105th was overrun, the Japanese attacking columns spread out over the entire field. Some joined the attacks on the combined perimeter; others hit the marine artillery battalions in the trees near Bloody Run; and large numbers branched off to the east and hit G Company. They moved into the area between G Company and the 3d Battalion CP, cutting off communications. After overrunning the 3d Battalion of the 10th Marine Artillery Regiment, the maniacal Japanese column came up against the 105th Regimental CP. Some from the beach column, bypassing the 1st and 2d Battalions of the 105th Infantry up on the combined perimeter, also hit the 105th CP but were repulsed with heavy losses.

Marine corps observers in the hills, watching the Japanese attack through field glasses, witnessed a strange phenomenon. Behind the enemy assault formations, moved a weird, almost unbelievable pro-

cession: the lame, the halt, and the blind. The sick and wounded
from the hospitals had come forth to die. Bandage-swathed men, am-
putees, men on crutches, and walking wounded helping each other
along. Some were armed, some carried only a bayonet lashed to a
long pole or a few grenades, many had no weapons of any sort. If
they could kill a few Americans, they would be happy; but their main
objective was to die in battle in the service of their emperor. Those
too weak to leave the hospital were killed.

From his vantage point on the heights above Hara-Kiri Gulch, 1st
Lt. Donald Spierling, G Company, 2d Battalion, could see the three-
pronged Japanese attack developing. He first heard what he thought
was a truck motor running, and then on the plain below, he saw
Japanese tanks with columns of Japanese soldiers behind them. He
thought these soldiers were about one hundred yards away from G
Company's position. From his position on the hillside, 2d Lt. Arthur
Hansen of G Company could see that the 1st and 2d Battalions of
the 105th had been overrun; he could also see "the enemy running
willy-nilly over the ground formerly occupied by our troops."
Hansen's carbine couldn't reach the Japanese, but an engineer attached to Company G "managed to pick off a few with his M-1." One
Japanese officer on his knees was looking like he was committing
hara-kiri with his sword, but the engineer picked him off and he fell
forward on his face.

First Lieutenant George H. O'Donnell of G Company, 2d Battalion, had a bird's-eye view of the Japanese *banzai* attack that morning. He wrote to his parents about a month after the attack stating:

Next morning, about 0430 all hell broke loose! It was their
big *Banzai* attack: Out from the draw, below us, came the two
remaining Jap tanks, followed by about four hundred Japs,
heading for the flats below us. It had just finished pouring, and
we were all soaked, with our teeth chattering. But, no sooner
had we dropped our eyes on that mob, than we forgot all our
discomforts! And then, from our right and below us, there
came thousands of Japs!!! For two hours they passed by, and
came right at us! It was like a mob moving after a big football

game, all trying to get out at once! We had a hard struggle keeping them from overrunning us, and we had a field day, firing, firing until our ammunition started to run low. The closest any of them came was ten yards; and we were hitting them at four and five hundred yards also.

Technical Sergeant J. F. Polikowski, a long-time member of G Company, was also on the high ground above Hara-Kiri Gulch that morning. He described the scene as follows:

Did you ever stand outside of a circus tent at about the time the evening show is over? That's just the way it was. It reminded me of circus grounds or maybe it was Yankee Stadium. The crowd just milled out on the field, pushing and shoving and yelling and shouting. There were so many of them you could just shut your eyes and pull the trigger on your rifle and you'd be bound to hit three or four with one shot.

Starting from Makunsha at 0400, it took the main body of attackers about forty-five minutes to reach the combined perimeter of the 1st and 2d Battalions dug in along the railroad tracks. They were hit from the front, flank, and, after moving through the gap between the 1st Battalion and G Company, they attacked the rear. Almost immediately, communications between the embattled two battalions and 105th Headquarters were cut. Major McCarthy, one of the few senior officers of the two battalions of the 105th to survive the attack, described it as follows in a later memorandum:

It was like the movie stampede staged in the old Wild West movies. We were the cameramen. The Japs just kept coming and coming and didn't stop. It didn't make any difference if you shot one; five more would take his place. We would be in foxholes looking up, as I said, just like those cameramen used to be. The Japs ran right over us.

The 1st Battalion CP had been set up astride the railroad tracks behind the frontline foxholes occupied by the three rifle companies and Company D of the 1st Battalion. At 0430, 1st Lt. Luke Hammond, 1st Battalion S-2, awoke in his foxhole to the sound of heavy rifle, machine-gun, and antitank gunfire blasting away in the darkness. Calls were coming in from the rifle companies up on the line for artillery fires. The whole battalion seemed to be firing at some invisible enemy. Captain Toft was calling back and forth across the railroad tracks to O'Brien, trying to find out how effective the artillery fire had been. Toft began calling for normal barrages and the shells began coming steadily, but slowly, into the area northeast of the CP where the Jap attack was taking place. The noise became so terrific that O'Brien and Toft could no longer hear each other. In order to communicate better with 1st Battalion headquarters, Toft and his men crossed the railroad tracks and moved straight toward Capt. Emmett Catlin's foxhole. Catlin, thinking that the men might be enemy, almost shot one of them with his pistol. When Hammond arrived on the scene, Catlin said, "Say Luke, let's go up to the front line where we can get a shot at these bastards."

Sergeant Ronald Johnson, O'Brien's radioman, who had earlier seen shadows and silhouettes of men moving up in the hills, recalled, "About four-thirty in the morning, the front lines ahead of us erupted with all kind of rifle fire, machine-gun fire, mortar fire, and what-have-you. . . . And the big battle began. It later turned out that the shadows and silhouettes that I had seen up against the mountains were moving through a gap between our line and the marines on our right flank. Somehow, some way—probably [because of] overconfidence I think now, [there was] this belief that there weren't that many Japanese troops left and so, as you know, we didn't have to be all that cautious. In any case, there was a gap in the line, and the Japanese troops did get through that gap and had gone to the rear, so that when they attacked in the morning they attacked us from three sides: from the front, and from our right flank, and to some extent from our rear."

By 0445, the firing on both sides had increased and intensified dramatically. Lieutenant Hammond recalled, "Everything we had and everything the Japs had was being thrown back and forth at very short ranges in the darkness. Jap bullets popped overhead, and occasionally they would send a stream of tracers over my foxhole as I tried to go deeper than it would let me. I wasn't on the line so that the best I could do was to lay low." His foxhole was alongside a concrete wall that was part of a cistern that had a concrete bottom about three feet deep. Many members of the 1st Battalion CP had slept in the building during the night.

On the front line, it was chaos. Sergeant Felix Giuffre, Company A, 1st Battalion, awakened in his foxhole to the sound of loud noise to his front. Two machine guns of Company A were shooting at the enemy and two antitank guns were firing canister at the advancing soldiers, killing twenty-five to thirty men with each round. Suddenly, the firing stopped. One machine gunner, Sgt. Edgar L. Theuman, was killed by enemy fire, as was the other gunner, Sgt. W. A. Berger of Company A. The Japanese were running all over the place, Sergeant Giuffre recalled.

Giuffre's M-1 jammed just as two Japanese soldiers crawled up to finish him off. He ran for it and caught a bullet in the leg, the first of his four wounds that day. As he lay there, a soldier from the 105th, whose name he did not remember, came up to him with two tommy guns and a rifle, giving him the rifle and then disappearing. Then Giuffre saw Pfc. Clement L. Mauskemo, a chubby, full-blooded Cherokee Indian, Company A, 1st Battalion, get killed. As he began to crawl away, he came across Pfc. William A. Priddy, a BAR man in Company A. Priddy had three Japanese soldiers trapped in a ditch near the front lines, but for some reason he could not pull the trigger of the BAR. Giuffre grabbed the BAR and killed all three. He gave the BAR back to Priddy and never saw him again. Priddy was later killed.

By 0445 the noise of the firing by both sides increased in tempo. From his foxhole, First Lieutenant Hammond could see "Jap tracers flying from several sources not far to our front." Machine gun bullets sharply crashed over his foxhole. As the firing increased, "grenades exploded and sent pieces of shrapnel screaming through the night air." Hammond remembered thinking, "We had the fire power and were giving them hell." Just then someone yelled, "Watch the railroad," and two men with tommy guns moved forward and let loose a burst of machine-gun fire. Hammond warned, "Now be sure you don't shoot our own men, they're over near that vehicle to your left front." The two men assured him that they had shot Japanese soldiers. Just then Captain Catlin rose up out of his foxhole and said, "Luke, I must be hit. Something warm hit me on the stomach." And then Catlin laughed. Hammond told him that he had better stay down. A few seconds later Hammond asked, "Emmett, are you hurt?" "No!" was the answer.

From his foxhole at about 0500, as it got lighter, Hammond began to see objects moving twenty to thirty yards in front of him. He could see men from the front line battalions falling back across the field. "What the hell is this?" he said aloud and sat up in his foxhole. O'Brien was talking to someone on the field telephone. The colonel waved and yelled, "Hold that line and stay up there!" and then he threw down the phone. The first soldier from the front line to reach the Battalion CP was from A Company. O'Brien yelled, "Where the hell are you going?" The soldier waved his arms and said, "I have no weapon!" and continued to the rear. He saw that he could not stop the men from running back. He turned and said something to First Lieutenant Hammond and moved off toward the front lines. O'Brien was later quoted as saying, "As long as one of my men is up there, I am going to be with them."

To avert disaster, Hammond insisted that they had "to fight and hold" the 1st Battalion CP at all costs. He crawled into the concrete cistern near his foxhole and peered toward the enemy. "Fifty yards away I saw a mass of people. I heard yells of thousands." There were several other men in the concrete cistern and all of the men agreed, "Let's hold here!" There were in fact thousands of Japanese soldiers coming toward them. Just thirty yards away, Hammond "saw two Japs in front of the mass jumping among our dead and wounded swinging their Samurai swords for all they were worth. It didn't take but a few seconds for someone to drop them." Later reports confirmed that "the enemy hacked our wounded with swords."

When a light machine gun that Hammond found lying in the cistern did not work, he picked up his carbine and began firing at the advancing Japanese. There were seven or eight other men in the cistern, including Capt. John Bennett, the naval liaison officer; Private Chin, a runner-messenger with Hammond's S-2 section; and one of the Headquarters Company cooks. Hammond recalled, "Targets were plentiful when I did get started and so close there was no excuse for missing. Sometimes I had to fire twice to stop them. I gave some of my ammunition to Captain Bennett who had run out. I thought two of us could use it to better advantage in such a case."

Hammond left the cistern and took a position behind the concrete wall. He was firing at Japanese targets less than thirty yards away, and it was starting to get light. Suddenly, "There was a slight jar, and I heard the plunking sound as the bullet smacked into my helmet. The pain was slight—I couldn't tell exactly where the wound was." There was blood streaming down from under his helmet, yet he felt no pain. After he emptied his carbine at the enemy, he removed his helmet and the cook gave him a bandage, which he applied to the wound on the side of his head. He put his helmet back on, picked up his carbine, and began to walk back along the railroad tracks looking for an aid station while a hail of bullets hit the ground behind him.

The antitank guns on the front of the perimeter that had been mowing down the Japanese in large numbers were finally overrun shortly after 0500. The guns were spiked by their crews for fear they would be captured by the Japanese and turned against the Americans. Sergeant Harry Enoch, commanding the antitank guns, came back to the 1st Battalion CP for medical assistance. Corporal Eddie Beaudoin, a medic assigned to the 1st Battalion, remembered that Enoch was wounded in the left arm and that his gunnery sergeant, "Rocky" Banks from Akron, Ohio, had been shot in the stomach. As Beaudoin was tending to Enoch, Pfc. Carmen J. Dagostino of Troy, New York, a member of the 1st Battalion's Headquarters Detachment, was shot and killed instantly by a Japanese sniper.

One of the last persons to see O'Brien alive that morning was 1st Sgt. Charles J. Stephani of Company B, 1st Battalion, 105th Infantry. After the Japanese broke through the perimeter in large numbers, O'Brien, though already wounded himself, ordered Stephani to take the walking wounded back about one hundred yards and there set up a new line. Stephani, along with TSgt. Andrew J. Kopsa of Cohoes, New York, immediately complied. Kopsa was then killed by a Japanese mortar shell. Once the line was set up, Stephani, a former professional baseball player, collected hand grenades from the walking wounded and began to throw them at the advancing hordes of Japanese. "I had the pleasure of getting more than fifteen of them," Stephani later recalled.

At about 0510 on July 7, after twenty-five minutes of fierce fighting, O'Brien finally got through his first, last, and only message to the 105th CP, informing them of the situation and asking that his men be supplied with food, water, and ammunition. One of the last men to talk with O'Brien that morning may well have been Capt. Carl E. Rohner of Weehauken, New Jersey, S-3 of the 3d Battalion. Rohner was in the hills overlooking the Tanapag Plain and had a clear view of the chaos going on below. When O'Brien learned that he could not contact the 105th Regimental CP, he contacted Captain Rohner who relayed his desperate message to Regimental Headquarters. By then, however, the situation in the front lines had deteriorated drastically. The two battalions of the 105th had been overrun and had suffered casualties of almost 60 percent. The men were out of ammunition and had left their positions. Many key commissioned and noncommissioned officers had been either killed or wounded. There was no longer any organized resistance to the Japanese suicidal onslaught.

The fighting was furious. It was a raging, close-quarters fight between individual groups of soldiers. Grenades, bayonets, firearms of all descriptions, fists, spears, and even feet were used by the participants. The whole perimeter was one boiling mass of individual fights. O'Brien, who was described by the 27th Division historian as a picturesque, irrepressible individual, idolized by his men, took the lead in opposing the attack. A slight, left-handed, bantam rooster of a man, he carried a pistol in a shoulder holster under his right armpit. He was already a legend before his death. On that fateful morning of July 7, he was, without doubt, responsible for the brave stand made by the men of his battalion when the Japanese attack first hit the perimeter. That gave the survivors of the massive attack time to pull back to Tanapag Village, where a new defense perimeter was established. This heroic action undoubtedly saved many lives.

O'Brien moved up to the front lines and ran up and down the line of foxholes with a pistol in each hand, patting his men on the back, uttering words of encouragement, and every now and then taking a shot at an oncoming enemy. At one point, he was seen atop an abandoned enemy tank, firing his pistols. His radio man was constantly with him, trying to get through to the 105th's Regimental Headquarters. While running up and down the line, he was seriously wounded with a bullet that went through the back side of his right shoulder, just near his spine. He refused to be evacuated and initially did not even allow a bandage to be applied. When he saw that the bandage was opened and ready, however, he allowed the medic, Walter Grigas, to apply the bandage. Grigas recalled that at the time he applied the bandage to O'Brien's right shoulder the colonel was on his right knee firing his pistol with his left hand and yelling, "Don't give them a damn inch!" After he finished putting on the bandage, O'Brien told Grigas to "Get the hell back where you belong." Another participant in the front line battle that morning, Sgt. John G. Breen, Company A, 1st Battalion, later said at a meeting of the 27th Division Association, that "Obie was one of the boys that day. He died right on the front line with us." Breen also recalled that O'Brien's last words heard over the shrieks of the charging Japanese, the cries of his wounded soldiers, and the deafening gunfire were, "Don't give them a damn inch!"

By the time O'Brien completed his last radio message at about 0510, the front lines of the perimeter had disappeared under the onslaught of the Japanese attack. He jumped into a nearby foxhole, grabbed a rifle from a wounded man, and fired away at the enemy until he was out of ammunition. He then ran to a jeep parked in the middle of the 1st Battalion perimeter, jumped aboard, and manned the .50-caliber machine gun mounted on it. One of the last things First Sergeant Stephani remembered seeing before moving back to set up a line of walking wounded was O'Brien firing the machine gun at the advancing Japanese. When last seen alive O'Brien was standing upright, firing into the Japanese hordes surrounding him. When his body was discovered the following morning, thirty dead Japanese lay around him. For these and other notable demonstrations of bravery on Saipan, Lieutenant Colonel O'Brien was posthumously awarded the Medal of Honor.

Sergeant Thomas A. Baker of Company A, 1st Battalion, 105th Infantry, was also a hero in the front line battle that morning. In command of a rifle squad on the Company A perimeter during the early morning hours of July 7, he was wounded early on by a grenade that almost blew off his foot. However, he continued to man his position until he had completely exhausted his ammunition. Although barely able to move, he left his foxhole and began to search for more ammunition. Sergeant Felix Giuffre recalled almost fifty years later that Baker came crawling toward him: "I asked him what he was doing and where he was going. He replied by asking if I had any ammunition to give him because he was going up to where the colonel was— in the thick of the battle. It was then I noticed the heel of one foot was shot off. I told him to come into the perimeter because he was wounded. He refused and said he had to join the colonel. Before he left, I told him that I had two bullets left; one for the . . . Jap that came for me and the other for myself. I wasn't going to be taken prisoner alive. With this answer, Tom disappeared. . . ." After crawling about ten yards farther, he was picked up by Pfc. Frank P. Zielinski of A Company, 1st Battalion. Though wounded himself, Zielinski carried Sergeant Baker for about 150 yards to the rear of the perimeter. When Zielinski was wounded a second time in the hip, he had to put Baker down. As he did this, Zielinski was again wounded by a clean shot through the chest, but he survived the battle.

Captain Bernie Toft then came by on his way to the new defensive position in the railroad cut. He picked Sergeant Baker up and carried him back along the railroad for thirty yards. Toft was then hit and Baker had to be laid down on the ground once again. A third unidentified soldier came up and offered to help, but Baker turned him down. "I've caused enough trouble already," he is alleged to have said. "I'll stay here and take my chances." At his request, Baker was propped up into a sitting position against a small telephone pole nearby. "I'm done for," he said. His last request to the men who had tried to save him was for a cigarette. Soon after that, Sgt. C. V. Patricelli from Troy, New York, came by and gave Baker a cigarette and TSgt. John McLoughlin, also of Troy, gave him a .45-caliber pistol and ammunition. When he walked away from Baker, Sergeant Patricelli looked back at him, with a pistol in one hand and a cigarette in the other, and thought he appeared "cool as a cucumber."

Two days later, after the battle was over, Sergeant Patricelli and 1st Sgt. Mario Occhienero of Company A were called up to identify the bodies of the dead Americans. They found Baker dead, but still propped up against the telephone pole, cigarette partially burned out in one hand, empty pistol in the other. Almost directly in front of him were eight dead Japanese. For his heroic actions Sergeant Baker was posthumously awarded the Medal of Honor.

Captain Bernie Toft, of the 249th FA Battalion, was later located by liaison one Sgt. Robert W. Smith shortly after he had been hit carrying Sergeant Baker. Toft had been shot in the stomach. Sergeant Smith said, "I told him that he would be okay, but he said 'I felt it hit me in the back. I'm dying.' He asked me not to let the Japs take him alive and I stayed with him until he died."

Once the Japanese had overrun the perimeter positions, many forward observers from the 249th FA Battalion who were up on the front lines found themselves acting as ordinary infantrymen. Sergeant Smith saw Japanese soldiers bayonet wounded American soldiers in their foxholes. In one incident, a Japanese swordsman jumped into Sergeant Smith's foxhole, his saber half out of its sheath. As he was coming down, Smith lunged up with his bayonet and got the Japanese soldier in the stomach. "When I withdrew the bayonet," Smith said, "the Jap half jumped, half stumbled away. It almost seemed to be just a nervous reaction on his part. So I shot him to make sure he wouldn't be any more trouble." Lieutenant Robert H. Laborde, twenty-three, of New Orleans, Louisiana, a forward observer, took over duties as a line officer when his communications with the rear were interrupted. He repeatedly helped organize lines of defense against the flood-like masses of oncoming Japanese soldiers. Once a mortar round landed close by, throwing him to the ground and knocking him unconscious for several minutes. He later found his helmet strap in two pieces, apparently cut by shrapnel. Armed with a submachine gun, he knelt along the firing line, furiously pumping quick bursts into the advancing hordes of the enemy. According to Sergeant Smith, "Laborde plunked down on one knee, fired for a few seconds, then moved on to a new location wherever he was needed."

Laborde saw a number of men from the 249th FA perform heroic deeds in the action that fateful morning. One of his artillerymen, Pfc. Glenn A. Barry, twenty-four, of Baker, Minnesota, calmly got up under a whistling rain of bullets to pick off a Japanese soldier who had crawled through the American forward line and was about to lunge at some helpless wounded men. Another of his men, Cpl. Oscar A. Jardin, twenty-five, of San Jose, California, stood by a wounded buddy until he could be evacuated, all the while picking off groups of Japanese soldiers as they frantically tried to get through. One almost did, tossing a grenade that just missed, trying to follow up a saber attack, but Jardin shot him a few feet from his slit trench. Nearby, Cpl. Joseph A. Ferrer, twenty-two, of Syracuse, New York, and Cpl. George S. Triebel, twenty-three, of St. Albans, New York, both with the forward observers, stayed in a trench firing at the Japanese attackers until an artillery barrage forced them back.

There were also many other heroes in the two battalions of the 105th who took the brunt of the Japanese suicide attack on that fateful July 7 morning. Most were killed or seriously wounded during the first half hour of the attack, including a high percentage of the officers and men of both battalions. Of the two battalions, 406 men died that morning and 512 were wounded, a majority of them two or three times.

From Company A, Pfc. David Boynton, twenty-one, of Honolulu, Hawaii, was in a foxhole along the railroad track and had repelled attack after attack by the enemy during the night. Although wounded seriously by a grenade an hour before the main attack, he stayed in the thick of the first charge by the Japanese. When last seen, he was standing up in his foxhole with blood streaming down his face, deliberately squeezing off each shot and yelling at the top of his voice, "Come on, you yellow bastards, and fight." No one saw him die, but his body was later found in the foxhole where he had fallen. Private Frank W. Gooden and Pfc. Leon B. Pittman, twenty-seven, of Valdosta, Georgia, of Company A, were both killed that morning. Gooden was killed in his foxhole fighting off the enemy attackers. Pittman had been hit the night before, but had stayed in his foxhole and fought off the Japanese when they attacked that morning. When he ran out of ammunition, he limped back to the 1st Battalion CP for more. On his way back with the ammunition, he was hit and killed by enemy rifle fire.

Also from Company A, Sgt. Edward A. Bogan, of New York, New York, was initially hit in the right shoulder. He then switched his rifle to his left shoulder and continued to fire on the enemy until his position was completely overrun and he was killed. With his passing, the company lost a talented musician, who had frequently entertained his fellow soldiers by playing the piano. Staff Sergeant Cleo B. Dickey of Company A, a close friend who had accompanied Sergeant Baker on many of his nocturnal reconnaissance missions and a tower of strength to his company, was one of the first men killed in the Japanese counterattack. Two of his close friends in Company A, SSgt. Harold M. Rehm and Pfc. Charles I. Keniry, were also killed in the attack.

Corporal Ralph T. Ross, a radioman for Company A, had gone back to the 1st Battalion CP for a reload of ammunition shortly after the attack began. While he was back there, the front line began to disintegrate. Once he was rearmed, he ran back to the front and jumped into a foxhole near O'Brien and fought from there. As things became worse on the front, Ross jumped from his foxhole and ran forward into the midst of the enemy. He was found dead two days later. His assistant radioman, also of Company A, Pfc. Olin H. Duncan, was found dead near him with Ross's radio in his possession. It is believed that Ross had seen Duncan killed and was trying to get back to retrieve his radio when he was killed. At least six other Company A men were known to have been killed in their foxholes during the initial Japanese charge.

B Company of the 1st Battalion, 105th Infantry, which had been dug in on the railroad tracks at the very top of the perimeter that night, was hit the hardest by the Japanese attack. Twenty-one men were killed in the initial fighting, including all eight men in a squad led by Sgt. Barney Stopera from Cohoes, New York. When his squad ran out of ammunition, the fighting became hand-to-hand. When it was over, thirty dead Japanese were found near the squad's position. Five of the men killed in the fighting had been members of Company B's undefeated touch football team at Schofield Barracks in 1943, including Sergeant Stopera; Pvt. Robert Rodriguez of San Diego, California; TSgt. Raymond D. "Lefty" Lefebvre of Cohoes, New York; TSgt. Andrew J. Kopsa of Cohoes, New York; and Pvt. Michael C. Posipanko of Munhall, Pennsylvania. A sixth member of the team, Sgt. Floyd E. Cox of Lee's Summit, Missouri, survived the initial attack but was wounded in the leg later in the day.

Sergeant John Domanowski of Company B, from New Hyde Park, New York, was on the front line early on the morning of July 7. Before it was fully light, he recalled that "He could make out a figure running and falling toward our lines and all the while calling out, 'Medic! Medic!'" Domanowski thought that it might be an American, but he could not be sure. Before Domanowski could fire, however, the individual running toward the American position fell down and was lost from view. As it got lighter, Sgt. Jay B. Hollifield of Company B, 1st Battalion, from Blowing Rock, North Carolina, raised his head out of his foxhole and was shot in the eye. He cried a little and stopped when his gunner, Pfc. Robert W. Hallaway, of Rock Lake, North Dakota, gave him first aid. Sergeant Hollifield later died. Sergeant Domanowski also remembered that at that time, "Bullets were flying over our heads. At times you can hear them pop over your head, and at times you don't hear them at all."

Domanowski went on, "I could see the enemy now and they are running toward us in groups, all the while yelling and screaming at the top of their lungs. There is hand-to-hand fighting not too far from my position." He picked up his rifle and immediately took a bullet in his left bicep. He recalls, "My rifle went into the air, and my bicep was shot up and splattered all over me. It looked like chopped meat. My arm was broken and it swayed like a pendulum on a clock. I had a hole in my left arm as big as a tennis ball, and I could see white bones poking through it." After being shot, Domanowski became disoriented. A medic who tried to bandage his arm was shot in the head. Private First Class Ralph J. Carpenter of Company B, from Farmington, Michigan, called to him and said he was hit. Domanowski recalled, "I yelled at him to get down, but he just stood there for a minute and was slow in doing so. I looked at him and just then, I saw his stomach being riddled by machine-gun fire. I can't explain the look on his face as he fell."

As Domanowski moved back to the rear with other members of Company B, he spotted some Japanese soldiers coming toward him. "I saw them running in single file with their arms on the shoulders in front of them. It looked like there were a dozen of them. I decided to go toward them. They weren't in uniform, but had tattered clothes and bandanas on their foreheads. They looked mean." Domanowski then knew that the Japanese had broken through. As he remembered it, "We had to fight to stay alive."

A man from Company B, Pvt. Erytell W. Lynch, of Greenville, South Carolina, miraculously managed to survive the Japanese attack even though he was wounded nine times. Lynch had been cut off when the men around him were killed. Alone and out of ammunition, he tried to fight his way back to the American lines through the turning, twisting mob of men. Finding his escape route cut off, he jumped into the nearest foxhole right on top of two Japanese soldiers. Before he could protect himself, he was shot in the chest and bayoneted nine times. One bayonet plunge went through his neck and out the ear on the opposite side of his head. He was shot once again and left for dead. The next afternoon, marines moving through the area found him alive. He was evacuated to Guadalcanal and later to the New Hebrides. Amazingly, he survived the war.

The members of C Company, 1st Battalion, were more fortunate than either A or B Companies. It was positioned at the extreme south side of the combined perimeter to the right of Company D and did not bear the brunt of the initial Japanese attack. However, before it could prepare its defenses, six of its men were killed in the attack when their position was overrun. One C Company man, Cpl. William J. Shaughnessy, was wounded in both legs and unable to walk. Sergeant Robert W. Smith of the 249th FA came across Shaughnessy and was trying to get him to the rear when they were confronted by a Japanese soldier with a sword. Sergeant Smith had to put Shaughnessy on the ground saying, "So long, Shaughnessy." With that Sergeant Smith engaged the Japanese officer in hand-to-hand combat and bayoneted him to death. Corporal Shaughnessy subsequently died of his wounds. Smith made his way back to the 105th Regimental Headquarters CP unscathed.

Company D, 1st Battalion's, heavy weapons company, commanded by 1st Lt. Charles T. Ryan, was hard hit by the Japanese thrust. The Japanese tactic was to target the machine gunners first. In consequence, Company D lost almost every gunner and assistant gunner. Private First Class Samuel Di Nova recalled: "Bullets were flying all around," and there was a lot of "screaming and hollering." The Japanese had pitchforks, clubs, sticks with bayonets attached to them, shovels, everything they could think of. When the machine guns jammed up because of overheating or ran out of ammunition, the machine gunners were sitting ducks for the Japanese. Di Nova remembers seeing two of his best friends from D Company, Pfc. William T. "Babyface" Carneal from Lexington, Kentucky, and Pfc. Edwin E. Hoyt from Rochester, New York, killed by the Japanese after their machine guns stopped firing and overheated. Both had their heads cut off by Japanese officers.

Di Nova also remembered seeing Sgt. Salvatore S. Ferino from Troy, New York, in a foxhole with Pfc. Frank Dagliere from Hartford, Connecticut, when the Japanese attacked that morning. Their machine gun had jammed due to overheating, so Sergeant Ferino got out of the foxhole and began to make his way to the rear. Inexplicably, Private First Class Dagliere stayed in the foxhole, and after being hit by Jap gunfire, was beheaded by a Japanese officer wielding a sword. Di Nova grabbed his carbine and with other members of D Company began to move back, stopping every now and then to form a line.

Sergeant Frank R. Pusatere from Troy, New York, Company D, was in a foxhole that morning near the 2d Battalion. The Japanese sprayed machine-gun fire in the area and he jumped into a ditch. As he jumped, he was hit in the face by fragments of a mortar round, which left him disfigured. A fellow member of Company D, Pfc. Michael Sabo from Gary, Indiana, picked him up and carried him to the beach where he was evacuated with others. Sabo later died of wounds he had received from a mortar shell explosion as he was attempting to get water for wounded men on the beach.

Sergeant Ernest L. Pettit of Company D from Troy, New York, was in his foxhole on the front lines with SSgt. Joseph J. Skiba on the morning of July 7 when an enemy mortar shell exploded near him. Pettit was hit with a piece of shrapnel in the neck and Skiba was hit in the chest. As Pettit later recalled, Skiba began mumbling, but he could not understand what he was saying. Pettit gave Skiba a cigarette, but it fell out of his mouth. Just then Skiba keeled over and said, "You dirty bastards!" and then stopped breathing.

The 1st Battalion Headquarters Detachment also had its share of heroes during the initial phases of the attack. Sergeant Ronald L. Johnson from Valley Falls, New York, was at the 1st Battalion CP with O'Brien when the Japanese juggernaut hit the front lines of the perimeter. During the first half hour of the attack, TSgt. James J. Garvin from Hoosick Falls, New York, was killed. Later after making his way to the beach, 1st Sgt. Bernard J. Zilinskas of Hoosick Falls, New York, was also killed. Sergeant Johnson, in his recollections of the Saipan battle forty years later, believed that Sgt. Herman Barnhart from Petersburg, New York, of Headquarters Detachment, 1st Battalion, and Ervin D. "Dale" Deadmond, Johnson's closest friend, were both killed by Japanese machine-gun fire shortly after the attack commenced. Johnson recalled, "We were on the right side of a road that ran parallel to the beach. Down this road the Japanese had concentrated their machine-gun fire." They were using red and blue tracers that were only about three or three and a half feet above the ground.

The 2d Battalion (less G Company), positioned on the west side of the railroad track closer to the beach, started to receive the impact of the enemy attack. Private First Class Seymour Krawetz of F Company, from Skokie, Illinois, recalled, "At or about 4:30 A.M. I was roused from my sleep by one of my foxhole mates." Because of the way we were dug in, the 1st Bn. received the initial brunt of the attack, and we could not fire for fear of hitting some of them. Then just as dawn broke, the 1st Bn. ran out of ammo and started to fall back through us." Sergeant Eugene "Mac" McCandless, Company E, 2d Battalion, was asleep when the Japanese hit. McCandless recalled, "I had no warning that the attack was coming. Someone in my platoon was yelling 'Mac, wake up!' There was great confusion and disorder with firing coming from all directions it seemed. Mortar fire was falling into our positions from the hills to the east."

Casualties in the 2d Battalion were also severe. E Company lost sixteen men and several were wounded in the first minutes. F Company lost twenty-three men, but did not give up an inch of ground. F Company's commander, 1st Lt. John E. Titterington from Green Island, New York, was hit early in the initial fighting. As in other parts of the line, machine gunners were the first targets of the Japanese. Titterington rushed from one machine gun to another, manning them until he could get someone else to take over. Although wounded, he refused to have his wound dressed saying, "I've got to go, I guess, but if I do, I'm going to take a lot of those sons of bitches with me." He died a true hero, while manning his machine gun.

There were other men from the 2d Battalion who put up a heroic defense that fateful morning and who deserve to be recognized. Sergeant Eli F. Nicosia, a battalion scout with Company H, recalled that he "spent the night on the front line firing my carbine and throwing hand grenades. By morning we had run out of ammunition and had to retreat." First Lieutenant Robert J. McGuire, a platoon leader in H Company, was wounded in the initial assault. When he saw his company's machine guns being overrun by the enemy, he rushed up to the front line and took over one of them, continuing to fire against the enemy's repeated charges. No one knows how many times he was hit before he was killed. Just before dying, he was asked by one of the H Company men to leave and return to the rear so that his wounds could be treated. He answered, "I'd rather stay here."

Captain Benjamin L. Salomon of Los Angeles, California, the 105th's dentist, was also a hero that day. Acting as the 2d Battalion surgeon, he was in the battalion aid station when the counterattack hit. In the first minutes of the attack, about thirty wounded soldiers walked, crawled, or were carried into his aid station, and the small tent was soon filled with wounded men. When he saw a Japanese soldier bayoneting one of the wounded soldiers lying near the tent, Captain Salomon picked up a rifle and killed the enemy soldier as well as two more who appeared in the tent's front entrance. Four more enemy soldiers crawled under the tent's walls. Rushing them, Captain Salomon kicked the knife out of the hand of one, shot another and bayoneted a third. He butted the fourth enemy soldier in the stomach who was shot and killed by a wounded American soldier.

Realizing the gravity of the situation, Captain Salomon ordered the wounded able to walk to make it back to the regimental aid station while he held off the enemy. After four American soldiers manning a machine gun were killed, he took control of the weapon and began to fire at the enemy. He fired so fast and well that the enemy bodies began to pile up in front of his gun forcing him to move it to another position. He was found two days later, slumped over the machine gun with his hands still on the trigger, his body riddled with bullets. Ninety eight dead enemy soldiers were piled in front of his position. Almost sixty years later, Captain Saloman was posthumously awarded the Medal of Honor for his heroic actions on Saipan.

The 2d Platoon, Antitank Company, attached to the 2d Battalion, had moved up to support the infantry rifle companies on the night of July 6 and set up a position near the battalion headquarters. Of the thirty-four men in the platoon who moved up that evening, ten were killed and twelve wounded so badly in the *Gyokusai* attack that they were evacuated and never returned to the platoon. Sergeant W. Taylor Hudson recalled what it was like that morning: "About four A.M., I was awakened by an increased volume of fire. . . . All types of weapons were being fired. Just over our heads tracers were passing and these were all colors of the rainbow. Huge parachute flares kept the scene as bright as day." All we could do was remain in the hole, watching and listening. After what seemed an eternity, one of the 2d Squad men called out "Rip," (the combat nickname for Second Lieutenant Young), "our guys are falling back!" Second Lieutenant Young said, "Stay here! I'll check the other squads." With that he left and Sergeant Hudson never saw him again. Young was killed in action that morning as was SSgt. John H. Schlagenhauf, one of Hudson's closest friends.

18 The Tide Runneth Over

After overrunning the 1st and 2d Battalions of the 105th, the Japanese attack rolled on like a great tidal wave seeking to overwhelm the other American forces in the area. At daylight on the morning of July 7, a group of about 500 men attacked up the Paradise Valley toward Hill 767. The 2d and 3d Battalions, 165th Infantry, positioned on the rugged, high ground near Hill 767, had a field day and massacred the attacking Japanese. At least 300 were mowed down in the first futile charge without any casualties suffered by the 165th. By early afternoon, the Japanese counterattacks began to taper off and many troops withdrew into the cave positions along the Paradise Valley, which they defended with fierce tenacity. Paradise Valley was not entered by American troops from the upper end until a month later when a large-scale mop-up attack cleaned it out. Small American parties who ventured into Paradise Valley were ambushed there as late as February 1945.

The 1st Battalion, 165th, situated on high ground near Hill 721, was attacked by Japanese forces from Hara-Kiri Gulch at or about the same time as the main attack hit the 1st and 2d Battalions, 105th, on the Tanapag Plain. From their excellent defensive positions, Major Mahoney's men slaughtered the oncoming Japanese. As one soldier in B Company, 1st Battalion, put it, "It was like shooting ducks on a rock." First Lieutenant Vincent E. Walsh, executive officer, Company A, 1st Battalion, was at the Company CP in a shell crater on top of the cliffs. He recalled, "During the *Gyokusai* attack some of the Japanese attackers attempted to climb to the top of the cliff but were killed by rifle fire from the men of Company A." At dawn on July 7, he "heard one of the water-cooled machine guns of Company D,

165th, firing from the top of the cliff into Tanapag Plain. I used my field glasses to observe the action on the plain and saw 1st and 2d Battalion, 105th RCT, intermingled with Japanese soldiers, sailors, and civilians. I ordered the gun to cease firing."

Situated behind the 165th Infantry, on high ground in excellent defensive positions, were the 3d Battalion, 105th Infantry, and G Company of the 2d Battalion, 105th, attached to the 3d Battalion. Company I of the 3d Battalion was on the right directly behind the main exit from Hara-Kiri Gulch. L Company was on the hump that formed the south wall of the gulch. G Company was to the left of L Company on the forward nose of the ground guarding Hara-Kiri Gulch and overlooking the coconut grove and the Tanapag Plain. To G Company's left, some 600–700 yards to the northwest, were the ill-fated 1st and 2d Battalions, 105th Infantry. Some 800–900 yards to the left behind G Company's left flank was the 3d Battalion, 105th's headquarters, including part of M Company, 3d Battalion Headquarters Company, and K Company. All of these units were in two or three deep winding trenches, particularly on the north side of the perimeter, facing the coconut grove.

A little after 0500 on the morning of July 7, just after the main thrust of the *gyokusai* attack had exploded on the plain below, each unit was hit by an unusual series of Japanese attacks. I Company, commanded by Capt. Ashley W. Brown, thirty-four, of Poultney, Vermont, was hit by a particularly vicious Japanese attack that came out of Hara-Kiri Gulch. The enemy soldiers worked their way stealthily up the tributary canyon, probing I Company's positions with small groups of men. Private John P. Kloberdanz, twenty-two, of Osage, Iowa, a member of Company I, recalled that a Japanese soldier with a sword got into his foxhole, grabbed him around the throat with one hand, and began drawing his sword out of its sheath. Kloberdanz tried to struggle free and reached for his rifle. The Japanese soldier knelt on his chest, put his other foot on the gun, and then tugged again at the sword. As the struggle continued, the Japanese soldier found that he could not free the blade, so he began hitting Private Kloberdanz with the sheath. Private Kloberdanz yelled for the other men in his squad to shoot the man. Staff Sergeant John J. Foley of Brooklyn, New York, obliged him when he was certain that he was shooting at the Japanese soldier and not a fellow American.

Shortly after 0600, a rifleman in I Company, Pfc. Peter G. Young, was killed by scattered rifle fire while guarding a light machine gun that had been set up to prevent an enemy attack. When the fire intensified, the other riflemen guarding the machine gun were forced to withdraw, leaving the Japanese free to scale the cliffs without being fired upon. Using grenades, the Japanese seriously wounded seven I Company men near the machine gun, forcing the gun crew to withdraw and leave the machine gun unmanned. More than 150 Japanese managed to climb up out of the gulch and attacked I Company essentially cutting it in two. I Company held its ground, however, and poured heavy, concentrated fire into the Japanese from both sides of the breach. After more than thirty minutes of bloody fighting, Sgt. Walter A. Drummond, twenty-seven, of Akron, Ohio, a rifle grenadier with I Company, moved forward and although wounded, reached the unmanned machine gun before the Japanese soldiers did. He sat down behind the machine gun and began firing. Within a few minutes, he had killed all of the enemy near the machine gun, but was himself killed by enemy fire.

One of Drummond's friends from I Company, Pfc. Herman V. Vanderzanden, had gone back to the I Company CP to get some medical supplies for the wounded sergeant. When he returned and learned that Drummond was dead, Vanderzanden went berserk. He borrowed a BAR and waded into the midst of the enemy below, firing his weapon from the hip. He drove the enemy back, but was killed before he could drive them over the cliff's edge. Drummond and Vanderzanden, by their heroic actions, blunted the Japanese counterattack and contained the attacking Japanese in a little pocket not more than thirty yards square. Captain Brown ordered his men to pull back fifty yards all along the line, and then for thirty minutes, I Company's mortars poured fire into the bunched Japanese, driving them back. By 0800, the Japanese counterattack against I Company had been repulsed.

L Company of the 3d Battalion, 105th, was situated on the reverse slope of the hump that formed the south wall of Hara-Kiri Gulch. It had low ground behind it and high ground in front. A little after 0500, this company's position, like I Company's position, was hit by a group of Japanese coming up from the floor of Hara-Kiri Gulch. The attack was easily repulsed, although the Japanese set up mortars on the opposite side of Hara-Kiri Gulch and poured fire on L Company's position for most of the day. At 0830 another group of Japanese that had slipped through the gap between G Company, 2d Battalion, and the 3d Battalion CP, set up a machine gun in the rear of L Company's position and proceeded to rake the line at intervals throughout the day. L Company was effectively pinned down. Although Captain Spaulding maintained good radio communications with Lieutenant Colonel Bradt back at the 3d Battalion CP, he was unable to get any men back and lost two men in the attempt.

At approximately 1000, several jeeps loaded with ammunition, water, and medical supplies arrived at the L Company position south of Hara-Kiri Gulch. They had been sent by Lt. Col. Joseph Hart, acting commander officer of the 165th, in response to the following radio plea that had been received at 165th Headquarters at about 0800: "There are only 100 men left from the 1st and 2d Battalions of the 105th. For God's sake get us some ammunition and water and medical supplies right away." Although initially skeptical about the truth of the message, Hart, whose best friend was O'Brien, moved up to his OP atop Hill 721 and looked down on the plain. The Japanese were "as thick as maggots." As soon as Hart saw the burning vehicles and dead men lying on the ground below, he immediately ordered four jeeps to bring needed supplies to the beleaguered 1st and 2d Battalions. Unfortunately, when the jeeps reached the L Company position at about 1000, they could go no farther due to the Japanese mortar and machine-gun fire. The supplies were turned over to Captain Spaulding who used them to resupply I, K, and L Companies of the 3d Battalion and G Company of the 2d Battalion. After conferring by telephone with Lieutenant Colonel Bradt, Spaulding kept his company where it was and did not make any attempt to move forward. The men of L Company spent the rest of the day taking pot shots at enemy targets of opportunity on the plain and in Hara-Kiri Gulch.

• • •

G Company, 2d Battalion, commanded by Capt. Frank Olander, was assigned on the night of July 6 to swing across the mouth of Hara-Kiri Gulch. They were to contain any Japanese from attacking the 1st and 2d Battalions, 105th, who were dug in on the coastal plain approximately 600–700 yards to the north and west. However, increasing darkness and heavy enemy fire that night forced Olander to take up a position short of that objective. G Company dug in that night on the nose of the ground above Hara-Kiri Gulch from which Olander's company could control the lower entrance to the gulch using firepower. Although this position exposed the company to enemy fire, it also afforded it excellent fields of fire. Olander placed one light machine gun directly on the nose, covering the entrance to Hara-Kiri Gulch. A second light machine gun was placed across the road to the left front and covered the entire face of the cliff that ran parallel to the beach to the north. This position could prevent any enemy movement along the base of the escarpment.

At 0445 when the main attack hit the 1st and 2d Battalions, 105th, the men of G Company could hear the heavy firing. As one man described it later: "In the dark we could hear a lot of people running. It sounded like a big herd of cattle. There were so many of them that the ground rumbled." When dawn came, almost twenty minutes later, the men on the high ground saw what "looked like a circus had just let out." The whole plain below them was filled with people. A sizable group of "at least 300" Japanese separated from the main body and started toward G Company. Captain Olander ordered his men to begin firing at once. Their concentrated fire thwarted the enemy's attack. No Japanese ever got to within 300 yards of their position, and most of the enemy were either killed or scattered within a matter of minutes.

Somewhere between 0700 and 0800, small groups armed with grenades tried to knock out the machine gun guarding G Company's left flank. After a frontal attack failed, several soldiers with grenades worked their way to the rear of the machine-gun position and threw a shower of grenades that wounded a rifleman guarding the gun. Sergeant Nicholas J. Grazioze, in charge of the machine-gun position, decided to withdraw the gun and its crew back inside the company perimeter to avoid being cut off. Grazioze was successful; however, while moving the machine gun back inside the perimeter, a second G Company machine gun covering the entrance to Hara-Kiri Gulch was knocked out of action and its gunner, Pfc. James J. Davis, was killed.

Technical Sergeant John F. Polikowski, in command of the G Company platoon, dug in at the base of the hill and ordered his men to move ten yards up the hill to give them an advantage of height against the oncoming Japanese. To get at the G Company men in their new foxholes, the Japanese attackers had to climb a steep knoll and make sure their grenades landed squarely, or else they would roll back down the slope and explode in their midst. The battle then settled down to a steady fire fight; the G Company men firing as fast as they could find targets and squeeze off their shots.

While most of the G Company men fired from foxholes or from behind rocks, four of Polikowski's men chose to get behind trees before they fired. Three of these were hit by an enemy sniper. Two—Pvt. James E. Lehman and Pfc. Charles Hruby—were killed and the other seriously wounded. First Lieutenant Donald Spiering from Beaverton, Oregon, a platoon leader in G Company, told Hruby "to stay down, but he wanted one more shot at the enemy and then he got it."

At 0800 on the morning of July 7, G Company began to run out of ammunition and Olander ordered his men to reduce their fire to conserve what ammunition was left. A resupply of ammunition from the 3d Battalion CP was not possible at the time because the Japanese had infiltrated through the gap between G Company and the 3d Battalion CP. Olander's orders were that no man was to shoot until the enemy was close enough that it would be impossible to miss. As one enlisted man of G Company described it, "that old 'whites-of-their eyes' stuff." As a result of Company G's diminished firepower, the Japanese were able to creep closer and closer to the company's foxholes, as close as fifteen yards in some cases. The enemy began to toss grenades, and just as quickly, Captain Olander's men picked them up and threw them back. It was a deadly game of baseball. By 0830 this game had resulted in heavy casualties for both sides. Five

Company G men were seriously wounded, including Olander who almost had his left arm blown off by an exploding grenade. Undaunted by his wound, he had a rough tourniquet placed on his arm above the break and continued to direct the defense of G Company's position.

With G Company's two machine guns knocked out and its lack of ammunition, the company was unable to prevent the Japanese from entering Hara-Kiri Gulch and bringing fire to bear against G Company from the rear. Private First Class Elmer A. Bornich was killed by this fire and two other soldiers from Company G were wounded. Sergeant Edwin L. Luck from Amsterdam, New York, took matters in his own hands. As he later recalled, he was at a listening post near the coral road on the hillside overlooking Hara-Kiri Gulch. At about 0800, he saw enemy soldiers carrying a big Hotchkiss-type machine gun trying to get across the coral road 150–200 yards away from his position. The gun was so heavy that two soldiers had to carry it using stretcher handles. Luck shot the Japanese soldiers with his M-1. When more soldiers tried to pick up the machine gun, Luck started picking them off one by one, firing clip after clip. All told he believes he killed or wounded nineteen or twenty Japanese soldiers that morning. He said, "Not bad for an old crow hunter from upstate New York." Shortly after this incident, Luck was wounded by a mortar fragment, hitched a ride to an aid station, and recuperated from his wounds on board a hospital ship.

At approximately 0900, G Company was in a precarious position. Hemmed in on three sides, it was almost out of ammunition, and its men had very little cover to protect themselves from the enemy fire; yet they continued to hold their ground and fight back. At about 1100, the Japanese began withdrawing and the front line became silent. One-half hour later, the enemy began placing heavy knee-mortar fire on the G Company position. Three men were hit and Captain Olander collapsed having lost a great deal of blood from earlier wounds. Following the mortar barrage, the Japanese machine guns opened up. First Lieutenant O'Donnell took command and immediately ordered the men to move back about 100 yards. O'Donnell recalled, "I watched a machine gun for half an hour, hitting a tree back of me, about ten feet off the ground." Lieutenant Arthur

Hansen also experienced machine-gun fire clipping tree limbs just above his head. He radioed the G Company CP for mortar fire. First Sergeant Jack Falkenstein said that there were only six rounds left from the mortar ammunition that SSgt. George T. Mole, G Company's mortar section sergeant, and one other man had brought up from the 3d Battalion CP. Second Lieutenant Hansen asked First Sergeant Falkenstein to have a test round fired. The first round was close and the second round was even closer. As Hansen recalled the incident, "Making sure there were none of our troops in the area, I told him to fire the remaining rounds, which I am sure had some effect because there was no answering fire from the machine gunner." Moving his wounded back with him, O'Donnell ordered his men to dig in that night alongside L Company, 3d Battalion, some seventy-five to one hundred yards behind G Company's original position.

Several years later, in a letter to the *Infantry Journal,* Capt. Frank Olander described the Japanese *Banzai* charge on the morning of July 7: "I think I saw more of the *Banzai*-charge battle than any other living man, for the simple reason that I was up on a slope that overlooked the fighting from right above it. I saw it all from the early darkness and dawn when the Japs first hit till a number of hours later when I was wounded and evacuated. It was a fight against terrific odds—an excellent delaying [action], followed by an attempt at envelopement [*sic*] which did not succeed and finally the breakthrough of the Japs and considerable disorganization as a result. My own company [G] did not give an inch. It stayed put and so did Company L, and we fought it out. The regiment fought with utmost bravery—a determined and glorious action. It cut the Jap attack to ribbons. It did the big part of the job of stopping the attack. We left many, many dead on that field."

The 3d Battalion, 105th Infantry Headquarters Group, which also contained part of M Company, the heavy weapons company, 3d Battalion Headquarters Company, and K Company, occupied a perimeter facing the coconut grove on the Tanapag Plain. K Company, which was dug in on the north side of the 3d Battalion perimeter, was hard hit by the *Gyokusai* attack just before daylight on July 7. At about 0500, a soldier from the 3d Battalion Headquarters Company heard a noise some fifty to one hundred yards ahead of his position. He took a BAR and decided to investigate. Some fifty yards forward, he found about thirty Japanese crawling on their hands and knees along a ditch, heading toward the 3d Battalion perimeter. The alert soldier got to his feet, set his BAR on automatic, and walked along the ditch spraying it with bullets until he had killed every one of the Japanese in the attacking party. This courageous soldier was never identified in the official reports of the battle and no one knows whether he survived the battle that day or the war in general.

Shortly after the sun came up on July 7, the enemy opened up on the 3d Battalion CP with machine-gun fire from the vicinity of the coconut grove. The first burst knocked out the whole machine-gun section of M Company, the 3d Battalion's heavy weapons company, guarding the perimeter of the 3d Battalion CP. One fatal casualty was 1st Sgt. Samuel N. Passero, forty-eight, of Johnstown, New York, a World War I veteran who had served with M Company of the 105th in France in 1918; in the Mexican Border War in 1916; and at Makin in November 1943. One of his men said that Passero was "tough, but if you did your job he was the best." Another member of M Company stated that his "example enhanced the morale and confidence of the entire company."

Within a few minutes, the full force of the left wing of the attack, which had slipped through the gap, hit the 3d Battalion CP positions along the perimeter. The battalion was pinned down in their foxholes all morning by harassing enemy fire coming from the hillside above their position. Eight K Company men were wounded during the morning attack. By noon on July 7, the men were virtually out of ammunition. Lieutenant Colonel Bradt was powerless to take any action to help the beleaguered 1st and 2d Battalions of the 105th until the large number of enemy on its front was eliminated. The 3d Battalion CP was entirely cut off from the outside world except by radio. K Company, Bradt's reserve company, was never able to reassemble and move out to help the two battalions of the 105th from being overrun farther up on the Tanapag Plain.

On the night of July 6, the mortar platoon of M Company, 3d Battalion, 105th Infantry, under 2d Lt. Joseph J. Meighan of Troy, New York, was up in the hills overlooking the Tanapag Plain about a 1,000 yards from the right flank of the 1st Battalion, 105th. Meighan spotted a heavy troop concentration forming about 1,500 yards in front of the 1st Battalion position and fired all of his platoon's 81mm mortar ammunition, effectively dispersing the enemy. He told the mortar-gun crews, "You guys are great and I'm buying the drinks when ever we get out of this stinking hell hole." The next morning Second Lieutenant Meighan "awoke to the sounds of MG and rifle fire and observed hundreds of Japs yelling and running toward our lines. It was like a turkey shoot as waves of Japs were running past my perch. I expended the ammo from my carbine, then worked my way down to the plateau and back to our MLR [Main Line of Resistance] that no longer existed."

At 0500 on July 7, the bulk of the column of Japanese attackers coming through the gap moved west and hit the three marine artillery batteries posted in the trees near Bloody Run. The marines were completely surprised by the attack, so their positions were overrun by the fanatical onslaught. They had not dug in for the night, which was standard practice for combat troops on the front lines. Two .50-caliber machine guns attached to the 3d Battalion artillery batteries were knocked out and their gunners were killed. The artillery pieces, which were initially captured by the Japanese during the attack, were recaptured later in the day by the 106th Infantry. There was no evidence that the guns had been fired that day, or that even one single breechblock had been removed to render the guns inoperable. The next day officers from the 3d Battalion, 105th, found that the ammunition for these guns was piled neatly and the only used brass was also stacked in neat piles. Not a round had been fired since the registration the night before.

Colonel M. Oakley Bidwell, division G-1, was an eyewitness to the tragedy the marines brought upon themselves that fateful morning. In a letter written twenty years later, he recounted what he saw:

On my way back to our CP, I was accosted by an almost hysterical marine lieutenant colonel. "You Army bastards!" he screamed, "You let them slaughter my battery!" He led me to a sickening sight. Slung between trees were dozens of green marine corps jungle hammocks. Most contained the bodies of young men whose throats had been cut. Nearby were the battery's 105mm guns. I did not see a single empty shell case. The guns had never been fired.

I later learned that this battery had been ordered forward to join the marines occupying the top of the ridge, but its commander decided not to try to climb the bad road after dark and decided to pitch camp for the night behind the 105th Infantry lines on the sea-level plain. I was assured by 105th Infantry survivors that the marine commander never made contact with the 105th, who were unaware that they were bivouacking behind them.

The marines obviously had set up no perimeter defense of their own or they would not have been surprised in their sleep.

The marine version of the attack is that while two of the artillery batteries of the 3d Battalion, 10th Marines, were overrun, the third battery held out and decimated the Japanese attackers, stopping the counterattack in its tracks. This assertion is manifestly clear in the G-3 periodic report issued by NTLF on the morning of July 8, 1944, and in the commendation given to the 3d Battalion, 10th Marine Artillery, by NTLF Headquarters on July 11, 1944. Robert Sherrod, a war correspondent for *Time* magazine, attached to NTLF Headquarters on Saipan, published an article in the July 19, 1944, issue. The article read in part:

> The artillerymen fired point-blank into the Japanese with fuses set at four-tenths of a second. They bounced their high explosive shells 50 yards in front of the guns and into the maniacal ranks. When the order came to withdraw, they sent this answer back, "Sir, we would prefer to stay and fight it out." They did.

Official marine reports describing the encounter state that the marine artillery battalion stopped the Japanese counterattack on the morning of July 7 by themselves. On July 11, 1944, Headquarters NTLF, commanded by Lt. Gen. Holland M. Smith, issued a commendation that credited the How, Headquarters, and Service batteries of the 3d Marine Artillery Battalion with not only repelling the Japanese attack by opening up "at point-blank range with cut fuses and continu[ing] to fire until the enemy approached to such a range that it was necessary to resort to ricochet fire," but also with recapturing "the guns which had fallen into enemy hands."

The marine version of who ultimately stopped the *gyokusai* attack on the morning of July 7 was quickly refuted by Maj. Gen. George W. Griner, the 27th Division commander. In a letter dated September 28, 1944, addressed to the editor of *Time* magazine, he stated, "The marine artillery battalion did not stop the attack. It fought very courageously and suffered 136 casualties. But it was likewise overrun. The number of enemy dead found in the position area of the marine battalion was 322." The marine artillerymen held out with small-arms fire until their ammunition ran out and then were forced to withdraw. At 0720 a number of wounded and frightened marines from H Battery came running into the 105th CP to report that their battery had been overrun and captured by the Japanese.

Early on the morning of July 7, Cpl. Edward H. Redfield and Sgt. H. La Dieu, members of the I&R Platoon, Headquarters Company, 105th, had just returned from a short patrol seeking information on the position and strength of the Japanese drive toward the 105th's headquarters. Although the tremendous stand of the 1st and 2d Battalions of the 105th had slowed the Japanese charge, the two scouts "found a very strong enemy force heading toward our regimental command post and we were soon under fire. It was obvious that we would quickly be overrun. So, we made our way back through the enemy fire with our report." After giving his report, Redfield went up to the perimeter defense line that had been set up by Headquarters Company. It consisted of a series of foxholes, bunkers, and trenches that had been dug by the Japanese to guard against a seaborne invasion against Tanapag Harbor. As Redfield moved up to the front, he spotted a lone American soldier staggering toward the front line. Fifty years later, he recalled:

> I ran out to him and saw his rifle near him. He was seriously wounded in several body areas. He seemed delirious and kept

calling for his rifle. I believe he was from our 1st Battalion. As I tried to apply sulfa powder to his wounds, my hand went well into a huge hole in his back. At that point, Captain John Baker, C.O. Headquarters Company, came up to me and the wounded man. Captain Baker tried to tell him he didn't need his rifle but he continued to yell for it. We made him as comfortable as possible and called for medical aid.

Sometime between 0530 and 0615, hordes of Japanese soldiers who had slipped through the 105th's front lines and overrun the marine artillery batteries to the north and east, or had come down by boat along the seacoast between Makunsha and Tanapag Village, began to attack the 105th Regimental CP's perimeter from the north and both flanks. The Japanese soldiers shouted and ranted, waving sabers and bamboo poles with bayonets tied to the end. They were drunk with sake, firing rifles and machine guns and throwing hand grenades as they approached. Every available man in the 105th CP group rallied to the defense of the perimeter. Cooks put down their ladles, and mechanics their tools. Wire-stringers and radio men left their communications equipment and picked up their rifles. Clerks dropped their red tape and pencils, and all snatched up their rifles. All normal activities within the CP were suspended. Ammunition parties kept a steady stream of ammunition flowing along the front lines. The firing was continuous and effective. The soldiers exchanged blow for blow, bullet for bullet, with their attackers. The defense perimeter was never penetrated. For the next six to ten hours, these men put up a fierce resistance against the Japanese onslaught. More than 1,600 Japanese bodies were counted in front of the 105th CP's position, but some were probably killed by the 106th Infantry later that day.

Some Japanese who attacked the 105th's CP that morning came along the coast by boat from the Makunsha area. First Lieutenant Francois V. Albanese, S-4 of the 1st Battalion, had established a supply dump about 1,000 yards behind the front lines and just forward of the 105th Regimental CP. At dawn on July 7, he began assembling supplies of food, water, and ammunition to bring up to the beleaguered battalions dug in 1,000 yards ahead. Suddenly, Albanese was startled by the sight of a large number of Japanese Imperial Marines landing on the beach near the 105th CP. One tall marine came at Albanese with fixed bayonet, threatening to run him through; Albanese shot him twice with his carbine, with no effect. The man kept coming. An American soldier nearby with an M-1 rifle dropped the Japanese soldier with one well-placed shot. Albanese threw his carbine into the sea and picked up an M-1 rifle, which he carried for the remainder of the Saipan battle.

Some inkling of the ferocity of the combat in front of the 105th CP that morning is reflected in a dispatch received from Saipan shortly after the battle. After describing the Japanese attack, the dispatch states: "The erstwhile cooks and mechanics, clerks and messengers bided their time, then cut loose with every weapon on the line." In Lt. John F. Armstrong's center section, he held its fire "until the enemy was within eighty yards and then loosed terrific machine-gun and rifle fire upon the enemy thereby wiping out a whole platoon of the enemy." The newspaper dispatch goes on, "One machine gun, with a crew of cooks and KPs, cut a wide swath along the right flank of the Japs. Wire-stringers turned machine-gunners did the same on the left. Antitank and Cannon [Company] men poured in their quota of lead." First Sergeant Lawrence J. Whalen, twenty-eight, of Whitehall, New York, Headquarters Company, 105th, fresh from making up his morning report "cradled a belching tommy gun as he stood up to get a better lane of fire at the enemy."

At noon on July 7, shortly after the fanatical Japanese attack had been beaten back, the defenders of Headquarters Company perimeter were startled to see a badly wounded American soldier, naked as a jaybird, pop out of the surf and begin running toward the perimeter. Private First Class George Herman who was on the beach at the time remembers the soldier yelling, "Don't shoot! Don't Shoot!" Herman, seeing that the soldier had a bullet in each thigh, each hip, and one in the right shoulder, yelled, "Medics! Medics!" According to Herman, the "Medics came in five or ten seconds and whisked him off to the aid station. After fifty-five years I still wonder if he survived, how far he had to swim, and how long he was in the ocean with five bullet wounds."

Once the enemy attack was broken up, the Headquarters Company men got out of their foxholes and at 1400 counterattacked the Japanese led by First Lieutenant Armstrong. During the afternoon, he remained out in front of his men, exposing himself to enemy rifle fire. At one point, the company commander called on him to take charge of the company and press the attack. Pulling what his friends later termed "a John Garfield stunt," SSgt. Howard D. La Dieu of Troy, New York, a reconnaissance platoon leader in Headquarters Company, picked up a light machine gun, looped the ammo belt over his shoulders, and advanced firing from the hip, routing the Japanese out of their trenches and dugouts. Captain Baker later said, "He used that machine gun as he would a rifle." Sergeant Vernon H. Houghtailing of Headquarters Company, 105th, from Torrington, Connecticut, was the chief grenadier for the headquarters troops. Men fed him the grenades and saw him clean out foxhole after foxhole as he advanced to within twenty yards of the Japanese line to make sure of his aim.

Private First Class Herman, a wire-stringer with Headquarters Company, 105th, was part of the counterattack on the afternoon of July 7. More than fifty-five years later, he recalled: "Late in the afternoon it was decided to form a line and sweep the area moving north. It was quiet. Nothing moved." The company was about one hundred yards in front of the 105th CP perimeter. Herman remembered that he was standing there when his buddy, T/5 Louis R. Reed, who worked in Headquarters Company's Message Center, told him to get down, which he did. Just then another soldier from Headquarters Company named Reif came up and stood where Herman had been standing and was shot in the groin. Herman recalled, "Reif yelled for help. Reed went to him. . . . Reed crawled to Reif's side. Then Reif screamed. I scrambled to them. Seconds later I rolled to the bottom of the ditch. Reed had taken a head shot when he took off his helmet to console Reif and was dead." After the medics came for Reif, Herman recalled, "Then we moved up. Nothing happened until we got to the 'crooked' tree. The Jap shooter crawled out of the brush and Lieutenant [Walter] Sluzas killed him with his pistol."

After advancing 500 yards, Captain Baker received an order to stop pursuing the Japanese and to return to the 105th CP area. At that time, the 105th Headquarters unit was relieved by the 106th, which spread out and deployed west across the road and to the shore. It was widely recognized that the fierce resistance put up by these men stalled the Japanese attack. According to Capt. Edmond Love, historian, "the sudden damming of the flood of the *Gyokusai* attack by the 105th Infantry command post resulted in a tremendous ebb tide."

It was at the 105th CP that the *Gyokusai* attack petered out. For ten hours, the cooks, technicians, supply men, and truck drivers stood their ground, never budging an inch, and not one Japanese advanced beyond the line they set up. For these heroic actions, Headquarters Company, 105th Infantry Regiment, was awarded the first Distinguished Unit Citation in the 27th Division for gallant and distinguished service on Saipan. The Distinguished Unit Badge, a blue ribbon set in a frame of gold laurel leaves, is issued in the name of the president "as public evidence of deserved honor and distinction," and is worn by all members of the cited organization.

For their individual heroic actions at Saipan in defending the 105th Infantry CP against the attack, Capt. John C. Baker was awarded the Silver Star for gallantry. His executive officer, 1st Lt. John F. "Jack" Armstrong, was awarded the Bronze Star. First Lieutenant Milton Latter, I&R Platoon, Headquarters Company, 105th Infantry, also distinguished himself that day and was awarded the Bronze Star.

19 The Withdrawal

By 0600 those men of the 1st and 2d Battalions of the 105th on the front lines began pulling back to gain better cover, ammunition, and medical assistance. They were not moving as battalions but as individuals, and the scene was chaotic. Savage fighting swirled around a dozen isolated pockets of American resistance. Some were overrun; others held out. The Americans moved back with the enemy soldiers running among them. The men of the 165th Infantry and the 27th Division Artillery on the cliffs overlooking the Tanapag Plain could not fire for fear of hitting the American soldiers who were alone or helping a wounded comrade. Some Japanese and American soldiers were hobbling along on crutches trying to keep up with the others. Everyone was mixed together. Sergeant Frank C. Cimaszewski of New York, a forward observer for the 106th Field Artillery on the heights above the Tanapag Plain, recalled setting up a firing mission to thwart the Japanese attack. But the Japanese and the soldiers of the 105th were all mixed together, so the firing mission had to be canceled.

Sergeant Ronald Johnson, O'Brien's communications sergeant, recalled that when the 1st Battalion of the 105th began to pull back, "The Japanese just swept over us. And many of those who did were directed to get as far to our rear as possible and to disrupt our rear. So you might be moving back, retreating say, and you would look to your right or your left, and you would see the Japanese soldiers running right along with you, and either because they were drunk—a great many of them were, a great many of them—they ignored you. They just ran on, right beside you. As I mentioned, their intent was to get as far to the rear as possible, so they weren't too concerned

267

about shooting a few people along the way. They were intent on getting back there and creating as much damage as possible."

The withdrawal was not entirely headlong. Every now and then a group of able-bodied men, with or without an officer, established a holding position behind a tree or bush to give the wounded men a chance to get back to the regimental aid station near the 105th CP. Several officers organized such a position in a small railroad cut just behind the initial perimeter to delay the Japanese. The effort, however, was futile against so many of the enemy and the position had to be abandoned within fifteen minutes. First Lieutenant Seymour P. Drovis, executive officer of Company A, 1st Battalion, 105th, and a Silver Star winner at Makin, was killed near the railroad cut while running up and down his improvised line, trying to get his men organized.

Wounded men helped wounded men. Those who could walk helped those who could not walk make it back to the rear. If a man could move, no matter how badly wounded, he crawled or hobbled along while the able-bodied men protected him. Sergeant Anthony A. Auzis, twenty-six, of Waukegan, Illinois, with Company A, 1st Battalion, was seriously wounded in the leg during the first stages of the fighting on the initial perimeter. After running out of ammunition, he went back looking for the 1st Battalion aid station but could not find it. He was wounded again, this time in the arm. On the way back to the 105th Regimental aid station, he found Sgt. Felix M. Giuffre of Company A, 1st Battalion, lying unconscious on the ground suffering from a head wound. Although he could barely walk, Auzis picked him up and brought him back along the railroad tracks as far as the minefield above RJ 2. Exhausted, he laid the unconscious man on the ground at the edge of the minefield. Auzis was then wounded again, this time in his good leg. Now forced to leave Giuffre at the edge of the minefield, Auzis dragged himself back to Tanapag Village and the second perimeter. He remained there the rest of the day and was again wounded when he was hit in the back by a large shell fragment fired unwittingly by friendly forces. That evening Auzis was evacuated from the beach back to the base hospital.

Sergeant Giuffre, meanwhile, regained some consciousness and began trying to move himself to the aid station. Captain Love's book states that Pvt. Joseph Gomes came running by at the time and saw Giuffre moving an inch or two at a time, literally tearing huge chunks of ground out with his hands as he tried to pull himself along. Sergeant Giuffre found himself in the middle of the minefield. Gomes, saying "to hell with it," jumped into the minefield, and carried Giuffre out of it and back into the perimeter. When interviewed later, Giuffre recalled that Tech 4 Medic Ramon T. Gonzalez carried him out of the minefield and into the perimeter where he was wounded a fourth time before he was evacuated from the beach late that afternoon.

Private First Class William Hawrylak, Company A, 1st Battalion, who was wounded earlier in the battle for Saipan, went AWOL from the hospital in order to return to his company the day before the attack. During the initial phase of the attack, he received a saber thrust from a Japanese officer that nearly cut off his buttocks. Although bleeding profusely and unable to walk, he continued to fire his submachine gun at the enemy, even though nearly everyone around him was killed or wounded. Staff Sergeant Dominic Daurio from Valley Falls, New York, his squad leader, ordered him to leave his foxhole while he could. Private First Class Hawrylak replied, "Hell, no! I like it here. Besides, I got no ass. How can I walk?" With that, Staff Sergeant Daurio picked up Hawrylak and carried him back toward the rear. Halfway down the beach, Pfc. Clayton E. Ernsthausen came along and helped Daurio carry Hawrylak back toward the perimeter. The wounded man was bleeding so profusely, he finally had to be laid down on the ground. Staff Sergeant Daurio gave Hawrylak a sulfa pill to prevent infection, carried him back to the perimeter, and placed him in a foxhole for his own protection. Hawrylak, however, refused to stay in the foxhole and spent the next several hours crawling around the perimeter on his stomach, collecting ammunition and cleaning weapons for the men still able to load and fire. He was eventually evacuated to the rear by one of Lt. Herman Schroder's trucks of the S-4 Detachment, 2d Battalion, and survived the battle.

Private First Class Cassie Hill, Company A, 1st Battalion, 105th, was wounded several times that day. At the initial perimeter, he was shot in the upper arm, shattering the bone, rendering him unable to fire his rifle. He teamed up with his foxhole mate, Pfc. Armin W. Kunde, to keep firing at the enemy. Hill would load the rifle with his good arm and Kunde would fire it. Once their ammunition supply ran out, the two moved back and forth picking up rifles and ammunition from the dead and seriously wounded as they went along. About halfway back to the perimeter, Hill was hit in his good arm and could no longer assist in loading the rifles for Kunde. Once they reached the perimeter, Hill continued to collect ammunition for those able to fire at the enemy. He was wounded again and again, but continued to assist in the defense of the perimeter. He was eventually evacuated by LVT late in the evening of July 7 and survived the battle. There is no record of what became of Kunde.

While B Company of the 1st Battalion, 105th Infantry, suffered heavy casualties in the initial Japanese attack, the company's casualties mounted as the men withdrew from the initial perimeter. Lieutenant George B. Dolliver from Battle Creek, Michigan, was hit by a stray bullet and killed instantly as he led his men during the withdrawal from the front lines. Technical Sergeant Michael Mele, twenty-six, of Albany, New York, stated: "We thought the world of Lieutenant Dolliver. We called him 'Daddy.' He took care of his men and led them. During the crucial period of waiting for the zero hour to come, he was an inspiration to us all. I was beside him when he got it. He died instantly. If the army ever had a braver officer, we would like to meet him."

First Lieutenant Hugh P. King from Hewlett, Long Island, New York, who had taken command of Company B, 1st Battalion, after Captain Ryan was killed on July 6, was himself killed while trying to organize the second perimeter at the northern edge of Tanapag Village. King was following SSgt. James F. Rhodes from Tell City, Indiana, during the withdrawal. When both stopped looking for a place to make a stand along the railroad tracks near RJ 2, Rhodes, who was in the lead, was killed instantly when a grenade hit him in the face. King was standing with Capt. Earl White, F Company, 2d Battalion, directing men coming south from the front lines into houses on the west side of the road north of Tanapag Village. As the two men stood there, directing traffic and shouting encouragement to the men, a mortar shell scored a direct hit on King, killing him instantly.

Sergeant John Domanowski of B Company, 1st Battalion, was shot in one arm during the initial Japanese attack. As he made his way back to the rear along the beach, he stopped to rest underneath a tree, facing the beach. A Japanese soldier in the tree above shot him in the other arm. He recalled, "I found a good spot on the beach where there were some bushes and small trees and decided to stay there. My left arm was useless and the pain was severe. My hand swelled quite a bit and I couldn't make a fist or use my fingers." As he lay there on the beach, many other wounded were brought in from the front lines for evacuation. Domanowski recalled what happened next: "I see a lot of soldiers going into about three feet of water. They are desperate men and want to hide. The Japs see them in the water, and open fire on them with machine guns. You could hear the bullets hitting their skulls." Another group of about forty American soldiers ran into the water trying to swim away from the Japanese fire.

Lieutenant John F. Mulhern, twenty-four, of Portland, Maine, B Company, 1st Battalion, the only officer of the 1st Battalion, 105th Infantry, to survive the Saipan battle unscathed, picked up a wounded soldier, Pvt. Anthony J. LaSorta from San Jose, California, and tried to bring him to the rear. LaSorta had suffered a broken leg from machine-gun fire. When Mulhern put him on his back, a Japanese machine gun opened up, literally blowing LaSorta to pieces, right off Mulhern's back. Amazingly, Mulhern did not receive a scratch.

Private First Class Gerald D. Ostrum, C Company, 1st Battalion, 105th, had a similar experience during the withdrawal from the front lines. He had picked up his badly wounded squad leader, SSgt. Louis S. Doddo, twenty-seven, of Norwalk, Connecticut, and was carrying him back fireman style when he heard footsteps behind him and a loud swish. A Japanese officer had run up behind him and with one clean stroke of his sword cut off Doddo's head. Ostrum dropped Doddo's headless body and killed the man with his carbine. Doddo had achieved some fame earlier in the fighting on July 4, when he captured Comdr. Jiro Saito, a member of the staff of RAdm. Takeshita Tsujimura, commander of the landing party on Saipan. Saito had headed the defense of the sector in which he was captured.

In Company D's sector, Pfc. Samuel Di Nova recalled that when the Japanese overran the front lines, he grabbed his carbine and began to run back along with others from Company D. Each time they stopped to form a line, they were attacked again. "There were Japs all around," he recalls. As he ran back, he jumped over the sugar cane railroad tracks. He even stumbled over a land mine hidden in the sand, but it did not explode. He recalled getting behind a coconut tree along the narrow stretch between the road and the beach twenty to thirty yards from the ocean with two big six footers from Company D who were from the coal mining regions of Pennsylvania. They were both replacements and had joined Company D at Fort Ord, California. Both of them, Pvt. Stanley Dopkiavich and Pfc. Paul Dubill, were killed shortly thereafter by enemy fire. Di Nova then moved out into the high grass with another soldier named Gans from Kansas. When he disappeared in the tall grass, Di Nova went back to the coconut tree and waited for help to arrive.

One of the more bizarre stories about the withdrawal from the front lines involved Cpl. Eddie Beaudoin, a medical corpsman. Corporal Beaudoin was at the 1st Battalion CP right behind the front lines when the attack hit. Once the front lines were overrun, Beaudoin left his foxhole and encountered four men from Company A, 1st Battalion, who were also withdrawing. Beaudoin had a rifle and a .45-caliber pistol and needed ammunition. One of the Company A men, who had two packs of M-1 ammunition, gave him one pack, and he started back toward the 105th Regimental CP. When he reached the "Little Perimeter," an area on the railroad tracks just south of the road to the coconut grove near the Tanapag Village, he killed a Japanese soldier and for the next three hours fought and killed a number of Japanese in hand-to-hand combat. When he finally arrived at the beach near Tanapag Village, he was covered with blood and disoriented.

In the 2d Battalion, 105th, sector of the line, the withdrawal took place in much the same way as it had with the 1st Battalion. Private First Class Seymour Krawetz, Company F, recalled: "Since we were in a sandy area [along the beach], after a while my M-1 jammed and I did not see any other live Americans near me, so I took off and caught up with the other guys. I cleaned the sand out of my rifle and fired until my ammo supply ran out. Now we [had] the ocean on one side of us and Japs on all of the other sides. After awhile we got hit with mortar fire that caused some horrible casualties and I wound up swimming and lost my empty rifle. The mortars stopped and I came back in and picked up a pistol and a bunch of us charged the Japs, but got stopped after awhile and I wound up sharing a foxhole with Major McCarthy, our battalion executive officer."

After he had been wounded in the initial Japanese attack, 1st Lt. "Luke" Hammond moved back along the railroad track toward the rear seeking an aid station. A hail of Japanese fire followed him, but fortunately he was not hit. Hammond spotted Capt. Bernard Toft, liaison one artillery officer of the 1st Battalion CP group near the railroad tracks. Hammond recalled, "He looked at me and quickly returned his attention to the Japs. Neither of us said anything. With pistol in hand he looked prepared to do his part in stopping the onslaught." As Hammond walked back along the railroad tracks, he came across a medic from the 105th Infantry treating another soldier. Hammond remembered yelling, "Where's the aid station?" The medic replied, "There's an aid station at regiment." The medic then examined his head wound and put another bandage on it. When he put his helmet on, the pressure of the bandage stopped the bleeding.

As he walked along the tracks, he saw to his left hundreds of Japanese soldiers rushing madly southeastward down the Tanapag Plain. They were moving around the right flank of the combined perimeter and were trying to get in behind the beleaguered 1st and 2d Battalions, 105th. They totally disregarded the Americans moving back along the railroad tracks, concerned only with getting in behind the trapped battalions. As Hammond walked along, he encountered some men from Company A and Company B, 1st Battalion, 105th. First Lieutenant King, in command of B Company, asked, "You think we ought to set up a line here, Luke?" Hammond agreed that they should try to hold at this point. Before they could get organized, however, a group of men [almost platoon-sized] from the 1st Battalion, came up from the direction of the regimental headquarters area. One of them said, "The Japs are all along back there." Someone else said, "We're surrounded." Another soldier suggested that the group should move down toward the beach and join forces with the 2d Battalion. Within a few seconds, there was a mass movement of men across the open field leading to the beach. Friendly artillery fire from the hills above the Tanapag Plain, which had been pounding the Japanese masses trying to get in behind the 1st and 2d Battalions, was now directed mistakenly against the Americans moving to the beach. American shells burst overhead forcing the men to hit the ground. Shrapnel was sprayed all around. When Hammond began to move forward, a calm, smiling soldier next to him said, "I'll have to stay here; my foot is cut off." First Lieutenant Hammond looked at him and said, "You can't make it any farther?"

"No," he said. There was nothing that could be done for the wounded man.

After the air bursts subsided, the men dashed across the road into an area by the beach near Tanapag Village. For cover, there were stone houses nearby as well as trees along the beach. The attackers had dug a number of zigzag trenches in the area and the men settled down in them. "We'll hold here," was the cry. Hammond recalled, "We placed our back to the ocean and built a half circle defense line. Throughout the remainder of the day that place was the hottest spot I had ever been in and ever hope to be. On three occasions I saw a Jap blow himself up with a hand grenade. Again I heard their fanatical yells as they charged. One [Japanese soldier] ran bewildered right into our midst, staring at the [American] soldier who was firing at him as if he wondered who he was. He [the Japanese soldier] stopped after he had run past the soldier, and stood holding his rifle and bayonet as if wondering what to make of it. This time the soldier's shot counted."

Sergeant Ronald Johnson of Valley Falls, New York, who had served as O'Brien's communications sergeant, recalled, "A number of us moved over to the beach. We went across the highway that ran parallel to the beach that was under fire. The way I did it, and the way I suppose others, [did] too . . . was to throw yourself across the road, just a few inches above the road, so that you were able to get under that fire. So you literally threw yourself across the highway there. You might take a little running start. . . . In any case, I got through and a number of others did, and we went over to the beach where we built up a little perimeter. You know what that looks like: a kind of half-circle with our rear anchored on the water and our front facing the Japanese, who as I mentioned came in and tried to eliminate all of these little perimeters that had been built up along the beach."

20 Defense of the Second Perimeter

By 0700, about two hours after the 1st and 2d Battalions, 105th, were overrun by the *gyokusai* attack, the survivors reached the northern edge of the village of Tanapag. There they encountered the left prong of the Japanese forces who had come down the plain along the cliffs skirting the positions of the combined perimeter. These Japanese had already overrun the three artillery batteries of the 10th Marines posted about 2,000 yards behind the front lines and attacked the 105th CP about 1,400 yards away on the right. There were also significant forces coming down along the beach and railroad tracks to attack the withdrawing Americans. Rather than fighting through this new enemy force, it was decided to take a stand on the railroad tracks just south of the road to the coconut grove near Tanapag Village. The men were initially directed by Capt. Earl White of F Company, 2d Battalion, 105th, who had already been seriously wounded, and 1st Lt. Hugh King of B Company, to take cover in the houses of Tanapag Village and in the trenches just north of the village. The wounded were dragged into the houses or into ditches inside the village. While directing this diversion, King was killed by enemy fire. Meanwhile, Major McCarthy, in command of the 2d Battalion, reached the village and took charge of the holding action, along with Captain Ackerman of A Company, 1st Lt. John Mulhern of B Company, and other officers and noncommissioned officers. By 0800 a perimeter had been organized that took up most of the village of Tanapag. For the next four hours, these men put up one of the great defensive fights in the history of the U.S. Army, fighting a bitter house-to-house battle with the Japanese who had surrounded it and were infiltrating the village.

By the time the second perimeter was set up, many line officers in the 1st and 2d Battalions had either been killed or wounded. In the 1st Battalion, Lieutenant Colonel O'Brien had already been killed. His executive officer, Capt. Albert A. Butkas, was alive and took an active part in the perimeter defense until he was seriously wounded during the first artillery barrage. Captain Ackerman, of A Company, was unhurt and played a leading role in initially organizing the men until he, too, was wounded. His executive officer, 1st Lt. Seymour P. Drovis, had already been killed in action. Of Ackerman's platoon leaders, 1st Lt. Kendrick "Fig" Newton of Greenville, Alabama, was wounded and largely ineffective. First Lieutenant Van M. Crocker of Albany, California, in command of the weapons platoon, was wounded as was 2d Lt. Sylvanus Brown. Second Lieutenant Albert Brockett had already been killed earlier in the Saipan battle.

In B Company, only 1st Lt. John F. Mulhern was fit for duty. Aside from 2d Lt. Martin L. Olsen from St. Albans, New York, who had been wounded, all of the other officers in B Company had been killed. In C Company, 1st Lt. Bernard Tougaw was still alive, but he would be killed later in the day. The rest of C Company's officers had either been killed or wounded by the time the second perimeter was established. In D Company, 1st Lt. Charles T. Ryan, who commanded the company, was wounded; 1st Lt. J. R. Stark and 2d Lt. Edwin Buelter had been killed; and 2d Lts. M. A. Sereton, W. A. Cash, and H. Scheer were wounded.

In the 2d Battalion, it was even worse. Major McCarthy was unhurt, but most of his other officers had been either killed or wounded by the time the second perimeter was established. Captain Clinton E. Smith, the commander of E Company, had been killed. His executive officer, 1st Lt. John L. Gill, was wounded and later died. First Lieutenant Braxton H. Freeland and 2d Lt. Henry S. Nadratowski of E Company were killed in the initial attack. First Lieutenant M. Mendelson, and 2d Lt. Chester W. Sillman had been wounded and were essentially out of action. F Company was in even worse shape. Captain Earl L. White had been seriously wounded before the perimeter was established, but continued to perform heroically. First Lieutenant John E. Titterington had been killed during the initial attack. First Lieutenant Ferdinando Savastono and 2d Lts. Charles

C. Magyar, R. Stadclasy, and Cecil A. Greenwell were wounded. H Company, the 2d Battalion's heavy weapons company, was equally devastated. All of its officers, except 2d Lt. L. E. Foster, were either killed or wounded during the Saipan battle. Captain William T. Ward, 1st Lt. Russell E. Nord, 1st Lt. Robert G. Womble, and 1st Lt. Robert J. McGuire were each killed during the initial attack. Second Lieutenant Claude M. Gregory of Hobbs, New Mexico, was wounded and out of action.

Much of the leadership at the second perimeter, therefore, devolved to the senior sergeants. From the 1st Battalion, there were: from Company A, TSgt. John J. McLoughlin, twenty-four, of Troy, New York, and SSgt. Richard W. Hoffay, twenty-two, of West Sand Lake, New York; from Company B, TSgt. Michael R. Mele, twenty-six, of Albany, New York, and SSgt. Robert H. Cortez, twenty-six, of Astoria, Long Island; and from C Company, TSgt Ralph N. Gannaway, twenty-seven, of Fort Worth, Texas. From the 2d Battalion there were: from Company E, 1st Sgt. Norman L. Olsen, twenty-five, of Hempstead, Long Island; from Company F, 1st Sgt. Arthur B. Bradt, thirty, of Schenectady, New York; from Company H, 1st Sgt. Allan W. Haverly, twenty-four, of Schenectady, New York, TSgt. Frank Mandaro, twenty-four, Jackson Heights, New York, and SSgt. Schmid, thirty-one, of Pattersonville, New York.

The second perimeter was a desperate affair. The whole area was surrounded by the enemy who made attempt after attempt to get inside the perimeter. The men, armed only with rifles, carbines, and some machine guns, did not have much time to dig in to protect themselves. They had to use whatever means were available to create cover and concealment. The concrete and wooden houses in Tanapag Village were obvious locations for defensive positions, but they were used almost exclusively for the wounded. The more seriously wounded were dragged to the center of the perimeter, and the rest took up positions around the fringes of the perimeter and foraged for ammunition, which they brought to the men on the firing line. Private First Class George L. Brown, a baker from Albany, New York, Company B, 1st Battalion, was always looking for bullets for the rifles and always came back with a handful. He seemed to be constantly exposed to enemy fire and would later die from enemy-fire wounds. Some of the wounded men set up a weapons cleaning line that operated all day, cleaning the weapons and clips of ammunition that were fouled up by the beach sand. First Sergeant Norman Olsen described the wounded men's activities as follows: "The wounded continued fighting, too. When they couldn't fire any more, they helped us by cleaning guns which jammed for some reason or other. None of them complained even though we were out of water and it was a brutally hot day."

Other men who had had their weapons shot out of their hands or who saw that their buddies were running out of ammunition ducked from hole to hole and from trench to trench picking up ammo from the dead and wounded to give it to the men on the firing line. Three men from E Company of the 2d Battalion stood out in this regard: Pfc. Thomas F. Daley, twenty-nine, Brooklyn, New York; SSgt. Homer Z. Simms, twenty-five, of Decatur, Alabama; and Pfc. Gerald O. Laucella, twenty-three, of Schenectady, New York. "We picked up the ammo from the dead and the wounded," Private First Class Daley recalled. "We also found some scattered about loose. Simms and I worked pretty much together; I collected the ammo, Simms put it in clips." When Private First Class Laucella saw that the men in his sector were well supplied with ammo, he began collecting first-aid packets for the hard-pressed medical-aid men. As he bent over to pick up one of the packets, he saw two Japanese soldiers trying to infiltrate the American line. "I shot one and he groaned," Laucella recalled. "Then I got the other as he tried to get away. Neither moved much."

There was also a serious lack of medical aid and medical supplies in the perimeter. Most medics had been killed or wounded, and only one or two were left. Most first aid was administered by one wounded man to another. The few medics there, however, performed in an outstanding manner. First Sergeant Arthur Bradt of F Company said: "Those medics did wonders with practically nothing after their initial supplies of medicines and bandages were exhausted. They used gun slings for tourniquets, made splints out of branches, and cut up captured Jap flags and the wounded men's clothes for bandages." Two received particular mention, Cpl. John J. Bloomfield, twenty-two, of Troy, New York, and Pfc. Egidio Torchio, twenty-three, of Santa Cruz, California. Both men dropped their weapons and constantly exposed themselves to enemy fire as they made their way from trench to trench, treating the wounded.

Other riflemen, though seriously wounded, continued to fight. Private First Class Mark W. Winters was wounded during the withdrawal and was hit again after reaching the second perimeter. Nevertheless, he had someone prop him up in a sitting position on the front line and slowly and deliberately picked off several Japanese soldiers with his carbine. When he ran out of carbine ammunition, he asked a fellow soldier for an M-1 rifle, which was lying nearby. The soldier refused, pointing out that Winters would be firing from an exposed position and that enemy bullets were landing all over the area. Winters replied, "I'll stay here and fire until I get the last Jap or they get me." Later in the day, he was killed on the spot where he lay, not by the enemy, but by friendly fire from the hills above the plain.

Some more seriously wounded who could no longer take part in the active defense of the second perimeter stoically suffered in pain alone rather than have someone come off the front lines to aid and comfort them. Sergeant Attillo M. Grestini, of Company B, from Cohoes, New York, fought throughout the morning, manning a rifle position on the northeast corner of the perimeter. When artillery fire began falling near his position about noon, a shell blew his left arm off and mangled his left leg at the hip. He lay there for some time without uttering a sound, biting his lip to keep from crying out. Sergeants John A. Sidur and John J. Goot, both of Company B and Cohoes, New York, discovered him and carried him back sitting on a rifle to the center of the perimeter. Grestini, however, refused to let them help him further. He made a tourniquet for both his arm and leg and lay absolutely silent in a foxhole in the middle of the perimeter for the rest of the day. He had no medical treatment whatsoever, nor did he have any drugs to ease the pain. Amazingly, he survived the war, moved to Chicago, and raised a family.

At 1000 on July 7, Pfc. J. C. Baird, a radio operator with C Company, reached the perimeter carrying his heavy SCR-300 radio on his back. This in itself was remarkable, but then, with bullets flying all around him, he fixed the radio, which had been damaged by enemy fire. With the radio fixed, he reported to Capt. Emmett Catlin, 1st Battalion, S-3, and Major McCarthy saying that he could get through to the 105th CP. Catlin then reported to Lieutenant Colonel Jensen, the executive officer, 105th, that O'Brien's battalion had been over-run and that most of it had been wiped out. He further said that he was at RJ 2 with about one hundred men and needed help quick. McCarthy, using Baird's radio, then begged Jensen for tanks and help in the form of ammunition and medical supplies. Jensen promised to do what he could, but at that time the 105th CP itself was under heavy enemy attack. Baird's radio was subsequently knocked out during an artillery barrage that landed in the area some-time between 1130 and 1200.

As the morning wore on, the level of combat intensified greatly in the second perimeter. First Lieutenant Luke Hammond recalled, "Bullets were popping fiercely overhead while the trenches were crowded with soldiers—many who were wounded. My trench must have been near the center of the perimeter for troops were on all sides. Next to the beach, grenade, rifle, and BAR fire was continu-ous." Periodically, the Japanese would rush the trenches only to be mowed down. Hammond said, "None of us were going to leave. We would hold." From his vantage point, he could see several soldiers walking back and forth on the beach and between the trenches. He saw two of them fall from Japanese rifle bullets. At least fifteen men watched these shootings take place, but they could do nothing about them; they simply looked at each other in a helpless sort of way. Just then Captain Ackerman came crawling into the trench where Hammond was situated. Ackerman had been wounded; a hole showed through the back of his helmet and he had a bandage around his neck. First Lieutenant Hammond said, "Hello Lou." Cap-tain Ackerman responded, "What say, Luke?" and then with a seri-ous look in his eye asked, "Haven't you got any communications?" Hammond shook his head from side to side. Ackerman repeated the question and then crawled out of the trench.

The second perimeter consisted of two main features: the small houses in Tanapag Village and a series of trenches that ran through the town. There were several problems: First, it was not a closed circle. There were large gaps along its entire length and not all were covered by fire. During the course of the day, parties of about ten enemy soldiers infiltrated the perimeter and attacked the wounded in the houses in the village. Second, the perimeter was not confined to one side of the highway. At least thirty-five men had been placed by Major McCarthy on the east side of the highway, guarding the small buildings on that flank and denying them to the enemy. Third, the side of the perimeter along the beach was not protected by either the 1st or 2d Battalions. The two main points where the Japanese consistently tried to break the perimeter in any force were along the beach and along the road to the south.

To protect against the Japanese penetrating the perimeter and killing the wounded inside the houses, Major McCarthy assigned an armed rifleman to each house where there were wounded men. Private First Class Charles E. Emig, twenty-five, of Lima, Ohio, Company A, who had been fighting on the front lines, was assigned this task. For the next four to five hours, he moved from window to window firing at any enemy soldier who lifted his head. When mortar barrages were launched against the house, he did everything possible to shield the wounded from mortar fragments. At noon, when artillery rounds came dangerously close to the house, he moved the wounded men out into a ditch nearby. He was able to cover most men as they moved out of the house, but was killed as he moved across a window opening to help one of the wounded.

A second problem was the need to cover the gaps in the line of trenches through which the Japanese could infiltrate. Tech Sergeant Frank Mandaro of Company H saw two of his unit's machine guns overrun. "The two guns covered a blind spot in our perimeter," Mandaro said. "When the Japs first started coming out of a small grove of trees close by the beach, the machine guns kept quiet, leaving it up to the riflemen. They didn't want to disclose their positions if it wasn't absolutely necessary. In a few minutes, however, they had to begin shooting. I'd never seen so many Japs. As the machine guns opened up, the Japs fell like ten-pins, but others kept coming. They ran, they crawled, they tried to get close enough to toss grenades." Mandaro fired his rifle until it grew hot in his hands. Between bursts, he saw a small body of Japanese soldiers jump into one of the machine-gun pits. After a few seconds, the gun resumed firing, "So I figured our boys had done all right," he said. But the short halt in the firing gave another group of Japanese time to move up and pepper the machine-gun pit with grenades. Mandaro recalled, "One of the gunners, his face bloody, continued firing until he toppled over. Another man took his place. Then several grenades exploded all around and inside the gun position, and the Japs swarmed in." His men in the other machine-gun position withdrew and ". . . we just plugged up holes in the general line."

Another major problem was the vulnerability of the beach to Japanese attack. The enemy made frequent attempts to break the perimeter by moving stealthily along the beach to get in behind the American positions. Two men were largely responsible for protecting the beach flank that fateful morning. Private First Class Willie Hokoana, thirty, a native Hawaiian from Paia, Maui, Hawaii, was a member of E Company. Although he started out as an ordinary rifleman, Hokoana obtained a damaged BAR from a wounded soldier during the battle for Nafutan Point and repaired it himself. At 0900, he noticed that large numbers of the enemy were trying to work their way south, using the narrow spit of sand along the beach. He found a tree sapling on the beach with a fork in its trunk. Hokoana was a tall man, more than six feet in height. He placed his BAR in the crotch of the tree, and proceeded to fire at the enemy all day as they came along the water's edge. He was credited with killing more than 140 Japanese from this exposed position by the time it became dark. For his gallantry, he was promoted to sergeant and recommended by Major McCarthy for an award.

Helping Hokoana defend the beach that day was Sgt. William A. Baralis of Troy, New York, of Company A. He had been the pitcher for Company A's baseball team back in Hawaii. According to one of his buddies, "He sure had a marvelous arm." When he spotted Japanese soldiers moving down the beach, he told Private First Class Hawrylak, the ammunition carrier, to get all the grenades he could find. Even though he was seriously wounded, Hawrylak went from man to man and obtained all their grenades. They were then passed up to Baralis in a sort of bucket brigade of wounded men. Baralis would wait until Hokoana's fire drove the enemy off the open sand spit and then throw a grenade to drive them back into the open again. It was estimated that he tossed about 150 grenades and killed approximately one hundred Japanese that day. Unfortunately, due to his exposed position, he was hit in the spine by a bullet at 1500 that day and died the next day in the hospital.

There were many heroes plugging the gaps that day. Private William J. Callahan, twenty-five, of New Haven, Connecticut, of B Company, was crouched in a foxhole toward the center of the beach defense perimeter north of Tanapag Village with his BAR. Every few minutes, he raised himself up, pushed out his BAR, and pumped a string of bullets at the advancing enemy. Sometimes he let them get to within twenty yards, to make sure that every bullet paid its way with Japanese blood. "He must have gotten more than one hundred in the five or six hours he was in that sector," said Private Callahan's superior officer, 1st Lt. John F. Mulhern, twenty-four, of Portland, Maine.

Private John M. Purcell, twenty-two, of Schenectady, New York, E Company, acted gallantly in the defense of the second perimeter. He aligned eight rifles along a trench to cover a clearing, then ran from one to the other, pulling the triggers as the Japanese attacked his sector. Between enemy thrusts, he rushed from gun to gun, reloading each. At times he had to collect loose ammunition and fit bullets into clips. He later said, "I felt like the proverbial one-armed paperhanger with the seven-year itch." His actions helped save the American line, which, whittled by day-long enemy attacks and constant sniping, was drawn tight around the beach position sheltering helpless American wounded. For his heroic actions, Private Purcell was awarded the Silver Star.

Amid rumors that friendly troops and tanks were coming up to relieve them, the men began to notice friendly artillery fire dropping dangerously close to their front lines where the Japanese attacks were being repulsed. Second Lieutenant H. Scheer, Company D, crouched in a sandy trench with First Lieutenant Hammond, cried out, "What can we do, Luke? I don't know anything we can do." Hammond shook his head and said he didn't know, but that something had to be done. Word moved through the men, "Pass it back, artillery fire falling in our front lines!" The word was passed back for a radio, but there was none available. For a while, the artillery fire resumed, falling among the attacking Japanese troops, but then it began hitting the front lines again. Hammond recalled, "We felt completely deserted." According to Sgt. John Domanowski of B Company, "We were shelled by artillery. It seemed to me that they came from back of us. . . . The shells would burst near us, and I could see the shrapnel skip over the water and into the heads of the men. A lot of bodies were lying on the beach by now. The shelling did not last too long, but it did kill a lot of the men."

One exploding shell set fire to a shack where hand grenades and ammunition were stored. The burning shack began popping like a giant firecracker. The men hugged their foxholes while shells continued falling. Captain Earl L. White, the commander of F Company, 2d Battalion, though badly wounded in the initial fighting, started alone for the burning shack. He plunged into it without hesitation and moments later came out carrying a limp American body. He set the man down, turned around, and went deliberately into the flames a second time to rescue another burned American soldier. For his heroics, Captain White was awarded New York's Conspicuous Service Medal, equivalent to the Bronze Star.

Shortly after 1100, the men along the northeast side of the second perimeter in the vicinity of Tanapag Village came under heavy artillery and mortar fire, which wounded several men. Hammond described the situation, "Suddenly more fire began falling in our area. You could hear the swish of the shell a fraction of a second before the terrible explosion." He concluded that the fire was coming from the hills to their right from SPMs. Men were being killed and wounded right and left by the murderous fire. Hammond looked up "to see someone all bloody raise up on his hands and knees as dust and leaves were falling around him. A shell had hit almost upon him." Ricochets from the falling shells screamed over into the ocean. Then a round landed ten feet from Hammond's trench next to a building: "I was literally lifted off the ground and let down again." Someone then yelled, "There's ammunition in that building!" Hammond checked, but found no ammunition.

Private First Class Samuel Di Nova recalled the shelling that day. "Shells were hitting the ocean and the beach," he remembered. One hit close to him and knocked him out. When he woke up, he saw the sky and the sun and thought he heard music. His left leg was torn up and a medic was putting sulfa powder on it and a stocking to keep it clean. All around him he saw men getting hit. One soldier would be alive, then minutes later dead. There were men running all around the perimeter. Sergeant Carlo Patricelli, Headquarters Detachment, 1st Battalion, from Troy, New York, came running up to help him, but Di Nova could not move. Another friend of his from Troy, Cpl. Salvatore Ferino, came running by being chased by a Japanese officer swinging his sword. The officer missed Ferino but hit another soldier, Pvt. Herschel Davis, in the rear end. The Japanese officer was then shot and killed by Capt. John Bennett, a naval officer assigned to JASCO, using his .45-caliber pistol.

Farther up the beach Sgt. Ronald Johnson and some other men from the 105th had set up a beach perimeter. First Sergeant Bernard J. Zilinskas of Headquarters Detachment, 1st Battalion, encountered him on the afternoon of July 7, and asked him, "What are you doing here? Why aren't you up there on the outside, firing?" Sergeant Johnson replied, "Well Barney, I just don't have any ammunition. And I might ask you the same question. I see you have your gun. Why aren't you up there?" Rather than argue with an old antagonist from their National Guard days, Johnson moved up toward the edge of the perimeter, about thirty feet away. At about the same time, the perimeter began to receive heavy friendly fire. About a half hour later, after the fire had lifted, Johnson went back to the area inside the perimeter where he had left Zilinskas. As he recalled almost forty years later, "There was Barney, propped up against the tree still, and at this point very near death. What had happened apparently was that while he was sitting there a mortar shell had landed between his legs, or very close to between his legs, and had shattered both of them, and he was bleeding to death. He may have had some other wounds from the shrapnel; I don't recall. In any case, I knew he was within a few minutes of dying, and he had no awareness of my presence, of course."

Back on the second perimeter, the constant shelling was making the men in the trenches extremely nervous. A few began to panic and started to move toward the beach. Others followed. The group ran into the woods bordering the beach, but the shell fire followed them. As more joined, the panicked men dashed back out into the open, farther down the beach. Shortly after that, another mass movement started toward the beach. Hammond recalled that all that was necessary to get the men to move was for someone to get up and say, "Damn it! Let's fight our way out of here!" In spite of urgings by Lieutenant Scheer and 2d Lt. W. A. Cash of D Company, and Tech Sergeant Levesque of F Company, Hammond was initially reluctant to leave the trenches, but when he saw that everybody was leaving, he went along taking up the rear. When the fleeing men encountered cannon and machine-gun fire coming from the right front, they turned down the road bunched together. Hammond recalled, "Crashing sounds were heard and black smoke appeared in the midst of these men. One man was stumbling forward slowly moaning in a helpless way, "Oh-h-h, will somebody help me?" Someone did try to help him along. Men were trying to signal the artillery in the hills to tell them that they were Americans, but the firing continued. Hammond found a piece of paper and began waving it, hoping the American artillery and SPMs up in the hills would see it and cease firing, but no such luck.

Shortly thereafter, Hammond was positioned in a shell hole at the edge of the woods when he saw Japanese soldiers running wildly between his position and the crowd of men who had gone down the road. He began firing at the Japanese soldiers with his carbine. Suddenly, one of the Japanese soldiers came running toward him "like a bat out of hell!" He recalled: "One of our guys was sitting directly in the path of the oncoming Jap, and of course he opened fire. The Jap kept coming carrying his rifle with bayonet fixed. A surprised Jap if I ever saw one. He continued around the right side of our soldier still as fast as his short legs could carry him, but with his eye firmly fixed on the soldier in a sort of intense wonder as if to say, 'What the hell are you shooting at me for?' Suddenly he stopped, still looking at his enemy. Then one shot and he was dead. Our soldier made some comment about him keeping coming after he had already put two slugs in him." Several other Japanese ran across the open field in front of First Lieutenant Hammond's position. Hammond fired at two of them, but missed both. Another soldier brought one of them down. "Black smoke from a grenade rose from his body as he finished himself off."

At noon, after almost an hour of constant shelling, Major McCarthy decided that if he could muster a force strong enough, the men could fight their way back to the 105th Regimental CP and bring up help for the more seriously wounded. He asked for volunteers and about one hundred men came forward, many of them already wounded themselves. Those not wounded were asked to stay back and protect the more seriously wounded. The organization of McCarthy's "flying wedge," as it came to be known, and its subsequent movements attracted artillery fire from friendly forces, including Cannon Company, 165th Infantry, and the 27th Division Artillery on the heights above the plain. The results were disastrous. There were two separate concentrations of fire that struck the group of men. The first concentration, most likely from Cannon Company, fell on the edge of the group, causing extremely severe casualties. The men panicked and began to run at full speed south along the edge of the road. About 200 yards south of Tanapag, almost to Bloody Run, the already frightened men were hit with a second concentration of fire, more deadly than the first. Several men received direct hits. Panic-stricken and without leadership, the men stampeded like a herd of cattle. Many, finding no place to go on the land, jumped into the lagoon and began swimming out to the reef. Of nearly one hundred men who started out, seventy-one managed to swim 250 yards from the shore.

Of the men who went into the water, two or three of the more seriously wounded drowned and some returned to shore after swimming out only a short way. Private First Class Thompson, F Company, was caught in the artillery barrage and headed for the reef. Before he dove into the water, however, he stripped off all of his clothes except his helmet. He had swum about one hundred yards out into the lagoon when a Japanese machine gun opened up on him. He zigzagged, swam underwater, but he could not escape the firing. He gave up and began swimming back to the shore. When he reached land, the Japanese machine gun opened up again, forcing him to run for it. Moving from ditch to ditch and bush to bush, he finally made it back to the 105th Regimental CP three hours later, stark naked except for his helmet. Private First Class Marcus H. Itano, C Company, 1st Battalion, was about to swim out to the reef, but he could see enemy bullets hitting the water all around his comrades, so decided to make it back to the 105th Regimental CP on foot by running down the beach.

About twenty-five other men who started to swim out to the reef decided to turn back and set up a perimeter, near the banks of Bloody Run below Tanapag Village, which became known as the little perimeter. During the afternoon, this group was augmented from time to time by additional soldiers who had been able to get through from the second perimeter. By the end of the day, this group numbered close to seventy-five men. Unfortunately, due to lack of communications equipment, this group remained out of touch with the main body of the survivors in the second perimeter and the 105th Regimental CP, which was still farther to the rear. The two American perimeters—the second perimeter at Tanapag Village and the little perimeter below it—could be best described as islands amid a sea of Japanese opposition.

Those who made it to the reef were eventually picked up at about 1400 on July 7 by boats from an American destroyer operating offshore. Captain Joseph W. Boulware, in command of the destroyer *Haywood L. Edwards*, which was conducting a fire mission off the coast of Saipan on the morning of July 7, 1944, recalled seven years later that his ship rescued about forty wounded soldiers of the 105th Infantry from a jetty in Tanapag Harbor after the *banzai* attack. In early 1951, while Captain Boulware was serving as a professor of naval science and commander of the navy R.O.T.C. at Rensselaer Polytechnic Institute in Troy, New York, he recalled the following events in a conversation with Brig. Gen. Ogden J. Ross, former assistant division commander of the 27th Division:

We were firing "call" fire, that is we'd fire any type of mission called for from the beach. The ship was about a mile from the breakwater in Tanapag Harbor. When light came, we noticed a bunch of men on the breakwater waving. We didn't know yet about the *banzai.* A small Cub plane came flying around, circled over the men on the jetty and then flew out to us, dropping a note. "It seems the men on the jetty, are in trouble."

We sent in a motor whaleboat to the breakwater. It came back loaded with wounded soldiers. Then we sent in both of the destroyer's whaleboats, one towing a life raft to get them all. Meanwhile, we radioed "Troops in trouble on the breakwater." Another destroyer sent in a boat.

Our whaleboats brought back forty-four G.I.s and one Jap prisoner. The other destroyers took off about twelve. It seemed every one of the men was wounded. Some were naked, for they had to swim at one time or another. We understood from them that they were part of a battalion that was cut off by the *banzai* charge. They estimated 5,000 Japs overran them. They told of firing their machine guns until the weapons got too hot to use. The Japs just piled up in front of them, but more kept coming. Then they were overrun.

I watched those wounded soldiers coming on-board. They ignored their wounds to climb up to the deck from the whaleboats. The ship's doctor and pharmacist's mate gave them first aid, we fed them and gave them clothing. I tried to talk to one little fellow who seemed to be the leader. He came up on the bridge where I was. All this time our guns had kept firing and I asked him, motioning with my hands, if he wanted cotton for his ears. He shouted that he didn't need the cotton. He had been hearing guns so long and loud that morning he didn't hear it anymore.

We radioed to the Amphibious headquarters that we had picked the men up. They sent a fast patrol boat to take off the wounded to a larger ship with better accommodations. That was the last I saw of them. We continued our mission of firing at the Japs all the time.

About 1230, almost an hour after the friendly artillery concentrations had disrupted Major McCarthy's "flying wedge," a jeep came careening down the road from the north toward the second perimeter. Behind the wheel was 1st Lt. Bernard Tougaw, commander of C Company, 1st Battalion. When he reached the second perimeter, he stopped and said, "I'm going to get help!" and asked if any men wanted to risk it by going with him to the 105th Regimental CP. Six or eight men, including a couple of BAR men, ran out of the houses and ditches and got on the jeep with him. One of them was Cpl. William Bowsh from Hudson, New York, a cook from Company B. Hammond recalled that the jeep was a medical jeep with the name *Lena Horne* painted on it. Tougaw asked Hammond if he wanted to come along, but Hammond declined and waved him on.

Before Tougaw arrived on the scene, Corporal Bowsh had been trying to escape the artillery barrage. When neither the road nor swimming out to the reef seemed feasible, Bowsh dove underneath a house in the village. There were already five seriously wounded men hiding under the house, three from Company B, 1st Battalion. Bowsh started to give two of the Company B men medical attention: Pvt. William Banko from Hellertown, Pennsylvania, and Pfc. John B. Produit from Idaho Springs, Colorado. Bowsh took off his undershirt and bandaged both men, putting sulfa powder on the wounds and giving each a sulfa pill. While he was working on the two men, he gave his carbine to one of the other wounded men and asked him to put it together and stand guard. While he was attending to the two men, the wounded man killed two Japanese infiltrators with a hand grenade. They had crawled in under the house trying to get at the wounded Americans.

When Tougaw drove up with the jeep, Bowsh and one of the wounded men got in with him. Then four other men ran out and climbed in the jeep. They went down the road toward the 105th Regimental CP. Miraculously, during the first one hundred yards, not a single shot was fired at them. Tougaw stopped the jeep at the bridge over Bloody Run and began to talk to 1st Lt. Seymour Shutzer, assistant surgeon, 1st Battalion. While they were talking, several more men jumped on the jeep, making a total of twelve men hitching a ride. Just about that time, an enemy machine gun opened up and Tougaw accelerated the jeep across the bridge running over dead Japanese soldiers lying in the road. Bowsh recalled later, "It was like we were riding on ties on a railroad track." After crossing, the jeep hit a tree lying across the road and began to stall out. As it began to stop, Tougaw was shot and killed with a bullet between the eyes. He slumped over the wheel and the jeep rolled off the road into a ditch, scattering the men in several different directions.

Bowsh ran back toward the bridge near Bloody Run. He couldn't go under the bridge, so he got up on the road and began to cross. Just then three medium American tanks came up the road from the south and, mistaking Bowsh for the enemy, began to fire at him with their machine guns. When the tanks recognized who he was and stopped firing, a Japanese machine gun covering the bridge opened up on him. Bowsh jumped into a ditch alongside the road and landed on top of two Japanese soldiers. When his carbine would not fire, he jumped out of the ditch and was about to dive into Bloody Run when an American soldier came up to the ditch and shot the two Japanese. It was then that Bowsh realized that his carbine had not fired because the safety was on. As he was moving along the road south toward the American lines, Bowsh encountered another American soldier, obviously wounded, limping down the middle of the road with a cane. Suddenly, a Japanese soldier jumped out of the ditch on the other side of the road and began to threaten the wounded man with a pistol. He was yelling and hollering and waving a pistol under the American's nose. Bowsh shot the Japanese soldier, but it took two rounds to do the job. The wounded American just kept walking down the road like nothing had happened. Bowsh never saw him again.

Because Bowsh's carbine was running low on ammunition, he took the pistol from the dead Japanese soldier. At that moment, the Japanese machine gun covering the bridge opened up again. Forgetting the pistol, Bowsh jumped from the road into the nearest ditch in which another Japanese soldier was hiding. The Japanese spotted him, and began yelling, "Suwendah! Suwendah!" Bowsh said, "Suwendah hell!" and let him have three shots that killed him. Bowsh then recrossed the road and jumped into the ditch on the other side on top of two Americans. When the Japanese machine gun opened up again, one of his ditchmates said to him, "Get the hell out of here. You're drawing fire." Bowsh got out of the ditch and made his way through the muddy fields to a cement building about 150 yards away toward the beach and what he thought were the American lines. When he got to the building (which had been a Japanese air-raid shelter), it was empty. Immediately after he arrived, he was joined by three other exhausted American soldiers, including two from the 1st Battalion, Headquarters Company. One had a BAR that he had picked up somewhere, which needed to be put together. Corporal Bowsh put it together, loaded it with a full magazine of ammunition, and gave it back to the man. As they started to leave the building, the soldier with the BAR who was in the lead ran into two Japanese soldiers who were coming in the door. Bowsh described what happened next: "This guy with the BAR got excited. He had the damn thing on full automatic and when he saw the two Japs, he just pulled the trigger and things happened. Do you know, that BAR did not stop firing until every round was gone! He cut those Japs square in two. I was mad at him, though, because he used up all his ammunition."

Bowsh then made his way back to the perimeter of the 105th CP, only about seventy-five yards away, and reported to Lieutenant Colonel Jensen what had happened to B Company. He was the first soldier from either of the battalions of the 105th to make it back.

Shortly after noon on July 7, the first sign of relief for the trapped men appeared in the form of a platoon of medium tanks that had moved up the road from the 105th CP. They rolled to a stop on the north side of the Bloody Run bridge and for two hours bombarded the Japanese positions, but without much effect. Neither McCarthy nor anyone else had any means of communicating with the tanks to coordinate rescue efforts. Finally, a tank came lumbering up the road near First Lieutenant Hammond's position. It was all buttoned up, so Major McCarthy had to run out to the tank and bang on its turret with his pistol to get the crew's attention. While bullets whizzed around his head, McCarthy persuaded the tank to open its turret and let him inside. After some conversation with Lt. Jack P. Lansford, the tank commander, he used the tank's radio to call the 105th Regiment CP for help, but got no intelligible answer. Determined to reach the CP, he then organized a group of thirty-five men, mostly walking wounded, under the immediate command of 1st Sgt. Charles J. Stephani of B Company, to fight their way back to the CP and report the status of the two battalions. The balance of the men in the second perimeter were to remain behind to protect the wounded who were to be evacuated either by trucks or by Alligators. Following behind one of the tanks, Major McCarthy and First Sergeant Stephani led the men down the road to the Regimental CP, suffering the loss of more than half their strength along the way. When they reached the CP at 1500, on July 7, they provided Lieutenant Colonel Jensen and Colonel Bishop with more precise information regarding the location and condition of the two entrapped battalions and requested that trucks and Alligators be assigned immediately to evacuate the wounded.

21 Relief of the 105th Infantry

Lieutenant Colonel O'Brien last contacted the 105th Regiment CP at 0509 on July 7. At 0530, Lieutenant Colonel Jensen, the 105th's executive officer, contacted Lt. Col. William M. Van Antwerp, forty-two, of Albany, New York, G-2, 27th Division Headquarters, and reported, "By the sound of the fire [he] knew the enemy to be near the CP." At 0615, Van Antwerp received another message from Jensen stating that the 105th CP was pinned down by enemy fire. After receiving that message, which included O'Brien's earlier, brief message, Major General Griner immediately called Col. Albert K. Stebbins, commander of the 106th Infantry, and ordered him to alert his two infantry battalions on the line to be ready to move up in support of the 105th Infantry. Griner also ordered the 762d Tank Battalion to rush all available tanks to the support of the 105th at once.

At 0920, after receiving further information from the 105th CP about the condition of the two forward battalions, Griner ordered the 1st and 2d Battalions of the 106th under Colonel Stebbins to attack northeast astride the railroad tracks to relieve the embattled battalions. When it was learned that H Battery, 3d Battalion, 10th Marine Artillery Regiment, had been overrun and captured by the Japanese, Griner, under severe pressure from Lt. Gen. Holland M. Smith at NTLF, ordered Maj. Almerin C. O'Hara, commander of the 2d Battalion, 106th, who had already reached the 105th CP, to break off all support of the 105th and recapture the batteries. O'Hara protested this order because it would force him to retrace the steps the battalion had already taken and to move inland from the coastal road where his battalion was located. Griner insisted, so the 2d Battalion, 106th, deployed its men east of the railroad tracks. By 1135, it had recaptured Item Battery, 10th Marines, and by 1540 a second battery was recaptured. At this time, the 2d Battalion, 106th, ceased its advance and dug in for the night.

It was not until 1000 that Colonel Stebbins reported that the 1st Battalion, 106th Infantry, commanded by Lt. Col. Winslow Cornett, had begun its attack up the left side of the railroad tracks along the beach, seeking out the 105th CP. After some confusion, on July 7, the 1st Battalion, 106th, finally established firm physical contact with the 105th CP at 1410. Upon arriving at the 105th CP, Cornett's battalion ceased forward movement and sent out patrols to the front. After conferring with Jensen, it was decided to sweep the remainder of the Japanese (mostly stragglers) to the north and to bring the remnants of the 1st and 2d Battalions, 105th, back to the American lines. Jensen ordered his clerks and technicians led by Capt. John C. Baker and 1st Lt. John F. "Jack" Armstrong of Headquarters Company, 105th Infantry, to organize a skirmish line and advance forward with the 1st Battalion of the 106th, to reach the perimeters that had been previously established by the 1st and 2d Battalions, 105th.

At 1600, the skirmish line reached Bloody Run about 400 yards in front of the 105th CP. Cornett dispatched his B Company, under the command of 1st Lt. Max W. Renner, to recapture the artillery pieces of How Battery, 3d Battalion, 10th Marine Artillery. The guns were found in perfect condition, although it was evident that the Japanese had tried to make use of them. Not a single breechblock had been removed by the marine artillerymen. There was still some enemy resistance in the area, which was immediately cleaned up by Renner's men. American casualties were minimal. At 1700, Griner called the 105th CP and ordered Colonel Bishop to withdraw his men to the rear because the 106th had bypassed the 105th CP, and thus became tactically responsible for the zone of action they occupied. Bishop protested because the 105th's Headquarters Company and Antitank Company were still manning the skirmish line. Griner reiterated the order and the 105th CP elements were withdrawn. In any event, the 1st and 2d Battalions of the 105th were completely disorganized, surviving personnel at the close of the day consisting of only one officer and one hundred men, mostly without equipment. The 105th, less the 3d Battalion, was relieved by the 106th Infantry at 1630 on July 7 and moved to a bivouac area. The 3d Battalion was relieved in the front line at 0630 on July 8 by elements of the 2d Marine Division and closed in to the 105th regimental assembly area at 1500.

The important role of army tank units in effecting the relief of the trapped two battalions of the 105th Infantry cannot be underestimated. At about 0530, Major General Griner ordered the 762d Tank Battalion to rush all available tanks to support the 105th Infantry. The tanks detached to the 105th Infantry on the morning of July 7 totaled three platoons—two of light tanks and one of medium tanks. After their hasty summons, all three tank platoons moved out and reached the 105th CP shortly after 0600. The two platoons of light tanks were commanded by Lieutenant Guffey and Lt. John B. Phalon, of La Crosse, Wisconsin. Lieutenant Jack P. Lansford commanded the platoon of medium tanks. Lieutenant Ralph W. Spears, who accompanied the tanks as the infantry liaison officer, reported to Colonel Bishop and was ordered to proceed up the road to locate the positions of the 1st and 2d Battalions, 105th. Spears returned to his jeep and started down the road, followed by a platoon of five light tanks under Guffey. After about one hundred yards, Spears sighted a group of Japanese ahead. He checked once again with Colonel Bishop and then got back into his jeep and, followed by the tanks, proceeded north toward the area where he thought he would find the 1st and 2d Battalions. When the column reached RJ 5, the rear tank in Lieutenant Guffey's column was knocked out by enemy gun fire.

After crossing the bridge at Bloody Run, Lieutenant Guffey, in the lead tank, stopped to make a reconnaissance of the area in front. His second tank stopped across the bridge to the north and his third tank commanded by Sgt. Oliver Hendricks stopped between the bridge and RJ 5. While Guffey was reconnoitering, a party of Japanese moving from the east disabled his second tank's track with a magnetic mine. Despite the blown track, the second tank's driver was able to move it forward and clear the bridge so that another tank could pass. By this time, the area was full of enemy soldiers trying to destroy the

tanks. Guffey radioed the commander of the second tank and ordered him to destroy the tank's guns and have his men escape from
the crippled tank under the protective gun fire of the other two
tanks. His third tank, under Sergeant Hendricks, meanwhile had
slipped off the road and bellied up on a concrete obstruction. Without infantry support, Guffey decided that his lone tank could not
function forward of the lines. Because he had already lost two tanks,
he withdrew down the road to the 105th Regimental CP.

After discharging his own crew at the 105th CP, Guffey took control of the tank himself and returned to the disabled one where Hendricks's men were still trying to fight off the encircling Japanese.
When Guffey arrived, Hendricks's tank had run out of ammunition
and the Japanese were all around the vehicle, trying to set it afire
and get at the men inside. Lieutenant Jack P. Lansford's platoon of
medium tanks came up and covered Hendrick's tank with fire, while
Hendricks's crew crawled out the escape hatch at the bottom of the
vehicle. Guffey's tank brought the men from Sergeant Hendricks's
tank inside and evacuated them to the 105th Regimental CP without any further casualties. With the exception of Lt. John B. Phalon's
platoon of light tanks, which remained to help guard the 105th CP's
perimeter, all tanks were pulled well back of the 105th CP's line of
defense. For the balance of the morning, the tanks provided fire support for the 105th's CP.

At 1100 General Griner requested that some marine tanks be released to the 27th Division from NTLF control to aid in the relief of
the two hard-pressed battalions of the 105th, but this request was almost immediately denied by Lt. Gen. Holland M. Smith. According
to Major General Griner, "Headquarters did not accept my version
of the importance of the action then in progress." However, not long
afterward, Lieutenant General Smith did order the two marine divisions to release 1,000 rounds of 105mm howitzer ammunition to
the army's 27th Division, which by now was running short.

Sometime between 1200 and 1230 on July 7, word reached the
105th CP that artillery shelling had forced many of the survivors of
the 1st and 2d Battalions (Major McCarthy's "flying wedge") in the
second perimeter to swim out into the ocean in order to survive. Guf-

fey's three light tanks were ordered to move up the beach and drive away the Japanese firing on the Americans in the water. When he moved his tanks into the water to get a better shot at the enemy, all three fell into a depression between the beach and the reef and, with their engines drowned, were put out of action. Guffey immediately radioed Lieutenant Lansford for help. Lansford's two medium tanks had moved up the coastal road about 800 yards, subject to constant enemy sniper fire and Molotov cocktails, and made contact with the remnants of the 1st and 2d Battalions of the 105th Infantry near the second perimeter. In a scene of unbelievable confusion, there were American infantry on both sides of the road in considerable numbers; many of them wounded. Lansford said later, "The men were utterly done up, but their faces bore an expression of great relief as they approached the tanks." After talking briefly with Major McCarthy, who used his radio to call the 105th Regimental CP, Lansford received an urgent radio message from Lieutenant Spears directing him to return and to help Guffey, whose tanks were still in the water near the 105th CP.

Once the attack on the 105th CP was repulsed, First Lieutenant Albanese, 1st Battalion, S-4, renewed his efforts to resupply the beleaguered 1st Battalion of the 105th with food, water, and ammunition. He commandeered a tank, loaded it with some food and ammunition, and ordered it to move forward. The tank driver refused to move off the road for fear of hitting Japanese land mines and then received an order to return to the 105th CP. Later that afternoon, after Major McCarthy managed to reach the 105th CP, Albanese and 1st Lt. Herman U. Schrader, twenty-four, of Browning, Montana, S-4 of the 2d Battalion, organized a convoy of trucks and jeeps loaded with medical supplies and ammunition. At approximately 1600, these vehicles made a mad dash up the road to the embattled men. On the way, Albanese observed a number of jeeps on the side of the road, each holding dead American soldiers. When the loaded trucks reached the first culvert, Japanese soldiers under the culvert opened up with machine-gun fire and hand grenades. Albanese was wounded by fragments from a grenade that exploded under his jeep and was taken to the rear for medical treatment. Schroeder, though wounded, managed to get three of his trucks to men who were still fighting the enemy. He loaded the trucks with the most seriously wounded and made it back to the 105th CP.

Major McCarthy's information convinced Major General Griner that the two battalions of the 105th could not continue fighting until they had been rested and reorganized. The problem was getting the embattled men back through the lines to the rear. Brigadier General Ogden J. Ross, assistant commander of the 27th Division, was given the task of rescuing the men trapped farther up the beach. Ross ordered elements of the 734th Amphibian Tractor Battalion to proceed up the lagoon and come ashore at the second and little perimeters. By 1730 the Alligators had reached the beaches where the weary defenders were still killing Japanese and began evacuating the wounded. Troops from the 27th Division Reconnaissance Troop came in with the Alligators and relieved the few men left of the 105th Infantry who had not been wounded and who were valiantly continuing the fight.

As they waited to be relieved, the men of the 105th, many badly wounded, were still engaged in heavy combat with the enemy. Lieutenant Luther Hammond recalled that from his position on the beach, "Machine-gun bullets popped in the air overhead and bursted [*sic*] into the trees," and "SPMs down the beach [began] firing on us." Somebody yelled, "Someone wave a white flag." Hammond recalled that Sgt. Luther V. Reese from Gallipolis, Ohio, Company C, 1st Battalion, "with determination and disregard for his own life, stepped out on the beach to wave a panel. That was the last I saw of him. He was shot down either by Japs or our troops. It was impossible to determine who was doing the firing. Japs were between us and them."

The presence of an American tank on the road near the beach encouraged some Americans who had been hiding in the woods to come out of hiding. One American soldier who approached the perimeter had no shirt, no helmet, and no gun. He did, however, have a weapon—a Japanese *samurai* sword. He seemed happy that he had reached the second perimeter and appeared confident of his safety. Then someone yelled, "Watch it Mac, there's a sniper in a foxhole over there." Suddenly, a shot rang out, and then another, and the man fell to the ground. Men nearby reached out and pulled him into the trench. Hammond later learned that the sword-bearing American soldier had killed three Japanese in hand-to-hand combat. Another soldier who came out of the woods about that time was 1st Lt. Charles T. Ryan, the executive officer of Company D. Hammond recalled that Ryan, "crawls out of the woods out into the open moving with determination and purpose. I spoke to him. He glanced at me, said something, and kept going. He was wounded so that he couldn't walk. Only a few seconds passed when a shot was heard just up the beach. A horrifying cry was heard and a muffled 'shot our own men' by a crying man. It sounded something to that effect. I still don't know the story."

About 300 yards down the beach, Hammond could see that the relief tanks and accompanying infantrymen were having trouble dealing with a Japanese pillbox on the beach. Two American light tanks were stuck in the sand after an attempt to move out on the reef and circle around the Japanese pillbox. The men with the tanks were firing tommy guns. The Japanese were intermittently firing machine guns and 75mm cannons at the tanks. When the firing abated for a while, Hammond observed two men crawling up the water's edge of the beach ahead of the tanks. It looked as though they planned to throw grenades at the pillbox, but in reality they were after the saber of a dead Japanese officer. One man picked up the saber, and stooping over, they both ran back a few yards. They then stood up and began walking back to their tank; the man carrying the saber strode proudly. Hammond recalled what happened next: "Suddenly, the fast chatter of a Jap MG sounded from the pillbox. The man in the rear was hit. His helmet flew off—his arms outspread—the saber flew to one side and down he went on his face." Hammond thought he was dead for sure, but a few seconds later he rolled over on his back and then rolled farther into the water. All the while yelling for help, he raised himself half up and dragged himself, falling and rolling toward the tanks. Before he could be run over, someone from one of the tanks moved him to a safe place.

When Cpl. Eddie Beaudoin arrived at the beach, after wandering around for three hours, he was in a daze and covered with blood.

He had killed a number of Japanese in hand-to-hand combat, but had no idea how many. As he was talking to a couple of American soldiers on the beach, two enemy soldiers burst out of the brush, one carrying a flag and the other a rifle. Beaudoin shot the Japanese soldier with the flag, but the soldier with the rifle shot him in the head. Beaudoin fell into the water, unconscious and paralyzed. Everyone assumed he was dead, but Pfc. Mickey Grevine of Scranton, Pennsylvania, Company D, pulled him out of the water. Staff Sergeant Walter Grigas, twenty-two, of Baldwin, New York, a medic attached to the 105th, pushed Beaudoin's brain matter back into his skull and placed a bandage on his head. Captain (later Major) Richard Charet, thirty-six, of Brooklyn, New York, 1st Battalion Surgeon, came over and helped Grigas with the bandage. Miraculously, Corporal Beaudoin was still alive and was evacuated from the beach shortly thereafter. He survived the war and would later have children and grandchildren.

At about 1730, with enemy fire still pelting the beach positions, five Alligators approached the beach behind the second perimeter. Several men waded out into the water to guide them. As the Alligators got closer, the men began loading the wounded on board. Stretcher cases were brought out first, and when the Alligators were fully loaded, they moved off. After helping with the stretcher cases, Hammond moved back to comfort the wounded men still waiting on the beach. Among them were Capt. Emmett Catlin, S-3, 1st Battalion, 105th, and 2d Lt. Kendrick R. "Fig" Newton, Company A, 1st Battalion. There also were 2d Lt. W. A. Cash of D Company, 1st Battalion, 105th Infantry, with his arm in a sling; 2d Lt. H. Scheer of D Company, being helped by one of his men; 2d Lt. M. A. Sereton of Company D, lying in a shell hole looking pale and weak; and TSgt. E. Hermans, a cook in A Company, 1st Battalion. Technical Sergeant Frederick W. Stilz, twenty-nine, of Brooklyn, New York, and a member of Company A, 1st Battalion, was moving among them offering water and consolation.

More Alligators arrived on the beach behind the second perimeter, bringing with them elements of the 27th Division Reconnaissance Troop. As Hammond was assisting in loading stretchers, someone said, "You better get on, Mac." Hammond waded out into the water and crawled into the next Alligator. Coincidentally, on board was Capt. Albert A. Butkas, executive officer of the 1st Battalion, who had been shot in the stomach and was in bad condition. Once the Alligator cleared the reef, it made its way down to the beach opposite the 105th CP. There the wounded were placed in trucks for transport to a field hospital. Captain Charet, 1st Battalion Surgeon, told Hammond to get into one of the trucks for transport to the field hospital. When they arrived at the 31st Field Hospital, there were rows of patients waiting to be treated. The more seriously wounded—such as Captains Butkas, Catlin, and Ackerman and SSgt. Harold Rehm (who later died of his wounds)—were evacuated to a hospital ship on July 8. Hammond's wounds were not treated until July 10 when he transferred to a hospital ship and was sent to Eniwetok for two weeks. Following that period of convalescence, he and other less seriously injured men were placed on a merchant ship and sent back to Saipan to await transportation to Espiritu Santo in the New Hebrides Islands.

Private First Class Samuel Di Nova, D Company, was wounded in the leg and lying on the beach waiting to be evacuated that afternoon. There was "fighting going on all around," and men were being hit right and left. For protection from air bursts, the wounded men were placed under palm trees. Di Nova recalled that Sgt. Nicholas A. Grinaldo of Troy, New York, C Company, grabbed him and dragged him thirty to forty feet to a safer place. "Hang onto this good leg, because it's the only way I'm going to get you out of here," Grinaldo told Di Nova. More than forty-five years later, Grinaldo was awarded a Bronze Star for saving Di Nova from almost certain death.

Di Nova remembers being carried from under the palm trees to the beach and then being lifted on to one of the Alligators by two men he knew only as "Bailey" from Watervliet, New York, and "Big John" from New York City. The fighting was still going strong and men were still getting hit by gun fire from the Japanese up and down the beach. Di Nova still remembers that the Japanese were shooting at the rescue vehicles as they came in and out of the lagoon. When the Alligator he was on reached land, Di Nova was put on a stretcher and tied on a jeep, which brought him to a large area behind the lines where the dying and wounded American soldiers were lying in rows. The doctors were operating on men out of the back of a big truck. His comrade from D Company, Cpl. Salvatore S. Ferino, was among the wounded. Di Nova was then taken out by boat to the hospital ship, the USS *Samaritan,* and his leg was operated on. The *Samaritan* was one of four hospital ships evacuating the wounded from Saipan; the others were *Relief, Solace,* and *Bountiful.*

From the ship, Di Nova was sent to the 29th General Hospital on New Caledonia and subsequently was flown to Hawaii. With him on the plane were other wounded men from Company D, including Pfc. Warren F. Garrett of Troy, New York; Sgt. Joseph L. Robitaille and Pfc. Leland Carrier from Lansingburgh, New York; and Pfc. Vito Furciniti and Cpl. Salvatore Ferino from South Troy, New York. Corporal John T. Hemmings of Troy, New York, Company C, 1st Battalion, 105th Infantry, was also on board the plane.

When his time came for evacuation, Sgt. John Domanowski of Company B, who had been wounded in both arms, recalled, "Just before dark, an amphibious tank drove up on the beach and started to pick up the wounded. It was almost full when I walked up to it, and there was just enough room for one more near the engine. With my two broken arms, there was no way that I could climb up there myself. I saw Terry Tarantino [Pfc. Nunzio R. Tarantino from San Francisco, California, and a member of Company B] and asked him to boost me up. With his help and the help of others, I did get on." While he was helping Domanowski, Tarantino kept repeating over and over again, "You should have see[n] Savage. You should have seen Savage." He was referring to Sgt. Orville R. Savage of Indianapolis, Indiana, of Company B. For the next forty years, Domanowski "kept thinking that Savage must have been some fighter."

Domanowski remembered riding on the Alligator for about a mile or more and then coming up on the shore. He remembered someone saying, "Watch it. This one has two broken arms." He was then laid down on the ground and immediately fell asleep. When he woke up the next morning, he was in a first aid station "that was put up in a hurry." One of his first visitors from Company B's Weapons Platoon was Sgt. James R. "Red" Howard from Jasper, Tennessee. Another visitor was Sgt. Joseph Claus Jr., Company F, 2d Battalion, an old friend from back home on Long Island, New York. The next thing Domanowski remembered was being on an operating table and thinking the doctors were going to amputate his left arm. When he woke up, he was relieved to find he still had both of his arms. He was then evacuated from Saipan by plane to Johnson Island and Hawaii. On board the plane with him was Pfc. Richard C. Tessnear from Mooresboro, North Carolina, also a member of Company B. Tessnear's leg had been amputated at the field hospital and unfortunately he died on the flight from Johnson Island to Hawaii. When Domanowski arrived at the hospital in Hawaii, a nurse came into the ward and asked if anyone had heard about 1st Lt. Seymour Drovis. She said that they had gotten married just before he left for Saipan. Although Sergeant Domanowski wasn't sure, he thought that Drovis had been killed during the battle, but he could not bring himself to tell the nurse what he suspected. (Drovis, was in fact, killed July 7, during the withdrawal from the initial perimeter.)

Staff Sergeant Felix M. Giuffre, Company A, who had been wounded four times during the battle, lay on the beach wounded for what seemed to be a long time before any effort was made to evacuate him to safe territory. He recalled that after he was evacuated from the beach, he was driven to the hospital by the brother of SSgt. Harold Rehm, Company A. With him at the hospital was TSgt. John McLoughlin of Company A, who had been wounded during the attack on July 7, when a mortar round exploded in front of him, mangling his left hand and forcing it to be amputated. McLoughlin survived the battle, and forty-five years later was awarded the Bronze Star.

22 The Last Days on Saipan

While the survivors were being evacuated from the beaches near Tanapag Harbor, the balance of the 27th Division prepared for the task of mopping up the Japanese left on the island. To shore up the line, the 3d Battalion, 6th Marines, was committed, late in the afternoon of July 7, to fill in the gap between the right flank of the 106th on the Tanapag Plain and the 3d Battalion, 105th, still fighting along the hillside above the coconut grove. As night fell on July 7, the 165th Infantry, with the 3d Battalion of the 106th attached, pushed through Hara-Kiri Gulch against only slight opposition and dug in along the cliffs overlooking the plain. Strong points consisting of machine guns, antitank weapons, mortars, and artillery pieces were set up every five yards along the line. There were still many enemy soldiers unaccounted for. Where were they and what were they doing? Most observers believed that the Japanese would regroup and renew the attack until they were all dead.

At 1900 on July 7, division headquarters received a report from the 165th Infantry that the Japanese would make another counterattack at 0300 on the morning of July 8. As the evening wore on, there were repeated reports from observation posts all along the high ground that the Japanese were assembling north of RJ 12, in the area near Makunsha. At 0047 on the morning of July 8, reports were received from the OP on Hill 767 that the Japanese were moving south to make an attack. This time the enemy's plan was simple. They used the beach exclusively, by-passing the plain with its wide-open spaces until they reached the village of Tanapag. There they moved inland to a point east of the road and waited. Patrols were sent out to probe the American lines. At about 0430, the Japanese launched their main attack primarily against the 1st Battalion, 106th, next to the beach.

The 106th had a field day that morning. All men in Company A opened up with their weapons and the mortars began pounding away. The enemy headed diagonally across the front of the battalion toward the beach again. Some reached the water's edge and tried to swim around A Company's flank. The battalion commander called it a "massacre." Company A estimated that its men killed about 700 Japanese in the next two hours, many at relatively long range. Company B, 1st Battalion, also took a terrible toll of the enemy, many of whom were able to get in much closer to the American lines before being killed. Estimates of those killed in the second counterattack were around 1,000, including the 700 killed by Company A. Many Japanese began to kill themselves with hand grenades. Just after 0700, the counterattack died out completely and only a few men were left in front of the 106th's line "yelling and jumping around among the bodies of their compatriots."

What has been described as "one of the most devastating single battles of the war" was over, and to the victor belongs the spoils. At 0800 on July 8, began the greatest single souvenir hunt of the entire Pacific War. By 1100 on July 8, nearly every soldier in the 106th Infantry had picked up swords, pistols, battle flags, and other keepsakes from the defeated Japanese. One soldier had his arms so full of sabers that he could barely carry them. At 1135 on July 8, the 27th Division was relieved by the 2d Marine Division with the 165th Infantry Regiment attached. The 27th Division was ordered into corps reserve.

Following the vicious fighting on July 7 and 8, there were literally thousands of dead Japanese soldiers lying on the Tanapag Plain. They needed to be buried immediately. One correspondent, who surveyed much of the battle area wrote: "The whole area seemed to be a mass of stinking bodies, spilled guts, and brains." Colonel M. Oakley Bidwell, forty-five, of Orlando, Florida, G-1, 27th Division, who was in charge of the burial detail, remembered the scene as follows: "I don't think I can draw a picture more horrible than my memory of Tanapag Plain. It appeared to be virtually solid dead soldiers. A creek ran through a shallow ravine, emptying into a beautiful turquoise-blue lagoon. The creek and its banks seemed filled with bodies. And while I watched, a huge crimson flower grew out of the mouth of the creek." Private George F. Herman of Headquarters Company, 105th Infantry, remembered seeing "Jap bodies in the sun for a week until they were as big as sumo wrestlers and bursting like balloons." Sgt. Stephen J. Behil from Binghamton, New York, remembers what it was like the day after the attack. On July 8, acting as a truck driver and bulldozer operator, he and another man from C Battery of the 249th FA went up to bury dead Japanese. Graves Registration people were separating the dead Americans from the dead Japanese. The bulldozers dug huge trenches and then pushed the stacks of dead Japanese soldiers into them and buried them in the mass graves.

There was an immediate controversy regarding how many Japanese took part in the attack on the morning of July 7. On the morning of July 8, NTLF Headquarters, under the command of Lt. Gen. Holland M. Smith, sent a dispatch to Admiral Turner which stated that the 1st and 2d Battalions, 105th Infantry, had been "overrun by a considerable force estimated to be at least 300 to 400 Japanese, supported by two tanks." Major General Griner immediately protested these gross underestimates and ordered Colonel Bidwell, 27th Division G-1, to supervise a very careful body count of the dead Japanese. Bidwell recalled, "We had an overlay on a large-scale map of the area, on which we recorded and numbered each enemy mass grave, with the number burried [sic] in each, the count was verified by two warrant officers or engineer officers in each case." One of those in charge of counting bodies was CWO4 Stephen A. Burns, who later received an official citation for his work in organizing "a detail of engineers, Japanese prisoners of war [including Japanese civilians], and incidental equipment in such an efficient manner as to accomplish the burial of several thousand enemy dead in less than four days. While supervising the burial, he shot and killed an armed Jap who had feigned death amid a pile of bodies awaiting burial, thereby preventing casualties to men working in the vicinity." On July 12, Colonel Bidwell submitted a letter to

NTLF, which stated that by actual count, 4,311 enemy soldiers were buried in the area between the 1st and 2d Battalions, 105th, and the farthest advance of the enemy. A further breakdown of the enemy dead indicated that 2,295 were killed in the combat area of the 1st and 2d Battalions, 105th, and 2,016 in the combat area of the 1st and 2d Battalions, 106th; the 3d Battalion, 6th Marines; and the 3d Battalion, 105th Infantry. These latter enemy dead represented the number of enemy that pushed beyond the defensive line of the 1st and 2d Battalions, 105th Infantry.

Lieutenant General Holland M. Smith, with typical ill grace, immediately questioned these figures, insisting that a large percentage of those buried were casualties from air raids, naval gun fire, and so forth that had taken place almost daily since June 11, 1944. Marine Major General Harry Schmidt, who succeeded Lieutenant General Smith as commander of V Corps, compounded the controversy when he stated in a letter to Major General Griner on July 15: "More than 300 freshly killed Japanese were counted on 8 July, in front of and in the positions of the 3d Battalion, 10th Marines [Artillery] which were overrun. It is probable that these Japanese constituted a large part of the enemy force which penetrated the positions of the 105th Infantry." Major General Schmidt further suggested that the very large numbers of enemy dead, due to the advanced state of decomposition, had apparently been in the area for some time.

Testimony from officers who visited the battle scene shortly after the attack, however, supported the higher figures of 3,000 to 4,000 participants in the July 7 attack. A committee of officers appointed by Admiral Spruance, which visited the scene on the morning of July 12, after the burial had been underway for almost three days, estimated the force to have been from 1,500 to 3,000. Major General Griner, who visited the scene on July 8, the first general officer to do so, put forth a compelling argument, based on the condition of the Japanese bodies when he visited the scene the day after the battle, that most of the Japanese dead were killed on July 7. In a letter that he wrote to marine Major General Schmidt on July 12, 1944, General Griner stated: "The assumption that the Japanese dead found on the ground in the area around Tanapag were killed by the action of our air arm and by naval gunfire since the preliminary strikes on the island on 11 June cannot be supported. As the only general officer to visit the scene on 8 July, I must insist that my observations in the case be given credence. I viewed personally upwards of one thousand enemy bodies and nowhere did I find marked decomposition of bodies which would indicate that the enemy had been dead for more than thirty-six to forty-eight hours."

There is no dispute, however, that out of the 1st and 2d Battalions of the 105th (less Company G), there were 406 officers and men killed during the *gyokusai* attack and 512 wounded. To preserve the morale of fresh troops coming up as reserves, Colonel Bidwell decided that no U.S. dead bodies would be sent to the rear by the road, as this would have required the bodies to be piled in open trucks like cordwood. Instead, he requisitioned and received a number of amphibious vehicles in which the American dead were placed. The bodies were taken to the rear by sea until they reached the Graves Registration section. On July 9, a muster roll was called from the eight companies of the two battalions of the 105th present on the night of July 6. Only 189 men answered the roll call. Another 200 were present from G Company and elements of both battalions not up on the line on the morning of July 7.

Once Marpi Point, the northernmost part of the island, was reached by elements of the 4th Marine Division, Admiral Turner declared that Saipan was "secured" as of 1600 on July 9. Although some 3,000 Japanese stragglers still remained on the island, the bloody battle was over after twenty-five days. On July 13, the 2d and 4th Marine divisions were pulled back into the center and southern portions of the island to prepare for the invasion of nearby Tinian Island. The task of rooting out the last remnants of the enemy forces on Saipan fell to the 27th Division. From the time Turner declared the island secured until the 27th Division left in August and September 1944, an additional 1,976 enemy soldiers were killed and almost 3,300 Japanese civilians captured.

When it was clear that the battle was over and that the Japanese forces were defeated, hundreds of Japanese civilians began to commit mass suicide. Saipan was the first island encountered by the

Americans where there was a large Japanese civilian population. Frightened by government propaganda that the American soldiers would rape Japanese women and kill the children, and urged on by Japanese military, many Japanese civilians chose suicide over surrendering. American soldiers watched in horror as hundreds of civilians made their way to the top of the bluffs overlooking the plain and hurled themselves to the rocks below. Others leapt from the cliffs of Marpi Point. At times the waters below the point were so thick with the floating bodies of men, women, and children that naval craft were unable to steer a course without running over them. Other civilians simply waded into the surf to drown and some blew themselves apart with grenades.

During the period between July 9 and July 16, 1944, each infantry regiment of the 27th Division was withdrawn to bivouac areas south of the general Tanapag-Donnay line. On July 9, 1944, the 105th was ordered to a bivouac area at Brown Beach 1 on the east shore of Saipan near the Kagaman Peninsula. The next day it was to begin antisniper patrols in the Kagman Peninsula area. While the 3d Battalion of the 105th was reasonably intact, the 1st and 2d Battalions were decimated. When Major Dolan attempted to regroup the two battalions on the morning of July 9, there was only one officer and 128 men in the 1st Battalion and 115 men in the 2d Battalion. These totals included all of the liaison men in the combat teams, such as tankers, artillerymen, supply men, and even naval personnel responsible for directing fire from naval ships at sea. Private First Class Arthur Herzog, Antitank Company, 105th, recalled that the two battalions had been so cut down that they "looked like two companies walking out." Staff Sergeant Walter Grigas, Medical Detachment, 105th, recalled that the 1st Battalion was whittled down to the point that it could be served food with only two cook stoves. Sergeant Angelo Rossi from Lafayette, California, Weapons Platoon, Company A, was wounded a week before the *gyokusai* attack. When he returned to Company A on July 9, he asked his friend, Sgt. Louis Campisi from Troy, New York, "Where is everyone?" Campisi replied, "They're all gone." Three out of five men in Rossi's machine-gun squad had been killed in the brutal suicide attack. Of the thirty-four men in the 2d

Platoon of Antitank Company who were up on the line the evening of July 6, ten were killed and twelve were wounded so badly they were evacuated and never returned to the unit.

Mop-up duty was dangerous. Second Lieutenant Joseph J. Meighan of Cohoes, New York, M Company, 3d Battalion, 105th, was leading an antisniper patrol on the Kagman Peninsula shortly after Saipan had been declared secure. "We were assigned a section to patrol and came upon a narrow footpath. A comrade and I were talking. We glanced at each other as we exchanged conversation, and just as he was about to turn his head to respond, a purple hole appeared in the center of his forehead. His eyes glazed in death before his body collapsed to the ground. About ten yards to our front center was a patch of camouflage. We dove into the underbrush, pinpointed the target, divided a squad into two sections, had it circle right and left, then closed in from the rear. Upon signal, they fired into the camouflage and it yielded two Japs, dug in, giving them a commanding view of our approach."

With the ranks of the officers of the 1st and 2d Battalions of the 105th seriously depleted, there were numerous reassignments from other units of the 105th during the mop-up period. Second Lieutenant Arthur G. Hansen, who had served with Company G, 2d Battalion, 105th, was given command of what was left of Company E, 2d Battalion, only thirty-three men out of a company strength of 183. Hansen recalled "taking out a patrol in the area called 'Suicide Gulch.' We came across a barn-like structure, which we could detect contained some Japs. We set it afire and none of the occupants chose to come out and perished in the fire." Hansen went on, "Later while moving alongside the gulch I was at the head of the column and drew some sniper fire, which hit the rocks alongside my face, spattering me with stinging bits of coral-limestone. We did an about face and worked our way into cover while additional shots were fired without effect. We never did locate the source of the fire because of the dense undergrowth, but I am thankful the source was a lousy shot. I understand they used smokeless powder so the only means of detection would be muzzle blast or any unnatural movement of the foliage."

Units of the 27th Division on mop-up duty averaged 150 Japanese killed or captured daily in isolated areas of Saipan. Captain Joseph W. Riegert, twenty-eight, of Troy, New York, S-3, Headquarters, 2d Battalion, 105th Infantry, led one army unit in a typical clean-up operation, killing twenty-three Japanese soldiers in a rock-bound hideaway. "I almost stepped on one of them," Captain Riegert said, "before I realized there were more than twenty of them, squatting under some low bushes amid a pile of rocks." Some were eating, while others were drinking sake. They were so absorbed in what they were doing, particularly the sake, that the Americans were able to flank them on two sides before killing them all. First Sergeant Norman L. Olsen, twenty-five, of Hempstead, New York, E Company, 2d Battalion, 105th, led another clean-up patrol that surprised a group of Japanese soldiers. "Some of them," Olsen recalled, "made a grab for their grenades and rifles. That was a mistake, because then we didn't have a chance to take them prisoners. So sorry, we had to shoot them!"

Around July 15, enemy activity in the northern part of Saipan became particularly annoying; consequently, the 105th Infantry was placed under the control of the army garrison force for tactical employment. On the following day, the regiment moved to a point in the hills east of Tanapag Harbor where it took over large-scale mopping-up operations in the northern half of Saipan Island, from a point just south of the town of Garapan. The 105th was disposed as follows: The 3d Battalion covered the northern half of the regimental sector; the 1st Battalion was responsible for the southwest corner of the regimental sector; and the 2d Battalion was responsible for the southwest quarter, less the town of Garapan, which was protected by one company of the 29th Marine Regiment. Colonel Bishop, still in command of the 105th, informed the G-3 of the army garrison force, "I consider the 105th Infantry at its present strength to be an inadequate force to accomplish the assigned mission."

On July 23, 1st Lt. Roger Peyre's platoon from Company K, 3d Battalion, 105th, was along the cliffs south of Marpi Point in the northern half of the 105th's sector. A message had come into division headquarters that Japanese soldiers hiding in a cave were holding more than one hundred women and children hostage. Could Division G-2 send down an interpreter? Technical Sergeant Bob Hoichi Kubo, a twenty-three-year-old, Hawaii-born, Japanese-American volunteered to go on the mission with Peyre's platoon. While on the way to the cave, Peyre and Hoichi Kubo encountered two Okinawan laborers who had escaped from the cave at the base of a cliff where the civilians—men, women, and children—were being held captive. Technical Sergeant Hoichi Kubo tried to persuade the men to return to the cave and convince the soldiers to release the civilians. Fearing the soldiers, they refused, so Hoichi Kubo went to negotiate the release himself. After removing his helmet, and borrowing First Lieutenant Peyre's .45-caliber pistol, Hoichi Kubo climbed down a rope to the base of the cliff and walked about seventy-five yards to the mouth of the cave and entered. While Hoichi Kubo was in the cave, a sniper across the valley shot and killed Peyre, and his body fell to the valley floor. Two hours later, the civilians were released and eight Japanese soldiers came out sans weapons and surrendered. Hoichi Kubo had single-handedly negotiated the hostage release and captured the enemy soldiers without incident. For his bravery, he earned the Distinguished Service Cross, the second highest medal awarded to members of the U.S. Army, making him the only military linguist recognized this way during World War II. When he learned that Peyre had been shot and killed, Hoichi Kubo ordered four young Okinawan laborers to climb down the cliff and recover his body. Peyre was one of the last Americans to be killed on Saipan.

On July 24, Col. Leonard Bishop of Scotia, New York, was relieved of command of the 105th Infantry Regiment and replaced by Col. Walter S. Winn from Shreveport, Louisiana, a graduate of West Point. Colonel Winn, a hard fighter, would command the 105th Infantry during the remaining action on Saipan and at Okinawa. In the fall of 1944, Bishop was returned to Oahu because of physical disability and was appointed chief of the special services section on the staff of Lt. Gen. Robert C. Richardson, the commander of army forces in the Central Pacific Theater. In February 1945, Bishop retired from the army and reverted to inactive status. He served as a pallbearer at Lieutenant Colonel O'Brien's funeral in Troy, New York, in May 1949, and passed away in Punta Gorda, Florida, on January 16, 1964, at the age of sixty-eight.

On July 30, 1944, due to widespread guerrilla activities in the northern part of Saipan, the 105th Infantry Regiment reverted to 27th Division control and the entire 27th Division was assigned to the garrison force to clean up the remaining enemy elements. The plan for this mission consisted of forming a skirmish line across the entire island from east to west along the Tanapag-Papako-Donnay crossroads north to Marpi Point. The clean-up action was initiated on July 31, with the 105th covering the area from the west coast to the summit of the ridge in the center of the island. At one point, the men of the 105th spread themselves across the width of the island and swept north, killing the enemy along the way. After that, the 105th went back to localized patrols and captured a number of Japanese soldiers who were still hiding.

During the period from July 31 to August 6, the 27th Division conducted a gradual sweeping operation with two regiments abreast from north of Mount Tapotchau to Marpi Point, thus concluding the organized mop-up. The 105th operated in its zone until August 3, 1944, when it was relieved by the 165th. All units of the 105th then went into bivouac for two days and were employed in building and improving their base camps. On August 5, the 3d Battalion, 105th, was assigned the mission of patrolling and mopping up the Mount Tapotchau area. While the 1st and 2d Battalions of the 105th were initially assigned this mission, the availability of transport for their movement to a rest and rehabilitation island in the South Pacific superseded these orders and the two understrength battalions were relieved.

On August 9, the remnants of the 1st and 2d Battalions of the 105th Infantry and the forward echelon of the 105th Regiment Headquarters boarded ship, and on August 11 sailed for a rest and rehabilitation area in a New Hebrides Island called Espiritu Santo. First Lieutenant George H. O'Donnell of Troy, New York, executive officer of G Company, 2d Battalion, 105th, was on that ship. He recalled that there were only 400 to 500 men on board from the 1st and 2d Battalions, including what was left of Antitank Company. The ship was a small Dutch merchant ship, the *Kota Baroe,* that had been interred at Saipan when the Germans invaded Holland in 1940. The trip to Espiritu Santo took almost a month, and it was a nightmare. While en route, the ship lost power, forcing a destroyer to go to the destination with a second troop ship. The other destroyer circled the *Kota Baroe* until it got underway. Private First Class Seymour M. Krawetz, F Company, 2d Battalion, 105th Infantry, recalled, "It was a most uncomfortable experience." To make matters worse, many of the men onboard ship came down with dengue fever, sometimes called "break-bone fever" because of the severe body aches associated with the illness. Sergeant W. Taylor Hudson, Antitank Company, 105th, recalled, "About all that could be done was give something for the fever, aches, and pains, and wait for it to wear off."

On August 23, the 3d Battalion, 105th, and other special units embarked for Espiritu Santo. While on board, the men suffered the same maladies the earlier contingents had suffered. Sergeant Major Jesse R. Bell from Saranac Lake, New York, 3d Battalion, 105th, recalled, "We had an outbreak of dyptheria [*sic*] and dengue fever and spent some time in isolation on Espiroto [*sic*] Santo." The last elements of the 27th Division left Saipan on October 4. In the period between the end of the battle on July 9 and October 4, 1944, the 27th Infantry Division killed a total of 1,972 enemy soldiers and captured almost 3,300 civilians.

The cost of the battle for Saipan was high. When the final tally of casualties was completed in early October, 1944, it showed the V Amphibious Corps had lost 3,119 men killed, divided almost equally among the three combat divisions: the 2d and 4th Marine Divisions and the Army's 27th Infantry Division. In addition, 10,992 men were wounded or missing. This total of 14,111 casualties represented about 20 percent of the combat troops committed, or roughly, the same percentage of casualties suffered at Tarawa and Peleliu, both renowned as bloody engagements. On the other side of the ledger, almost the entire Japanese garrison on Saipan (approximately 30,000 men) was wiped out.

The 27th Infantry Division suffered 1,053 dead and 2,617 men wounded, more than half of whom would never return to duty. Almost half of the officers and men of the 27th Division killed on Saipan (20 officers and 410 enlisted men) were from the three infantry battalions of the 105th Infantry Regiment. The 1st Battalion of the 105th alone suffered 546 total casualties—208 killed in action (KIA), 291 wounded in action (WIA), and 47 missing in action (MIA); the 2d Battalion suffered 513 casualties—177 KIA, 307 WIA, and 29 MIA; and the 3d Battalion suffered 221—45 KIA, 166 WIA, and 10 MIA, totaling 1,280 killed, wounded, or missing in action for the 105th.

In early August, the War Department finally released information concerning the casualties suffered by the 105th Infantry at the Battle of Saipan. The news of the terrible toll the battle had taken on the soldiers from northeastern New York was devastating to their families and friends. The announcement of Lieutenant Colonel O'Brien's death, the ranking Troy soldier in the 105th Infantry Regiment, brought forth many words of praise from his former comrades in arms. Upon learning of O'Brien's death, Col. Christopher B. DeGenaar (who commanded the 105th Infantry when the regiment left Troy in October 1940 and while it was stationed at Fort McClellan) said:

> Bill O'Brien was one of the finest officers in the regiment. I considered him outstanding. As an officer he had initiative, good judgment, and excellent practical sense. He was a natural leader and men always followed where he led. He was "full of vim and vigor," and we will never forget him.

Colonel Lester C. Higbee, commanding the 2d Regiment, New York State Guard, was captain of Company A, 1st Battalion, 105th Infantry, during the 1920s when O'Brien was first sergeant of Company A. Remembering O'Brien, Higbee said, "He was a fine soldier. He set an example of soldierly conduct for the men of the regiment to follow. Colonel O'Brien was a strict disciplinarian. He was particularly characterized by the snap and dash with which he drilled his men. He kept them on their toes."

Colonel Leonard E. Bishop, his commander on Saipan, called O'Brien "the greatest soldier on Saipan." Brigadier General Ogden

J. Ross, assistant commander of the 27th Division on Saipan, and former colonel of the 105th, was a close personal friend of Colonel O'Brien's. On August 26, 1944, he wrote to O'Brien's brother, Frank and said "His death was a tremendous blow to me personally. We had been associated together so long and [I'd] known him so well. In my opinion, he was the ideal battalion commander—energetic, fearless, and possessing great powers of leadership. We all miss him very much. Officers and men of his battalion and regiment speak of him in the highest possible terms. The soldiers, who had been under his command, all spoke of him in terms of greatest affection and respect."

Epilogue

In a letter dated March 17, 1945, the U.S. War Department notified my father that his brother, Lt. Col. William J. O'Brien, had been awarded the Medal of Honor for his conspicuous gallantry and heroism at Saipan. One of Lieutenant Colonel O'Brien's men, Sgt. Thomas A. Baker, Company A, 1st Battalion, was also awarded the Medal of Honor for his valor during the same battle. This was the first and only time that the Medal of Honor was awarded to two army men from Troy, New York, for heroic conduct in the same battle while serving in the same unit during World War II.

The awards ceremony was held in Troy on Sunday, May 27, 1945, on the campus of Rensselaer Polytechnic Institute (RPI). The medals were presented to the widows of Lieutenant Colonel O'Brien and Sergeant Baker by Robert J. Patterson, the under secretary of war. Patterson, who was originally from Glens Falls, New York, had served in the 105th Infantry and was a wounded and highly decorated veteran of the 27th Division in World War I. At the same ceremony, a beautifully designed and engraved Japanese sword that had been captured on Saipan was presented to O'Brien's only son, William J. O'Brien Jr., as a gift from the officers of the 105th Infantry.

While the ceremony was taking place, many of O'Brien's and Baker's comrades from the 105th were heavily engaged in the bloody battle for Okinawa. Some would never make it back to Troy. However, several members of Company A, 1st Battalion, 105th Infantry, who had served with O'Brien and Baker before and during the war were present at the ceremony. O'Brien's widow, Mrs. Marjorie Baird O'Brien, was escorted by Capt. John B. Prout (a former member of

Company A) and his brother-in-law. Mrs. Charlotte O'Brien, Lieutenant Colonel O'Brien's mother, was escorted by Maj. Edward J. Maguire, a longtime member of Headquarters Company, 105th. Mrs. Constance Cecelia Baker, widow of Sergeant Baker, was escorted by Lt. William Dippo, longtime member of Company A. Mrs. Emma Baker, Sergeant Baker's mother, was escorted by Lt. George Schongar, former member of Company A, 1st Battalion, 105th, who had been wounded on Saipan.

I was proud to be present at that ceremony. Between 6,000 and 7,000 persons gathered on a rainy day at RPI's '86 Field to honor the dead heroes. The crowd listened spellbound as Secretary Patterson began to read the citations, first for O'Brien and then for Baker. The loudspeakers carried Patterson's message beyond the field, to open windows for blocks around, blocks that were lined with people. I can still hear his voice as he honored O'Brien and Baker with phrases such as ". . . conspicuous gallantry . . . at the risk of his life . . . above and beyond the call of duty at Saipan . . . in the highest traditions of the service . . ." As Patterson read the citations, he moved forward to where the widows stood with their military escorts and presented their respective husbands' medals to them. To each he spoke briefly, "I am proud to bestow this honor in the name of the President of the United States, but I am saddened, too, by the occasion which makes it possible." Each woman bowed slightly and in a barely audible voice replied, "Thank you, Mr. Patterson."

On July 14, 1948, the Department of the Army, in General Orders No. 49, awarded a Distinguished Unit Citation to the 105th Infantry Regiment (less 3d Battalion and Company G) and the Spears Detachment, 762d Provisional Tank Battalion. The award was given for exceptionally outstanding performance of duty in combat against the enemy at Saipan, on July 7, 1944, and the citation reads:

> The regiment attacked north toward the village of Makunsha on the west coast of Saipan against increasing enemy resistance. At dawn on 7 July, this unit was subjected to one of the greatest Japanese mass attacks attempted in the Pacific theater. The 1st and 2d Battalions fought furiously, as the enemy, at-

tacking in great numbers and with fanatical fury, penetrated the combined perimeter defense and inflicted overwhelming casualties on the units. Forced to yield, the survivors of that fierce assault formed successive defensive positions and continued to engage the attacking forces. These units, faced with a dwindling supply of ammunition, water, and medical supplies, fought off incessant enemy attacks throughout the day. Meanwhile the Japanese drive had carried on to the regimental command post where it was completely stopped and contained by the determined stand of Regimental Headquarters and special units. Every available man engaged in the action. Through the courage, tenacity, and endurance displayed by all ranks, this unit and its attachment, suffered severe casualties, repulsed the powerful assault launched by a numerically superior enemy and contributed materially to the defeat and destruction of the Japanese forces at Saipan. The conduct of the 105th Infantry Regiment (less 3d Battalion and Company G) and the Spears Detachment, 762d Provisional Tank Battalion, attached, throughout the battle reflects great credit on itself and is in keeping with the highest traditions of the armed forces of the United States.

On Tuesday, May 10, 1949, almost four years after the Medal of Honor ceremony, a casket containing the body of my uncle, Lieutenant Colonel O'Brien, arrived in Troy for a proper military funeral. The flag-draped casket, with my uncle's personal saber on top, lay in state at the National Guard Armory on 15th Street in Troy from 7 P.M. to 10 P.M. on May 11, 1949, while members of the 105th Infantry, family, and friends paid tribute. Former enlisted members of Company A of the 105th Infantry and two uniformed members of the Troy Citizen's Corps alternated every fifteen minutes standing honor guard at the armory.

Two days later, on Friday, May 13, 1949, the casket, lying on a weapons carrier, which served as a caisson, was escorted from O'Brien's mother's home on Fourth Avenue to St. Augustine's Church. On either side of the caisson were current officers and former officers of the 105th Infantry and representatives of the New

York Adjutant General's office. Lined along the street were the surviving members of Company A and other units of the 1st Battalion,
105th Infantry. The honor guard was commanded by Lt. Col. John
J. Purcell of Troy, New York, commander of the 105th Infantry since
July 17, 1948. Purcell had served with my uncle on Saipan and had
been a long-time friend of the family in Troy. The honor guard was
composed of 200 enlisted men from the 1st Battalion, 105th Infantry;
current officers and former officers of the regiment; the Troy Citizen's Corps; and the LaSalle Institute Guard of Honor.

Marching alongside the caisson carrying my uncle to St. Augustine's Church, the honorary and active pallbearers (many of whom
had served with my uncle in both war and peace) were led by Brig.
Gen. Ogden J. Ross, assistant division commander of the 27th Division.

A solemn requiem Mass for my uncle was celebrated by the Rev.
Lafayette W. Yarwood, former 27th Division chaplain, assisted by the
Rev. Paul G. Brunet, former chaplain of the 105th; both priests were
old friends. My uncle's casket was then escorted out of the church
by the active pallbearers and placed on the caisson for the trip to St.
Peter's Cemetery.

I was only twelve at the time, but I remember the gravesite ceremony being highly emotional. The images are forever burned in my
memory: flags waved, flowers covered the grave, officers saluted, rifles fired, and grown men and women cried. There the dead hero
was honored with a volley fired by a squad of men from Company
A, 1st Battalion, who had left Troy with O'Brien nine years earlier in
1940 and served with him on Saipan. My uncle was laid to rest with
a headstone that reads, "William J. O'Brien, Medal of Honor, Lt. Col.
U.S. Army, World War II, 1899–1944." It is hard to believe that more
than fifty years have passed since my uncle's burial. In the summer
of 1995, I visited his gravesite in a special section the cemetery has
devoted to World War II veterans.

More than fifty years after my uncle's remains were buried at St.
Peter's cemetery in Troy and more than fifty-five years after his death
in battle on Saipan, the remains of Sgt. Thomas A. Baker, Company
A, 1st Battalion, 105th Infantry, were brought home and interred in

the new Saratoga Military Cemetery in Stillwater, New York. In a solemn, windy ceremony held on Veteran's Day, November 11, 1999, more than 200 people—veterans groups, government officials, family members, and friends—gathered together to honor Troy's second Medal of Honor winner. I attended that ceremony and found it just as moving and emotional as my uncle's fifty years before.

"Sergeant Baker, you are now present and accounted for," said 1st Lt. Joseph Meighan from Cohoes, New York, who had served with Baker on Saipan as part of the 105th Infantry. Also speaking at the tribute were two local congressmen, Rensselaer County Executive Henry Swack, Troy Mayor Mark Pattison, and Sgt. Brian Baker of the Troy Police, nephew of the Medal of Honor winner. Their words were interrupted only by the sound of American flags snapping in the November wind.

Throughout the ceremony, a pair of military combat boots sat underneath the cemetery's central flagpole. A rifle was stuck into the ground behind the boots with a soldier's helmet on top, the soldier's way of identifying a comrade who had fallen on the battlefield. A contingent of soldiers from the 105th Infantry Battalion, 27th Infantry Enhanced Brigade, provided a six-soldier rifle salute and a bugler closed with "Taps."

Over the years since World War II, the various elements of what had been the 105th Infantry Regiment, the Apple-knockers, have been reorganized, redesignated, converted, and/or consolidated into a number of military configurations. Currently, many units of the Apple-knockers are part of the 1st Battalion, 105th Infantry of the 27th Infantry Brigade of the New York National Guard. The brigade is one of fifteen elite enhanced brigades in the Army National Guard training to defend our country in time of war and protecting it in time of peace. The 1st Battalion, 105th Infantry, is still carrying on the traditions and lessons learned from the 105th Infantry Regiment, and its members proudly wear the Apple-knocker insignia on the front of their dress uniforms.

Notes

To avoid an extremely cumbersome and unwieldy endnotes section, I have adopted, at the urging of my editors, the new citation practice of a collective reference, rather than numerical citations. For each chapter of the book, I have listed, generally in the order in which they were used, those books, monographs, military reports, diaries, newspapers, and journal articles that I have relied on, accompanied by appropriate page references. Where quotations appear in the text of the chapter, I have identified the sources in a cryptic manner. Complete identification of the sources is contained in the bibliography.

Chapter 1: Prelude to World War II

For the pre–World War II history of the 27th Division, including the 105th Infantry (the "Apple-knocker" regiment), I have relied on Kaune, *The National Guard in War: An Historic Analysis of the 27th Infantry Division in World War II*, pp. 15–18, 21–22, 26–28; Love, *The 27th Infantry Division in World War II*, pp. 7–9, 12; *The Tibbits Cadets of Troy, New York*, pp. 7, 23–28, 31–33; and the *Times Record*, Troy, New York, Oct. 7, 10, 15, 19, 24, 1940.

Something "big" was up, Plante interview, Sept. 24, 1998; "I was in awe and very appreciative," Kelly Ltr., Dec. 10, 1997; "trucks broke down a lot," Luck interview, Sept.11, 1998; "a short officer with a trench coat on," Wirmusky interview, Sept. 21, 1998; "hollering and drinking," Dauro interview, Sept. 22, 1998; "raising the devil" . . . "card games" . . . "crap games," Pettit interview, Sept. 21, 1998.

Chapter 2: Training at Fort McClellan

In addition to Kaune, pp. 34–37, 45–47; *Tibbits Cadets*, pp. 45–46, and Love, pp. 11–14, which describe the 27th's training at Fort Mc-Clellan in 1940 and 1941, I have referred to Gabel, *U.S. Army GHQ Manuevers of 1941,* for information regarding the Tennessee, Louisiana, and Arkansas maneuvers of 1941, pp. 52–54, 59, 64–90, 96–111, 116.

Fort McClellan was a "mess," a "hellhole," and a "dirty, stinking, muddy hole," Standarski telephone interview, Oct. 3, 1998; O'Brien "walked over to this big recruit . . . ," Domanowski Ltr. Oct. 6, 1996; "Look at those SOBs . . . ," Whalen interview, March 4, 1997; Captain O'Brien a "soldier's soldier," ibid.; ". . . endless marching up and down . . ." Haag #300, Kelly Survey; ". . . asshole of the world," Wirmusky interview, Sept. 21, 1998; ". . . if it wasn't for the shootin' . . . ," Love, p. 13; ". . . the soldier of 1941 will give a better account of himself . . . ," "The Papers of George Catlett Marshall," Vol. 2, pp. 590–591.

Chapter 3: The Japanese Attack on Pearl Harbor

Following the Japanese attack on Pearl Harbor, the 27th Division was put on alert and moved to Hawaii. For information describing these movements, I have relied on Love, pp. 14–17, 18–21, 43; Kaune, pp. 49, 50–51, 53, 56; and *Tibbits Cadets,* p. 48. See also, *Times Record,* Troy, New York, Dec. 8, 15, 1941; April 5, 1943; Feb. 23, 1945; and the *Troy Observer-Budget,* Aug. 5, 1944.

Captain O'Brien "complained like hell . . . ," Busone interview, March 1, 1997; Tent City "where you roasted . . ." Hudson Mem., p. 2; *Aquitania* a "beautiful ship," but many got "sick as dogs" and "deathly ill," Daurio interview, Sept. 21, 1998 and Hudson Mem., p. 3; ". . . all those beacons sticking out of the ocean . . . ," Giuffre interview, July 31, 1998; ". . . if the army had more officers like him . . . ," Orion Gallivanter, Dec., 1996, p. 9; ". . . blew it to smithereens . . . ," Pettit interview, Sept. 24, 1998; ". . . Hello. I'm Ralph Smith, your new division commander . . ." *Orion Gallivanter,* June, 1998, p. 7; Schofield Barracks "a beautiful set up . . ." Giuffre interview, July 31, 1998; ". . . we were billeted in a big gymnasium complex . . ." Hudson Mem., p. 4; "Everyone in the regiment envied our good fortune.," ibid.; ". . . shoot at the first thing you saw," Luck interview, Sept. 11, 1998; training "a period of just work and more work." Herzog #543, Kelly Survey; "I was over to the Old Company today [Company A] . . ." O'Brien Ltr., July 4, 1943; "We have a good outfit, Frank, . . ." O'Brien Ltr., July 23, 1943.

Chapter 4: The 105th at Makin

The narrative describing the 105th's participation in the Makin battle is based, in large part, on two sources: *The Capture of Makin, 20–24, November, 1943,* Center of Military History, United States Army, 1946, and *Seizure of the Gilberts and Marshalls,* by Philip Crowl and Edmund G. Love, Center of Military History, 1955, pp. 44–45, 47, 56–57, 60, 62–63, 71–72, 75–76, 77–79, 82–83, 85, 87–88, 91, 95–96, 106–108, 116, 124–125. In addition, I have referenced Kaune, pp. 44–48, 61–62, 65–68, 69–70; Love, pp. 23–36, 40–41, 44–45, 47–49, 50–55; and Melynk, *Infuriatingly Slow? The 27th Division and the Debate over Makin,* pp. 8, 10, 12–14, 25, 30, 47, 49.

"From small unit problems . . ." Melynk, p. 10 citing Marshall and Makin, p. 24; the 27th Division "has been in Hawaii for over a year and is a well trained division with excellent leaders . . ." Marshall Papers, Vol. IV, pp. 73–74; "the designation of the 27th Division for the Gilbert operations . . . is agreeable . . ." ibid, p. 74; General Ralph Smith was "very much liked by Admiral Nimitz and Admiral Spruance . . ." ibid, p. 81; the Makin naval bombardment achieved "a high degree of neutralization . . ." Crowl and Love, p. 76; "The effect of naval and air bombardment was highly satisfactory . . ." ibid; "However, there was not enough of it . . ." ibid; "I jumped down from my boat . . ." Crowl and Love, p. 77; "I remember being hung up on a coral pinnacle . . ." Lighthall #354, Kelly Survey; ". . . when our LTV came ashore on the left flank of Yellow Beach . . ." Hansen Ltr., Sept. 25, 1998; "It was a moon-lit night . . ." ibid.; "Psst! Hey, Sarge! . . ." Love, p. 45; Makin, pp. 93–94; ". . . there's a hundred and fifty Japs in the trees . . ." Makin, p. 95; "Later that morning as our advance continued . . ." Hansen Ltr., Sept. 25, 1998; ". . . he felt an extra piece of something . . ." *Honolulu Star-Bulletin,* March 4, 1944; "Heil Hitler" and "Blood for the Emperor," Love, p. 52; ". . . Lt. Hansen went over the side to wade in water . . ." Hansen Ltr., Sept. 25, 1998; ". . . Yeah, the 27th landed at and took Makin . . ." O'Brien Ltr., Jan. 8, 1944.

Chapter 5: Return to Oahu

This chapter, which describes the 27th's preparations for the Saipan invasion, is based on Love, pp. 55–57, 112–115, 117; Crowl and Love, pp. 301–304; and Kaune, pp. 95–97. It also refers to Hough, *The Island War: The United States Marine Corps in the Pacific,* pp. 221–222; Sherrod, *On to Westward, The Battles of Saipan and Iwo Jima,* pp. 28, 35; and Hoffman, *Saipan: The Beginning of the End,* pp. 21–23, 32.

"We have got the Japs beaten . . ." Marshall Papers, Vol. 4., p. 200 (quoting *The New York Times,* December 23, 1943, p. 3); "We not only had to build . . . ," Hudson Mem., pp. 7–8; " The finest lagoon in the Pacific," Love, p. 56 (quoting Admiral Nimitz); "This is where the serious phase of the war in the Pacific begins." Sherrod, p. 28; ". . . we don't have much time to write . . ." O'Brien Ltr., March 28, 1944; ". . . we painted our combat packs in camouflage colors . . ." Domanowski Ltr., Oct. 18, 1996; ". . . some thought that Japan was next . . ." ibid.

Chapter 6: Target: Saipan

This chapter describes the geography of Saipan, its history, and the Japanese defenses as well as the preliminary naval and air bombardment of the island by the American forces. In addition to Love, pp. 115–119, 124–125; Hoffman, pp. 2–5, 6–8, 11–13, 34–38; Hough, pp. 224–225, 227; Sherrod, p. 59; and Kaune, p. 101, it refers to Crowl, *Campaign in the Marianas,* pp. 21–22, 26, 53, 58, 62–67, 72–73; and Denfeld, *Hold the Marianas,* pp. 1, 19–21, 22–24, 29–30, 32, 44, 47–48.

"We were packed like sardines in a can . . ." Domanowski Ltr., Oct. 18, 1996; "We boarded our troop ship at Pearl Harbor . . ." Krawetz Ltr., May 5, 1997; "We were all impressed by the sight of the battleship *Oklahoma* . . ." ibid.; "Now hear this—this is Colonel O'Brien . . ." Domanowski Ltr., Oct. 18, 1996; "Target Saipan . . ." ibid.; ". . . we felt as though we had been there before." Krawetz Ltr., May 5, 1997; "I am considering study of landing our Division on Tinian . . ." 105th Unit Journal, June 4, 1944; "Control of the air . . ." Hoffman, p. 35; "Second air raid since landing on Saipan Island . . ." Tarao Kawaguchi diary (TKD), June 11, 13, 14.

Chapter 7: The Marines Hit the Beaches

The narrative of the marine's bloody attack against the Saipan beaches on June 15–16, 1944, is based primarily on Hoffman, pp. 45–46, 49, 50–59, 60–71, 71–74, 77–79, 84–85; Crowl, pp. 79–81, 83, 85–87, 90, 95–96, 99–100; Denfeld, pp. 49–50, 53–55, 58; Sherrod, pp. 36, 44, 47–48, 60, 63; Hough, pp. 227–231; and Love, pp. 125–128.

"All we heard was bad news from a marine officer . . ." Cimaszewski Ltr., May 7, 1986; "During the evening, the unit commander . . ." TKD, p. 18; H. M. Smith ". . . it is always better to get them [Reserves] on the beach . . ." Hoffman, pp. 84–85; "Will we have to call in the Twenty-Seventh Division? . . ." Sherrod, p. 63; "The big flashes . . . It looked like an atom bomb . . ." Di Nova interview, Sept. 25, 1998; ". . . they must have hit the aviation fuel dump . . ." Krawetz Ltr., May 5, 1997; "My first glimpse of Saipan . . ." O'Donnell Ltr., Aug. 5, 1944; "It was the huge explosion of a Jap aviation gas dump . . ." ibid.; "Navy guns are in action . . ." Domanowski Ltr., Oct. 18, 1996; "It was at night. I am leaning on the railing . . ." Giuffre interview, July 31, 1998; "How in heaven's name can anyone survive? . . ." ibid.; "Be prepared to land your unit [less RCT 106] . . ." Crowl, pp. 99–100.

Chapter 8: The 27th Division Comes Ashore

My account of the 27th Division's landings on the Saipan beaches on June 16–17, 1944, is based on Love, pp. 130–133, 135, 145, 157–158; Crowl, pp. 98, 100–104, 109–110; Hoffman, pp. 80, 86–90, 94–95, 97–98; and Denfeld, pp. 50–51, 56–58.

"Great difficulty was encountered . . ." 165th Operations Report, Saipan, p. 1; "My first glimpse of Saipan occurred at daybreak on the morning of June 16 . . ." *Times Record,* Troy, New York, Dec. 5, 1944. "Our mission was to get ashore . . ." ibid; "We were told that we were going to land on the Magicienne . . ." Giuffre interview, July 31, 1998; "This time they told us . . ." ibid.; "It was determined that it would soon be dark . . ." Rregilo Ltr., Apr. 23, 1997; ". . . for some reason we were not permitted to land . . ." Krawetz Ltr., May 5, 1997; "We climbed down at least forty feet over rope ladders . . ." Domanowski Ltr., Oct. 18, 1996; ". . . had to push the bodies aside . . ." Standarski, Oct. 3, 1998; ". . . there were bodies floating around in the water

. . .", Giuffre interview, July 31, 1998; "The marines had taken a terrible beating . . ." Beaudoin interview, July 8, 2000; "Boy! Are we glad to see you guys . . ." Pettit interview, Sept. 24, 1998; "The first dead Jap to come before my eyes . . ." Hammond Ltr., Aug. 10, 1944; ". . . the beach was alive with people . . ." Hammond, "Saipan Notes," p. 6; "I will never forget the way he walked to the front lines . . ." Domanowski Ltr., Oct. 18, 1996; "the beach was so cluttered with gasoline drums . . ." Speiring Mem. undated; "A Japanese Tojo . . ." ibid.; "There were so many tracers . . ." ibid.; "We disarmed the Marine . . ." *Orion Gallivanter,* Sept., 1999; Antitank Co. ". . . sailed around for a couple of days . . ." Hudson Mem., p. 10; "Most of the equipment of the 105th Infantry was still aboard . . ." Kovalski #505, Kelly Survey; ". . . people hit the deck. . . . the stink [of dead bodies] is terrible . . ." Hammond, "Saipan Notes," pp. 6–7.

Chapter 9: The 105th Joins the Attack

The narrative in this chapter traces the advance of the 105th Infantry on June 18 and June 19, 1944, along the right flank of the 27th Division line in southern Saipan. It is based on Love, pp. 153–154, 155–159, 160–166; Crowl, pp. 111–114, 137–138, 139–141; Hoffman, pp. 101–102, 105–108; Hough, pp. 232–234; Sherrod, p. 81; and Denfeld, p. 45. Also cited in this chapter are quotations from notes taken by David A. Benz, a war correspondent, assigned to the 27th Division on Saipan. They were provided to me by the New York State Military Museum.

"Where is O'Brien's Bn?" 165th Unit Journal; "O'Brien's Bn has not been in action" ibid.; ". . . the 105th's Baptism of Fire . . ." Hammond, "Saipan Notes," p. 8; "Moore [S-2 Squad] and I are looking through telescope . . ." ibid.; "I was lying prone on a ridge . . ." Hammond Ltr. Aug. 10, 1944; ". . . the 1st Battalion, 105th Infantry . . . the most colorful and the most busiest . . ." Love, p. 160; "A cocky little rooster . . ." ibid.; ". . . head was sliced in half . . ." Domanowski Ltr. Oct. 18, 1996; "His stomach was torn up . . ." ibid.; ". . . we heard planes overhead . . ." Hammond, "Saipan Notes," pp. 10–11; "Over it went. . . ." ibid.; "Later we arrived at the bunkers [near the airfield] . . ." Rregilio Ltr. April 23, 1997; ". . . joined up with some marines . . ." *Orion Gallivanter,* Sept. 1999; ". . . got some valuable information from a Jap Major . . ." ibid; "The patients are coming in . . ." TKD, p. 18; "Coast line filled with cover . . ." 105th Unit Journal; "Jap tanks reported approaching area . . ." ibid.; "We didn't even see the Jap pillboxes . . ." Benz Notes on Nafutan; "A rifle squad had assaulted . . ." Rregilio Ltr. April 23, 1997; ". . . a volley of mortar shells . . ." ibid; ". . . after the first barrage . . ." ibid.; "It was a much bigger dump . . ." O'Donnell, Aug. 5, 1944.

Chapter 10: The Attack on Nafutan Point

This chapter describes the activities of the 105th Infantry on the Nafutan Peninsula on June 20–21, 1944. The narrative is based on Love, pp. 167–170, 174, 176, 177–182, 183–185, 187–195, 222; Crowl, pp. 141–144, 145–146, 147–149, 150–151; Hoffman, pp. 113–114, 117–118, 122–123, 126, 131–132.

"Send vehicles to 1st Battalion to evacuate casualties . . ." 105th Unit Journal, June 20; "1st Bn CP under Jap fire . . ." ibid.; ". . . enemy has come forth displaying white . . ." ibid.; "Japanese had taken the Marine uniforms . . ." Herzog interview, Sept. 25, 1997; "He said that he only wanted . . ." *Orion Gallivanter,* Dec. 1996; his "attitude and concern for his men" ibid.; "Shoot me! Shoot me!" Love, p. 174; ". . . in order to maintain . . ." Hoffman, p.118; "I witnessed an old time mass attack . . ." Hammond, 1st Battalion Intelligence Report, pp. 3–4; "I saw a dead Cpl. of Company A . . ." ibid., p. 4; ". . . be ready to attack at 1000 . . ." Spierling Mem. on Saipan, p. 2 undated; ". . . when all hell broke loose . . ." *Orion Gallivanter,* Sept. 1999, pp. 4–5; ". . . all small-arms fire . . ." ibid.; "who in hell gave orders to dig in here? . . ." Hansen Ltr. Sept. 25, 1998; " Battalion said not to give any ground." ibid.; ". . . but the Japs opened up . . ." ibid.; ". . . anyone who moved would be dead . . ." ibid.; ". . . severely disappointing. Only the 1st Battalion 105th showed any gains . . ." Kovalaski #567, Kelly Survey; ". . . like pins on a bowling alley . . ." Love, p. 189; "The buggers had, off and on, been pestering me all day . . ." O'Donnell Ltr. Aug. 5, 1944; ". . . difficult terrain and Jap positions in caves . . ." Crowl, pp. 150–151; Nafutan Point cleaned up "in a couple of days." ibid.; "Large amounts of bombs and ammunition . . ." 105th Unit Journal; "It sounded like the whole island blew up . . ." Beaudoin interview, July 8, 2000.

Chapter 11: Second Battalion, 105th: Alone on Nafutan

The narrative set forth in this chapter, describing the 2d Battalion's fight against superior Japanese forces on Nafutan from June 22 to July 3, is based on Love, pp. 195–199, 200–213, 214–222, 287–288, 661–663; Crowl, pp. 151–154, 155–160; Hoffman, pp. 139, 144–147, 161–163, 173; Denfeld, pp. 77–78; and Hough, p. 241.

"Getting our supplies . . ." Hudson Mem., p. 12; "The ground there was so rocky . . ." Krawetz Ltr. May 12, 1997; "You fellows know what we're up against . . . " Benz Notes on Nafutan; Brownie ". . . you better take a lot of stuff with you . . ." ibid.; "Our first action was on Nafutan Ridge . . ." Krawetz Ltr. Feb. 24, 1997; "My platoon commander, Lt. Cecil Greenwell . . ." Krawetz #488, Kelly Survey; ". . . keep moving and stop holding up the movement." Hammond, 1st Battalion Intelligence Report, p. 4; "Earlier, following the over-running of the strong point . . ." Hansen Ltr. Sept. 25, 1998; "The division is advancing against a determined enemy . . ." 105th Unit Journal; "The Battalion will carry out an attack at midnight tonight . . ." Denfeld, pp. 77–78; Crowl, p. 159.

Chapter 12: The Fight for Central Saipan

This chapter traces the movements of the 27th Division, including the 105th Infantry, in central Saipan from June 22 to June 29, 1944, and is based on Love, pp. 223–225, 227–231, 287–289, 331–333, 338, 340–347, 350–353; Crowl, pp. 170–172, 174, 211, 220–221, 225, 228; Denfeld, pp. 73, 76–77, 80–81, 82–83; Hoffman, pp. 158, 169–171, 177, 185–186, 191–192; Kaune, pp. 116, 177; Hough, pp. 240–241; and Sherrod, p. 110.

". . . he was up against the strongest position yet encountered on Saipan." Love, p. 228; "Cannon to right of them, Cannon to left of them . . ." Crowl, p. 174; "The fight on Saipan as things stand now . . . " Denfeld, p. 77; "Give me more information . . ." 165th Unit Journal; O'Brien ". . . was raising hell with C Company . . ." Hammond, 1st Battalion Intelligence Report, p. 6; ". . . provide information on planes that caused casualties . . ." 165th Unit Journal; ". . . it is imperative . . ." 165th Unit Journal; ". . . several parties as large as twenty men . . ." Kovalaski #507, Kelly Survey; "If there were no naval gunfire . . ." Denfeld, pp. 80–81; "Establish strong perimeter defense in your areas . . ." 165th Unit Journal; "Slept good because of the saki . . ." TKD, p. 19; ". . . a small Kasserine Pass situation . . ." 105th Unit Journal; "Obie's Ridge . . ." Love, p. 347; "The morning of July 5 arrived . . ." *Times Record,* Troy, New York, Dec. 5, 1944; ". . . a dismal failure as a fighting division . . ." Love, p. 331; "We found the main strength . . ." TKD, p. 19; "Tell the regiment . . . the 105th and 106th gained . . ." 165th Unit Journal, Sherrod, p. 112; "Dug foxhole due to scare . . ." TKD, p. 19.

Chapter 13: The Drive to Tanapag

This chapter describes the movement from June 30 to July 4, 1944, of the 105th Infantry from central Saipan to the Tanapag Plain on the west coast of the island. The narrative is based on Love, pp. 357, 361–369, 370–375, 377–378; Crowl, pp. 230–232, 241–242; Hoffman, pp. 179, 192–193, 195–196, 201–202, 206–207; Hough, pp. 241–242; Denfeld, p. 84; and the 105th Operations Report.

"No one had any tougher job to do . . ." Crowl, p. 230; ". . . every place but . . ." O'Donnell Ltr. Aug. 5, 1944; "The following officers were reported to have distinguished themselves in combat . . . "Lt. Col. William J. O'Brien . . ." 165th Unit Journal; "Toward the morning we reached . . ." TKD, p. 19; ". . . we are moving back into assembly area . . . " 105th Unit Journal; ". . . while working, everybody seemed . . ." TKD, p. 19; "Leading elements pinned down . . ." 105th Unit Journal; "Fight your way to it if it takes all night " ibid.; "At dawn visited the place . . ." TKD, p. 19; ". . . we had made a thousand yard gain . . ." Standarski, Oct. 3, 1998; *Times Record,* Troy, New York, Aug. 5, 1944; "The Japs and our artillery were dueling . . ." ibid.; "A party of four got close enough . . ." ibid.; "Company D never had any kick . . ." ibid.; "This is our last trip . . ." "Pipe down or it will be . . ." "I hollered . . ." " . . . and we dove out of the jeep." ibid.; ". . . with a moon out . . ." O'Donnell Ltr. Aug. 5, 1944; "Halt! Who Goes There . . ." ibid; "All those not already in their foxholes . . ." ibid.; "At daybreak, the sound of . . ." TKD, p. 21; ". . . we'll spend the 4th on the beaches at Tanapag . . ." Love, p. 371; "We advanced on a front . . ." Benz Notes, July 4, 1944; "We were lucky there was no heavy fire . . ." ibid.; "The Japs all ran from us . . ." ibid.; "I guess they figured they could swim . . ." ibid.; "He asked for a knife or any other weapon . . ."

ibid.; ". . .the Japs fired at us from most of the houses . . ." ibid.; ". . . the sergeant was one of my best men . . ." Love, p. 375.

Chapter 14: The Final Battle for Saipan

The narrative set forth in this chapter traces the actions of the 105th Infantry on the Tanapag Plain from July 4 to the morning of July 6, 1944, and is based on Love, pp. 378–380, 386–389, 390–392, 394, 395–397, 398–399, 409, 430; Crowl, pp. 243–245, 247–248, 250–251, 252–253, 287; Hoffman, pp. 208–209, 210, 213–216; Denfeld, pp. 83–84; and *Small Unit Action: The Fight on Tanapag Plain*, (SUA), pp. 69, 71–77, 78–85, 86–88.

"General Saito was feeling very poorly . . ." Crowl, p. 244; "Seven Lives for the Emperor! . . ." Love, p. 430; "In the afternoon, I happened to be crossing . . ." O'Donnell Ltr. Aug. 5, 1944; "It was so light it bounced . . ." Hammond Ltr. Aug. 10, 1944; ". . . 1st Lt. Matsumi came to our dugout . . ." TKD, p. 21; "Up and at 'em! . . ." Love, p. 389; "Tiger Hughes, a combat engineer lieutenant . . ." Benz Notes, Nov. 1944, p. 56; ". . . could see daylight through their tanks . . ." SUA, p. 77; ". . . ran for it . . ." ibid., p. 85.

Chapter 15: The Afternoon Attack on July 6

The afternoon attack by the 105th Infantry on July 6 set the stage for the climatic Japanese suicide attack the next morning. The narrative is based on Love, pp. 410–412, 413–416, 417–419; Crowl, pp. 253–254, 255–256; Hoffman, pp. 214–215, 217; SUA, pp. 101–105, 106–109, 111–113.

"At the navy base there were a number of stores and supplies . . ." R. L. Johnson interview tape, Sept. 29, 1984; "I can see him clearly now . . ." ibid.; "I don't think I'm going to make it . . ." ibid.; "He had a look on his face that I will never forget . . ." Albanese interview, Mar. 6, 1999; "Obie was nervous and restless, as usual . . ." Crowl, p. 254; "Whatever you do, don't stop—keep moving . . ." Domanowski Ltr. Oct. 18, 1996; ". . . anyone would be lucky to get back alive . . ." Sidur interview, Aug. 13, 2001; ". . . the 105th has broken through . . ." SUA, p. 105; "The machine-gun fire went by my ear . . ." Beaudoin interview, July 8, 2000; "A Company and C Company are on our flanks . . ." Domanowski Ltr. Oct. 18, 1996, p. 9; ". . . just couldn't seem to realize . . ." SUA, p. 108; "We had to walk across that ditch . . ." Love, p. 414, "Since the base units had . . ." Hudson Mem., pp. 5, 13; "All were securely dug in . . ." ibid.; "At about 1700 we were trying to clean out . . ." O'Donnell Ltr. Aug. 5, 1944.

Chapter 16: Prelude to *Gyokusai*

Several hours before the *gyokusai* attack, things were relatively calm on the Combined Perimeter; then ". . . all hell broke loose." The narrative covering from 1800 on July 6 to 0400 on July 7 is based on Love, pp. 420–428, 429–431, 433–440, 461–462; Crowl, pp. 256–258; Hoffman, pp. 217–218, 222–223, 257; Hough, pp. 243–244; Denfeld, pp. 87–88.

"It was just before sunset on July 6 . . ." Krawetz Ltr. April 15, 1997; ". . . just a little behind the front lines," Herzog interview, Sept. 25, 1997; Beaudoin interview, July 8, 2000; "Nobody worried about who, what . . ." Herman Ltr. Feb. 21, 2000; ". . . the muzzles were hanging right out in the road," Love, p. 428; ". . . before the *banzai* charge . . ." Cimaszewski interview, March 3, 1997; Ltr. May 7, 1986; ". . . the intelligence which . . ." R. L. Johnson interview tape, Sept. 29, 1984; ". . . sat down on the lip of his slit trench . . ." ibid.; "For more than twenty days since the American Devil . . ." Love, pp. 433–434, ". . . advance with those who remain . . ." Love, p. 434, ". . . the additional regiment of marines . . ." 105th Operations Report, p. 10; "I was ill prepared for this . . ." R. L. Johnson interview tape, Sept. 29, 1984; "Prisoner says that his unit has been ordered to attack . . ." Love, pp. 435–436, 105th Unit Journal; "Captain Ackerman came back from seeing Colonel O'Brien . . ." Love, p. 438; "We were told to dig in . . ." Domanowski Ltr. Oct. 18, 1996, p. 10; "For God's sake, Bernie . . ." Love, p. 462; "To start from the beginning . . ." Smith Ltr. Nov. 28, 1997; ". . . probably the biggest and best fourth of July . . ." Di Nova interview, Sept. 25, 1998.

Chapter 17: Day of Hell

This account of the massive Japanese counterattack on the morning of July 7, 1944, is based on Love, pp. 441, 443–445, 453–457; Crowl, p. 258–259; Hough, p. 244; and Denfeld, p. 91.

"The enemy running willy-nilly over the ground . . ." Hansen Ltr.

Sept. 25, 1998; "... managed to pick off a few ..." ibid.; "Next morning, about 0430 ..." O'Donnell Ltr. Aug. 5, 1944; "Did you ever stand outside of a circus tent ..." Love, p. 433; "It was like the movie stampede ..." ibid.; "Say Luke ..." Hammond, *Gyokusai Attack*, p. 8; "... about four-thirty in the morning ..." R. L. Johnson interview tape, Sept. 29, 1984; "Everything we had and everything ..." Hammond, *Gyokusai Attack*, p. 9; "Jap tracers flying from several sources ..." ibid.; "... grenades exploded and sent pieces of shrapnel ..." ibid.; "We had the fire power ..." ibid.; "Now be sure you don't shoot ..." ibid.; "Luke, I must be hit ..." ibid., pp. 8–9; "Hold that line and stay up there! ..." ibid., p. 9; "Where the hell are you going? ... I have no weapon! ..." ibid., p. 9; "As long as one of my men ..." Wesack interview, Nov. 18, 2000; "Fifty yards away I saw a mass of people ..." Hammond, "Saipan Notes," pp. 9–10; "... saw two Japs in front of the mass ..." Hammond Ltr. Aug. 10, 1944; "... the enemy hacked our wounded ..." 105th S-2 Summary, p. 1; "Targets were plentiful ..." Hammond Ltr. Aug. 15, 1944; "There was a slight jar ..." ibid.; "I had the pleasure of getting ..." Stephani interview, March 6, 1999; "Don't give them a damn inch! ..." Grigas Ltr. June 16, 1999; "Get the hell back where you belong ..." ibid.; "I asked him what he was doing ..." Giuffre interview, July 31, 1998; "I have caused enough trouble ..." Love, p. 454; "I'll stay here ..." ibid.; "I'm done for ..." ibid.; "He was cool as a cucumber ..." ibid.; "I told him he would be okay ..." R.W. Smith Ltr. Nov. 28, 1997; "When I withdrew my bayonet ..." Benz notes, July 25, 1944; "La Borde plunked down ..." ibid.; "Come on, you yellow bastards ..." Love, p. 455; "... could make out a figure running ..." Domanowski Ltr. Oct. 18, 1996, pp. 10–11; "Bullets were flying ..." ibid.; "I could see the enemy now ..." ibid.; "My rifle went into the air ..." ibid.; "I yelled at him to get down ..." ibid.; "I saw them running in single file ..." ibid.; "... we had to fight to stay alive ..." ibid.; "So long, Shaughnessy ..." R. W. Smith Ltr. Nov. 28, 1997; "Bullets were flying all around ..." Di Nova interview, Sept. 25, 1998; "Why let him die? ... You dirty bastards! ..." Pettit interview, Sept. 24, 1998; "... we were on the right side ..." Johnson interview tape, Sept. 29, 1984; "At about 4:30 A.M. ..." Krawetz Ltr. April 15, 1997; "I had no warning that the attack ..." McCandless Ltr. Sept. 7, 1987 [quoted at Denfeld, p. 91]; "I've got to go, I guess. . . ." Love, p. 456; ". . . spent the night on the front line . . ." Nicosia #552, Kelly Survey; "I'd rather stay here . . ." Love, p. 457; "About four A.M., I was awakened . . ." Hudson Mem. p. 13; "Our guys are falling back . . . Stay here . . ." ibid.

Chapter 18: The Tide Runneth Over

After overrunning the 1st and 2d Battalions, the Japanese attack spread out like a great tidal wave seeking to overwhelm the other American forces on or near the Tanapag Plain. The narrative of this action is based on Love, pp. 447, 473–474, 476–481, 482–489; Hoffman, pp. 225–226; *Times Record,* Troy, New York, Aug. 5, 7, 1944.

"It was like shooting ducks on a rock. " Love, p. 474; " During the *Gyokusai* attack . . ." Walsh Ltr. Sept. 20, 1996; ". . . heard one of the water-cooled machine guns . . ." ibid.; "There are only 100 men left . . ." Love, p. 447; ". . . thick as maggots . . ." ibid.; "In the dark we could hear a lot of people running . . ." Love, p. 479; ". . . looked like a circus had just let out . . ." ibid.; ". . . at least three hundred . . ." ibid.; " . . . we had a field day, firing . . ." O'Donnell Ltr. Aug. 5, 1944; ". . . to stay down, but he wanted . . ." Spierling interview, Oct. 4, 1998; ". . . that old whites-of-eyes stuff . . ." Love, p. 480; "Not bad for an old crow hunter . . ." Luck interview, Sept. 11, 1998; "I watched a machine gun for half an hour . . ." O'Donnell Ltr. Aug. 5, 1944; "Making sure there were none of our troops . . ." Hansen Ltr. Sept. 25, 1998; "I think I saw more of the banzai-charge battle . . ." *Infantry Journal,* Jan. 1949, p. 23; "You guys are great and I'm buying . . ." Meighan Mem. Sept. 30, 1998; ". . . awoke to the sounds of MG and rifle fire . . ." ibid.; "On my way back to our CP . . ." M. Oakley Bidwell Ltr., July 30, 1984; "The artillerymen fired point-blank . . ." Love, p. 484; ". . . until it was necessary to resort to ricochet fire . . ." ibid.; ". . . the marine artillery battalion did not stop the attack . . ." ibid.; ". . . found a very strong enemy force . . ." Redfield Ltr. May 31, 1997; "I ran out to him and saw his rifle . . ." ibid.; ". . . the erstwhile cooks and mechanics . . ." *Times Record,* Troy, New York, Aug. 5, 1944; ". . . until the enemy was within eighty yards . . ." Armstrong Ltr. July 31, 2001; "One machine gun, with a crew of cooks and KP's . . ." *Times Record,* Troy, New York, Aug. 5, 1944; ". . . cradled a belching tommy gun . . ." ibid.; "Don't shoot! Don't shoot! . . ." *Orion Gallivanter,* Dec.

1999, p. 16; ". . . a John Garfield stunt . . ." *Times Record,* Troy, New York, Aug. 5, 1944; "He used that machine gun as he would a rifle . . ." ibid.; "Late in the afternoon . . ." Herman Ltr. Feb. 21, 2000; " Reif yelled for help . . ." ibid.; "Then we moved up . . ." ibid.; ". . . the sudden damming of the flood . . ." *Times Record,* Troy, New York, Aug. 7, 1944.

Chapter 19: The Withdrawal

After being overrun, the survivors of the 1st and 2d Battalions, bringing their wounded, withdrew to secondary positions along the coast, fighting the enemy all the way. The general narrative describing these heroic actions is based on Love, pp. 445, 449, 452–459, 460–462.

"The Japanese just swept over us . . ." R. J. Johnson interview tape, Sept. 29, 1984; ". . . to hell with it . . ." Love, p. 459; "Hell, no! I like it here . . ." ibid.; "We thought the world of Lt. Dolliver . . ." *Times Record,* Troy, New York, Aug. 5, 1944; "I found a good spot on the beach . . ." Domanowski Ltr. Oct. 18, 1996, pp. 12–14; "I see a lot of soldiers going into about three feet of water . . ." ibid.; ". . . there were Japs all around . . ." Di Nova interview, Sept. 25, 1998; "Since we were in a sandy area . . ." Krawetz Ltr. Apr. 15, 1997; "He looked at me, and quickly returned his . . ." Hammond, *Gyokusai Attack,* p. 11; "Where's the aid station? . . ." ibid.; "You think we ought to set up a line here, Luke? . . ." ibid.; "The Japs are all along back there, . . . We're surrounded . . ." ibid; "I'll have to stay here, my foot is cut off . . ." ibid.; "We placed our back to the ocean . . ." ibid.; "A number of us moved over to the beach . . ." Johnson interview tape, Sept. 29, 1984.

Chapter 20: Defense of the Second Perimeter

The narrative of the fighting at the Second Perimeter on the morning and afternoon of July 7 is based on Love, pp. 444–450, 456, 459–460, 462–467, 470–471, 488–490; Crowl, pp. 259–260.

"The wounded continued fighting, too . . ." Benz Notes, July 17, 1944; "We picked up the ammo . . ." ibid.; "We also found some scattered . . ." ibid.; "I shot one . . ." ibid.; ". . . then I got the other . . ." ibid.; ". . . those medics did wonders . . ." Benz Notes, July 18, 1944;

"I'll stay here and fire . . ." Love, p. 466; "Bullets were popping fiercely overhead . . ." Hammond, *Gyokusai Attack*, pp. 15–16; "None of us were going to leave . . ." ibid.; "Haven't you got any communications? . . ." ibid.; ". . . the two guns covered a blind spot . . ." Benz Notes, July 18, 1944; ". . . when the Japs first . . ." ibid.; "One of the gunners, his face bloody . . ." ibid.; ". . . then we plugged up . . ." ibid.; ". . . he sure had a marvelous arm . . ." Love, p. 464; "He must have gotten . . ." Benz Notes, July 18, 1944; "I felt like the proverbial one-armed paperhanger . . ." *American Legion Magazine*, Oct. 1944, p. 45; "What can we do, Luke? . . ." Hammond, *Gyokusai Attack*, pp. 17–18; "Pass it back, artillery falling in our front lines . . ." ibid.; "We felt completely deserted . . ." ibid.; "We were shelled by artillery . . ." Domanowski Ltr Oct. 18, 1996, p. 15; ". . . suddenly more fire began falling . . ." Hammond, *Gyokusai Attack*, pp. 18–19; ". . .to see someone all bloody . . ." ibid.; "I was literally lifted off the ground . . ." ibid.; ". . . there's ammunition in that building . . ." ibid.; ". . . shells were hitting the ocean and the beach . . ." Di Nova interview, Sept. 25, 1998; "What are you doing here? . . ." Johnson interview tapes, Sept. 29, 1984, pp. 10–12; ". . . and there was Barney, propped up against . . ." ibid.; "Damn it! Let's fight our way out of here . . ." Hammond, *Gyokusai Attack*, p. 20; "Crashing sounds were heard . . ." ibid.; ". . . like a bat out of hell! . . ." ibid., pp. 20–21; ". . . black smoke from a grenade . . ." ibid.; ". . . flying wedge . . ." Love, p. 449; "We were firing 'call' fire . . ." *Orion Gallivanter*, July, 1951, p. 3; "I'm going to get help! . . ." Hammond, *Gyokusai Attack*, p. 23; "I think everybody was just too surprised . . ." Love, p. 468; "It was like we were riding on ties on a railroad track . . ." ibid.; ". . . yelling and hollering and waving . . ." Love, p. 469; "Suwendah, Suwendah!" ibid.; "Get the hell out of here . . ." ibid.

Chapter 21: Relief of the 105th Infantry

This chapter, which discusses the relief of the remnants of the 105th Infantry on the afternoon of July 7, is based on Love pp. 451–452, 487–488, 489–494, 495–497. ". . . by the sound of the fire . . ." Love, p. 487; ". . . headquarters did not accept . . ." Crowl, p. 261; ". . . the men were utterly done up . . ." Love, p. 495; ". . . machine gun bullets popped in the air . . ." Hammond, *Gyokusai Attack*,

p. 24; "Someone wave a white flag . . ." ibid.; ". . . with determination and disregard for his own life . . ." ibid.; "Watch it Mac . . ." ibid., pp. 24–25; ". . . crawls out of the woods . . ." ibid.; "Suddenly, the fast chatter of a Jap MG . . ." ibid., p. 26; "You better get on, Mac . . ." ibid., pp. 27–28; ". . . fighting going on all around . . ." Di Nova interview, Sept. 25, 1998; "Hang on to the good leg . . ." ibid.; *Times Union*, Albany, New York, Sept. 20, 1996; "Just before dark, an amphibious tank . . ." Domanowski Ltr. Oct. 18, 1996, pp. 16–17; "You should have see [n] Savage . . ." ibid.; "Watch it—this one has two broken arms . . ." ibid.

Chapter 22: The Last Days on Saipan

This chapter covers the period from the afternoon of July 7 until late Aug. 1944, when the last units of the 27th Division embarked for Espiritu Santo. The narrative is based on Love, pp. 431–432, 451–452, 472, 498–501, 518–520; Hoyt, *To the Marianas, War in the Central Pacific: 1944,* p. 255; Crowl, 261, 263–266; Hoffman 226, 233–234, 268–269.

A "massacre" Love, p. 500; ". . . yelling and jumping around . . ." ibid., p. 501; ". . . one of the most devastating single battles of the war . . ." Hoffman, p. 226; "The whole area seemed to be a mass . . ." Sherrod, p. 140; "I don't think I can draw a picture . . ." Bidwell Ltr. July 30, 1984; "Jap bodies in the sun . . ." Herman Ltr. Feb. 21, 2000; ". . . overrun by a considerable force . . ." Love, p. 431; "We had an overlay on a large-scale map . . ." Bidwell Ltr. July 30, 1984; "A detail of engineers, Japanese prisoners of war . . ." Burns Citation, Aug. 9, 1944; "More than 300 freshly killed Japanese . . ." Hoffman, p. 234; "The assumption that the Japanese . . ." Love, p. 433; ". . . looked like two companies walking out." Herzog interview, Sept. 25, 1997; "Where is everyone? . . . They're all gone . . ." Rossi Ltr. June 22, 1999; "We were assigned a section to patrol . . ." Meighan Mem., Sept. 30, 1998; ". . . was given command of what was left . . ." Hansen Ltr. Sept. 25, 1998; ". . . taking out a patrol . . ." ibid.; "Later while moving alongside . . ." ibid.; "I almost stepped on one of them . . ." Benz Notes, July 23, 1944; "Some of them . . ." ibid.; "I consider the 105th Infantry . . ." 105th Unit Journal, July 16, 1944; "It was a most uncomfortable experience . . ." Krawetz Ltr. June 2, 1997; ". . . about all that could

be done . . ." Hudson Mem., pp. 18–19; ". . . we had an outbreak of
. . ." *Orion Gallivanter,* March, 1997, p.11; "Bill O'Brien was one of
the finest . . ." *Times Record,* Troy, New York, Aug. 5, 1944; "He was a
fine soldier . . ." ibid.; ". . . the greatest soldier on Saipan." *Times
Record,* Troy, New York, Feb. 23, 1945; ". . . his death was a tremendous blow . . ." Ross Ltr. Aug. 26, 1944.

Epilogue
The final chapter is based on Love, pp. 520–521, 523–529,
543–544, 552, 614–626, 630–639, 640–641, 646–651, 666–672, 677;
Kaune, pp. 139–140, 144, 150–152; Sherrod, pp. 229, 299; Gailey,
Howlin' Mad vs. The Army: Conflict in Command, Saipan 1944, pp. 8–9,
249; Appleman, *Okinawa: The Last Battle,* pp. 26, 43, 115, 202–204,
235–238, 240–243, 247, 490.
". . . froze in their foxholes . . ." Love, p. 666; ". . . had our spirits
at rock bottom . . ." Hudson Mem., p. 20; "The evidence points con-
clusively . . ." Gailey, p. 249; "I went too far in questioning . . ." Sherrod, p. 299; ". . .one of the most memorable . . ." Krawetz Ltr. Aug.
13, 1997; ". . . conspicuous gallantry . . ." *Times Record,* Troy, New York,
May 28, 1945; "I am proud to bestow . . ." ibid.

Bibliography

Primary Sources

National Archives, College Park, Maryland Record Group 407, File 327-0.3.

Operations Report, GALVANIC, Makin Operations, TF 52.6, November 16–25 1943.

27th Division Operations Report, June 17–August 6, 1944, "Battle for Saipan."

27th Division G-3 Periodic Reports, July 6–7, 1944.

105 RCT Operations Report, FORAGER Operation, Saipan, June–August 1944.

105 RCT Unit Journal, FORAGER Operation, June 1–August 23, 1944.

165 RCT Operations Report, FORAGER Operation, Saipan, June 16–July 7, 1944.

165 RCT Unit Journal, FORAGER Operation, Saipan, June 16–August 6, 1944.

105 RCT Operations Report, ICEBERG Operation, Okinawa, April 10–June 30, 1945.

105 RCT Action Report, TSUGEN JIMA, April 9, 1945.

249th F.A. Operations Report, FORAGER Operation, April–August 1944.

249th F.A. Battalion Unit Diary, FORAGER Operation, June 15–July 18, 1944.

Adjutant General Reports, New York, 1931, 1936, 1939.

Twenty-Seven Division Pictorial History, U.S. Army, Fort McClellan, Alabama, 1940–1941, Army-Navy Publishers, Inc., 1941.

Interviews by Author

Capt. Francois V. Albanese, S-4, 1st Battalion, 105th Infantry, Syosset, New York, March 6,1999; Telephone Conferences, April 27, 1997, June 2, 1999.

Capt. John A. Armstrong, Headquarters Company, 105th Infantry, St. Petersburg, Florida, March 3, 1997; Jacksonville, Florida, April 25–26, 2001; Telephone Conferences, August 13, 1996, April 22, 1997, various E-mail messages.

Cpl. C. Edward ("Eddie") Beaudoin, Medical Detachment, 105th Infantry, Saratoga, New York, July 8, 2000.

Sgt. Stephen C. Behil, 249th F.A. Battalion, Albany, New York, September 24, 1997, September 26, 1997.

Richard Bishop Jr., Telephone Conferences, August 1, 1996, September 11, 1996, December 9, 1998.

Vincent Busone, Company A, 105th Infantry, Northport, Florida, March 1, 1997.

Sgt. Frank Cimaszewski, 106th F.A., St. Petersburg, Florida, March 3, 1997.

Sgt. Arthur P. Conlon, Company A, 105th Infantry, Albany, New York, September 25, 1997.

Sgt. John J. Daurio, Company A, 105th Infantry, Valley Falls, New York, September 22, 1998.

P.f.c. Peter Davendonis, Hdq. Detachment, 1st Battalion, 105th Infantry, Hoosick Falls, New York, September 22, 1998.

P.f.c. Samuel Di Nova, Company D, 105th Infantry, Troy, New York, September 25, 1998, Beaver Falls, New York, November 18, 2000.

Sgt. Felix M. Giuffre, Company A, 105th Infantry, Chesapeake, Virginia, July 31, 1998.

Sgt. Walter Grigas, Medical Detachment, 105th Infantry, Telephone Conferences, Chicago, Illinois, June 30, 1999, July 2–3, 1999.

Capt. Luther C. Hammond, S-2, 1st Battalion, 105th Infantry, Gainesville, Florida, February 27, 1997; Jacksonville, Florida, April 25–26, 2001.

Sgt. George Herman, Headquarters Company, 105th Infantry, Telephone Conferences, Chicago, Illinois, January 5, 2000, May 2, 2000.

P.f.c. Arthur Herzog, Antitank Company, 105th Infantry, Albany, New York, September 25, 1997.

Sgt. W. Taylor Hudson, Antitank Company, 105th Infantry, Telephone Conference, Louisville, Kentucky, June 16, 1999.

Sgt. Edwin Luck, Company G, 105th Infantry, Vienna, Virginia, September 11, 1998, March 4, 2000.

Joel La Vallee Telephone Conference regarding Paul La Vallee, Company M, 105th Infantry, March 14, 1999.

TSgt. John Mc Loughlin, Company A, 105th Infantry, Telephone Conference, August 13, 2001.

1st Lt. Joseph J. Meighan, Albany, New York, June 22, 2000; Troy, New York, July 6, 2000; Beaver Falls, New York, November 18, 2000.

Cpl. Joseph A. Marano, Company D, 105th Infantry, Albany, New York, September 24, 1997.

Major Robert H. Mc Kay, 1st Battalion, 105th Infantry, Jacksonville, Florida, March 5, 1997, April 25–26, 2001.

1st Lt. George O'Donnell, Company G, 105th Infantry, Albany, New York, September 26, 1998.

SSgt. Ernest L. Pettit, Company D, 105th Infantry, Wynantskill, New York, September 24, 1998.

Sgt. Charles A. Plante, Company A, 105th Infantry, Averill Park, New York, September 24, 1998.

Maj. Carl E. Rohner, Executive Officer, 3d Battalion, 105th Infantry, Telephone Conference, Hilo, Hawaii, August 30, 1999.

Sgt. John A. Sidur, Company B, 105th Infantry, Cohoes, New York, Telephone Conferences, July 26, 2001, August 13, 2001.

Sgt. Robert W. Smith, 249th F.A Battalion, Telephone Conference, September 17, 1997.

1st Lt. Donald P. Speiring, Company G, 105th Infantry, Telephone Conference, April 25, 1999.

P.f.c. Frank Standarski, Company A, 105th Infantry, Telephone Conference, October 3, 1998.

1st Sgt. Charles J. Stephani, Company B, 105th Infantry, East Patochgue, New York, March 6, 1999.

Pvt. Donald Trudeau, Company B, 105th Infantry, Bear Mountain, New York, November 18, 2000; Telephone Conference, August 13, 2001.

Sgt. Adam Weasack, Company D, 105th Infantry, Bear Mountain, New York, November 18, 2000.

1st Lt. Vincent A. Walsh, Company A, 165th Infantry, Weeki Watchee, Florida, March 2, 1997.

Sgt. Charles A. Whalen, Company A, 105th Infantry, Ormon Beach, Florida, March 4, 1997.

Cpl. A. J. Wirmusky, Headquarters Detachment, 1st Battalion, 105th Infantry, Hoosick Falls, New York, September 21, 1998.

Letters to Author

J. A. Armstrong, Company A, 105th Infantry, August 17, 1996, February 5, 1997, March 11, 1997, May 8, 1997, May 12, 1997, June 7, 1997, August 12, 1997, August 30, 1997, September 17, 1997, November 5, 1997, February 14, 1998, March 24, 1998, October 30, 1998, July 31, 2001.

Stephen Behil, 249th F.A. Battalion, December 23, 1995.

Richard Bishop, March 28, 1997.

Vincent Busone, Company A, 105th Infantry, November 18, 1996.

Melvin Carnell, 249th F.A. Battalion, September 8, 1997, September 17, 1997, enclosing 249th F.A. Battalion material.

Floyd D. Cox, Company B, 105th Infantry, March 25, 1997, June 24, 1998, October 24, 1999.

Sgt. John Domanowski, Company B, 105th Infantry, September 16, 1996, October 6, 1996, October 18, 1996 (with enclosure).

Sgt. Felix M. Giuffre, Company A, 105th Infantry, April 25, 1997, May 8, 1998, June 5, 1998, August 17, 1998, September 7, 1998.

Sgt. Walter Grigas, Medical Detachment, 105th Infantry, June 16, 1999.

1st Lt. Luther C. Hammond, S-2, 1st Battalion, 105th Infantry, July 5, 1997.

Sgt. George Herman, Headquarters Company, 105th Infantry, February 21, 2000.

Sgt. W. Taylor Hudson, Antitank Company, 105th Infantry, June 4, 1999, enclosing *Four Years and a Week*.

1st Lt. Arthur G. Hansen, Company G, 105th Infantry, September 25, 1988.

Dr. June Hoyt, August 24, 1998 (enclosing transcriptions of Ronald

Johnson tapes of Autumn 1984, September 8, 1984), December 2, 1998 (enclosing transcription of Johnson tape of September 29, 1984), March 19, 1999.

George Kelly, Headquarters Company, 105th Infantry, December 10, 1997.

Seymour Krawetz, F Company, 105th Infantry, February 24, 1997, April 15, 1997, May 5, 1997, May 12, 1997, May 22, 1997, June 2, 1997, June 16, 1997, June 30, 1997, July 7, 1997, July 14, 1997, July 24, 1997, August 2, 1997, August 13, 1997, September 2, 1997, September 29, 1997, October 19, 1997, November 14, 1997, December 3, 1997, January 1, 1998, February 12, 1998, March 8, 1998, April 12, 1998, August 8, 1998.

Charles Laing, Lima, Ohio, June 15, 1998 (enclosing correspondence with Company A survivors), Charles Laing, Lima, Ohio, October 24, 1996, (enclosing correspondence between Charles Emig, Company A, 105th Infantry, and members of his family).

1st Lt. Joseph J. Meighan, January 11, 2000, numerous E-mail messages in 1999, 2000, and 2001.

Robert W. Novak, Company B, 105th Infantry, December 19, 1997, March 18, 1997, April 3, 1997, December 2, 1997, December 11, 1997, September 21, 1999, August 21, 2000, December 8, 2000.

Sgt. Ernest L. Pettit, Company D, 105th Infantry, August 20, 1998.

Sgt. Angelo Rossi, Company A, 105th Infantry, September 7, 1998, October 13, 1998.

Sgt. Nicholas Rregillo, Company B. 105th Infantry, March 22, 1997, April 23, 1997.

Major Carl E. Rohner, 3d Battalion, 105th Infantry, June 22, 1999.

David Reese, April 20, 1998, June 11, 2000, re: Sgt. Luther Reese, Company C, 105th Infantry, KIA at Saipan.

Sgt. Robert W. Smith, 249th F.A. Battalion, November 28, 1997.

P.f.c. Frank Standarski, Company A, 105th Infantry, April 7, 1999, April 19, 1999, April 30, 1999, February 15, 2000.

1st Sgt. Charles J. Stephani, Company B, 105th Infantry, March 18, 1999, November 17, 1999.

1st Lt. Vincent A. Walsh, Company A, 165th Infantry, September 4, 1996, September 20, 1996.

Miscellaneous Letters

Lt. Col. C. Oakley Bidwell, G-1, 27th Division, to Dr. June Hoyt, July 30, 1984.

Frank C. Cimaszewski, 106th F.A., to George H. Rogers, May 7, 1986.

Albert P. Conlon, Company A, 105th Infantry, to Charles Laing, February 24, 1998.

Sgt. John Domanowski, Company B, 105th Infantry, October 17, 1996, to Charles Laing.

Sgt. Felix Giuffre, Company A, 105th Infantry, September 8, 1944, to Charles Laing.

1st Lt. Luther C. Hammond, S-2, 1st Battalion, 105th Infantry, to parents, August 10, 1944.

Dr. June Hoyt to Charles Laing (enclosing Love book index).

Edward H. Redfield submitted by William "Red" Langton to the *Orion Gallivanter*, September 1999.

Sgt. Charles Mazzarella, 102d Medical Detachment, 105th Infantry, to the *Orion Gallivanter*, December 1996.

1st Lt. George O'Donnell, G Company, 105th Infantry, to parents, August 5, 1944.

Sgt. Angelo Rossi, Company A, 105th Infantry, to Charles Laing, June 22, 1994, February 17, 1998.

D. W. Roche to the *Orion Gallivanter*, December 1996.

Books

Alexander, Joseph H., *Storm Landings,* Naval Institute Press, 1997.

Denfeld, D. Colt, *Hold the Marianas,* White Mane Publishing Company, Inc., 1997.

Department of the Army, U.S. Army in World War II, The War in the Pacific, Washington, D.C., U.S. Government Printing Office.

Appleman, Roy E. *Okinawa: The Last Battle,* 1949.

Crowl, Philip A. and Edmund G. Love, *Seizure of the Gilberts and Marshalls,* Center of Military History, United States Army, Washington, D.C. 1955.

Crowl, Philip A., *Campaign in the Marianas,* Washington, D.C. Historical Division, U.S. Army 1960.

Eisenhower, Dwight D., *Crusade in Europe,* Garden City, New York: Doubleday, 1948.

Gabel, Christopher R., *The U.S. Army GHQ Maneuvers of 1941,* Center of Military History, U.S. Army, Washington, D.C., 1992.

Gailey, Harry A., *Howlin' Mad vs. the Army,* Presidio Press, 1986.

————., *The Liberation of Guam,* Presidio Press, 1988.

————., *War in the Pacific,* Presidio Press, 1995.

Glidden, William G., *History of the Schenectady Militia and the 105th Infantry Regiment,* Self-published, August 8, 1976.

Hoffman, Carl W., *Saipan, The Beginning of the End,* Washington, D.C., Historical Division, U.S. Marine Corps, 1950.

Hough, Frank O., *The Island War: The United States Marine Corps in the Pacific,* New York: J. P. Lippincott, 1947.

Hoyt, Edwin P., *Storm over the Gilberts,* New York: Mason/Charter, 1978.

Hoyt, Edwin P., *To the Marianas, War in the Central Pacific, 1944,* New York: Avon Books, 1983.

Love, Edmund G., *The 27th Infantry Division in World War II,* Washington, D.C.: Infantry Journal Press, 1949.

The Papers of George Catlett Marshall, Volume 4, "Aggressive and Determined Leadership," June 1, 1943–December 31, 1944, Johns Hopkins Press, 1996.

Morison, Samuel Eliot. *History of Naval Operations in World War II,* Boston: Atlantic, Little, Brown, Vol. VII, Aleutians, Gilberts & Marshalls, 1951; Vol. VIII, New Guinea and the Marianas, 1962.

O'Ryan, Maj. Gen. John J., *The Story of the 27th Division,* New York: Wynkoop, Hallenback & Jack Crawford Co.,1921.

Scott, Jay. *American War Heroes.* Monarch Books, Inc. 1963.

Sherrod, Robert. *On to Westward: The Battles of Saipan and Iwo Jima.* New York: Duell, Sloan and Pearce, 1945.

Smith, Holland M. and Percy Finch, *Coral and Brass.* New York: Random House, 1969.

Spector, Ronald H. *The American War with Japan, Eagle Against the Sun,* New York: MacMillan, Inc., 1985.

Sutliffe, Robert Lewis, *The 71st New York, in the World War,* date and publisher unknown.

Stewart, William, H., *Saipan in Flames, June 1944 Invasion,* J. M. Guerro & Associates, 1993.

War Department. *The Capture of Makin,* November 20–24, 1943, Washington, D.C.: Government Printing Office, 1946.

Unpublished Works

Kaune, Charles S. *The National Guard in War: An Historical Analysis of the 27th Infantry Division (New York National Guard) in World War II.* Fort Leavenworth, Kansas. 1990.

Hammond, *Intelligence Activities–Saipan,* June 17–26, 1944.

———., *Japanese "Gyokusai" ttack,* pp. 8–29.

———., *Last Resting Place.*

———., *Saipan Notes,* June 15–18, 1944.

Hudson, W. Taylor, *Four Years and a Week,* 1992.

Kelly, Professor Thomas O., II, Survey of 27th Division Members in World War II, Siena Research Institute, Loudonville, New York.

Mac Naughton, Donald S., *The Tibbits Cadets of Troy, New York: 100-Year History, 1876–1976.* 1976

Melnyk, Les, *Infuriatingly Slow: The 27th Division and the Debate over Makin.*

Meighan, 1st Lt. Joseph J. Company M, 105th Infantry, *Apple-knockers-Mike-3,* Saipan, Okinawa 1998.

Spiering, 1st Lt. Donald P. Company G, 105th Infantry, Memorandum regarding Saipan unknown.

Spiering, 1st Lt. Donald P. Company G, 105th Infantry, Memorandum regarding Okinawa unknown.

Periodicals

The Orion Gallivanter, Official Publication of the 27th Division Association, Inc., published quarterly at Baldwinsville, New York.

Love, Edmund G., "The 27th's Battle for Saipan," *Infantry Journal,* September 1946.

Love, Edmund, G., "Smith vs. Smith." *Infantry Journal,* LXIII, November 1948.

Sherrod, Robert, "Answer & Rebuttal to 'Smith versus Smith': the Saipan Controversy," *Infantry Journal,* LXIV, January 1949.

Smith, Holland M. and Percy Finch, "My Troubles with the Army on Saipan," *Saturday Evening Post,* November 13, 1948.

Benz, David A., "A Christmas Letter Home." *Paradise of the Pacific,* Holiday Number 1944, *American Legion Magazine,* October 1944.

Newspapers

The Times Record, Troy, New York, October 7, 10, 15, 19, 24, 1940; October 4, November 13, December 8, 15, 1941; April 5, 1943; August 5, 7, 1944; September 12, 1944; January 21; February 23, 1945. December 5, 1948

The Troy-Observer Budget, August 5, 1944, August 8, 1944.

The Albany Times Union, February 5, 1943, February 23, 1945.

Honolulu Star-Bulletin, March 4, 1944.

The New York Times, December 23, 1943, May 28, 1945.

The Messenger, Athens, Ohio, June 29, 1990.

Index